Ladakh in the Twentieth Century

Ladakh in the Twentieth Century

by

Dr. Sudhir S. Bloeria

Vij Books India Pvt Ltd
New Delhi (India)

First Published in India in 2021

Published by

Vij Books India Pvt Ltd
(Publishers, Distributors & Importers)
2/19, Ansari Road
Delhi – 110 002
Phones: 91-11-43596460, 91-11-47340674
M: 98110 94883
e-mail: contact@vijpublishing.com
Web : www.vijbooks.com

ISBN: 978-93-89620-82-5 (Hardback)

ISBN: 978-93-89620-83-2 (Paperback)

ISBN: 978-93-89620-84-9 (ebook)

Dedicated to

the memory of

Rigzin Namgyal Kalon

(9th Dec. 1923 – 8th Apr. 2002)

Contents

Introduction

My association with Ladakh and knowledge about few places there started quite late in life; in fact till after completing my college and joining the Officers Training School, Madras I was ignorant about the place. It was there that for the first time one heard of a place situated in the region; and I have graphically described this in the 'Preface' of my first book as, "Zojila, I heard this name for the first time in July 1965 while undergoing pre-commission training in the Officers Training School Madras. We cadets were grouped into four companies, each named after a famous battle. Mine was Zojila Company. Our Company Commander belonged to 4 RAJPUT, one of the battalions which had taken part in the famous operations in that area in November 1948. He gave us a talk on those operations, but being raw soldiers we understood very little of it... Seven years later, I left the army and joined the civil service, and got my first posting as Sub-Divisional Magistrate, Kargil. Before taking up the new assignment I read a number of books on Ladakh which provided sufficient information about the region, including the campaigns of Zorawar Singh and the battles fought in that area during 1947-48. My first journey over Zojila, on the way to Kargil, was memorable. Awe-inspiring massive cliffs rising sharply on both sides of the defile almost cast a spell on the travellers passing through the Zojila. Over the years I have had the experience of traversing over this fabled pass in different modes of transport and also on foot; in extremely pleasant weather and under very difficult conditions of snow blizzards and howling winds."[1] I stayed in Kargil, then a subdivision of Ladakh district for two harsh winters; from July 1974 to February 1976.

It was here that I first heard of Rigzin Namgyal Kalon, as a leading light of the entire region – he was almost a legend in his lifetime, and

1 Sudhir S. Bloeria, *The Battles of Zojila, 1948,* Har-Anand Publications Pvt Ltd, New Delhi, 1997, p. 7.

during that period he was actively engaged in encouraging the local Leh area farmers to grow surplus vegetables and sell these to the army at negotiated price and terms. The twin aim was – as it appeared to me at that time, and later confirmed by him – that the army would get fresh vegetables during the winter months at reasonable rates and the local growers also got suitably benefited. As a young and keen person, on his first assignment, I was interested in trying to follow this example and made efforts to motivate the local Agriculture officers and farmers in this regard and get them ready to grow and sell surplus vegetables to the army garrisons in the Kargil area through a cooperative societies network. This required lot of groundwork of first persuading the farmers to grow some surplus vegetables of identified varieties; then providing them with necessary inputs and finally organizing Cooperative Marketing Societies so that middle man is removed and the grower gets maximum benefits from his produce. The planning and preparations for this initiative started well in time, in the month of September, so that in the next working season, during the summer months of 1975, a modest beginning could be made of selling potatoes etc. to the army worth two lakh rupees.

Kalon Sahib, as the secretary of the Leh Vegetable Marketing Society, must have heard about this lead on our part and rang me sometimes towards the end of December; expressed his happiness about these tentative steps by the local farmers and also wanted details of the goods that we could offer to the army, so that he could prepare and discuss with the local army headquarters in Leh a consolidated list of the entire region. I was highly impressed that this person, on whom the Kargil farmers would be depending on for various marketing services and liaison with the army, himself rang up and showed keen interest in our scheme. That created a very positive impression in my mind. I had a more substantive chance to work closely and interact happily with him during my next tenure in the area as the Development Commissioner, Ladakh from October 1978 to February 1981. This was the period that I saw him more closely and carried much positive image of his imposing personality, downright humility and consistent efforts to keep away from the field of politics – and this in spite of very considerable following among the Ladakhi masses in general and the local farmer community in particular. He would always consider himself as a farmer; first and last, based on his large landholdings in Leh and Nubra regions of Ladakh; which he managed very competently and efficiently. He was ever a notable facilitator in the welfare schemes aimed at improving the condition of locals; being particularly keen on increasing income of the local farmers and extending greater benefits to them. Together we would negotiate with the local and higher army authorities; the ways and means of increasing the quantum and variety of farm products which could be sold to them – any worthwhile deal which would be beneficial to both sides in terms of money as well as diversity; vegetables, fodder, milk and the like. During my stay in Leh, I learnt a lot about him.

I gathered that Kalon Sahib, an icon personality in his lifetime, was born on December 9, 1923. Before 1947, he had travelled extensively in Ladakh and outside; generally with his flocks as also on business trips, to the Northern and Eastern extremities of the region – often also crossing over to the Tibetan territory as the borders were neither well-marked nor sufficiently patrolled by the security forces of either side then. He really came into his own, literally bloomed, during the darkest period in the history of Ladakh when the tribal raiders from Pakistan invaded the region; which was practically undefended, from Gilgit and Skardu side. Panic was then the predominant feeling in the entire area, from the beginning of 1948 till the very end of that year, and the Pakistani intruders had once reached the village Taru, hardly 20 kilometers away, practically on the outskirts of Leh town. Under his inspired leadership, also that of his father and a handful of community elders, the local residents appealed to Jawahar Lal Nehru and Sheikh Mohammad Abdullah to send help for the beleaguered population. Without waiting for the arrival of the Indian Army – which started coming in gradually from the beginning of June 1948 – he raised a voluntary force of over one thousand strong to defend their homes and hearths in and around Leh and Nubra regions. These people were imparted rudimentary training in handling arms and explosives and then deployed in defensive positions to first secure the main town of Leh and then go on the offensive in this and Nubra sectors. He and his volunteer scouts not only succeeded in halting the enemy advances but were also instrumental in boosting morale of the general masses – both Buddhists and Muslims – persuading them not to leave their homes in and around Leh. In fact, Kalon Sahib has been well regarded as the most important personality responsible for defending Leh, during those hopeless days and weeks of 1948, due to his personal courage, optimistic attitude and practical vision. Kalon Sahib also provided free provisions to the local scouts, raised by him, from his own grain stores for months together. He was undoubtedly a moving force to ensure communal harmony in the region as well as provide safety and security to the Muslim population of the area.

It was also during the period my posting there as the Development Commissioner – as the Deputy Commissioner Ladakh was called at that time - that I looked at the area and its peculiarities carefully. The town of Leh does not appear to be that high in the beginning; although situated at around eleven thousand feet. However, once a person has reached there, by any means, the first indication of the height and lack of oxygen in the atmosphere is the labored breathing. Even a short walk leaves one almost panting and there is a marked tendency to take deep breathes while just talking. For the first couple of nights, there is almost a scary tendency to feel a load on the chest as also perceptible shallow breathing. It takes a few, at least two, days to acclimatize to the place. Any outsider is well advised to take a lot of fluids, ample rest and enough lemon squash for the first few days; and also repeat all these precautions even if returning after leaving the area and visiting the plains, for a short period. The air - the atmosphere in fact – at the whole of Ladakh region is rarified and markedly free of dust. During the day the sky appears bluer than anywhere else in the plains. In fact, many people realize what the actual color called sky blue is, when looking at the sky in Ladakh. During nights, the full moon manifests as a precise circle of brilliance with sharp edges and one can see more stars on a dark night, than anywhere else, against the backdrop of a black canopy. It would be no exaggeration to mention that only in Ladakh one can observe and behold a three-dimensional view of the stars at night.

An account of the first visit by an army officer to Ladakh in the summer of 1956 includes, "… till then Ladakh was my only experience of Buddhist culture and ambience; and a constant source of new experience and wonderment. Where else for that matter was food so monotonously unvaried and simple – crushed or milled barley, a few roots such as giant-size turnips and radishes; hard, dried cubes of solidified yak's butter; occasionally a strip of dried mutton or yak-flesh (for though the Buddhist may not kill, there is no ban on eating flesh killed by others)? Where else is all food eaten uncooked, at least by the common people (for whom the only cooked item in their daily diet is tea)? This is because there are few trees or bushes in that desert-mountain terrain and wood is a rare commodity."[2]

It was almost a decade and a half after I left Leh on finishing my tenure there that a desire sprouted in my mind to write a biographical account of his life; in the backdrop of developments in the region during the twentieth century. After reaching Leh from Jammu, in the first fortnight of September 1998, we met at his residence and I outlined the contours of my project and also requested him for a longish interview so that I could faithfully record various notable happenings in his momentous life. He heard me in silence; went into a mood of serious contemplation and after few moments spoke softly and clearly – in his typical modesty – saying that he considered himself an ordinary person and whatever little he had accomplished for the area and its people was the outcome of a natural urge; which anyone else in his place would have also done. Not prepared to give up easily, I persisted with my counter-arguments and while justifying my scheme of things, again briefly profiled the plan and its framework – hoping that these would somehow make him agree to my request. After patiently hearing me out and again reiterating his regards for me and appreciating the project I had in mind; he drew a clear demarcation which stipulated that he would talk about various facets of his life only on the condition that I would agree not to pen down his biography, but instead write about the Ladakh region – which in his opinion was not only a much wider canvas but was also a more appropriate course. After both of us concurred on this 'gentlemen's agreement'; he opened up without any inhibitions and we talked about his life and other happenings in the region in considerable details.

The interview with Kalon Sahib continued for the next four days.

This book, in the current form, is not only about Ladakh region in the last century; but is also a glowing tribute to his multi-faceted persona and, above all, his well-known humility. Ladakh and many generations to follow would always be grateful to him and all that he did for his region and his people; irrespective of their place, caste, creed or religion.

On his death on April 8, 2002, at the age of seventy-nine, a moving tribute was written by Kachu Asfandyar Khan – a retired IAS officer who

---

2 Maj. Gen. D.K. Palit, VrC (Retd), *Out of This World: Ladakh or Little Tiabet,* Journal of the USI of India, October-December 2001, pp. 560-61.

hailed from Kargil and was also once Deputy Commissioner of that district. This 'obituary' appeared in a local daily and in parts read, "... Though, he never took part in the active politics of Ladakh, whenever the people of Ladakh faced any grave problem, he never shirked his responsibility and like a beacon of light guided the people towards safety.... Though he is no more with us, the loving memory of his magnanimity, his simplicity, his vision and wisdom will guide us in building a modern Ladakh based on the principle of peaceful co-existence..."[3] Each word of this piece rings true; as the writer and many others who expressed similar sentiments reflect the essential spirit of what Kalon Sahib stood for in the course of his eventful life.

I have also had the privilege and good fortune to be acquainted with and knowing well two other iconic personalities who have been virtually revered in Ladakh for their valiant, effective and sustained operations against the enemy. The first one was Lt. Col. Hari Chand, MVC; who got this gallantry award as a young Major in 1948 for brave actions in the Khaltsi-Leh sector. He was my Battalion Commander in the Officers Training School, Madras, when I was a Cadet there. During our training, he took a special lecture and explained important points relating to operations undertaken by him in that area; especially the guerrilla tactics and the concept of operations behind the enemy lines. While serving in Ladakh; both I and Kalon Sahib had decided to request him to come again to the area and accept a 'Civic Reception' in his honour, around the Independence Day of 1980. To our lasting regret; we came to know while working out the details of this program that he had expired by then. The second person in this category was Lt. Col. Chewang Rinchen, MVC and Bar, SM; who belonged to the Nubra valley of Ladakh and became a legend in his lifetime. In 1968 – when I was still in the army - he was posted in my Battalion, located in the Tangdhar sector of Kashmir; and I had the good fortune to be the number two man in his Company. Once we were asked to be prepared to raid an enemy post which was creating problems in the area. The operation was cancelled later; but I remember his short and crisp orders while the preparations were going on. He simply asked us to follow him to the target. I am absolutely sure that if tasked, we would have achieved our objective. Great self-confidence and an air of invincibility around the persona were his hallmarks. While serving with

3 Kachu Asfandyar Khan in, *Hero of Ladakh Passes into History*, published in Daily Excelsior, Jammu, dated April 14, 2002.

him I realized his personal qualities as a soldier; which enabled him to reach the stage which he had. Couple of years later he was to win another MVC, during the 1971 operations in the Turtuk sector. Till his very end, we maintained a happy and cordial relationship that I am proud of.

Ladakh, for centuries, has been a land of mystery for the people of many ethnicities. Numerous travelers, traders, historians, preachers and sociologists have attempted to unravel its mystique; with each succeeding only partly in this endeavor. This region has always been an area of significant strategic and geo-political importance; a place of considerable relevance in the Great Game that took place between major world powers in the nineteenth and the first half of twentieth century. Up to 1947 Leh, the principal town of Ladakh, was an important trade and transit point with good deal of traffic and trade moving on the routes leading to Tibet, Chinese Turkistan, Yarkand, Baltistan and Srinagar; in fact a significant entrepot for traders and travelers which traversed this vast region as part of their exertions on the famous – and often desolate – Silk Route for many centuries. It was, in fact, from Nubra valley that a route going over two major passes in the Karakoram Range connected Kashgar, an important trade centre on this trail.

Notwithstanding a rich historical background, Ladakh today is a vast land with its own unique culture and traditions which offer challenges and opportunities to the visitors. Known by many names like the Land of Lamas, Moon land, Land of High Winds, Cold Desert and the like; Ladakh is truly the Nature's workshop, studio and art gallery all rolled in one. From Zojila to Hanle and Padam to Turtuk the huge expanse is a collage of lofty mountains, high passes, exquisite lakes, quaint and picturesque Gompas – some of them perched on hilltops or precariously constructed on steep mountain slopes. The landscape is also dotted with beautiful green valleys and patches. Tsomoriri, Tsokar and Pangong are the famous trio of lakes in the region. Driving along the last one a person can see all possible hues of blue and green. Local legends apart; chemical analysis of the water of these lakes provides enough food for thought. The whole place is also a challenge and delight to the mountaineers and trekkers; some of the finest trekking routes and lofty mountain tops exist here. Driving from Zojila to Leh, one can see a series of high mountains barren and clad in different shades of cream, yellow, rust and brown; some of these appear to have been recently swept by a huge broom. In fact, mountains are the crowning glory of Ladakh. They stand majestic in myriad colors, shapes and sizes forming three famous mountain ranges of the mighty Himalayas, Zanskar and Karakoram. The peaks of Nun-Kun with massive glaciers rolling down to the edge of a rivulet near the village of Parkachik – on the Kargil – Zanskar road - is a sight to behold. Equally mesmerizing is the scenery from Darbuk to Demchok covering a distance of over two hundred kilometers at an average height of fifteen thousand feet of highlands pastures and wilderness. This area is the home of famous Pashmina bearing goats and also very sturdy *Nomads* who rear them; as well as the Zebra-like *Kiang*.

The lofty mountains of Ladakh are drained by a multitude of rivers and streams; foremost amongst them being the mighty Indus; which flows through this region rather lazily and appears almost brooding till it is met by the noisy and turbulent Zanskar River near Nimu. During the closing decades of the last century; a fairly extensive network of roads and bridges was developed and now dots the landscape. Leh is connected by fairly good roads with Srinagar and Manali; but due to heavy snowfall, these main highways are generally closed for at least five months of winter, from December to April-May every year. With the proposed tunnels at Rohtang and Zojila Passes, in Manali and Kashmir respectively, it is expected that in the coming decade or two the year-round motorable traffic to this area would become a reality. The high mountain passes; at least four of which, namely Khardung La, Chang La, Taglang La and Bara Lacha La are over seventeen thousand feet high and would continue to pose the 'high altitude' challenge to the road traffic passing over them.

The Ladakh region is endowed with huge natural resources; some well known like the potential for solar energy, wind energy and geo-thermal assets and others yet to be discovered like minerals etc in this vast stretch of land. But the biggest collective wealth of the area is, undoubtedly, the people who inhabit this rugged, and in most part, bleak landscape. Leading a landlocked and almost isolationist existence over the many centuries, they have devised techniques and means of cultivation, irrigation, animal husbandry and entertainment which are ingenious in concept and need determined hard work to ensure sheer survival in those hard conditions. To further appreciate this point an observer has to learn about and understand the extremely tough living conditions of the nomads of Changthang highland pastures and have a look at the old irrigation channels of Kargil and the Gompas; which are dispersed all over the place. A mere sight of the many kilometers long functional watercourses built along the sheer rock face almost a century ago, may be longer in some cases, without the use of any cement or steel invoke wonder and admiration for this engineering marvel. Similarly, one is amazed at the ingenuity and hard labor that must have gone into the construction of such beautiful and large Gompas, particularly in getting big logs of timber for the roofs and pillars; each one of which had to be brought in from outside the region without the help of any of the modern gadgets, means of communication and locomotion. A local tale, for instance, describes that the Rangdum Gompa, located near the village bearing the same name – at the northern bottom of Penzi La pass on the Kargil-Padam road – was erected a few centuries ago. At that time the timber required for its pillars and roofs was hauled all the way from the forests near Paddar belt of Kishtwar area in Jammu division; over the snow-clad high mountain ridges of Zanskar. Seen from that point of view; as also taking into consideration the oldness of this structure, the construction feat is a wholesome tribute to the commitment, tenacity and resolve of the people who built it.

In the closing three decades of the last century, two important things happened in Ladakh which changed the region forever. The first one was the opening of this area to the tourists in July 1974. The entire local population seized this opportunity with characteristic enthusiasm, resourcefulness and determination. In the beginning couple of years, the arrival of mere ten thousand tourists in a season would put tremendous strain on the available resources of the region and presently almost two lakh outsiders can be easily provided with residential as also transport facilities all over the place. This infrastructural capacity is still growing in an expanding circle. The main 'bazaar' of Leh is bustling with activity during the summer months with well-stocked modern stores and consumer outlets. The wide pavements on both sides of the road are dotted with small vendors selling fresh vegetables including some of the juiciest and tastiest apricots – the delicacies of Ladakh. It would now be difficult to believe that till about seventy years ago, this unusually wide street was sometimes the venue of Polo matches. The second game-changing event for the entire region was the formation of Ladakh Autonomous Hill Development Council (LAHDC); first organized for the Leh district in the mid-nineties and later for Kargil district also during the year 2003. These very potent experiments were aimed at providing inclusivity, speedy improvement of infrastructural facilities, enhanced educational and medical services, as also help in unleashing the local entrepreneurial skills. The LAHDC concept of empowered local administration has considerably achieved all this; while also taking into consideration the local needs, inputs as well as sensitivities. Ladakh can today provide an example of functioning and elected model of local self-government to the rest of the country.

Of course, in the face of ever increasing tourists' arrivals as also modernization; the challenges of environmental protection and maintaining the social and cultural fabric of the region are palpable and very real. Ladakh is certainly struggling to find answers to many questions; but importantly it is on the move. This in itself is a hugely positive sign.

For Ladakh, with all its glory and splendid isolation; the twentieth century has been a period of great trials and tribulations, crisis and opportunities; and in the final analysis a number of downs and many more ups. The region has flourished but is still not clearly out of the woods. There are issues; social, cultural, political, environmental and the like, which need to be addressed on priority. The people of Leh district very wisely and consciously started investing in the education of their children from the nineteen seventies. Kargil followed suit a couple of decades later. This collective sagacity is now paying handsome dividends. There are today competent Ladakhi professionals in diverse fields, and the number is happily growing.

Both I and my wife have been big admirers of this region for decades now. We have a long list of local friends and acquaintances; people with whom we have shared different emotions of life. This book is kind of saying a big Thank You to this huge area and its doughty inhabitants.

CHAPTER I

Background - Ladakh Region up to 1900

Ladakh Region: A Comprehensive Description

Ladakh, the northern most region of India forms a part of the Outer Himalayas. It is one of the most elevated areas of the earth, with huge landmass and high mountain ranges oriented in parallel chains. More famous amongst them – apart from the Himalayas - are known as Zanskar Range, Ladakh Range and Karakoram Range. It lies roughly between 32 – 36 degrees North latitude and 76 – 79 degrees East longitude. This landmass has one of the lowest population densities in the world; of just over 2 per square kilometer. Leh and Kargil being two districts of the area as also the two principal towns; which presently form this 'cold desert'. Geologists estimate that the mountain ranges in this remote part of the country were formed over a period of forty-five million years; with the folding of the Indian tectonic plate into the Eurasian plate.

The mountain tops are usually around 20,000 feet high – if not of greater altitude – while the level of valleys varies from eight to fifteen thousand feet. The Indus River, which drains the entire region, enters the area at an elevation of 14,000 feet and flows through the territory at progressively decreasing levels – like all water courses do – till it takes a sharp bend towards the plains and by this time coming down to an altitude of around five thousand feet above the sea level.

The area endures a harsh climate on account of its geographical situation. There are considerable daily and seasonal extremes of temperature and very marked differences at any time of the year between sun and shade temperatures. Winters are severely cold with recorded temperature in the inhabited areas varying between minus twenty to minus 45 degrees Centigrade; though there is plenty of sunlight during the day time. In spite of bitter cold conditions from December to April, it is remarkable that no one has ever died in Ladakh due to exposure to low temperatures. This one parameter speaks a lot about the efficacy of mutually supportive community living in the region. Rainfall is scanty and the landscape is arid.

Ladakh of the nineteenth century, and traditionally, looked east towards Tibet; as also north to eastern Turkistan (Xinjiang); south to the plains of India; and west to the regions of Baltistan and Gilgit.

People of Ladakh region are hardy, gentle and extremely simple in habits; those inhabiting the Leh area, in addition, exude happiness around them. Their main source of livelihood had traditionally been agriculture supplemented to a large extent by animal husbandry. Rearing of cattle assumes a new importance at altitudes of over 12,000 feet, where it is not possible to raise the agricultural crop. The farming activity is mainly confined to river valleys and *nullah* plains and includes cultivation of wheat, barley and husk less barley. Cattle which are reared for their milk, wool and meat as also serve as beasts of burden are Yak, Sheep, Goat, Donkey, Cow and Zomo. Horse and Pony have traditionally been treated as proud possessions by local families. Pashmina goats are famous for its wool throughout the world.

The population in this area is basically of the Tibeto-Mangol, Dard and Mon stocks. Over the ages there has been quite an intermingling of the different tribal identities, but an overwhelming majority is of Tibeto-Dard lineage. Majority of the people speak the Tibetan with dialectic variations in different areas; along with Dard and Shina languages.

A thoughtful observer of Ladakhi way of life, during the olden days, has commented, "... One may only find tiny villages huddled together in the crevices of the numerous valleys like small oasis in a vast arid desert of a frozen turbulent sea of mountains. But to those who visit the area and keenly observe, may find that these villages are full of life revolving around a system regulated by climatic conditions and natural laws for thousands of years. Yes, despite the most inhospitable terrains and harsh climatic conditions, one may find that these villages have survived and thrived for centuries together. The people living in these villages have succeeded in evolving a society based on the sublime human feelings of understanding and peaceful co-existence...the Ladakhis have managed to survive in such inhospitable conditions in this part of the earth and not only have evolved an indigenous method of survival but also produced a unique culture and civilization during its journey through the ages. They had learnt to live with Mother Nature, cultivating the available land and rearing live-stocks and cattle... every Ladakhi had a roof over his head and means of subsistence for his family from the land as well as from the live-stock...the Ladakhi society was a unique example of peaceful coexistence and mutual brotherhood. People shared their joys and sorrows with each other. All the members of the society worked together like the members of a big family in which every member cared for each other. The village affairs were looked after by the village committee of elders consisting of members from all the households. Every year men were nominated to discharge the duty of village watchman and water regulator. Even the village artisans had to go to each household to mend household articles and agricultural implements. These men were paid in kind for their services by each household at the time of harvesting. In this way, the whole society manifested mutual understanding and cooperation. There were no competitions, confrontations and animosity among the members of that society... Since Ladakh is bounded by lofty mountains from all sides with few fare weather tracks connecting it to other neighbouring countries, so in old days it was essential for the residents of Ladakh to produce almost everything by themselves or barter them from the neighbouring countries during the short summer months, before the closure of all exit routes due to heavy snowfall. Under such compelling circumstances, it was obvious that every member of the family ought to have been well-versed in the art of agriculture and animal husbandry so that they could contribute something to the family coffers within the short summer months. Right from stocking of food grains to the collection of fuel and fodder, everything had to be completed well before the onset of the severe winter months."[1]

An important area of the Ladakh region has always been Baltistan. It is also the name of an old kingdom in this territory; roughly denoting that where the Dard race ends, the Baltis begin. With Skardu as the major town in the belt; the other well known places include the names of Khapalu and Chorbat. An important and largish village in this zone – Rondu – has been expressively described by a European traveler as, "...over that small

1 Kacho Asfandyar Khan, *Ancient Wisdom from Ladakh,* Kacho Publishers Kargil – Ladakh, 2014, pp. 48 to 51, 57 and 58.

area crops bear abundantly and fruits grow in luxuriance. Apricots and mulberries are the most common, and, indeed, they flourish wherever in Baltistan water can be brought to freshen their roots; but here is added pomegranate, which is rare in these hills; weeping willow too lends its graceful form to the varied collection of trees that almost hide the fields from view…The river flows past, some hundreds of feet below the level of the village, between perpendicular rocks of massive gneiss; in a narrow part of it is spanned by a rope-bridge, made of birch twigs, which is 370 feet long in the curve, with a fall in it of some eighty feet, the lowest part being about fifty feet above the stream. The approach to the bridge is over slippery rocks; the path is narrow and difficult…"

The houses in this region were generally built of stones and mud, with flat roofs. A portion of the first floor, more so in cases of comparatively affluent people, was commonly built into another storey, to be used during the summer months. The abundance of fruits here helped significantly in the local economy; as the dry fruits were a valuable commodity in the entire Ladakh region – as also beyond.

May be due to less severe winter and consequently easier life; the Baltis appear more thick-set and taller than the average Ladakhi. Also due to their embracing the Muhammadan religion – most of them belong to the Shia sect; the Baltis adopted the custom of polygamy; even though the local economy did not support an increasing population. Hence in the majority of poor population; polygamy did not become very popular. By virtue of their depressed economic condition; many of the locals went as far as Simla, in search of employment and consequently the hope of making some money through working as labourers there; as also selling their stocks of dried fruits. The Baltis also inhabited the entire Suru valley, including the town of Kargil. In fact those days; the centre of commercial activity in Kargil revolved around a cluster of shops called 'Balti Bazaar'. Kargil was positioned almost halfway; with Srinagar on the western and Leh situated on the eastern side. The Kashmir approach passed over the Zoji La, Dras – along the Valley of Dras River – till the mountains on both sides gave way to a wide plateau of Kargil. The town being on the banks of the Suru River and also its confluence with the stream coming from Wakha side; the availability of irrigation facilities in the cultivated terraced fields of villages around has been plentiful. This situation ensured abundance of crops – of course from Ladakhi standards – of barley and wheat. There are plenty of fruit trees - mainly apricots – as also good growth of willows and poplars; primarily used for construction activity. It was an important halting and a place of rest for the people traveling from Srinagar, Skardu and Leh sides.

This area has also been fittingly mentioned as, "From village Kharul where the Dras river pours its tribute of waters into the Suru river and where the river is spanned by a bridge, the starting point for the road to Skardu, we enter the valley which goes by the name of the river Suru. This river rises in the Penzila glacier, receives numerous tributaries and ends its fairly long course at Nurla where it meets the Indus. The Suru valley is co-extensive with the limits of the Kargil tehsil. Though sharing in full the general rugged mountainous character of the entire area, this valley is on the whole more fertile than most other parts of it."[2]

A brief description of some other areas of Ladakh, in addition to above, is made in the succeeding paragraphs. It also included the Deosai plateau, which lay south of Skardu and was surrounded by high mountains having an average height of about 16000 feet. The table land in between the mountains ranged from 12,000 to 13,000 feet high. Generally, the route from Srinagar to Skardu followed over Gurez and Deosai plains.

Skardu has been described in the 'Gazetteer of Kashmir and Ladakh' (1890), as "Skardu is situated on the left bank of river Indus; it occupies a nearly level plain of fine alluvial clay elevated 150 feet above the river, and extending from one of two isolated rocks, which overhangs the Indus towards the mountains on the south side of the valley. This rock rises to a height of 1,000 feet above the river. The neighbourhood of the rock of Skardu was doubtless selected as the site of the principal town of the kingdom of Baltistan from the advantage it afforded as a place of defence."

The area of Dras can be taken as a thin slice of territory located between the villages of Shams Kharboo, Dras and Matayan; primarily drained by Dras River and bounded on both sides by tall mountains with an average height of sixteen to seventeen thousand feet. This narrow valley got broadened only at one place at Dras; where a track from there leads to the plateau of Mushkoo. This belt is mostly populated by the people of *Dard* origin.

2 Shridhar Kaul and H.N. Kaul, *Ladakh Through the Ages,* Indus Publishing Company, New Delhi, 1992, p. 22.

Zoji La; a depression in the Himalayan Range – and the eastern approach to the Ladakh region; more particularly the access to Kargil and Leh. A peculiarity of this place is the steep rise from the Valley side but only a slight gradient on the Ladakh section. Zoji La has been comprehensively described as, "One of the most striking contrasts in nature manifests itself in the valley of Kashmir and Ladakh being set next to each other. The lush green verdant valley, dotted with blue lakes and capped with glacier topped mountains, is adjacent to barren, windswept cold desert highland region of Ladakh. The principal towns of Srinagar and Leh are connected by a traditional trade route running west to east. The most important landmark, on this route, also being the watershed and dividing line between the two regions, is Zoji La. In the native language "Zoji La" means "Path of Blizzards", a befitting name for the pass, as would be sufficiently evident after studying its topography. The Zoji La is known by other names also, such as Seoji La, Baltal Kotal, Dras Pass, Zogi La and Zwaje La etc. In the great Himalayan mountain range starting from Mount Everest in the east to Nanga Parbat in the west, Zoji La is the lowest depression being 11,578 feet above sea level. All other passes are over 14,000 feet high. Though such a low pass and a simple walk under summer conditions, the Zoji La is also one of the most dangerous. It accounts for a large number of animal and human lives, taking its deadly toll by means of sudden avalanches or engulfing its victims in bottomless drifts. For the major part of a year all these passes including Zoji La remain closed due to snow and avalanches...The route from Baltal to Zoji La was just a mule track going up the steep slope of the hill overhanging the gorge of the Sind river and was usable only from May to December. In winter this was impassable and a temporary pathway, rarely traversed, used to be made over the snow which filled the gorge below Zoji La until the snow melted and the summer route became available...After the snow had fallen, only the very brave could venture to walk through, ignoring the howling winds, blinding blizzards and thunderous hurtling of avalanches. The minimum temperature there became sub-zero from mid-October and could be as low as -50 degrees Centigrade during winter months."[3]

Zanskar has been a largish area situated in the south westerly direction of Leh and drained by the river bearing its name. The Zanskar river met Indus near village Nimoo and after the confluence the entire stream

3 Dr. Sudhir S Bloeria, *The Battles of Zoji La, 1948,* Har-Anand Publications, New Delhi, 1997, pp. 20, 21 and 22.

became Indus. The area was closed for all traffic during the winter season and remained approachable only in the summer months; from Kargil side over the high Penzi La and from Leh direction, upstream the Zanskar river. At least two ancient *Gompas* – Sani and Karsha – bear testimony to the social interaction of locals with outsiders. Zorawar Singh also made use of the route from Kishtwar-Paddar to Zanskar for his forays into Ladakh.

Nubra – the area is also known as Nubra valley – is drained by the Nubra and Shyok rivers, mainly by the latter and is separated from the Indus basin in Ladakh, by a great ridge of mountains. The track from Leh to this area crosses over a very high pass called Khardung La – the highest point on this being 18,300 feet; and on both sides the ascent is quite steep. The first village, a largish one, after crossing over from Leh side also bears the name Khardung. However, the average altitude of the plains of Nubra and Shyok valleys - the two parts which form the Nubra region - is lower than Leh and hence the climate here is comparatively more moderate. This, in turn, makes the area greener with the luxuriant growth of trees and crops. The most famous animal of this region being the 'double humped camel'; although the farmers keep ponies, sheep, goats and yaks like other places.

The Nubra area has been fittingly described in the following manner, "The valley is reached from Leh by two routes; one of the routes leads over the Khardong La and the other over Digar La. The Khardong path traverses a glacier on the Nubra side and is on that account more difficult. It opens later and closes earlier than Digar pass. But this route being shorter is generally preferred by travelers between Leh and Nubra valley…In summer in fine weather it is full of charm. It grows apricots, apples, walnuts and some other fruits. The water supply is abundant but a large part of the valley which could be easily irrigated remains uncultivated because of want of manure. Unlike Leh the valley is rich in fire-wood being largely covered with bush-wood jungle. Panamik which is practically the last village on the route to Yarkand contains hot water springs where people suffering from certain ailments take bath under the direction of native physicians."[4]

Leh had, undoubtedly, the distinction of being the principal town in Ladakh region. Located at a height of 11,554 feet above sea level, it was

4 Shridhar Kaul, *Op., cit,* pp. 36 and 37.

an important commercial point between India, Tibet and Central Asia. Leh was connected with Srinagar, Jammu and Manali by three different routes – Central Asian trade route, south-western and southern route. The south-western passage linked Jammu with Leh via Kishatwar and Zanskar. It was primarily a foot track; however, horses or ponies could be used for short stretches. The southern path ran from Leh, going east over Taglang La and Bara Lacha La; through Keylong to Rohtang Pass and then to Manali. The Central Asian trade route; can be said to be a traditional and age old pathway connecting with Srinagar and Leh. Also, from Leh there were routes to Tibet, Chinese Turkistan, Yarkand and Baltistan. These have been described by Cunningham as:[5]

> The south-eastern road from Lhasa to Garo and the Indus to Leh. A branch from India, via the Niti pass joins this road at Garo;
>
> The eastern road from Chinese Territory, through Rudok and the valley of Chushul and Sakti to Leh;
>
> The northern road from Yarkand and Kotan, over the Karakoram mountains and down the Shyok and Nubra rivers to Leh; and,
>
> The north-western road from Balti, via the Shyok and Indus rivers to Leh.

Because of the centrality of its location; Leh has at times played an important part in the Central Asian affairs.

In the books, mostly written by the British travelers, the Ladakhi subsistence habits were generally described as, "…the grain which is mostly grown in the area is Grim, or loose-grained barley and it is this grain that most Ladakhis eat. Grim is a hardy plant which can be cultivated even up to a height of fifteen thousand feet…At lower levels, besides grim, wheat is also grown; but little of this is consumed by locals themselves; they grow it for the market and the travelling merchants. Peas and barley is also sown and the latter is generally given to horses. Every crop requires irrigation for its growth…The drink of the Ladakhis is *Chang*, a light sort of Beer made without hops, usually sour in taste. People enjoy it more during the winters…A strong decoction out of this is made by the process of distillation; and is called the 'local whisky'…Tea is another favourite drink in this region; it is made in a churn, with butter added."

5 Alexander Cunningham, *Ladakh,* W.H. Allen and Co., London, 1854, p.148.

The word of praise and acclamation written on the occasion of laying the foundation of a *Gompa, Chorten or Maney wall,* in that order, is an important source of historical knowledge of the region. The eulogy is generally in respect of the King, Queen, crown prince and other princes and princesses; the *Kalons,* head of the local area, town or village and also down to the workers – so that they may reap the reward of this good work, which in turn would help in saving them from the cycle of births. In order to gain merit; the names of the people who donated silver, gold, grain, butter and the like; are also recorded.

Gompas – monasteries – are almost a living heritage of Ladakh with most of them being centuries old. They are virtually living institutions of the region and for ages have been the centers of economic, religious and social activities. In a way, the monasteries are inseparably entwined in the Ladakhi way of life. These are generally built upon a rocky outcrop or at an elevated point outside the village. Such locations are selected mainly to ensure sanctity, solitude and security. A large number of them are antiquated and picturesque structures. Gompas provide residential quarters to the monks – which average to more than a hundred at each location - as well as are a principal place of worship and meditation. A typical day at the Gompas starts with morning prayers; with collective and deep throated voice of Lamas chanting Mantras creating a spiritual ambiance around. In these Gompas auspicious days are celebrated, almost throughout the year – though majority of them during the winter months – in accordance with the dates determined by Tibetan lunar calendar. Two significant days being the Buddha Jayanti; commemorating Buddha's birth as also enlightenment and Losar, which is Tibetan – and hence Ladakhi - New Year. During these celebrations; the traditional chanting and music is, at times, supplemented with famous 'mask dances' by the monks symbolizing the victory of good over evil. Generally, the interiors of Gompas are decorated with admirable *Thangkas* – Tibetan cloth paintings, at times embroidered, depicting religious figures in different positions. In some cases, the *Thangkas* are directly painted on the Gompa walls. The Gompas do play a prominent role in Ladakhi village life – in all major events of a person's existence right from birth to death. The Gompas are held in high esteem by the local population. The people would not withhold even a small part of butter or grain dedicated to the Gompa – this is the case in respect of all villages in relation to the Gompas of their affiliation throughout Buddhist Ladakh – and these offerings are the major source of sustenance of the Gompas of the region. Apart from the usual material offerings given to the Lamas; some devotees also donate part of their lands to Gompas. With the result that a particular Gompa may have in its possession agricultural tracts also far away from where it is located. Such dedicated lands are in turn given to the local tillers and a fixed portion of the produce comes back to the Gompas; and stored in the granary. The grains, thus stored, feed the Lamas of the Gompas and the surplus stock is carried forward for use of the locals around; during the times of need. The Gompa granaries have been recorded to feed the locals of villages in the vicinity, during times of famines, or similar conditions, in Ladakh.

Most of the Gompas are centuries old and are the central focus of heritage of Ladakh. At some of them, though, a bit of modern restoration works has been done; but most still retain the original architecture and considerable charm. Ladakh has some of India's most historically and architecturally noteworthy Gompas; few of the more famous ones include the names of Hemis, Thiksay, Spituk, Pheyang, Likir, Alchi, Lamayuru, Rangdum and Karsha.

The significance of Gompas in the local milieu gave rise to the institution of Lamas in Ladakh. The affairs of every monastery were managed under the directions and supervision of the Head Lama; he was the final authority in the social and religious affairs of the Gompa, as also the areas around. If he was a reincarnation of a senior religious head, he was known as the 'Kushok' in the local parlance and also extended so much more respect as well as reverence. The other Lamas also were placed in different categories starting from the lay entrants to the very top. The top bracket, generally, consisted of those Lamas who after finishing their education in Tibet returned to their respective Gompas. Their services were utilized in teaching the younger initiates; and senior Lamas who were good artists, their talents employed in decorating the Gompas with *Tankhas* and floral designs. In the Ladakhi society, all Lamas enjoyed considerable respect. He was expected to be a good orator; well versed in 'chantings' and rituals and capable of presiding over religious ceremonies in the society or individual household. His services were also utilized at the time of distribution of land, water and settlement of disputes; as an uninterested party, and his decision was agreed to by the parties. He was also called at the time of disease, gathering of harvest and similar events. For these services the peasants normally offered a portion of their crop production and sometimes gave cash also; all of which went to the assets of the Gompa. In short, they were spiritual leaders and counselors of the lay people and exercised considerable benevolent influence over the society. It was indeed a relationship of mutual dependence.

Chortens, sometimes also referred to as *Stupas*, are structures; semi-permanent in nature and located on the out skirts of almost every large village in the Buddhist area. These are generally made of stones and sun-dried bricks, plastered over with mud, whitewashed and partly painted. Its thick walls cover both sides of a track; the walls are roofed at an appropriate height. The top of *Chortens* is designed like a small temple; complete with floral designs. Passing underneath it and between the two walls is considered auspicious in the local lore. These also mean objects of offering or meditation; signifying the Buddhist concept of three jewels, that is, *Buddha, Dharma* and *Sangha.* The *Chortens* are built in the memory of Kings, high spiritual Lamas and prominent citizens whose contributions to the society are well recognized.

Maney Walls are generally the long and thick built up stone walls – loose and dry stones gathered and put together – and covered with thousands of flat slabs bearing a holy inscription. One may also find some biggish stone slabs there on which important teachings of Buddha are carved. These are almost an integral part of every village; but also sometimes found alongside frequented tracks. The paths divide and go on both sides of the Maney walls; the passers-by keeping the wall on his right as per the local traditions.

Until 1834, Ladakh was an independent kingdom, though considering the terms imposed on it by the Treaty of Tingmosgang – in 1684 – this independence was rather illusory. By the beginning of 19th century, Jammu region was under the control of Dogra rulers. In 1834, General Zorawar Singh who was a celebrated commander of the Jammu ruler Raja Gulab Singh invaded Ladakh. The probable reasons for undertaking this risky and difficult venture were to gain possession of the lucrative Pashmina trade of Ladakh as also to expand the boundaries of Jammu kingdom. In practical terms this meant the end of Ladakh as an independent entity.

The Census of this region was conducted in the year 1891. As per report published by the Census Superintendent, Kashmir State, dated 17th

December 1891; the population figures of Ladakh, Skardu and Gilgit were shown as 28,274; 110,325 and 16,769 respectively.

In the latter half of the 19th century; Ladakh had Tibet in the north-east, its borders touched Sinkiang in the north, in the north-west lay Uzbekistan and Afghanistan – the well known Wakhan corridor – and in the west it was neighbored by North West Frontier Province of the British India. This region, then as also now, possesses great strategic significance because of its location. It is surrounded presently, moving from West to North to East, by Pakistan, Afghanistan and Tibet (China) respectively. Illegal occupation of part of it by Pakistan and China and the 1962 Chinese aggression also allude to its strategic prominence.

The overall scenario was comprehensively summed up by a local respectable as, "In Ladakh there are separate names for specific regions and the Indus valley belt between Nimoo and Sukurbuchan is generally referred to as the 'Sham' area. There is a prevalent belief amongst locals that people of these villages are intellectually much superior to their counterparts elsewhere in Ladakh. There may be some logical reasons for this.

"Traditionally, the land holdings in this entire region are much smaller thereby making it difficult for a family to survive only on agricultural operations. So, in a way sheer out of compulsion, alternative sources of income had to be resorted to; and this led to the people engage in the service or take to long distance travelling with their live stock. Both these vocations – apart from providing extra money to the family – added to the knowledge and expanded the breadth of vision of the general people; and over a period of time they became a much better informed group…The story of transformation and change in Ladakh is indeed unique and fascinating in some ways. In the local language it is very aptly described as a case of jumping from 'Boonglu (Donkey) to Boeing'. The local inhabitants were used to taking the donkey as the fastest means of travel and suddenly – on 24th May 1948 to be precise – the people saw the spectacle of an airplane landing in Leh airstrip. So the change was not sequential and gradual from animal transport to mechanical means of conveyance; like in other places of the world. In case of Ladakh; the people saw aircraft first and the road-bound mechanical transport a few years later."[6]

6 Interview with Col (Retd) Wangdus of Leh, on 8th November 2018.

Ladakh in Ancient Times

The earliest history of Ladakh is practically shrouded in mystery. In the rest of India, the recorded history indicates of the huge 'Magadh' empire in the third century B.C. Thereafter followed the famous Gupta dynasty and Imperial Kanauj in the northern parts; as also the ascendance of the Pandyas and Cholas in the south India. After tenth century, the Muslim invasions resulted in the rule in Delhi by various dynasties; the Mughals being the most famous; who ruled effectively from the middle of sixteenth century for almost two hundred years. There were also three important 'Sultanates' in the south; called 'Nizamshahi' in Ahmednagar; 'Qutbshahi' based in Golconda (present Hyderabad area) and 'Adilshahi' located in Bijapur. However, Ladakh remained untouched by these momentous developments in the rest of the country; only having brief brushes with mostly Kashmir.

At the same time it is also a fact that some prehistoric tools and artifacts have been found in this region; particularly on the banks of Indus river coursing through this area. These do provide evidence of the belt being inhabited in the Neolithic period; although other details about the kind of people that inhabited the place and their way of life are not yet available. From the rock carvings and related sources it can be deduced that Buddhism came to Ladakh from the north-west side around the beginning of Christian era. The 'Kanika Chorten' in Zanskar, almost a standalone structure of its kind, is believed to be from the time of emperor Kanishka; who ruled over a vast tract from the beginning to middle of the second century AD. His rule extended from Tajikistan, in Central Asia to almost the entire northern India, right up to Bengal. Kashmir was also part of his kingdom and then an important centre of Buddhist learning and theology.

On the other hand, in the early few centuries, this region was practically steeped in the phenomenon of 'stand alone' and hence developed its societal ethos and community conduct almost in isolation. The first significant influence in the place has been, according to folk-lore, that of Guru Padmasambhva – a renowned Tantric scholar steeped in Buddhist traditions; he reportedly belonged to Lahaul- Spiti region of the Manali area. He is the first contact that Ladakh had with Buddhism. Padmasambhva was followed, over the next few hundred years, by a string of Kashmiri scholars of this religion, who spread Buddhism in Ladakh and further east to Tibet. The first formal mention of this area is found in the travel accounts of few Chinese monks who passed through on their way to the Indian heartland in the search of Buddhist sites, philosophy and literature. Fa-Hien, in the 4th Century identified Ladakh as "Mountainous and so cold that no grain ever ripened."

A keen observer of the old history of Ladakh has thus commented, "…it is remarkable to note that contact between India and Ladakh has been very ancient. From Ashoka's time when the first Buddhist's monk came to Ladakh for spreading Buddhism, India has been in contact with Ladakh. The Buddhist monks from India were responsible for converting the Ladakhis to Buddhists. These monks came to Ladakh via Kashmir… After 10th century AD, Kashmir started coming under the sway of Islam. Consequently one finds that the cultural relations between Ladakh and rest of India have not been so strong thereafter… started having closer cultural relations with Tibet after 10th century AD. The nearness of Tibet might have also been a factor in bringing closer relations between the two regions…During the seventh and eighth centuries AD, several Chinese Buddhists made pilgrimages to famous Buddhist shrines of North India. The diaries kept by the Chinese pilgrims on their Indian tours are of the highest value for the study of ancient Indian geography and archeology… these references do throw some light on the events that were taking place in Ladakh at that time."[7]

It can be safely surmised that Buddhism reached Ladakh, some centuries before it spread in Tibet; as the source of this religion was the same, that is, Padmasambhva followed by scholars of Buddhist philosophy mainly of Kashmiri origin. Therefore, going westwards from Kashmir to Tibet via Ladakh, only appears natural. Cementing the Kashmir connection in the first millennium; king Lalitaditya there, according to historical accounts, made it a part of his realm in the eighth century. It is now believed, beyond dispute, that the 11th century paintings on the walls of Alchi *Gompa* are the works of Kashmiri painters and carry no influence whatsoever of Tibet; as is evident in the *Tankhas* and floral designs in other monasteries of Ladakh. Some scholars even go to the extent of saying that traces of 'Gandhara' art can be discerned in Alchi. Similarly, the rock statutes just outside Dras town and the 8th century huge stone carving of Bodhisattva Maitreya at Mulbek, adjacent to the highway, bear ample

7 Rajendra Nath, *Strategic Ladakh,* Vij Books India Pvt Ltd, New Delhi, 2016, pp. 7 and 13.

testimony to the artistic capabilities of the skills of artisans from the south of this region; devoid of any Tibetan effect or bearing.

The religious influence of Kashmir on the Ladakh region, however, substantially declined from the end of the first millennium. There were two reasons for this. The first pertained to the rise of Adi Shankaracharya (788 – 820 AD.) and the ascendency his *Vedanta* philosophy achieved over the prevailing Buddhist spread in the country. This resulted in considerable decline of Buddhism in India; including in Kashmir. The second reason was the incursions of Muslim warriors; from the western side and steady spread of Islam in India. Kashmir also, in time, came under the sway of the new waves. Therefore it can be reasonably surmised that from 11th century onwards, Ladakh established closer religious and political links with Tibet. This trend continued uninterrupted for almost five hundred years. Under the Tibetan influence the local religious practices also went through a process of transformation. In addition, institutional links were established between the monasteries of the two regions. Tibetan Buddhist texts were copied and brought to Ladakh. The Ladakhis also started sending monks to Tibet for advanced monastic training; and this trend continued till the Chinese occupied Tibet. More importantly; roughly from 15th century onwards, the new Gompas in Ladakh were built as representatives of one or the other Tibetan monastic order. The Buddhists of Ladakh generally came to belong to three different sects of Gelugpa; Drugpa and Degung – with each one having its monasteries. Spituk, Likir, Rangdum and Karsha monasteries belong to the Gelugpa; whereas Hemis, Stakna are amongst the more famous ones coming under the banner of Drugpa and Lamayuru, Phyang, Shachukul are categorized as part of Degung sect.

For the next over six hundred years, Tibet dominated various aspects of Ladakh; but it remained politically independent till 1834 invasion of Zorawar Singh.

Ladakh from 12th to 19th Century - including the Treaty of Tingmosgang of 1684 between Tibet and Ladakh – and up to 1834

The Central Asian trade routes passing first over the ZojiLa, from Srinagar side; were always hazardous. But this axis was, however, quite effectively used by intrepid traders and adventurous warlords. King Sikander of Kashmir reportedly followed this route to conquer Baltistan in 1405 A.D.

and forced conversion on Buddhist population there with violence. His son, Zain-ul Abidin – also popularly known as Budshah, the great king, in the Kashmiri lore – also invaded Ladakh, twice, forcing the local king to acknowledge Kashmiri supremacy.

The reverse traffic started in 1533 when Kashmir was successfully invaded by the Kashgari army of Sultan Abu Sayed Kashgiri, under his general Mirza Haider Dughlat. The tide turned once again when the ruler of Kashmir reconquered Ladakh and Baltistan and annexed these to his possessions in 1545.[8] The next recorded military confrontation with forces from the plains took place in 1680s, when the troops of Aurangzeb, from Kashmir, moved into Ladakh and defeated the Tibeto-Sokpa invaders pushing them to the traditional Ladakhi – Tibet border at Tashigong.

This armed confrontation amongst three entities of Kashmir (on behalf of Mughal Emperor), Ladakh and Tibet; continued intermittently for almost four to five years ultimately resulting in the famous Treaty of Tingmosgang in 1684.

Ferguson; in his publication named 'Kashmir' has mentioned this, at pages 93 and 94, "In an invasion by Ali Sher, the ruler of Skardu, in the early part of the seventeenth century, the gompas were sacked and their records destroyed. In the latter part of the same century Ladakh was again invaded by the Sokpos, a Central Asian tribe. The ruler of Ladakh then appealed for help to Ibrahim Khan, Governor of Kashmir under the Emperor Aurangzeb. Assistance was promised on condition that the Ladakh ruler should become a Muslim. Hence when the forces of Ibrahim Khan had expelled the invaders, the ruler received back his throne and in accordance with his agreement, adopted the Muslim faith. At this time also – A.D. 1687 – the boundary between Ladakh and the Tibetan district of Rudok was marked by heaps of stones which were still in position in the nineteenth century...After 1687, later rulers of Ladakh reverted to Buddhism, but continued to pay tribute to the Governor of Kashmir. The Afghan and Sikh rulers of Kashmir still continued to receive this tribute until Ladakh was conquered for Gulab Singh in 1841 by his general Zorawar Singh."

The history of Ladakh, till about the invasions of Zorawar Singh, has generally been speculative and vague; sort of shrouded in mystery

8 S.D.S. Charak, Indian Conquests of Himalayan Territories, Jammu, 1978, p. 67.

and 'curtain of fog'. For the period of around five hundred years; till the 1830s it can broadly be divided into three distinct groupings. The first phase lasted for about two hundred years till 1554; in which the rulers of Kashmir took quite a lot of interest in this region. After this period came the era of Ladakhi – Balti engagements and finally the series of Ladakhi wars with Tibetan; starting in 1679 and ending with the Treaty of Tingmosgang in 1684. Thereafter, till the 1830s; Ladhaki kings retained their political independence – though they were heavily influenced by the Tibetan religious and cultural sway and dominance.

The primary elements in the consideration of Kashmiri kings in keeping Ladakh under their control related to this region falling in the north-east of Kashmir, therefore securing Ladakh meant taking care of this flank of their domains; the second logic, of course, was economic as this arrangement enhanced the revenues of Kashmir by virtue of annual tribute coming into its treasury. There were other reasons too. Firstly, rebellious elements of Kashmir used to take shelter across Zoji La – Kashmiri descendents having settled in the village of Matayan across the pass is an example of this. Secondly, in order to check the plundering attacks by Ladakhi tribes; it was felt necessary to keep this area under control. Also, for smooth trade activities to and from Central Asia and Tibet; it was imperative to have cordial relations with Ladakh. However, at every possible opportunity, Ladakh revolted and was again brought under control by a powerful king in Kashmir. This ding-dong battle continued; till Ladakh was last invaded and forced to pay tribute to Kashmir by Daulat Chak in 1554. After that the Chak rulers remained busy in their struggle with the Mughals; who ultimately prevailed in Kashmir in 1586, when Akbar defeated Yusuf Shah Chak and occupied Kashmir.

Thus for few decades; Ladakh was under the rule of local kings till the next fight with Baltis. This has been graphically described as, "The first battle between the Ladakhis and Baltis took place in the reign of Jamyang Namgyal (1560 -1590 AD). Although the Ladakhis fought well, the Baltis carried the day. The Baltis being Muslims, destroyed as per their beliefs quite a few monasteries in and around Leh after their victory. However, there was a settlement between the conquerors and the conquered which is unique in history. The daughter of the Balti king was married to Jamyang Namgyal and the Ladakhi kingdom was left intact. It seems that the main idea of the Balti king was to spread Islam in Ladakh valley by this strange settlement. However, this attempt did not achieve much by way of the spread of Islam, though a few Ladakhis did embrace Islam…"[9]

The same author has cited the rulers of Ladakh during the crucial two hundred years up to 1840. He mentions, "Though the kings of the Namgyal dynasty were ruling over Ladakh as far back as 1560 AD and also during the Balti Wars, yet according to the Ladakhi chronicles the true Namgyal dynasty starts from 1640 AD. The following kings ruled over Ladakh during the periods as shown against them:-

Delegs Namgyal	….	1640 – 1680
Nyima Namgyal	….	1680 – 1720
Deskyong Namgyal	….	1720 – 1740
Puntsog Namgyal	….	1740 – 1760
Tsewang Namgyal II	….	1760 – 1780
Tsentan Namgyal	….	1780 – 1823
Tsepal Namgyal	….	1823 – 1840

The period of Namgyal dynasty is full of wars which were fought…"[10]

During the period Delegs Namgyal was ruling in Ladakh; the 5th Dalai Lama was governing in Tibet. The latter's territorial ambitions got better over Tibet's religious and spiritual influence on the people of Ladakh and he decided to invade it. For this purpose he launched the Tibeto-Mangol expedition to Ladakh in 1679 under the command of Galdan Chhewang. The Tibetan general made good progress and defeated the Ladakhi army which had been sent to stop him. The next year, in 1680, Chhewang advanced further and brought Leh also under his control; but the Ladakhi army held out at the fortress of Basgo. Here the local troops gave stiff fight to the invaders; and a stalemate ensued which lasted for the next three years. In the meantime, the king and the Ladakhi government had shifted to the palace and fortress at Tingmosgang – and this position also successfully resisted the Tibetan onslaught. To break this stalemate; the Ladakhi king was practically forced to ask for the help of Ibrahim

9 Rajendra Nath, *Op.,cit,* p. 16.

10 Ibid.

Khan, the Mughal governor of Kashmir. With the help of Mughal forces of Kashmir, the Ladakhis defeated the Tibetam army and liberated its areas by pushing the aggressor far beyond Leh and eastwards – according to some accounts on the other side of Pangong Lake.

For securing the Mughal help; the Ladakhi king had to accept their stiff conditions which included his becoming a Muslim and taking a new name of Aqibat Mahmud Khan; striking the coins in the name of Mughal emperor; sending a prince to Kashmir as an indemnity as also repairing the mosque at Leh. In addition he gave virtual monopoly of wool – Pashmina - export and transit trade to Kashmir, so essential for the important shawl industry there.

Although, Delegs Namgyal had become Muslim only in the name and also not many people around Leh had converted to Islam; these developments greatly disturbed the Tibetans who soon became keen to wean away the Ladakhis from Muslim and Kashmiri influence. In the meantime the 5th Dalai Lama died and Tibet was being ruled by a Regent till the next Dalai Lama came of age. As a part of this plan; the Tibetan forces waited for the Mughal troops to return and confronted the Ladakhi king again with the arrival of fresh reinforcements. The Ladakh army, by itself, could not effectively face the Tibetan military might and their king sued for peace. This also suited the Tibetans, who had by then softened their stand and resultantly the famous Treaty of Tingmosgang took place in 1684. These developments effectively ended the five year Tibet – Ladakh – Mughal war of 1679 – 84.

Without going into the literal meaning of the stipulations detailed in this document; the Treaty of Tingmosgang essentially and practically meant the following:-

- The frontier between Ladakh and Tibet was to be demarcated as mutually agreed upon and also the boundary respected by both sides.

- The Ladakhis were to accept the religious supremacy of the Dalai Lama.

- The Ladakhi kings were to treat both sects of Buddhism on equal footing.

- The king of Ladakh would never call in foreign armies again.
- The Ladakhi wool, including Pashmina, would only be sold to Kashmiri traders and four Kasmiris were allowed to settle near Leh for this purpose. No Kashmiri was permitted to enter the western Tibet. Ladakh was also to receive favorable terms for its tea trade and other produce.
- The king of Ladakh would send a mission, once in three years, carrying presents for the Dalai Lama.

Fascinatingly, the terms of this treaty were duly implemented and respected by both sides till about the early 1950; when the Chinese occupied Tibet. From 1684 onwards, Ladakh retained its political independence; though in religious and spiritual matters the Tibetan influence almost reigned uncontested. Towards the latter half of 1830, came the series of victorious battles fought in the area by Zorawar Singh. He also put in place an administrative structure to run the affairs of Ladakh region on more sound lines; also giving due recognition to handpicked local officials. Magana Thanedar, one of the trusted commanders of General Zorawar Singh was nominated as the first Governor of Ladakh; after the latter's death in December 1841.

It would be interesting as also appropriate to make a separate mention of the spread of Islamic influence in areas of Ladakh and around Leh town. This religion came to the region primarily by way of persuasion of few renowned Muslim saints as well as through the military might; and spread basically in the belt of Baltistan – Purig (the old nomenclature of Kargil area) as also few pockets in and around Leh town. The first lot of conversions took place; inspired by the famous personality of Mir Syed Ali Hamdani – who is credited with profoundly influencing the people of Kashmir and their conversion to Islam. It is said that after his second visit to Kashmir; he passed through Ladakh, in 1394, on his way to Kashgar. He converted some local people and also built few mosques in far off places like Padam in Zanskar and Shey, near Leh. However, the main work in this regard was done by his notable disciple, Syed Mohammed Noor Baksh; who essentially functioned in the Baltistan and Purig areas and converted bulk of the people there to Islam. His followers came to be known as 'Noorbakshi' and had a predominant position in this belt before the area came under the Shia influence in the Nineteenth century. The eastern part of Ladakh; including Leh and villages around did not get much affected by this phenomenon of conversions to the Muslim faith.

In the closing years of 16th and the beginning of 17th century, Islam began to take some roots in Leh region after king Jamyang Namgyal was defeated in war by Balti chief Ali Sher Khan of Skardu. The Muslim ruler of Sakrdu, offered his daughter, Gyal Khatun, in marriage to king Jamyang as a part of the settlement with him. Along with his daughter, the Skardu ruler also sent a large retinue of maids, male servants and local musicians to Leh. Gyal Khatun retained her religion even after marriage and mosques were built in Leh and Shey village for her and her servants. Later also, the Muslim queens of Ladakh used to offer prayers in these mosques. During the reign of Jamyang Namgyal as also his successors; a number of Balti Muslims migrated to Shey and nearby Chhushot village. The king also granted land to selected Kashmiri Muslim traders to settle down in Leh.

More coercive methods of conversion to Islam were employed by the Mughals in the course of their involvement in Ladakh's confrontation with Tibet – Mongol army during the early part of 1680s. Before the requisite help was provided; the Mughal emperor stipulated severe religious conditions and their acceptance by the Ladakhi king. Notwithstanding the fact that within a couple of years the local ruler embraced back the Buddhist religion and Ladakh firmly returned to the Tibetan orbit of influence; this considerably strengthened the position of Muslims in Ladakh; particularly in and around Leh.

Over the past centuries; a number of Muslim merchants on the Central Asian trade routes also settled and married local ladies in and around Leh. Adding to this number was also the category of individuals who were invited to Ladakh for specific purposes like striking coins; making correspondence in Persian with the governor of Kashmir as also working as butchers, and the like. In the late nineteenth century; some descendents of these people produced distinguished adventurers who accompanied the European expeditions to Central Asia and Tibet. The most famous among them is Galwan Rasul; after whom the Galwan valley in Ladakh is named.

No doubt there have been occasional confrontations between the rulers of Ladakh and Skardu; but these did not result in any long term acrimony and bitterness. On the other hand there were long periods of friendship and co-existence. Occasional matrimonial alliances between

Muslim chiefs of Baltistan - Purig area and the Buddhist royal family of Ladakh also helped reduce tensions. Consequently, the common people too followed the example of religious tolerance set by their rulers. All these factors resulted in a significant population of Muslims in Leh as also nearby villages of Shey, Thicksey and Chhushot.

Zorawar Singh's Campaigns

Zorawar Singh Kahluria was born in 1786, in a Dogra Rajput family in Kahlur, Bilaspur a small erstwhile state, now part of Himachal Pradesh. Not many details about his early life are available. He is said to have gone to Haridwar, at a young age, following a domestic quarrel in his native place. From there he reportedly came to Jammu area and spent couple of years in the service of the Ranas of Marmat Jagir in the present Doda district of J&K; where he learnt and honed his combative and martial skills. After this, he came to the notice of Maharaja Gulab Singh who employed him. For his demonstrated acts of bravery as also administrative acumen; Zorawar Singh, in a few years rapidly rose in the ranks. One successful appointment followed another in quick succession and he became governor of Kishtwar in 1821, with the title of Wazir. The topography of Kishtwar (now a separate district), a plateau at 5,500 ft. above sea level and surrounded by lofty mountains, rugged terrain and cold climate, gave Zorawar Singh an ideal opportunity to train his troops for operations at high altitude. He also perfected the tactics of mountain warfare and, equally important, the art of managing the supply requirements of large bodies of troops in difficult areas separated by considerable distances from their base. According to a historian of repute, the conquest and acquisition of Kishtwar by Gulab Singh had "opened the gateway to further conquests across the Inner Himalayas which were to follow soon after. In a way Kishtwar served as a springboard from which Zorawar Singh leapt on to his career of military exploits which marked him as one of the greatest generals and military strategists, India has ever produced. It was through Kishtwar that he advanced towards Ladakh, Baltistan and Tibet and made a history in the annals of warfare."[11]

The historical accounts of that time do not clearly indicate whether the expeditions towards Ladakh were undertaken under his own initiative by Zorawar Singh or he was goaded into this venture by Gulab Singh. In

11 Charak, *Op., cit,* p. 53.

either case, Zorawar Singh was to change the face of Ladakh as also the contours of Gulab Singh's domains.

The first campaign of Zorawar Singh started in the summer of 1834 when he set off from Kishtwar at the head of about five thousand strong army. He followed the route from there to Paddar; then over the high Zanskar mountains and reaching at the head of Suru valley of Kargil, probably near the village Panikhar. A major engagement with Ladakhi troops took place at Sankoo, in which the Ladakhis were defeated. Some interesting facts about this conflict have been described as, "On 16 August, 1834 Zorawar Singh was opposed for the first time by a Ladakhi force of about 5,000 strong which had been mobilized in haste. It is interesting to note as to how the Ladakhi army was raised at that time. Since the days of Senge Namgyal under whom fire-arms are mentioned for the first time, every household was furnished with a match lock. This old weapon and a certain supply of powder had to be kept in readiness for times of war. When the call to arms was sent around the country, one man with the match lock had to come from every house, carrying on his back provisions to last him for a whole month (chiefly parched grain) and blankets for the night. The load was so heavy that the mobility of the army was considerably impeded by it. There was no artillery. Cavalry it would have been easy to raise, but it was not of much use in the mountainous country..."[12]

Zorawar Singh halted at Sankoo, built a small fort and resumed cautious advance to Pashkum, through Lankarchey and Minji. Pashkum was occupied after overcoming a spirited defence by the local forces; who got demoralized after their leader died in the encounter. By November a stalemate ensued when both sides opened negotiations for a settlement. When Zorawar's representatives were killed and his position attacked; he realized the precarious situation including the vagaries of the oncoming winter. These prompted him to retreat to Lankarchey and take shelter in the fort. His forces remained there for the winter months.

In the spring of 1835, probably in the month of April, a large body of Ladakhis marched towards Lankarchey to attack him. Zorawar Singh pre-empted their plans to put an effective siege around his fort; by attacking them before this force could reach their destination and at a time when these troops were preparing their evening meal. In the ensuing battle, the

12 Rajedra Nath, *Op., cit,* pp. 19 and 20.

Ladakhi force was decisively defeated and fled the battlefield. This led to the unopposed entry of the Dogras to Pashkum for the second time. From there, practically on the heels of the fleeing Ladakhis; his troops embarked on a long march towards Leh. At Lamayuru, a letter offering peace was received from Tsepal, the king of Ladakh, whom Zorawar Singh met at Bazgo. After settling the terms of truce; the hostilities were suspended and Zorawar went up to Leh and installed Tsepal as a ruler holding power on behalf of Gulab Singh. An annual tribute of twenty thousand rupees was demanded and obtained from him; in addition to the war indemnity of Rs. 50,000. After making peace thus, Zorawar Singh returned to Lamayuru.

But, this treaty did not ensure a lasting peace in the region and Ladakh exploded time and again seething in discontentment and rebellion. Zorawar Singh spent next five years, leading his armies over difficult passes and under inhospitable conditions – once he appeared unexpectedly at the door steps of Leh from behind the high mountains, through Gya and Meru side – suppressing revolts in various parts of Ladakh and periodically changing the local rulers in an effort to find a suitable person to run affairs on his behalf. In these efforts, Zorawar Singh also fortified Leh by building a fort and keeping his troops there (the fort still exists and is presently manned and maintained by the army). The last uprising in Ladakh he faced was during 1939; but before the rebellion could mature Zorawar Singh again appeared on the scene with a sufficient force. The rebel leader was caught and publically executed. He also arrested several potential trouble makers and sent them as prisoners to Jammu. Thereafter, he formally annexed Ladakh to Jammu dominions and appointed his own officer as the administrator of Ladakh. The king, Tsepal, was divested of all powers; granted a pension as also allowed to retain his palace and the nominal title of royalty. Thus, Ladakh was pacified and never rose in revolt again.

After ensuring peace in Ladakh; Zorawar Singh diverted his attention towards Baltistan, where the Raja of Skardu provided reasons to him to intervene and attack the place. Zorawar Singh set out to conquer the region and his troops now included Ladakhis also; though commanded by his own officers. The Balti forces were defeated after putting up stubborn resistance at a number of places. The results indeed could have been catastrophic for him; but for the famous crossing over a make-shift snow bridge over the freezing Indus. His enterprise and undaunted spirit triumphed in the end and by June 1840, Zorawar Singh was back in Leh, having completed his mission successfully. He was careful enough to leave a strong Dogra garrison in a newly constructed fort at Skardu to ensure his authority.

Zorawar Singh was, however, not satisfied with these victories. Probably a mixture of the economic factors and a growing appetite for military adventure, made him to undertake expedition into Tibet. The combatants of his force did not exceed five thousand. Only two thousand of these were Dogras and the rest were from Ladakh and Baltistan. On 5th June 1841, he conquered Rudok, and then moved ahead and occupied Gartok during the beginning of August, after overcoming the local resistance. Further advance was made to take over Karing and Taklakot.

His bold forays into Tibet had met with success. The occupation of area west of Mayum Pass was completed by the middle of September and his troops had taken in more than five hundred miles of Tibetan territory in about four months time. Zorawar Singh had not expected that a serious attempt to dislodge him would be made by the Tibetans. But, in this he was proved wrong and the Tibetans reacted with dispatch and determination. In November, when the cold had become unbearable for his troops, he heard that a Lhasa force was approaching to confront him. The two probing detachments of his army were badly mauled by Tibetans. In a desperate attempt to stem the tide, Zorawar Singh advanced with his whole available force to meet the enemy. The final show down took place at To-Yo on 10th December, 1841 and continued for three days. On 12th December, he fell fighting on the battlefield.

In his book, Franckie has vividly described the last battle of this valiant commander and connected subsequent events as, "Zorawar proceeded further and encamped at Tirthapori on the Sutlej river. A Tibetan force numbering 10,000 soldiers arrived on the spot. News about the arrival of a further army came from Mehta Basti Ram, who had been posted at *Takla Khar* on the river *Gogra* near the Nepal frontier. One night there was very heavy snowfall and many soldiers died. A severe winter had set in and Zorawar realized the danger of utter annihilation. He deputed a small force of 600 men under Ghulam Khan to face the Tibetans, but it was surrounded by the Tibetan army and cut to pieces. He had no alternative but to attack. On December 10, 1841, he led an attack on the Tibetan army. The fighting continued for three days. He said, 'Either the Tibetans will take my head or I shall take it myself !' Wounded by a bullet in the thigh, he fell to the ground with his sword in his hand and fought fiercely to the end. A javelin pierced his heart and he died. His dead body was cut into pieces by the Tibetans who carried off his head and pieces of his flesh as souvenirs. It is said that they pulled out his hair and kept it for the sake of good fortune. Thus died the fearless man. Having lost their leader, his soldiers fled away in order to save their lives but most of them were killed. Only about a 1,000 escaped alive. The Tibetans pursued the fleeing Dogra soldiers and 700 were captured and dispatched to Tibet. Among the prisoners were Ahmed Shah of Baltistan, General Rai Singh, Ghulam Khan and Nono Sodnam and Prince Ali Mohammed.

"After Zorawar's death, the Tibetans sent a warning to Ladakh to prepare for war. It produced adverse political reaction in Ladakh. The Government of India became anxious and Captain Cunningham, Assistant to the British Resident, was asked to proceed to Ladakh to negotiate for an amicable settlement. Mehta Magana sent a plea for help to Gulab Singh who dispatched a new and better equipped army of 8,000 soldiers under Dewan Hari Chand and Wazir Ratnu. A call to arms was issued to Ladakh and Baltistan. The peasants were ordered to mobilize for transport work. The attack was launched and fort after fort was taken by the Dogra army. The Tibetan army was pursued. They were either killed or captured at different forts. But the Tibetan government sent 3,000 soldiers to invade Ladakh. Both the armies met at Drangste. On the advice of Thanpa Sodnam, the stream was dammed up by the Dogra army with the result that the Tibetan camp was flooded; as this camp was situated in the lower part of a narrow valley. Their arms and ammunition became wet. After a fierce battle the Tibetans suffered defeat. Their Commander Ragasha was captured and his head was severed with a sword. Besides Peshi (also spelt as Pishi) and Zurkhan fifty others were taken prisoner. Peshi committed suicide by swallowing his diamond ring. The Tibetans agreed to make peace.

"By now, the British government had become alarmed and directed Gulab Singh to cease all hostilities. They deputed Cunningham to Ladakh. The old boundary between Ladakh and Tibet was re-established and it was agreed to provide facilities for trade. Exchange of prisoners was also agreed to.... a peace was concluded with the Tibetans, according to which the annual trade between Lhasa and Leh was reinstituted, the Dogras taking the place and obligations of the Ladakhi kings. Jigsmed Namgyal had to be satisfied with the village of Stog and the taxes of its few peasants and hardly a single one of the old Ladakhi state officials remained in office…"

The achievements of Zorawar Singh have been comprehensively described by a scholar, as "To have marched an army not once or twice, but six times over the snow-clad ranges of Ladakh and Baltistan, 15,000 ft. above the sea level where the air is so rarified, people from the plains can hardly live with comfort, is a wonderful achievement. To have conquered that country after successive campaigns and reduced it to a peaceful province is an exploit for which there is no parallel in Indian History."[13]

The campaigns of Zorawar Singh achieved a lot and also hold a number of lessons for his coming generations; the important ones are enumerated as :-

- During the six years of victorious campaigns in these remote and high areas; Zorawar Singh added Ladakh and Balti regions to the Jammu territories. These yielded revenue to Gulab Singh and also added to his stature as a powerful local ruler; important enough for the British to take note of.
- These campaigns also laid the foundations of and became precursors to the subsequent additions of Gilgit, Chilas and Chitral etc. areas to the territories of J&K state.
- This entire region; from Gilgit to Damchok[14] and Karakoram Pass to Zoji La is critical for the defence of India and geo-strategic indivisibility of this huge tract is an integral part of this premise. The strategic importance of such a region can hardly be over emphasized.
- Zorawar Singh's conquests also resulted in the formation of a multi-ethnic, multi-religious and multi-lingual Jammu kingdom; and later the J&K state itself. This was an extremely commendable enterprise.
- He used his considerable political as well as administrative skills in bringing about the pacification of the conquered people. His

13 K.M. Panikkar, *The Founding of the Kashmir State,* George Allen and Unwin Ltd, London, 1953, p. 82.

14 It is the easternmost village of Ladakh.

treatment of the Ladakhis and Baltis provide a lesson in how to manage and win over a people proud of their heritage and conscious of their cultural identity. He never harassed the people and strictly enforced the moral code of conduct on his troops. He showed consideration towards his opponents and administered the conquered areas through local rulers; making them partners in further conquest of Baltistan and later Tibet.

- No force can operate in these areas, leave aside win battles, unless adequate administrative back up is available to it. His efficient and resourceful provisioning establishment, logistic management, careful planning and optimum use of local resources has been remarkable. Zorawar Singh's military genius, in fact, can only be matched by his administrative and management accomplishments.

- The planning, preparation and execution of these campaigns hold useful lessons in high altitude and mountain warfare, which are quite valid even today.

A little over 150 years after the death of Zorawar Singh, a local intellectual in Leh made realistic assessment of his impact on the Ladakhi milieu; and said, "With the advent of the rule of Dogras in the Ladakh area, the society also underwent a transformation. Till then the ruling elite were the king of Leh and his nobles. Since these people offered tough resistance to Zorawar Singh and his forces on occupying their lands, these nobles and their families, particularly those who had taken active part in resisting and leading the local troops were strongly suppressed. Importance was also given to Argun families, who were the off-springs of the Muslim merchants and their Buddhist wives. Since reading and writing Urdu came almost naturally to them; this also helped members of this community to get into the government service. Slowly they came to acquire considerable influence and prosperity much greater than their proportion in the population. For historic and economic reasons their settlements were concentrated in and around Leh town… However, the Dogra rule also brought with itself a sense of security to the local population as because of centralized administration, law and order situation improved and people could feel secure in their homes."[15]

15 Interaction with Tashi Rabgias, in Leh on 12th September 1998.

Although there is no clinching historical evidence to this effect; it is quite probable that Gulab Singh had obtained the British acquiescence for his Ladakh enterprise. By 1834, the relevant year, he had come to consider himself a friend of the East India Company and it is prudent to assume that he made confidential inquiry whether they would have any objection to such a campaign. For the British; Ladakh area was almost an unknown territory and they could not have been interested in that region. All the same; Gulab Singh did carefully weigh different aspects of this historic offensive. The severe cold – at least during the winter months; barrenness of the terrain, high altitude and lack of knowledge about passes and internal tracks were certainly the negative factors which reduced the efficiency of soldiers from the plains as also restricted the mobilization of a large army. On the positive side; the Dogra troops possessed better fighting qualities than their Ladakhi counterparts; they were more experienced in the art of war and also better disciplined; their equipment was up to date whereas Ladakhis were few centuries behind in this respect. In addition, the other two notable advantages with Dogra army were the elements of surprise and the guidance of an experienced and dynamic leader. The last was their greatest asset; whereas the Ladakhis had none. All these factors made Gulab Singh to take a decision to go ahead with his ambitious plan. Zorawar Singh, to his credit, faithfully carried out the desires of his master till the very end.

The saga and legend of Zorawar Singh lives, even so long after his death; not only in Ladakh but also much beyond the confines of its territories.

Ladakh during 1840 – 1899

After Kashmir came under the control of the Dogra ruler in 1846, with the Treaty of Amritsar, the administrative amalgamation of this region with Jammu and Kashmir State became complete. The system of administration introduced in Ladakh by Wazir Zorawar remained in force for some years even after his death. The administrative heads of the place exercised both civil and military powers and were designated as Thanedars; their seat of power being the fort constructed by the Dogra troops, just outside the Leh town. Maharaja Ranbir Singh is generally credited with bringing peace and tranquility in the entire region and removing strife – otherwise so endemic there – from this part of his state. Kaul has aptly narrated the ruler's wise handling of this vast expanse as, "The period of consolidation of the conquest of Ladakh and Baltistan synchronized mostly with the reign of Maharaja Ranbir Singh, a sagacious and far-sighted ruler. He kept a watchful eye on this newly conquered territory and made the welfare of its people one of his principal concerns. He selected men of high caliber as its administrators who organized the administration and introduced reforms with tactful gradualness. The people were thus spared the shock of abrupt changes and given an administration which was infinitely better than any they had known before. They gradually got reconciled to the new order of things and, in course of time, became loyal and staunch supporters of Dogra rule over them."[16]

Fredric Drew was a British officer in the employment of government of India. In the decade of 1860; his services were lent to Maharaja Ranbir Singh who was keen to organize effective administration in his vast and disparate kingdom. In this role, Drew extensively travelled in the entire state; and was also for few years – starting in 1871 – posted as the Wazir of Ladakh. The frontier regions of Gilgit and Ladakh were then part of the same administrative unit called the Ladakh Wazarat. Drew has recorded a vivid account of the J&K of his time; in a book titled, "Jummoo and Kashmir Territories"; which was published from London in 1875. The Indian edition of this work came out from Jammu in 1971, under the name, "The Northern Barrier of India". According to him, "It was these raids (primarily by the people of Chilas in the Astor valley area) that determined Maharaja Gulab Singh to send a punitive expedition against Chilas; this he did in 1851 or 1852. The Dogras at last took the chief stronghold of the Chilasis, a fort two or three miles from the Indus River, and reduced those people to some degree of obedience; and there has been no raid since... Returning to Astor itself, we find it a place that used to be the seat of a Dard Raja, but is now a cantonment of the Maharaja's troops, the chief station for the Gilgit Brigade. It is a collection of hundreds of small huts, which the soldiers inhabit in twos and threes; these huts are huddled or crowded together in two or three separate clumps. The number of troops is about 1200; the object of keeping them here, rather than nearer the frontier, is to save carriage of the supplies, which mostly come from Kashmir; the force is on the right side of the snowy Pass, and is always ready to advance to Gilgit if required... The Dards are now Muhammadan. Formerly they had some kind of idolatry, of which we know not much; nor do we know at what period they were converted to Islam... It is a fact that before Nathu

16 Shridhar Kaul, *Op., cit,* p. 106.

Shah came (say in 1842) the Astor people used to burn their dead, and not bury them as Muhammadans should. A curious remnant of the custom still remains there – when they bury they light a fire by the grave; it is true they will now tell you they light the fire to keep off jackals; this may be in some sense true, that is to say they could hardly reconcile themselves to leaving the body in its grave undestroyed, so they lit the fire as they had been used to, and this satisfied them in giving some security as against the beasts of prey, and at the same time making a link with the past."[17]

The same person picturesquely described the journey from Skardu to Leh in the following words, "From Skardu to Leh, the capital of Ladakh, is some two hundred miles by the road. It is a route little frequented, and is seldom traversed by any but foot passengers. Persevering Baltis are to be met with, who bring this way the sweet produce of their orchards, the dried apricots, which are in great favour and demand in the cold countries of Ladakh and Tibet; or some may be seen returning from their tour of labour in parts strange to them, high laden with the manufactured things which will find a good market in Baltistan…Next above the part of the Indus we have been speaking of, we come to Khalsi, where the road from Kashmir reaches the Indus Valley; hence, onwards, that road coincides with our own. Four days' journey is still before us. At Khalsi the Indus is spanned by a wooden bridge, where rocks narrow it up to a width of sixty or seventy feet only. The bridge is commanded by a small fort on the higher bank; the path from the bridge is, indeed, led along the covered way half round the fort. The village of Khalsi is on a plateau about 250 feet above the river. There is here a long strip of cultivated land watered from a side stream; crops and fruit-trees grow on it well, and even luxuriantly; walnuts and apricots ripen, though the height above the sea is something over 10,000 feet…As before said, the valley and the higher roads meet at the next village, Bazgo; this, as one looks down on it from the edge of the neighbouring plateau, has a picturesque and strange appearance on account of the position of some of its buildings, as of the monastery, on a towering rock. The Zanskar River, of great volume, here joins the Indus on the opposite side.

17 Frederic Drew, *The Northern Barrier of India,* Light and Life Publishers, Jammu, 1971, pp. 148, 151, 172 and 173.

"As we approached Pitak[18] we came to a more open part of the valley. Pitak is the last village before Leh….Entering from the direction of Kashmir we pass through a small gateway and find ourselves in a long, wide, and straight bazaar, the houses regularly built and uniformly whitewashed. This has been erected since the Dogras took the country, and is now the place that is most frequented. At the farther end of this bazaar one passes into the old part of the town, among houses separated by narrow winding passages… Outside the city are several gardens, or what are here so called; in truth they are plantations of willow and of poplar. These plantations are extremely useful, both for their grateful shade – which is the first thing a traveler will look for in these parts in summer time – and as a reserve of timber for building, a thing in Ladakh extremely scarce. On the east of the town the mountains are near and there is no cultivation; but to the west, the whole width of the valley, about three-quarters of a mile, is of cultivated land, descending in terraces, with small hamlets scattered over it."[19]

Frederic Drew also in his book, succinctly elucidates as to why the northern boundaries of J&K state – and consequently of the British Indian Empire – were extremely difficult to breach or trespass; he closes the narrative with a flourish, as, "Kashmir, when reached, could afford forage and supplies for a large force; but a large force could yet more easily be poured in from the other side by the power who holds the Panjab, and unless the invader could advance to, and command immediate victory in, the Plains, his position in Kashmir would soon become precarious. The Passes he came by would close behind him; snow would be his enemy, to cut off his retreat, while in the early spring his opponent might over the less lofty mountains, advance from the Panjab before aid could arrive from the north.

"Hence it seems to me that an invasion of India itself through these mountains would be one of the wildest of undertakings. A small and lightly equipped force, if well armed, might indeed find their way far through the hills, and overcome the troops of the Maharaja if they remain in their present state. But such victories as would bring the invaders as far as Kashmir, if he did not quickly give up the fruits of them and retire, would cause his destruction. Our Northern Barrier is one through which but two or three passages lead; and the gates that guard them, if opened by

18 Presently called Spituk.

19 Frederic Drew, *Op., cit,* pp. 239, 245, 247, 248 and 250.

a stranger, may close behind him, while the door in front might prove too strong to be forced."[20]

References of similar nature can be found in abundance in the written works produced during the second half of Nineteenth Century.

After Maharaja Ranbir Singh extended his territories in this area and occupied Gilgit and beyond; the British became alive to the strategic importance of this region as also its utility to keep the Russian southward influence in check. They rightly calculated that the whole place could become a sort of fulcrum in the unfolding Great Game. They worked hard and were able to persuade Maharaja Ranbir Singh, in 1870, to agree to make significant improvements in the Srinagar – Gilgit route, via Gurez, to enable it to take regular traffic; and called it the 'Treaty Road'. With this started the active British interest and involvement in these places. They steadily built upon their knowledge about the Central Asian region. As a part of this effort, Lord Mayo sent a large mission to Yarkand, in 1873, with the twin purposes of securing a commercial settlement on terms agreed by the local ruler with the Russians; as also to obtain as much information about the whole area as possible. Almost simultaneous to the Srinagar – Gilgit section; the Srinagar – Leh track and beyond to Karakoram was also declared as a 'Treaty Road' and later as a 'free highway'. The British also wanted to take advantage of the considerable Central Asian trade on this axis. Consequently, a Joint British Commissioner (JBC), generally an officer of their political department, was appointed and positioned in Leh. His main jobs were regular maintenance of this road; enforcement of the regulations and settlement of disputes between traders and travelers; particularly when both or one of them happened to be a subject of the British Indian government.

For the convenience of the travelling people using this route, government Sarais were established at each stage of travel, roughly twenty miles apart, starting from Sonamarg and right up to the Panamik village in Nubra valley. These were managed on contract under the authority and supervision of the JBC. Each Sarai was looked after by a chowkidar and the local contractors were bound to provide grain and grass for the pack animals and supplies and firewood for the merchants on payment. This was done according to a rate list displayed in each Sarai; and the system

20 Frederic Drew, *Op., cit,* pp. 330 and 331.

worked efficiently. Earlier, the Hoshiarpuri traders used to go to Leh and on to Yarkand etc. through the Kulu- Manali route. Later, as the travel from Rawalpindi and Srinagar became quicker and easier; they also took advantage of the improved infrastructure and transport facilities on the Srinagar – Leh sector and switched a bulk of their trade operations this side. The whole system stabilized well by the closing years of the fourth quarter of the century. In fact the then JBC, Captain R.L. Kennion, went on a visit to Rudok in 1899 and saw some traders buy and collect wool from the local graziers under the arrangements arrived at the Treaty of Tingmosgang. He sent a detailed report to the government; parts of which have been quoted by Janet Rizvi and read as, "…Many of these are in accordance with old custom considered 'State traders' and are not taxed, though the ancient privilege of having their goods carried free has for some years been withdrawn. Owing to this and to their more intimate connection with the country, they are able to trade with more advantage to themselves than the Kulu men. They make advances of money to flock owners and are themselves the proprietors of large number of shawl-goat sheep put out to graze in charge of Tibetan herdsmen on the extensive pasture lands of these parts. The Kashmiri looms derive their wool supplies almost entirely from this source."[21]

For effective control and administration of the far-flung areas; it is always required that authorities at the decision making level are kept abreast of all the developments on regular basis. For this, the importance of a dependable, secure and regular system of two way deliveries of messages and reports can hardly be over emphasized. The Britishers had put in place a workable mechanism in this regard; which served them and the J&K government amply well – almost splendidly. This has been officially described in the following manner, "The communication on the lines between Srinagar and Gilgit is maintained, not by regular runners, but through village agency, and therefore cannot be depended on for speed, though, so long as there is no snow on the road, the variation in time is slight. Between Srinagar and Leh, there are regular runners during the summer, but in winter, when the men cannot camp out, they go from village to village…Mr. Ney Elias, in 1878, made the following report on the postal routes to Leh:- 'The Kulu route is closed to traffic for eight months in the year, and during the remaining four months, cannot be used

21 Janet Rizvi, *Trans-Himalayan Caravans,* Oxford University Press, New Delhi, 2000, pp. 73 and 74.

as a dak road, owing to its length and natural difficulties in the form of high passes. The Kashmir road, on the other hand, is in ordinary seasons open for dak service the whole year, with the exception of a week or two during the winter, when heavy snow is falling, or when exceptionally boisterous weather prevails at a certain point. It is, moreover, a somewhat shorter route to Lahore than the Kulu route. But two serious obstacles to the Kashmir route exist – (1) the necessity of crossing the Zoji La pass in its present uncared-for condition; (2) the absence of an undivided and effectual control of the dak service between the limits of the jurisdiction of the *wazir* of Kashmir (*viz*., Sonamarg) and Ladak.' ...From the account given of the Zoji La, it will be seen that the 7-mile section between Baltal and Greman (probably means Gumri here) is too long for the safety of the dak men, and is the chief cause of the delay in running the mails between Kashmir and Ladak'...From Sonamarg to Leh there are thirty-two dak stages, to each of which in the summer two men are appointed, while between Sonamarg and Matayan sixteen extra men are employed during the winter...Except on the part of officials, *Europeans*, and a few merchants, there does not appear to be much written correspondence in Kashmir."[22]

In administrative terms, till the end of the 19th century, the whole of Ladakh – Gilgit area came under the jurisdiction of one district known as the Ladakh Wazarat, which was part of the Jammu province. It had Tehsils at Leh, Kargil, Skardu and Gilgit; with regular hierarchy going down to the level of Patwaris. It is educative to note that according to the Census report of the Jammu and Kashmir Territories for 1873, the population figures for Ladakh, Skardu and Gilgit areas are shown as; 2,569 Hindus; 81,662 Muhammadans and 20,254 Buddhists.[23]

Some fascinating information can be gleaned from the Administrative Report of 1954 Samvat (corresponding to 1897-98 AD) for the whole state. Parts of this document dealing with Ladakh provide interesting details about the administrative functions in this area, and read as,

"405. Following administrative changes took place during the year under report :-

1. Appointment of an Assistant Wazir-i-Wazarat at Ladakh.

22 Gazetteer of Kashmir and Ladak., published in 1890.

23 Ibid.

2. Creation of a sub-division at Skardu and another in the Bhimber Tehsil, with consequent appointment of Naib Tehsildars with opening of sub-treasuries at those places…

"429. Following reforms were introduced in the Skardu Tehsil of the Jammu Province :-

1. The abolition of Thanedars and the appointment of Naib Tehsildars in their stead, the former being always a source of danger to the administration, owing to the lowly paid officials being appointed on these posts.

2. Appointment of ten Patwaris on Rs. 10 per month each, and of one Qanungo on Rs. 15 per month, and levy of a Patwar cess at the rate of Rs. 3-2 per month for meeting these charges.

3. Raising the pay of Kothialas and taking security from them, in order to avoid misappropriation of the State revenue as well as introduction of proper weights, and construction of new Godowns.

4. Commutation of the system of collection in gold to cash payment, necessitated by the fact, that commutation rate, on the gold taken as part of revenue, having been raised from Rs. 12 per Tola to Rs. 18 per Tola, the Lambardars made recoveries from the Zamindars at the old rates of Rs. 12 per Tola; whereas they charged the State at the new rate of Rs. 18 per Tola, the excess between the old and the new rates going to the Lambardars concerned.

5. Curtailing, to actual requirements, the collection of fuel and grass, taken as part of revenue, in order to meet the demand from local state officials, replacing the collections thus done away with by cash assessment…"[24]

Thus Ladakh had seen cataclysmic political changes in these hundred years; as also increased economic activity. The people of the region were better prepared than ever before to enter the next – twentieth– century; that was to bring even greater changes.

24 Accessed from the records of the State Archives in Jammu, in September 2018.

Gilgit and Beyond

Gilgit was located in the north-west part of the princely J&K state and the area had predominantly Muslim population. Gilgit and tribal belts beyond effectively remained under the British control from the latter part of nineteenth century till the Independence in 1947. This was due to the strategic interests of the Empire and the British perception that the Russians were interested in making southward expansion; which could include incursions into Afghan territory as also tribal belt north of Gilgit. There was no network of roads to and within Ladakh and Gilgit. The traffic to and from this area was only on foot or by horse, yak, etc. over bridal tracks which were narrow, rough and hazardous; and hence no wheeled traffic over these was possible. Gilgit was connected with Ladakh by a mule track which ran over passes 12,000 to 14,000 feet above sea level; Leh to Gilgit was around 480 kms. From Leh, this track went west to Kargil, turned northwards from Kargil to Skardu-Gilgit and then onwards led to Wakhan province of Afghanistan and also to Sinkiang over the Pamirs. This route was also followed by Zorawar Singh who conquered Baltistan in 1839-40. Drew estimated and recorded that Gilgit was about 130 miles from Srinagar as the crow flies, but was 230 by road and the march took twenty two days. He further wrote about Gilgit as, "The fort of Gilgit is the Maharaja's chief stronghold in Dardistan. It has been at different times taken; destroyed, rebuilt, added to, and altered...this is built in the Dard style. Of a wooden framework for the wall, filled in with stones; it was really a strong work for the country... in the spring of 1871 a severe earthquake threw down a considerable portion of the fort, and it has now, I believe, been rebuilt on a better plan."[25]

The British interests, at that time were peculiarly served by passing on the Kashmir valley and other areas to Maharaja Gulab Singh. It is abundantly clear that British concluded the treaty of Amritsar on 16th March 1846 and handed over the territories mentioned therein; not out of any consideration for Gulab Singh but as a well thought out policy alternative. As shrewd businessmen they looked at it as another transaction; carefully weighing the whole deal in monetary pros and cons. The rationale behind this move becomes clear from the following extract of the communication sent by the Governor-General, dated 14th March, 1846, to the 'Secret Committee' of his masters in London. In this dispatch, he outlined and conceptualized the

25 Frederic Drew, *Op., cit,* pp. 157 and 159.

proposed line of action as, "It will be seen by the draft of the Treaty now forwarded that, in consequence of the inability of the Lahore Government to pay the sum stipulated as indemnification for the expenses of the war, or to give sufficient security for its eventual disbursement, the Hill territories, from the Beas River to the Indus, including the provinces of Kashmir and Hazarah, have been ceded to the British Government.

"It is not my intention to take possession of the whole of this territory. Its occupation by us would be, on many counts, disadvantageous. It would bring us into collision with many powerful chiefs, for whose coercion a large military establishment at a great distance from our provinces and military resources would be necessary. It would more than double the extent of our present frontier in countries assailable at every point, and most difficult to defend without any corresponding advantages for such large additions of territory. Now, the distant and conflicting interests would be created and races of people, with whom we have hitherto had no intercourse, would be brought under our rule, while the territories, excepting Kashmir, are comparatively unproductive, and would scarcely pay the expenses of occupation and management.

"On the other hand, the tract now ceded includes the whole of the Hill possessions of Rajah Gulab Singh and the Jammu family. Its possession by us enables us at once to mark our sense of Rajah Gulab Singh's conduct during the late operations, by rewarding him in the mode most in accordance with his desires, to show forth as an example to the other chiefs of Asia the benefits which accrue from an adherence to British interests, and to meet the expenses of the campaign, which we declared our determination to exact, and which, excepting by the cession of territory, the Lahore Government is not in a condition to afford.

"Rajah Gulab Singh had engaged to pay the crore of rupees demanded from the Lahore State, on being put by us in possession of the territory ceded by the 4th Article of the draft Treaty, on such terms and conditions as we may approve...."[26]

Also, historically speaking; the British had sufficient and compelling reasons for transferring Kashmir to Maharaja Gulab Singh at that point of time in 1846. But, in the next little over a decade two significant events materially changed the ground situation. In 1849 the British annexed Punjab

26 K. M. Panikkar, *Op.,cit*, pp. 161 and 162.

and made the erstwhile Khalsa kingdom as a part of their Indian domains; thus extending the western borders right up to Afghanistan and also taking in some of the restive areas and tribes of the North West Frontier. Secondly, in the aftermath of the Uprising in 1857, the British Government directly assumed responsibilities of East India Company's possessions in the sub-continent; making India as a part of the Empire. These developments substantially altered the validity of earlier assumptions and the British generally looked upon the Amritsar treaty and the deal struck under it, with considerable regret; especially giving away of the 'Switzerland of the east' – the Kashmir valley. Somehow they wanted to undo what they had done in 1846; and their future exertions need to be seen in this light.

From the early part of the 19th Century, even though the British kept a wary and discreet eye on the Czarist Russian interests to the south of their kingdom; in political analysis of the former, these did not pose material threats either to borders of Afghanistan or the Chitral-Hunza regions. The Russian threat, in British calculations, became palpably perceptible after the occurrence of Panjdeh episode in 1885. This incident which took place on the borders of Afghanistan and Russia; though was resolved peacefully but it increased British apprehensions about the security of Afghan boundary. It also highlighted the strategic importance of the entire Gilgit region and evoked almost panic reaction from the British Indian establishment about the need to undertake effective defensive measures against the Russians. The famous 'great game' was nearly at its peak. Gilgit was to become, and remain, a strategic fulcrum to the British calculations in this regard. Providentially for them; the Panjdeh incident took place near the time of Maharaja Ranbir Singh's death. Though he had not shown any hostility towards the British or their interests; but all the same passionately guarded his independence, like his father, and resisted all attempts to get a British Resident posted in his state. However, he had consented to a mutual relationship with the British; especially to allay their concerns about the Russian interests in the Gilgit area. Probably he also came to realize that, influences amongst the chiefs of the region apart, it was beyond his resources to effectively deal with the Russian power and it was more prudent to let the British manage them. In the decade of 1870s; work on the 'treaty road' from Srinagar to Gilgit – via Gurez – was taken in hand; state forces as also Imperial Service Troops and British officers stationed in various forts and secure places in Gilgit area and beyond; a British Joint Commissioner placed in Leh to look after as also regulate trade with Central Asian region; and a British officer positioned in Gilgit in 1877. Though four years later, in 1881, this functionary was withdrawn.

As already mentioned; with the Panjdeh occurrence, the British alarm further heightened and with the intention of securing more direct control over the affairs of J&K state as well as taking developments regarding Gilgit area in hand; the British explicitly linked the issue of recognition of the natural accession of Maharaja Pratap Singh to his accepting the posting of a Resident in his realm. The ruler of the state had no choice but was literally forced to accept this arrangement. Under this overall structure, the Gilgit Agency was revived and established again in 1889 under Colonel A. G. Durrand; including the areas of Hunza, Nagar, Punial, Yasin, Koh-Ghizer and Ishkoman. This time the system stayed in place for good over five decades and the Empire was thus able to secure its strategic interests; without spending any money on the civil administration of the area, which continued to be the responsibility of the state government – a typical Imperial model.

Various moves in this region and justifications thereof, from the British point of view, have been competently described by an Englishman – E.F. Knight - who visited almost the entire belt in 1891. In the last paragraph of the Preface of his celebrated book he mentions, "Kashmir has been called the northern bastion of India. Gilgit can be described as her farther outpost. And hard by Gilgit it is that, in an undefined way, on the high Roof of the World – what more fitting a place! – the three greatest Empires of the Earth meet – Great Britain, Russia, and China. Hence the title I have given to this book."[27]

This system was rigorously tested few years later, in 1895, when the rebel tribesmen laid siege to the Chitral fort; with about four hundred troops inside including British Officers, J&K state forces men and Sikh soldiers. The fort was encircled and threatened for full 47 days from 3rd March 1895 till effectively relieved by two columns. The first one comprised little over 400 soldiers from Gilgit garrison under the command of Colonel Kelly; which reached Chitral on 20th April 1895 – a day after the rebel elements, in knowledge of the coming troops, had lifted the siege and melted into adjoining hills. The larger force, marching from Rawalpindi, a division strong headed by General Sir Robert Low reached there about a week

27 E.F. Knight, *Where Three Empires Meet,* Longmans, Green and Co., London, 1919, p. viii.

later. Mobilization of military might of this level – which was certainly beyond the resources of J&K state – was a sure enough way to convince the Afghan and Russian governments as also the restive mountain tribes to keep away from making trouble in this region as the British considered it a part of their area of influence. The move apparently did serve the desired purpose; as the entire region remained comparatively quiet till 1947.

The Relief of Chitral was, in a way, an effective demonstration of the British resolve and capacity to marshal their resources and expeditiously deploy these to secure their essential and stated strategic interests. It was also a message to friends and foes alike that when the chips were down; the Empire could be depended upon to react in a predictable and declared manner. The message had actually reached well in the intended quarters; as the future developments in the region would amply prove.

All the same, British policy with regard to interests of the Empire in the far-flung mountainous regions was aptly described by Captain Francis Younghusband – he was officially holding this rank of the army then – during a lecture in the Royal Colonial Institute, London, on 12th March 1895. The subject being 'On the Kashmir Frontier'; referring to the Great Game, he said "In Asia we cannot stay still, another power on the North is advancing steadily step by step towards us, and we have been compelled to throw forward outposts…There are some Englishmen, however, who ask what is the use of our pushing out into all these remote parts, and interfering with all these wild tribes. They should realize that men who have studied the question most deeply were sure that in order to guarantee quiet in the plains of India we must have a control over the mountains bordering on them."[28]

The country side of Gilgit and small principalities around had historically remained a restive and volatile region; prone to treachery, deceit and betrayal by different personalities. These often included the rulers of little kingdoms; their brothers, sons, step-brothers, step-sons and the like. The tumultuous scenario of the whole place has been succinctly described in pages 330, 331 and 332 of the "Gazetteer of Kashmir and Ladak" published in 1890. The relevant narrative, in parts, reads, "The history of Gilgit – that is, its reliable history – does not go back further than the commencement of the present century, when it was conquered by

28 Patrick French, *Younghusband,* Harper Collins, London, 1994, p. 115.

the Yasinis under Suliman Shah, Khushwaktia. Azad Khan, of Payal, or Punial, displaced the Yasinis, and Tahir Shah of Nagar family overturned the Payal *raj.* Tahir left Gilgit to his son Sikandar Khan, who was ousted by Gauhar Aman of Yasin about 1841. Thereupon Karim Khan, brother of Sikandar Khan, sought aid from the governor of Kashmir, who, with the sanction of the Lahore darbar, sent a force of 1,000 men under Nathu Shah to assist him. In the meanwhile Sikandar Khan had been murdered; so Nathu Shah, feeling doubtful of success, sent for reinforcements. When these arrived, he assaulted the fort and took it by storm. Gauhar Aman, on hearing of this, fled precipitately to Mastuj...In 1852, however, the Gilgitis, tired of Sikh oppression, called the Yasinis and other tribes to their aid, and, rising in revolt, drove the Kashmiri troops out of the valley with a loss of 1500 men. Thus, for the third time, Gauhar Aman became master of Gilgit. In 1856 Gilgit was recaptured. But in the following year Gauhar Aman once more took the place. The Indian Mutiny and other matters now fully occupied the attention of Gulab Singh, and it was not till 1860 that his son Ranbir Singh sent a force to recover the country. Gauhar Aman suddenly dying, the fort was taken without much difficulty. The Dogras followed up their victory by going as far as Yasin, which they held for a few days and then abandoned. In 1863 some messengers of the maharaja having been robbed and imprisoned by Mulk Aman, the son and successor of Gauhar Aman, another expedition was sent against Yasin. The Yasinis were defeated and tribute exacted.

"In 1866 Hunza was attacked by the Dogras in alliance with Nagar, but, owing to the treachery of the latter State, the attack completely failed. A general alliance against the Dogras seems now to have been formed by Chitral, Yasin, Tangir, Darel and Hunza, and all Punial was wrested from them. Gilgit was then besieged, but the garrison, 2,500 strong, held out successfully till reinforced. As a punishment for this conduct, an expedition was sent into Darel by the Chonchar and Dodargali passes, which dictated terms to the Darelis... From 1867 to 1880 the history of Gilgit may be characterized as uneventful. In 1876 Captain Biddulph was sent on a mission to Gilgit and Hunza, and in the following year he was appointed Resident at Gilgit. This arrangement lasted till 1880... Revenue is raised in the shape of grain for the garrison, also the people are bound to furnish personal service according to the number of houses, which, it is believed, is nearly 1,000, every one of which can boast of a matchlock.

In this way about 600 or 700 men are actually employed in various duties, such as patrolling roads, guarding posts, and conveying supplies."

Thus, the historical fact remains that it was only during the reign of Maharaja Ranbir Singh that peace was brought to the otherwise restive region of Gilgit; conditions of tranquility prevailed there and remained in place till 1947.

The Dogra Kings

This write up covers few details about the rulers of J&K state from 1834 to the end of nineteenth century. That is the period when Ladakh came under the sway of Jammu kingdom; and later in 1846 – after the treaty of Amritsar – became part of the J&K state. Apart from Jammu and Kashmir; it became third distinctive part of this largest princely kingdom under the overall supremacy of the British Indian government. It briefly describes the reigns of Maharaja Gulab Singh and Maharaja Ranbir Singh as also the first fifteen years of the rule of Maharaja Pratap Singh; particularly those aspects which had a bearing on the Ladakh region. The remainder regime of Maharaja Pratap Singh in the next – 20th - century and that of his successor Maharaja Hari Singh till the state acceded with India on 26th October 1947; is narrated in the next chapter.

Maharaja Gulab Singh (1792 – 1858). Starting with humble beginnings in the service of the Khalsa kingdom of Maharaja Ranjit Singh; Gulab Singh's meteoric rise reflects his personal bravery, winsome courtly manners and plucky good fortune. By his untiring efforts, political manipulations, blessings of his master Maharaja Ranjit Singh and shrewd management of the developing political situations; he was able to carve the Jammu kingdom for himself – which also included Ladakh area from 1834 onwards – and the state of Jammu and Kashmir, on 16th March 1846 by virtue of the treaty of Amritsar. Apart from the Punjab and NWFP of the British India in south and west respectively; his state also touched borders with Afghanistan, Uzbekistan, Sinkiang and Tibet. The campaigns of his favorite and loyal general Zorawar Singh in Ladakh, Baltistan and western Tibet from 1834 to 1841 from the Kishtwar side; are unique in their planning, execution as also administration aspects and have no parallel in the Indian history. After the death of Zorawar Singh in December 1841, fighting the Tibetan forces; the rebel elements in Ladakh joined hands with the Tibetan commanders and rose against the Dogra regime. Gulab

Singh dispatched a strong contingent of the army from Jammu under the command of Dewan Hari Chand which was successful in suppressing the revolt and also throwing back the Tibetan troops. The Tibetan government approached for peace and in September 1842 a peace treaty was signed by Dewan Hari Chand and Wazir Punnu on behalf of Gulab Singh and Kalon Surkhan as also Depon Pishy on behalf of the Dalai Lama. By this treaty the traditional boundary between Ladakh and Tibet was reorganized and recognized by both sides.

While in the service of Khalsa Durbar of Maharaja Ranjit Singh and also his successors; Gulab Singh suffered the anguish of losing his two younger brothers, two sons and one nephew. Maharaja Gulab Singh created a seldom followed example in history by installing his only surviving son, Ranbir Singh, on the throne of J&K state during his life time. The British Governor General in India also confirmed this arrangement and Ranbir Singh as his legitimate successor. Thus Ranbir Singh ascended the throne on 20th February 1856, with requisite rituals and royal ceremonies. Gulab Singh spent rest of his life in service of the new Maharaja; his son. Ranbir Singh on his part; not only gave due respects to his father but also faithfully carried out the latter's wishes. Maharaja Gulab Singh' biographer has narrated last couple of years of his life as, "The Maharaja suffered from dropsy for a long time... The disease became worse with time, and in 1856 Gulab Singh's health began to fail. As a result he decided to entrust the administration to his only surviving son, Ranbir Singh, and to retire completely from the affairs of this world. In February 1856, he formally installed Ranbir Singh on the gadi and himself accepted the position of Governor of Kashmir, and left for Srinagar to lead a quieter life. But even in the seclusion of Srinagar he was rudely awakened by the news of the great Indian Mutiny. As soon as this news reached him, though he was on his death-bed, he ordered Dewan Jwala Sahai to proceed immediately to Rawalpindi and offer all the resources of the State to the British Government in his name. He was specially ordered to offer free hospitality to all European women who might like to leave the plains. The offer of military and financial help was accepted, and Maharaja Ranbir Singh, together with Dewan Hari Chand, was ordered to go with a large force to help in the siege of Delhi. This was the last public act of Maharaja Gulab Singh. Soon afterwards his illness became worse and he died on the 25th Sawan, 1914 (Samvat), or August, 1858, at the age of sixty-six."[29]

29 K.M. Panikkar, *Op.*, cit, pp. 149 and 150.

Maharaja Ranbir Singh (1830 – 1885). Though he did not enjoy the advantages of friendly diplomatic relations, influence and status his father had developed with the British; Ranbir Singh, at the young age of twenty-six, had behind him sufficient experience and rigorous training acquired under his father. Thus he confidently assumed the onerous responsibility of running the administration of the largest princely state in the entire British India. His first major success was to get the repatriation of about one hundred and six soldiers of his army who, as a part of general Zorawar Singh's force, had been made captive and held in Lhasa since December 1841. The Maharaja managed this through the good offices of the British Resident in Nepal in the year 1857.

Ranbir Singh mostly devoted his time to consolidate the boundaries of the kingdom he had inherited and also put the administration of these areas on as sound a footing as possible. In his time; all round progress was made on every aspect of importance to the regime from communications to education system as also collection of taxes and the like. He did not show the adventurous streak of his father and undertake the expansion of his realm; all the same the State forces did carry out operations in the Gilgit area and beyond; mostly to consolidate the farther boundaries of the kingdom. By the end of the decade of 1860; Gilgit, Punial and Yasin had firmly came under his control. Also a long conflict ended in 1870 with agreements and treaties with Rajas of Hunza and Nagar. The mountain chiefs had realized that their strength was no match to the forces of Maharaja Ranbir Singh. Towards the end of his regime, even the Mehtar of Chitral – as the ruler of this principality was called – accepted the suzerainty of the Kashmir Durbar and agreed to pay an annual token tribute. With this, the extreme northern and north-western portions of the state were brought under effective control. However, these extremities did become restive occasionally causing wearisome problems to the Dogra as also British commanders; though in all skirmishes, the local trouble creators had to face the rout.

The British did recognize Ranbir Singh's prestige and influence in the Gilgit region and beyond; but were more worried about the Russian perceived interest in this as well as Afghanistan region. Maharaja Ranbir Singh also did not agree to the British proposal to have a Resident positioned in his kingdom; diplomatically maintaining that no such mention was found in the treaty of Amritsar of 1846. As a concession though, he agreed to have a bilateral arrangement by which commerce, trade and political affairs were more directly put under the British control in the Gigit – Ladakh region. A 'treaty road' – even though it was an enlarged track – was also made, under this agreement from Srinagar – through Gurez - to Gilgit and beyond in the 1870s. Trade with Central Asia was henceforth controlled by the British Joint Commissioner (BJC) headquartered in Leh. In a mutual agreement between him and the British Governor-General Lord Lytton; Gilgit Agency was established in 1877 and a British Political Agent was posted there, for the first time, to look after the political affairs and safe guard British interests in this region; where they feared increasing Russian influence. The British officer posted in Gilgit was later withdrawn in 1881; and it was almost a decade later that the Gilgit Agency was re-established; this time on more regular and permanent basis. In spite of all this; it is also a known fact that though he extended usual courtesies to them; Maharaja Ranbir Singh was mistrustful of the British - particularly their senior functionaries.

In the decade of 1870 Maharaja Ranbir Singh also agreed to post two British officers – Drew and Johnson - as commissioners in Ladakh. This too was a major concession he made to them. It is incidental that both the officers acquitted themselves very well in the region and made a name for themselves; for good governance and keeping welfare of the locals in mind.

A noteworthy achievement for this frontier region took place in 1882; when telegraph services were extended from Srinagar to Gilgit and thence to Skardu.

Maharaja Ranbir Singh died, in Jammu, on 12th September 1885 after ruling over the extensive territories of the state for over twenty-nine years. A comprehensive evaluation of his reign mentions, "Maharaja Ranbir Singh was a judicious and liberal-minded ruler who initiated a plethora of wide ranging innovative measures for the benefit of his subjects. Through his sincere, sustained and consistent efforts he achieved incredible success for the overall development of the state and morphed the socio-economic conditions of his subjects during his ruler ship. He would be acknowledged as the most popular ruler who was conscious of his duties and obligations towards his subjects. He improved the status of his administration with dedication and lofty ideals of service."[30]

The same author, in a Jammu Daily, has further described his rule as, "Ranbir Singh's administration was required to remove the scars of many centuries of maladministration, mismanagement and harsh rules of the Afghans and the Sikhs under whom the conditions of the local inhabitants had deteriorated... He completely overhauled the administrative machinery, made an attempt to demarcate the various functions of the administration and established several separate departments for the Army; foreign relations; home affairs; civil departments besides religious endowments...During his rule he achieved unparalleled prosperity for his subjects, he remained unruffled and unfazed, successfully foiled all British strategies to impose the Resident in the State and throughout his rule maintained complete and unrestricted independence in the internal matters and gave to Jammu and Kashmir an enviable political identity."[31]

Maharaja Pratap Singh (1850 – 1925). Ranbir Singh was practically on his death-bed, when in 1885 the Panjdeh incident took place. This involved the Afghanistan and Russian forces as the episode happened on the border between these two countries. All the same it heightened the British concerns about the Russian interests – as also possible advance – southwards. This turned their misgivings on this count to anxious apprehensions; as also increased the importance of keeping Gilgit and areas around under their more direct and effective control. On the death of Maharaja Ranbir Singh; his eldest son Pratap Singh ascended the throne on 25th September, after the mourning period was over. Pratap Singh became ruler of the state in the shadow of the rising British demand for more closely managing the affairs of J&K; particularly its northern extremities. Their foremost requirement was to position a Resident in the state and they linked this issue with the formal recognition of Pratap Singh as the new king. Almost bluntly it was conveyed to Pratap Singh that posting of a Resident was a necessity due to the potential danger of Russian interests and influence on the Pamirs. Notwithstanding his well reasoned and polite objections; Sir John was posted as the first Resident in J&K and the Maharaja was virtually forced to accept the new arrangement.

30 Sat Prakash Suri, *The Dogra Rulers of Jammu and Kashmir*, Shubhi Publications, Gurgaon – India, 2011, p. 50.

31 Sat Prakash Suri in the *Daily Excelsior*, Jammu, dated 12th September 2018.

The successor Resident, C. Plowden, who joined in March 1888; started a series of events and leveling trumped up charges which ultimately, and virtually, forced Maharaja Pratap Singh to cede his rule to a State Council headed by his younger brother Raja Amar Singh in April 1889. Amar Singh was considered more pliant and accommodating by the Resident and his masters in Calcutta. Thus, the British succeeded in their design of virtual dismissal of the ruler of the state from the seat of power; the real authority passing on to the Resident, in the garb of State Council. It also considerably helped them to deal more directly with; what they perceived as the Russian threat. This way the British Indian Government managed to regain control of the areas; of strategic interests to them and which they were compelled by domestic and political reasons to part with almost half a century ago, in 1846.

Maharaja Pratap Singh was virtually reduced to an appealing, beseeching and complaining individual; requesting the British Governor-General in India, and the Supreme Monarch in London, for the restoration of his powers so severely curtailed on false and fabricated charges. He had, in the normal course of events, outlived his two younger brothers and his powers were fully and formally restored by Lord Chelmsford, in a Durbar in Jammu on 4th February 1921. Over four years later; Maharaja Pratap Singh breathed his last on 23rd September 1925.

The overall and panoramic view of Ladakh can best be squeezed in the few words of a local intellectual as, "Geographical isolation of the region, nurturing the confluence of two races, has helped Ladakh become the crucible for a distinctive socio-cultural entity. The challenges and inspiration provided by the harsh but picturesque Ladakhi environment have had their telling impact in shaping of the unique Ladakhi ethos. Besides, at one point of time in history, Ladakh had become an entrepot of trade from all four directions and thereby a tributary as well as distributary of the Silk Road. The merchandise goods traded in Ladakh included Pashmina, felt (Namda), salt, borax, sulphur, spices, brocades, pearls, metals, carpets, tea and dry apricots. Being on such a trade cross-roads has helped the people of this region acquire their own characteristic outlook. They have come to acquire something of a cosmopolitan air which, many feel, both the Tibetans and Dards conspicuously lack."[32]

32 Interaction on 8th November 2018, with Chewang Phonsog; the first IAS officer from Ladakh, who rose to become Chief Secretary of J&K State.

CHAPTER II

Ladakh up to Independence (1901 - August 15, 1947)

Ladakh at the Beginning of 20th Century.

Though the process of the conquest of Ladakh was started in 1834 by Zorawar Singh, it became part of the Jammu and Kashmir state in 1846; even though officers and soldiers were retained there for the defence of the region, as also to carry on the administration. The army officers, who also took care of the administration, were generally called Thanedars and the civil officials came to be known as Wazirs. The entire Ladakh area, including the Gilgit region, was a single administrative unit until the very beginning of the twentieth century. Some of the better known names in this period are as follows;

- Magna Thanedar – 1841 to 1846.
- Mehta Basti Ram Thanedar – 1846 to 1859. He was also a part of Zorawar Singh's army when that famous general died in the battlefield in December 1841. Basti Ram had been made in charge of the rear camp of the forces and hence was saved and returned to Leh, to recount and report back story of the debacle.
- Mehta Mangal Thanedar – 1860 to 1865. He was an able administrator and made a name for himself amongst the locals for his welfare activities and developmental works. There is still a village in Kargil district, at present, called Gund Mangalpur. It is said that the place was established by him and he insisted on

planting trees there. He reformed the tax system and made revenue settlement of the whole of Ladakh for the first time.

- Mr. Johnson Wazir – 1873 to 1882. As the name suggests he was a Britisher, employed in the tourism department of Government of India, in which capacity he had once visited Ladakh. Later, he joined the service of the state and was sent in this area as the Wazir. He is well known for his construction activities in the region, including building of the first European type of bungalow – for his own residence – there. He also reorganized the government granaries and reformed the system of land settlement introduced by Mehta Mangal. His accessibility to high and low, his sociability and quick dispensation of justice won enviable popularity for him and his administration.

- Pandit Radha Kishen Koul Wazir – 1882 to 1886.

- Choudry Khoshi Mohammad Wazir – 1906 to 1909.

By the sixth decade of the 19th century, the British Government of India started interfering in the administration of the state; particularly in Ladakh and Gilgit regions in view of their trade potential and strategic locations. In pursuance to this policy and against the wishes of Maharaja Ranbir Singh, they appointed a British Joint Commissioner in Ladakh. His duty was to supervise the trade relations with Tibet and Central Asia, as well as to keep a watch on the movements of the Russian military across the border. This arrangement was formalized in 1870 by the conclusion of a commercial treaty between the Maharaja of J&K and the Government of India. Thus the British got what they wanted in the region to safeguard their Imperial designs. Subsequent British exertions in the region; right up to 1947 and even beyond, amply prove this point. All the same, it is also a fact that some of the British Joint Commissioners posted in Leh did some good work, particularly in the field of streamlining the goods trade in the region; as also to put the postal and telegraph services in this far-flung area, on sound footing. Whereas the journey between Leh and Srinagar would take up to 21 days, the important official mail would reach these two points in mere three days. So well was this system organized and implemented. It is recorded that once the BJC was unhappy because some significant dispatches were received 'full three hours late'. Of course, the official retributions followed. It is also a matter of record that the first sub-post office in Leh was established in June 1876; kind courtesy of the then BJC. They would, of course, not permanently stay there but visit Leh for a few months every year; till this annual journey ended with the British rule in 1947. As an aside, it may be mentioned that the State had its own Telegraph Department at that time which dealt with messages not only in English but also in Urdu. It is also another measure of the deep British interests in this State to note that in 1901 there were 590 miles long telegraph lines belonging to the State and 367 miles to the former. In the next ten years, these comparative figures were to inter-change.

An interesting background of the State of Jammu and Kashmir has been briefly described at page 4, Chapter I of the Census of India - 1911, as "...Gulab Singh was made Raja of Jammu in 1820, in consequent of his defeating and capturing Agha Jan, the Rajput Musalman Raja of Rajauri, who was fighting the Sikhs. Dhyan Singh obtained the principality of Punch, and Suchet Singh the Ramnagar *ilaqa.* With this as a nucleus, the State began to expand. Basohli, Bhadarwah, Kishtwar, Bhimber, Rajauri were conquered and absorbed one by one, and the Dogra power travelled across the heights of the north-eastern hills until it reached the Ladakh country in 1840. The Buddhist Raja ruling there succumbed to the Dogra forces under Wazir Zorawar. The Mohamedan Rajas of Kharmang, Kiris, Skardu, Khaplau Shigar, etc. in Baltistan were subdued one after the other, and there remained only Kashmir with its appurtenances to be incorporated to make this extensive State complete. This was accomplished on the occasion of the war between the British and the Sikhs in Punjab. Appearing on the scene first only as a mediator after the battle of Subraon in 1846, Maharaja Gulab Singh acquired from the British, on payment of Rs. 75 *lacs*, not only Kashmir (with Mozaffarabad, the land of Bambas and Khakas) but all the country lying between the Ravi and the Indus. This included the turbulent *ilaqa* of Hazara; while, on the other hand, under Major James Abbot's demarcation Manawar and Garhi *ilaqas* had been transferred to Punjab. An exchange of these in 1847 made the State quite a self-contained and compact territory."

Similarly, in the Census of India – 1901 Report, at page 12 the Ladakh region has been mentioned as, "55. Frontier Districts. – The frontier of His Highness formerly consisted of only one district, as stated in the Introduction to this Report, but has recently been split into two districts of Ladakh and Gilgit. The frontier district is bound on the north by a chain of the Mustagh mountains and Chinese Turkistan; on the east by Tibet; on the south by Kashmir and Jammu Provinces of the State; and on the west by Yaghistan and Chitral." Thus division of the Frontier Area of J&K State was with the purpose of carving out a separate unit of Gilgit, and areas around especially in the north and west, for a more effective control of the military related matters – there by retaining as well as having a meaningful say of the British Empire in the ensuing Great Game being played by major powers in the region – as also simultaneously acquire a firmer grip over the trade with Tibet and Central Asian segments. It was in pursuance to this general policy that, even though the Maharaja's government of J&K posted a Wazir in Gilgit, the real control over the levers of power there were in the hands of the British Political Agent. He was generally a handpicked army officer who worked under the overall supervision of the Resident in the State.

The final and formal decision in this regard was taken on 12 April 1901, in a meeting of the State Council held in Jammu.[1]Accordingly, the Wazarat of Frontier District was abolished and "creation ordered of Ladakh Wazarat and Gilgit Wazarat, each under a Wazir-i-Wazarat who were to be directly responsible to the Revenue Member for all execution administration."By virtue of the same order, Pandit Vasa Kak Dar was posted as the Wazir-i-Wazarat of Ladakh and Durga Parsad as Wazir-i-Wazarat of Gilgit. There were also some minor changes made in the territories of these districts. The Ladakh Wazarat came to comprise Tehsils of Ladakh, Kargil and Skardu. The Zanskar tract, which was till then a part of Kishtwar Tehsil, was ordered to be henceforth a part of Kargil Tehsil. Thus, for the first time Zanskar became an administrative unit of the Ladakh region. Similarly, the Gilgit Wazarat included the territories of Gilgit and Astore Tehsils and the existing Niabat at Bunji. Interestingly, it was clearly mentioned in the proposal for consideration of the State Council that an effective push for this step came from the British Resident. Thus, by the first decade of twentieth century J&K state consisted of ten districts, of which five were in Jammu province; namely Jammu, Jasrota, Udhampur, Riasi and Mirpur districts. The Kashmir province comprised three districts, namely Kashmir North, Kashmir South – including Tehsil Khas, meaning Srinagar area – and Muzaffarabad. In addition, there were two frontier districts of Ladakh and Gilgit.

1 C.S. Old Record File No: 21/7-A of 1901 (accessed in the Archives at Leh in September 1998).

The constant British desire to acquire an increasingly firmer grip over affairs of this strategically located State; more so the frontier areas, in the background of the Great Game in the region, has been written about and commented on extensively by many persons and writers. It would be of interest to see what the Census of India – 1911 says in this regard. About the Political Status; it mentions "...., in the reign of the late Maharaja Sir Ranbir Singh, a 'Political Officer on special duty in Kashmir' was appointed to grant passports to European visitors and to serve as a medium of communication between the Durbar and the Government of India. With the accession of His Highness the present Maharaja in 1885, a Resident in Kashmir was appointed in place of this special officer. In 1887, at His Highness the Maharaja's own request, a Council was constituted to conduct the administration of the State, under the general control of the Resident. This Council consisted of His Highness's brother, the late Raja Sir Amar Singh, K.C.S.I., and two selected officials from the British service. In 1891 the Maharaja assumed the Presidency of the Council, with Raja Amar Singh as the Vice-President. Full powers were resumed by His Highness the Maharaja in 1905, since when he has himself carried on the administration. The State, amid all these changes, has all along enjoyed full sovereign powers so far as its internal administration is concerned, and is under the suzerainty of the British Government, through the Government of India, in respect to its foreign affairs." This document further mentions, "There is another isolated unit, Mansar village, which, though lying in Tibetan territory, belongs to the State, paying revenue to it. This village is under the Wazir-i-Wazarat of Ladakh. To guard the interests of the Central Asian trade a Political Officer, designated the British Joint Commissioner, is stationed at Ladakh. In the event of disputes between the foreign traders this officer exercises coordinate jurisdiction with the State Wazir at Ladakh. He also directs the maintenance of the treaty road between Yarkand and Kashmir, through Ladakh."[2]

The first authentic population survey figures of the people in this sparsely inhabited region are available for the year 1911; and the total came to 263195 souls. This number increased a bit to 272973 in 1921 and ten years later showed again a marginal increase to 288584. The census in 1911 showed the religion wise break-up as; 225476 Muslims, 36200 Buddhists, 1300 Hindus, 84 Christians and 135 in 'others' category. The entire Gilgit Wazarat was predominantly Muslim; whereas in Ladakh

2 Census of India - 1911, Chapter I, pp. 6 and 7.

Wazarat, Kargil and Skardu Tehsils belonged to this bracket and Leh Tehsil was mostly consisting of Buddhist. The population mix in the present Leh and Kargil districts has, more or less, remained the same.

As per the records available, cash payments in the land revenue collection system were introduced in J&K in the 1880s; but even then the local administration was given the freedom of accepting this in kind also. In Ladakh area the grain payment system was encouraged. This not only suited more to the farmers but was also helpful in the larger picture; as in the interest of the Central Asian trade the State had to maintain granaries at important halting stages and the same could well be ensured only through this means. This task was taken so seriously by the State Government that in the 'Gradation List' published in 1916, one Munshi Mirza Mohammed – a Naib Tehsildar – was shown posted as Inspector Granaries Ladakh. The settlement operations in the entire frontier region of Ladakh and Gilgit were completed between 1894 and 1911; the last being Kargil Tehsil. The main source of income for the State continued to be the land revenue collections, as in the rest of the state, but in this area custom and excise duties also were quite significant. By the beginning of twentieth century, it is estimated that the total income from Ladakh neared about one and half lacs annually, the expenses on army and civil officials hovered in the range of rupees eighty thousand. The rest was remitted to the state treasury.

In so far as the spread of education is concerned, the picture was quite dismal at the end of nineteenth century. Although fairly accurate statistics in this respect are not available; it would not be wide off the mark to presume that then the literacy rate in Ladakh was somewhere in the range of ten per thousand. This later on, reportedly, climbed to 19 in 1921 and 31 in 1941. This one set of figures significantly indicates the level of ignorance and deprivation the whole area was steeped into before the independence. The efforts of some enlightened *Thanedars* and Wazirs were few and far between to make only a marginal difference in this respect. The Moravian missionaries started a missionary school in 1889. Their purpose, of course, was to win over the local population to Christian faith through this route. The move did not make a material difference in either case. But it did jolt the State Government into action and, a decade later, the first primary school was opened in Leh as also a teacher appointed. In 1908 it was upgraded to Middle Class and another teacher was added.

Thereafter the spread of schools and education was steady but still not sufficiently effective. Almost six-seven decades were to pass before this situation could be satisfactorily turned around.

A 'Gradation List' of revenue officers of the state was issued in Jammu on 29th November 1916, by Makkbul Hosain, Revenue Minister, Jammu and Kashmir State. It showed S. Sultan Mohammed Khan as Wazir-i-Wazarat Ladakh (1903) and M. Mohammed Abdullah as Wazir-i-Wazarat Gilgit (1904). At a step lower were mentioned the names of Lala Mathra Das being Tehsildar Skardu (1899), Lala Udho Ram as Tehsildar Gilgit (1909), Sheikh Ata Mohammed posted as Tehsildar Kargil (1909) and B. Lachhman Singh Tehsildar Leh (1909)[3]. It is interesting to find in this document that Wazir-i-Wazarats were placed in four grades of pay of rupees 500, 400, 350 and 300 per month. Similarly, Tehsildars in the state were divided in four categories of pay per month of rupees 200, 175, 150 and 125. In addition, the Officiating Tehsildars were entitled to a pay of Rs. 120 per month. In the same vein, Naib-Tehsildars – forty of them in total – were divided in three monthly pay packets as rupees 75, 60 and 50 per month.

At this point of time, as also for many decades later, the main source of income for the entire region was based on agricultural activities. But the fertile tracts of land being limited, these were not sufficient to support the entire population; which had to depend upon their flocks of different animals for earning extra sources of livelihood as also getting their household stock of essentials replenished from a well established internal trade regime, based on barter system as also sometimes payments, in areas like highlands of Chang Thang, Leh town and Skardu etc. In this activity, people of 'shaam *ilaqa*' an area between Nimu –Khaltsi villages and further south in the Indus valley played a major role, as they owned and kept a good number of animals in their stock. A largely imaginary description is made in the succeeding account; though mainly based on the facts culled from various authentic sources, of a typical journey undertaken by the villagers of Ladakh to the distant highlands of Changthang for replenishment of items for their daily needs. The village under question is Khaltsi, just across the Indus river on the Srinagar – Kargil – Leh road; the time of the journey is the summer season of the early years of twentieth century and the group of villagers planning to proceed ahead under the leadership of their

3 Copy of this 'Gradation List' is in the Archives Section of Leh.

village-head, who 'in spite of his youth, he was the undisputed leader of the trading expedition as of other village affairs'. The interesting sequence of events is graphically described, in considerable details as, "Now the last preparations were made. Bags were filled with wheat, barley and apricots. A few had acquired cotton goods, cloth, coloured sashes, dyes, spices and tobacco from an Indian merchant in Srinagar. Everything was packed into bags. Each participant kept his own goods rigidly separate. Several of the villagers had brought out weapons – old flintlocks and muzzle loaders. Then the horses were fetched from the mountain pastures. That in itself took two days because the horses had scattered far on the bare hillsides in their search for food. Saddles and bridles, bags, blankets and tents were repaired by the men. At last everything was ready. In the last few days the horses had been fed with barley to strengthen them for the journey as well as their usual food of clover mixed with chopped up straw. They looked healthy though some were wild and unruly when they were being shod. This task was taken care of by the villagers themselves. The wildest horses had to be bound and shod on the ground. All this was carried out by the men with great skill and confidence.

"Then the people drove about 200 sheep and goats out of their stalls. They were to join the expedition as the beasts of burden. Each animal was loaded with a double bag consisting of 14 to 15 kg of grain, dried apricots or the equivalent weight of other goods. Moreover, every one of them was literally carrying his own fleece to market. The mountain sheep are strong and particularly good climbers. Nevertheless many succumb to the strain of the long journey or are torn apart by wolves or snow leopards…

"In order to spare both man and beast the journey was divided into easy daily marches, reaching Leh in three days mostly by following the Indus. Most of the men went by foot. Drogpa Namgyal (the headman) and two others had a horse for riding as well as their pack horses. The men on foot undertook to take care of the pack horses, guiding them on the narrow track. They also had to lead and keep together the herd of laden sheep and goats. In Leh bazaar they made their last purchases of provisions and trade goods. Then they continued along the Indus – through bare valleys, narrow gorges, sandy snowy deserts, over high passes and through rushing torrents, now in the burning sunshine, now in icy cold and even a fierce snowstorm. So, trading on the way wherever they had a chance, they reached Changthang after about a month….

"There the Ladakhis visited a succession of scattered nomad camps. Year in, year out these nomads live in their brown tents woven out of yak wool. They tend and protect a long-legged variety of sheep, and herds of goats, horses, donkeys and yaks. They move from one pasture to another, wherever there happens to be grazing and water. Great, strong, long-haired dogs help the nomads to keep their flocks together and protect them from wild beasts. Their whole wealth consists of these herds together with rock salt which they break out of the many old sea-beds, and rock soda which is also found on the plateau...

"The villagers had done good business; almost all their own and Indian goods had been exchanged. They still wanted to find a bigger camp where yet more soda (for making tea) could be obtained. This camp lay beyond the usual trade route in a broad valley"[4].

Imperial Service Troops

The British devised an ingenious plan to effectively control these difficult and mountainous terrains by using the troops raised and trained at the expense and expertise of the native rulers; with the effective and active involvement of selected young British army officers, as 'stiffeners'. This phenomenon has been described as "... the Imperial Service troops, who compose the Gilgit garrison (this was written in 1891). It will be remembered that, according to the recently-organised scheme, the fundamental principles of which were settled by the present Foreign Secretary in India, Sir Mortimer Durand, some of the important native States now place a certain portion of their armies at the disposal of our Government for the purpose of Imperial defence, the drilling and training of the men supervised by selected British officers. The State of Kashmir supplies three regiments of Imperial Service troops and a mule battery, in all about two thousand men, who, like the regulars, are Gurkhas and Dogras. They are well equipped, and are armed with Sniders. Thanks to the energy with which the officers of the Agency have taken them in hand, the men now know their duties as disciplined soldiers, and have a smart appearance, which is more than can be said of the sepoys of the other Kashmir regiments... The Dogra General, Suram Chand, who commands the Gilgit Brigade, arrived this day with his staff. The somewhat anomalous system with which the Imperial Service troops are employed in the field

4 S.H. Ribbach, *Culture and Society in Ladakh,* Tr. John Bray, Ess Ess Publications, New Delhi, 1986, pp. 146-148.

was now on its first trial. We had with us Dogra officers of high rank, but in action, at any rate, they were practically superseded by the British officers, generally subalterns attached to the Kashmir regiments, who led the men. No friction or other difficulty apparently resulted, and it seemed to me that great tact and sense were displayed on either side in dealing with these delicate relations."[5]

A mention of this ingenious scheme of force management is made in a later Indian publication as, "The armies of the State of Kashmir enjoyed a peculiar position by virtue of its geographical situation. Its troops garrisoned their own frontier districts and engaged themselves constantly with the tribes on its borders and thus saw a considerable amount of frontier service. The defence of Chitral was largely carried out by the Kashmir troops, consisting of Imperial Service Artillery and Mountain Batteries, for the defence of the Gilgit frontier. The various states, while retaining regular troops, reduced their numbers to meet the extra cost of the Imperial Service Corps. The Gwalior contingent was one of the crack forces of India. It was decreed that the Imperial Service Troops should be exclusively the subjects of the Gwalior Ruler for the purpose of being commanded by him."[6]

Thus the British, by this mechanism, were able to use effectively the forces maintained and paid for by the Indian rulers, for potently taking care of their Imperial interests in the north and north-west of the Indian peninsula; without spending their own money. The basic concept of Imperial Service Troops was conceived and fleshed out by the then Viceroy, Lord Dufferin in 1888. It was envisaged that selected units from few chosen states would be helped by the Government of India to modernize the weapons and equipment and by sending British officers to these states to train these men to ensure their performance levels be in consonance with the British Indian Army. Till the First World War, Jammu and Kashmir State provided the largest contingent of Imperial Service Troops comprising one infantry brigade and two Mountain Batteries. Most of these, of course, were deployed and used by the British in Gilgit area. "By 1894, the British agent in Gilgit, Mr Bruce, was able to report that

5 E. F. Knight, "Where Three Empires Meet", Longmans Green and Co, London, 1919, p. 317 and p. 380.

6 H. H. The Maharaja of Jaipur, "A History Of The Indian State Forces", Orient Longmans, New Delhi, 1967, p. xiv.

the Imperial Service Troops in Gilgit had become an efficient force and 'the Dogra officers were very keen and loyal. They were well-fed and disciplined and active'."[7]

Gilgit

Gilgit and regions north and west of it – like Chitral, Hunza and Nagar etc – although were under the sway of Maharaja of Jammu and Kashmir, in terms of sovereignty and suzerainty, the British right from the beginning kept a close watch in the region; as part of their overall strategy of keeping the territories' secure from the suspected southward expansion of the Russians, under what has come to be known as "the great game". The contours of this scheme of things have been clearly enunciated in the Defence of India Plan, in 1927, as "His Majesty's Government are of opinion that the preservation of the existing frontier of Russia and Afghanistan is of vital importance to India and the British Empire, and in certain eventualities would be prepared to develop the whole forces of the Empire to preserve the integrity of Afghanistan and resist the extension of Russian dominion southward….."[8]. The British interests and movement of troops in this belt were always within these parameters and in pursuance to this overarching policy. It was in this context that the British interests in the frontier areas of J&K State, particularly in the Gilgit region, came to acquire a special significance and they started exerting pressure on the ruler to accept positioning of their representative, preferably the Resident. But, as long as Maharaja Ranbir Singh was ruling the state, he thwarted all such attempts. With his death and Maharaja Pratap Singh ascending the throne in 1885, the British renewed their efforts with greater vigor to increase their influence in J&K. Notwithstanding the opposition and objections by Maharaja Pratap Singh, the British appointed Sir Oliver St. John as the first resident in Kashmir; who arrived in the state in March 1888. The British interference in the exclusive matters of the state reached a material high with their establishing Gilgit Agency in 1889. This also included areas of Hunza, Nagar, Punial, Yasin, Koh-Ghizer and Ishkoman. The military responsibility of the J&K State forces, thereafter, extended up to Bunji in the frontier region and beyond that the charge of defence

7 Major General D.K. Palit, VrC, *Jammu and Kashmir Arms,* Palit & Dutt Publishers, Dehradun, 1972, p. 71.

8 As quoted in, "Defence of India: Policy and Plans", published by Combined Inter-Services Historical Section (India & Pakistan) – 1963, New Delhi, p. 23.

functions was assumed by the British. Even though the civilian matters continued to be managed by the state administration as heretofore.

In this context, at least till the region remained under the control of the Maharaja of Jammu and Kashmir up to late 1947, it may be proper to treat these areas as part of Ladakh rather than be combined with the regions of either Jammu or Kashmir. The British made Gilgit as the secure base of their northern extremity of Imperial influence in the Indian sub-continent. Even though their presence in the region started around eighth decade of the nineteenth century; this was formalized by a commercial treaty with J&K in the year 1870. The importance of Gilgit as a strategic location and its significance for the British Empire has been explained by a contemporary author as, "The value of Gigit to the Kashmir State, commanding as it does the Indus Valley and the mouth of the Hunza River, and so holding in check the unruly on either side, is obvious enough, but it is only recently that the great strategical importance to the Empire of this position has been fully realized.... The Russian expeditions are exploring the passes of the Hindoo Koosh on the northern side.... while we are ever hearing of fresh movement and gatherings of Czar's forces on our frontier.... Should we submit to this trespassing of Russian troops into states which we guarantee against foreign invasion, the natives cannot but lose faith in us.... and here a very small body indeed could prove the nucleus of far-spreading mischief... Gilgit, the northern most outpost of the Indian Empire, covers all the passes over the Hindoo Koosh, from the easternmost one, the Shimshal, to those at the head of the Yasin River, in the west.... But the possession of the Gilgit Valley does more than this: it afford us a direct communication through Kashmir territory to the protected State of Chitral, which would be otherwise removed from our influence by the interposition of countries at present practically closed to us. We now guarantee the independence of Chitral against Afghanistan, as we that of Afghanistan against Russian aggression...."[9]

The purposeful British exertions started with the commercial treaty signed between the Governments of India and Kashmir in 1870. This paved the way for more orderly conduct of the existing mercantile discourse between various states of the region, passing through the Ladakh area; as also expediting the infrastructural improvements in this territory. This, in turn facilitated the movement of troops and ordnance; particularly to

9 Knight, *op., cit.* pp. 288 – 291.

Gilgit and beyond including Chitral, Hunza and Nagar; as also paved the way for a British representative to be stationed at Leh, known as Joint-Commissioner. He oversaw the trade with Central Asian region as also with Tibet; as well as settling all disputes whenever these arose between different trading parties; which were not very often. A contemporary account records, "The presence of this officer at so important a centre has already produced excellent results: most of the abuses that hampered the trade on this route have been swept away, and the merchants are no longer so outrageously blackmailed as before on their way through Kashmir territory. The duties that were once levied on caravans passing through Leh were abolished some years ago by the Maharajah's Council..."[10] Also in pursuance to this Treaty, a new and much improved 'road' was constructed between Srinagar and Gilgit. This came about as a result of the contract drawn between an English firm, Messrs Spedding & Co. and the Kashmir Durbar. This mountain track of significant strategic value passed over two high passes – the Rajdiangan and Burzil – as also traversing a distance of about 380 kilometers between Srinagar and Gilgit and going through Gurez valley and Deosai plains; was ten feet wide throughout, and with a maximum incline of one in ten. The whole project was completed in 1893; considerably facilitating the movement of troops and supplies up to the endpoint. This was an important enterprise for which nudging came from the Empire and cost was borne by the State of Jammu and Kashmir – a classic pattern of colonial dispensation.

By the last decade of the nineteenth century, 1891 to be precise, the British domination, and in some cases forceful exertion of their military power, had extended west and north of Gilgit to the principalities of Chitral, Hunza and Nagar. These areas were inhabited by unpredictable, capricious and often hostile people; with strong tribal bonds, whose passions could be aroused by the local chieftains without much difficulty. The British policy was not to physically govern them; that job was sensibly and deliberately left to the local rulers or chiefs, but deny the benefit of their alliance to an inimical power – the Russians. This, the British achieved with the help of Imperial Service troops, mostly comprising J&K State forces, commanded by selected British officers and located in secure fort-like structures right up to the Wakhan Corridor of Afghanistan and the Karakoram ranges.

10 Knight, *op., cit.* p. 159.

The main British base of course always remained at Gilgit, from where officers of the Empire kept a wary eye on this region and effectively projected the Imperial power as and when required. Even otherwise the rulers of Chitral, Hunza and Nagar had accepted the suzerainty of the J&K Maharaja and paid annual tributes to him; as also the over lordship of the Empress of India – the Queen Victoria. All the same, the British also knew that these local tribes would always side with the mightier military power and therefore this military superiority needed to be projected all the time; more particularly so, when challenged. They had followed similar policy also in the North West Frontier region with good results and understood that any laxity in this respect, in any particular sector, would end up in unraveling this careful model. A serious breach, however, did take place in the mid 1890, which amply tested this British resolve.

In March 1895 the garrison at Chitral, an unalloyed representation of the British Empire, was besieged; in the midst of a mountainous region and hundreds of kilometers away from the nearest support. It was a direct challenge to the British prestige, as also military might, and the Empire picked up the gauntlet. Not doing so would have not only resulted in their losing face but also seriously and adversely affecting their policy in the entire area; including the NW sector as well as Afghanistan – if not against Russia itself. The British counteraction was swift and decisive; leaving no doubt in the minds of friends and foes alike that they meant business and an effective one at that.

The problem started with the death of the ruler of Chitral, Aman-ul-Mulk; and the British political agent at the time there was Surgeon Major G.S. Robertson. In order to influence the power change-over as also to effectively deal with the ensuing local intrigues; Robertson brought a force of about 400 soldiers and some British officers from Gilgit and housed them in the Chitral fort. This body of troops – the maximum that could be spared from Gilgit at that time - included a contingent of 300 from Kashmir Infantry and 100 of the 14th Sikhs. In the on-going succession struggle, a local chieftain influenced the Chitrali tribesmen to encircle the small British force, inside the Castle, and attempted to subdue it by force. Thus started a siege of this garrison which lasted for 47 days, from March 3 to April 19, 1895; till the relief force, under Colonel Kelley, arrived from Gilgit and dispersed the hostile tribesmen. A much larger body of troops, a division strong from Peshawar, was still few days' march away from

Chitral. "When it became apparent how critical the state of affairs were, the Government of India saw that it was necessary to move up as many troops as could be spared from Gilgit to afford some relief to the Chitral garrison till the large force under General Low, which was to march from Peshawar direction, could reach Chitral…"[11] As per this plan; Colonel Kelley marched about 350 kilometers from Gilgit over rough and mountainous terrain, with 400 troops and two guns – as only this much force could be spared from that station – to reach Chitral. Because of difficult topography and administrative problems, each soldier was allowed fifteen pounds of baggage and carried a greatcoat and eighty rounds of ammunition. His immediate aim was to help the besieged force there and to bolster up the defences till larger body of supporting troops could arrive from Peshawar. Starting from Gilgit on March 23, he reached Chitral on April 20 and came to know that a day before the siege had been raised by the local tribesmen; who had fled from the scene learning about his force and also in the knowledge that a much larger body from Peshawar was only few days' march away.

Strategic philosophy of the whole operation has been described in a book, by two brothers, who closely watched the events, as "… the maintenance of our influence in Chitral was a matter of the first importance. To abandon Chitral to the possibility of foreign occupation would involve a risk which ought not to be run, and it would be unjustifiable to ignore our pledges to preserve the suzerainty of Kashmir…. Just on the brink of a disaster the British forces came out triumphant… and the story of the defence and relief of Chitral will be handed down to posterity as one of the most brilliant chapters in the annals of Indian military history."[12]

All said and done, the British presence and machinations in the entire area were not based on any sound footing; but largely depended on the goodwill of the J&K Maharaja. Being cognizant of this fact, the policy planners of the Government of India – with full backing of the Imperial strategists – started working to devise a model which would give them a more formal foothold and say in matters relating to this sensitive region. This desire became more urgent after September 1925 when Maharaja Hari Singh became ruler of the State. His general attitude

11 G.J. Younghusband and F.E. Younghusband, "The Relief Of Chitral", Macmillan and Co., London, 1895, p. 136.

12 Younghusband, *op., cit,* pp. 177 and 175.

to the British presence in the State and various statements attributed to him - more particularly his stated desire to abolish the Gilgit Agency and resume control of that territory - made the British uncomfortable. This apprehension turned into alarm with the Maharaja's stance at the First Round Table Conference held in London, during November 1930 and January 1931. Thereafter, the British almost became desperate and started feverishly working for the transfer of Gilgit to the Government of India. What followed was like a complicated game of 'chess' in which moves and counter moves were controlled by the Viceroy in New Delhi. In this encounter of no holds barred of wits and ideas – also impinging strongly on the law and order scenario of the state – Maharaja Hari Singh was roundly by-passed, beaten and cornered. The Viceroy "seems to have laid himself open to the suspicion, that he may have been, if nothing else, fishing in troubled waters….. The Ministry was ultimately changed and while EJD Colvin was appointed the Prime minister of Kashmir with effect from 22 February 1932, three other British nominees took over Home, Revenue and Finance departments."[13] The new Prime Minister of J&K purposefully devoted himself to work out a suitable and practical formulation about Gilgit, keeping British interests fully in mind. By August 1933 he was able to send a suitable proposal to the Viceroy; as is evident from the latter's telegraphic message to the Secretary of State for India, in London. It read as follows, "My official telegram dated 31 August 1933 Gilgit. Alternative proposal of Kashmir Government to transfer entire control of civil and military administration to Government of India seems to provide excellent opportunity for permanent stabilization of position in Gilgit which is recognized to be so desirable…."[14] It did take some more time for both parties to work out mutually acceptable formulations of certain matters; and finally on 3 April 1935, these terms of agreement were ratified by the Viceroy. This deed took effect from 1 August 1935; which meant that from that day the strategic territory of Gilgit was transferred to the Government of India on lease for sixty years. The very first clause of this accord, which said it all, read as "That the civil and military administration of the entire Gilgit territory would be resumed by the Viceroy and the Governor General of India, although the territory would continue to be included within the dominions of the Maharaja of Kashmir." Thus, notwithstanding the fact

13 Major Dr. K. Brahma Singh (Retd), "British Diplomacy in Kashmir", Reliance Publishing House, New Delhi, 1998, p.154.

14 *Ibid*, p.155.

that his flag was allowed to fly there, ruler of the State lost Gilgit region to the British. Though the deal was to remain in operation for sixty years – practically till August 1995 – the British paramountcy lapsed on India gaining independence on 15 August 1947; and with that this agreement also became redundant. The Gilgit region was formally handed over to the nominee of Maharaja on 1 August 1947. It is a different story that this was done only in name and the British game was much too deeper in the region. It is also a fact that after stitching the Gilgit agreement; the British lost all interest in the developments taking place in the State and left it to the Maharaja to deal with the emerging scenario.

Durbar at Gilgit

However, notwithstanding the life of Gilgit lease deed for sixty years from August 1935; the British interests, presence and exertions in the region had been effectively taking place since more than half a century earlier. Over the years it had developed a peculiar momentum and protocol; which reflected the pageantry, pomp as also the arrogance of power of the Empire. Most important manifestation of this phenomenon was the ritual of Annual Political Durbar at Gilgit presided over by the Political Agent; who naturally was a selected British officer of the Political Department of Government of India. To understand various nuances of the region and official decorum etc., it would help to go through an entire 'Durbar Order' issued by the Military Assistant to the political Agent. This document, mentioned here only as a sample, is dated 4 February 1925[15] and reads as,

"1. All British officers will be at the Agency House at 4-40 p.m. on Thursday the 12th March 1925 and will attend the Political Agent mounted to the Durbar which will be held in front of the Fort at 5 p.m.

Dress British officers Review order (Military).

2. On arrival at the parade ground the Political Agent will dismount. The drums will then play a roll and all present at the durbar will stand up.

3. The Political Agent accompanied by the Military Assistant and the Colonel Commandant will inspect the Guard of Honour. The Assistant Political Agent will rejoin the Political Agent after he has completed the inspection. The remaining officers having taken up a position as shown by

15 This group of papers is titled as C.S./G.B./ File No : 279/F-11/ of 1925 – Annual Political Durbar at Gilgit; and was accessed in the Archives Section of Leh in September 1998.

the small squares on the sketch map, will salute the Political Agent as he passes up the centre and joining in behind him take their seats on the Dias.

4. The Wazir-i-Wazarat and officer Commanding units will await the arrival of the Political Agent on the Dias and will salute him as he reaches the steps and move off to their seats.

5. The Military Assistant, a few moments after the Political Agent has taken his seat, will advance in front of the Political Agent; face him, salute and ask if the Durbar may be declared open. On the Political Agent's giving his assent the Military Assistant will face the people, declare the Durbar open and resume his seat.

6. The Wazir-i-Wazarat will present a nazar and the Colonel Commandant Gilgit area, his sword. The officers of the Kashmir State forces will then present their swords to the Political Agent.

7. The officers of the Gilgit Corps of Scouts will then present their swords to the Political Agent.

8. The Chiefs will then in order of seniority noted below present nazars which will be touched and remitted except in the case of the Chiefs of Hunza and Nagir, who will present their tribute :-

1. Mir Sir Mohamad Nazim Khan K.C.I.E, Mir of Hunza.
2. Mir Shah Sikandar Khan, K.B.E., C.I.E., Mir of Nagir.
3. Khan Bahadur Raja Mohammad Anwar Khan, Governor of Panial.
4. Raja Shah Abdur Rahman Khan, Governor of Yasin.
5. Mir Ali Mardan Shah, Governor of Iskkoman.
6. Khan Bahadur Raja Murad Khan, Governor of Kuh-Ghizar.
7. Raja Jafar Ali Khan of Gilgit.
8. Raja Hasan Khan of Astor.

9. The Political Agent will then deliver an address in English to the Chiefs and headmen. On the Political Agent rising to make his speech all present will stand up and remain standing until permitted to resume their seats.

The Indian Assistant will then bow and resume his seat.

10. After a few moments the Indian will ask leave to present recipients of Khillats and when permitted to do so will call out names of recipients.

11. Every one attending the Durbar will be in his place by 4.40 p.m.

12. The Military Assistant will then ask (as in Para 5) if the Durbar may be closed and on being given assent by the Political agent will turn and declare Durbar closed.

13. At the conclusion of the Durbar the Political Agent will take his departure accompanied by the British officers. All others will stand up and keep their places until he has gone.

14. Durbaris (chiefs and headmen) would not wear boots of any description or native shoes while attending the Durbar but the recognized English shoes as ordered by the Government of India or Paboos. Native shoes should be left outside the limits of the Durbar. Ammunition boots will not be worn except by soldiers on duty of whose uniform they form a part.

15. All ponies are to be kept off the Parade ground.

16. The orderlies or servants of spectators will be allowed inside the ring of Military Police round the Durbar ground. The body guards of Chiefs will be drawn up as shown in the sketch map."

The above are the detailed instructions regarding programme and protocol to be followed at the annual durbar of the Political Agent of Gilgit; which in this case took place on 12th March 1925. Herein a speech was also delivered by the Political Agent; opening lines of which indicated the official precedence from his point of view. It began with, "Wazir Sahib, Colonel Sahib, Chiefs, Motabars and guests."

Other important and salient portions of this speech, covering a broad panoramic scenario of the region, included "...I am pleased to be able to announce that the Resident hopes to pay a visit to the Agency in the autumn. Unfortunately, the time at his disposal will not be enough for him to travel all over the Agency, but he will visit Hunza and Nagar and return to Kashmir through Chilas. He regrets that he cannot go further afield, but hopes to meet here at Gilgit all those to whose districts he cannot go himself...I will now turn to the internal affairs of the Agency – the past year has been generally uneventful and the administration of the Agency has been satisfactory. The harvest has been excellent and we are fortunately relieved from the anxieties of the last few years...The second matter is the entry into the Agency, from Chitral, of some 150 Maulais who fled from their homes for religious reasons. I have not full enough information to enable me to judge of the rights or wrongs of the case, but I am glad to say that His Highness the Mehtar[16] recently gave a written assurance that the refugees and their property would be safe if they returned to Chitral, and that they have now gone back to their homes...Our friend Mir Shah Sikandar Khan has received the honour of being created a Knight of the most excellent Order of the British Empire in 1923; and it falls to me today to present him with the Insigma of his Knighthood. Our friend Raja Mohamad Anwar Khan was made a Khan Bahadur last year and I have the pleasant duty of presenting him with the Badge and Sanad of the title."

Thus ended the speech and ceremonies of the Annual Durbar of the Political Agent of Gilgit; undoubtedly an occasion of importance in itself. But the reporting of this event through the State administrative channels and due notice at different levels of hierarchy, does tell its own story. The entire proceedings - along with copies of the 'Durbar Order' and speech of the Political Agent – were reported by the Wazir-i-Wazarat Gilgit, Pandit Dina Nath, on 28th March 1925, to the Foreign Member of Council of the State. The latter, in turn, endorsed a copy of this report – on 8th April - for perusal of the Ruler. Maharaja Pratap Singh is documented to have 'seen' and retuned the papers on 15th May 1925.

Marriage of a Princess

Considering the harsh climate, geography, low population density, huge area and volatility of the region; as also long distances from centre of the power; Ladakh has always been considered a difficult place to govern. That is the reason which prompted the rulers of the State to send very competent officers there after this region became a part of Jammu and Kashmir. Most of the administrators after the middle of nineteenth century were men of high caliber and known capabilities. Even of such handpicked officers, in the beginning of 20th century, one name certainly stands out and that is of M. Hashmat Ullah Khan, who became Wazir-i-Wazarat Ladakh in the year 1911. He was not a resident of the state in the strict sense; and was born

16 The ruler of Chitral was traditionally called "Mehtar".

near Lucknow in the U.P. In his youth he took up employment with J&K State and rose to administer the district of Udhampur and then was sent to Ladakh. In that region, even after a century, he is still remembered with affection, especially amongst the older people. He was dark in complexion and therefore the local people fondly refer to him as Wazir 'Nakpo' (Nakpo means black in Ladakhi). It is said that he could fluently understand as also speak the local language and dialects. There are a number of stories connected with the man; most famous of those is the one about Khurbathang canal near the town of Kargil. It was undoubtedly a very ambitious project taken in hand at a time when keeping public peace and *status quo* was the main job of high officials like him. Hashmat-Ullah was different; he thought big and acted with decisiveness. Just outside Kargil, there was this huge and barren plateau, called Khurbathang, which he thought of making green and fit for cultivation; and in Ladakh all cultivation is dependent upon assured source of irrigation. He conceived of bringing water from many kilometers away, from a local stream, through a gravity canal. It was certainly an audacious plan; considering the technical and financial resources involved and their availability to the local administrators then. But, these limitations did not deter Hashmat-Ullah and he went ahead with his plan; completed this work and almost succeeded in getting water at the Khurbathang plateau. His failure in the end was due to the faulty alignment in a portion of the canal – generally believed to be an act of sabotage by the concerned engineering staff. Be that as it may; the fact is that it was a bold and daring undertaking and the man was certainly much ahead of his times. Khurbathang plateau did get water ultimately, but only a hundred years later; through the same water source and also along a higher contour than originally envisaged. However, even now the old configuration of the channel is faintly visible all along the course; a silent and standing tribute to the efforts and genius of Hashmat-Ullah and his concern for the welfare of local population.

One of his almost unknown, delicate and complicated tasks was to try and find a bride, of high origin, for the Maharaj Kumar of Sikkim. This assignment lasted for almost nine months, from June 1911 to March 1912, and is based on the recorded correspondence between the Resident's office, Chief Minister of Jammu and Kashmir State and Wazir-i-Wazarat Ladakh.[17]In this regard a letter dated 8th June 1911, originates

17 The details of this episode are based on the correspondence available in the Archives Section of Leh; as accessed in September 1998.

from the Chief Minister of J&K State – Rai Sahib Dewan Amar Nath. It is mentioned therein "Maharaj Kumar of Sikkim has expressed his desire to the Government of India in regard to his intention to marry a Buddhist lady of some respectable family from Ladakh, the Govt of India have asked the Resident to arrange through the Darbar to find out some suitable match for the Maharaj Kumar. The Maharaj Kumar is of 34 years of age and a devout Buddhist, and wishes to marry a grownup Buddhist lady, if possible an English knowing one." The Wazir is further asked to make confidential inquiries about the proposed match from the areas of Ladakh, Zanskar, Purig etc; obtain full particulars – and if possible a photograph of the girl – in such a manner that the parents of the girl may not come to know about the matter till it is finally settled. The letter ends with two directions; that the reply should be sent back before end of the month and that the whole matter may be treated 'strictly confidential'.

A suitable reply is sent by Hashmat-Ullah, on 2nd July 1911. In view of the secrecy involved in this sensitive matter, this communication is personally written by the Wazir, in which he rightly pointed out, "...The most respectable family of Buddhists in Ladakh, Zanskar and Purig is that of the Raja of Stok whose grandfather Giapu Tandup Namgyal was the ruler of Ladakh at the time of conquest. He has no daughter of his own..." The Wazir singles out another suitable spouse for the Maharaj Kumar (name and identity of the lady have been deliberately withheld) and expressed hope that soon enough he would, through his contacts in the high places, be able to get a photograph also.

In the beginning of October, 5th to be precise, a letter from office of the Resident reminds Chief Minister of the State "... if possible, a photograph of the lady....may be obtained, as the Maharaj Kumar is desirous of seeing a copy." Few days later a suitable, but courteous, reminder is addressed to Hashmat-Ullah by the State Chief Minister. This letter is replied to on 15th November in which, apart from other matters, the Wazir said, "I beg to enclose herewith a photograph..... The photo, I am sorry to say is not a good one. There are no professional photographers in Ladakh and as the matter had to be managed without giving the least opportunity to the lady or to her parents to suspect the real object, no better could be arranged. I, however, hope that it will serve to give the Maharaj Kumar at least some idea..." Here again, keeping in mind the requirement of confidentiality of the matter, this letter and the enclosures were personally written by

Hashmat-Ullah in his own hand. Apart from the photograph; he also sent three other papers including the Gyneological Tree of the said family which confirmed their high status, characteristics of the lady in question as also a reference to the expectations of the family for State help in case of finalization of the marriage.

All this was passed on to the Resident, by the State Chief Minister towards the end of November 1911. After that the latter is informed by the Resident, on 19th March 1912, "....that the Political Officer in Sikkim has reported that the Maharaj Kumar does not desire marriage with the lady....." Thus the whole issue came to an end without any material change in the current situation. But, one can imagine how much strain this subject must have put on the Ladakh Wazir; considering the need for keeping the whole matter under wraps, limited resources available then as well as extreme conservativeness of the persons involved. No one would be able to logically guess as to whether the Maharaj Kumar actually changed his mind or political considerations of the Raj prevailed. In any case had this alliance materialized, then how it would have affected the future of Sikkim; is a matter of endless speculation. That Hashmat-Ullah was an important part of this initiative is almost like an act of natural justice; considering his undeniable talents.

In the end it needs be mentioned that after retirement he did write his reminiscences and put in print his vast knowledge about this region. The book was published in Urdu and the stock quickly exhausted. It remained out of print for more than five decades. It was, few years ago, translated in English by Zain-ul-Aabedin Aabedi and published by Atlantic Publishers, New Delhi, in 2014; under the title "History of Tibet and Great Tibet". As a tribute to the legendry civil servant, that Hasmat-Ullah certainly was, in those by-gone days of the early twentieth century are these comments about the book by a scholar, "Penned by such a person of eminence, who was also the Wazir-e-Wazarat of Ladakh, the book is the authentic chronology of history and an anthology of significant socio-political events of the past and present which shaped both these regions and Baltistan. The book presents to the reader a comprehensive canvas as the author minutely observes the people's traditional way of life; together with their rich and distinct heritage."

Polyandry

The custom of Polyandry, that is, a woman keeping more than one husbands – usually brothers – has been widely prevalent amongst the Buddhists of Ladakh since ancient times. The exact roots and origin of this norm have not been determined with any finality; except that in certain societies and under certain circumstances such a practice found acceptability amongst the people. In the Muslim society, though, the prevalence is of exactly opposite nature in the form of Polygamy; which means a man having more than one legally wedded wife.

The system of Polyandry has not been limited to the Buddhists of Ladakh only, but was practiced over the centuries by many tribes and people living in the higher altitudes of the Himalayan region as also the Tibetan plateau. Though many scholars have written about it; the most authentic and celebrated work in this field is certainly by Dr. Y.S. Parmar, who rose to be the first Chief Minister of Himachal Pradesh. He acquired his Ph.D. from Lucknow University in 1944 and the topic of his thesis was "Polyandry in the Himalayas". This was later published also as a book by the same name. Dr. Parmar has deeply gone into the rationale and various forms – as also derivations – this practice took, over a period and among different people residing in the upper reaches of the Himalayan belt.

Coming back to Ladakh and without going into the merits and de-merits of this custom; it is true that Polyandry coupled with the acceptance of the ancient Hindu tradition of *Primogeniture*, that is, of the eldest brother becoming sole owner of the entire property as also shouldering the responsibility for upkeep of the whole family; became a stabilizing influence on the socio-economic scene for centuries together. In a land-locked society with very few means of subsistence, these two customs taken together prevented fragmentation of the scarce land resource, kept the family cohesion intact as also ensured a regular entry of *monks* and *chomos* (female monks) in the various monasteries. In fact almost every Buddhist family in Ladakh thought that it was blessed if one of its members joined a monastery to become 'lama'. In each family; on account of the custom of polyandry and the law of primogeniture – prevailing then – it was usually one of the younger brothers who left the family to enter a monastery. But, the fact remains that such a practice is certainly an anathema to any modern and progressive society and had to go one day. Even though it was largely practiced in the region till the fourth decade of 20th century; it was declared a legal offence and banned by a law promulgated by Maharaja Hari Singh in 1941. After that though this practice was observed surreptitiously in the interiors of the region; Polyandry slowly disappeared from the whole of Ladakh during the second part of the 20th century.

Trade with Central Asia Region, Tibet and Internal trade

Trading activities in the Ladakh region have been the resultant outcome of the twin factors of agro-climatic conditions and the strategic location of Leh town. Harsh climate, high altitude and scanty rain fall were mainly responsible for low yield of the land and that too was limited to areas with heights lower than Leh; which meant less than eleven thousand feet. Even then the out-put was limited, to being single crop as also based on assured irrigation of the flowing streams during the short period of summer months. At the higher altitudes, Changthang plateau and areas around, the population was totally dependent upon the animals they kept and reared; earning from the load carrying capacity of these creatures and different by-products got from them. The animal husbandry activities even at lower levels, were a subsistence necessity as only agriculture there could merely support a limited population and these people also had to meet their daily needs of goods other than agriculture produce. For this also, in a society where dealings were primarily based on barter system, a portion of the agricultural produce of the lower areas got invested in the exchange of goods of daily use – and even luxury - from other parts of Ladakh and areas outside the region. Every family in Ladakh, therefore, kept a herd of animals ranging from sheep and goat to donkey, yak, horses and camels etc; their numbers depending upon the family resources, place, trading interests and requirements. Keeping Leh as the central fulcrum of the trading milieu, one finds that these activities covered all the four directions.

The trade towards the south and western direction was mainly home bound as the areas in this category included down the Indus valley, Baltistan in general – including Skardu and Kargil sectors – as also Kashmir and parts beyond. The highland regions in the immediate north and Nubra valley were a part of this dispensation. Towards the east Ladakh traditionally had flourishing trade relations with Tibet; which were centuries old. In the north lay the Central Asian region and Ladakh had a thriving commercial interaction with different entities there – the most famous being Yarkand. It was usual for the traders, of all kinds, to exchange or sell their goods at

Leh; making that place an important terminal point of multilateral trade between India – J&K included – Tibet and Central Asia. In other words there was the intra-regional trade in Ladakh as well as its forays into Tibet and also strong trade links with Central Asia, in particular with Yarkand and Sinkiang areas.

All trading activities in this region were carried out on the basis of mutual trust and cordial relationships amongst the parties concerned; and even the places and households not directly connected with this activity well understood the collective benefit of it for the entire region. It is a great learning, as also humbling, experience to now read or learn about the collective wisdom of these people and their concerted endeavour to build relations and friendship; as also keeping these above any effort to make immediate gains. All business was transacted verbally as trust was the underlying principle – which importantly was never betrayed – and human bonds held high premium. At every halting place the traders and locals made friends with each other; so that at any time of difficulty the help was available. At the end both sides benefitted; and well understood the advantage of this scheme of things. This worldly wisdom has been comprehensively explained by a perceptive observer as "…. trades that I have been describing were conducted on the basis of mutual trust, with an acknowledgement of mutual need, and as an extension of the participants' everyday range of relationships. Profit of course – if each party to a transaction were not to make a profit on the deal, then what was the point? But profit was never at the expense of a relationship. In a harsh natural environment like that of Ladakh good relationships between neighbors and acquaintances are – apart from anything else – a survival mechanism; this was surely even more true of the traders with their months-long peregrinations on trails often the most rudimentary… As with much else in Ladakhi life, in trade too the human dimension came first."[18]

The internal or domestic trade in Ladakh effectively covered the whole region and included areas like Changthang, Nubra, Zanskar, Kargil and Skardu. It generally followed two directions of Leh – Indus Valley – Skardu, including Kargil area and the other being Leh – Nubra plus areas beyond. Most of this trade would take place round the year though the major part was transacted during the summer months. From the lower

18 Janet Rizvi, *Trans- Himalayan Caravans*, Oxford University Press, New Delhi, 2000, p. 141.

regions the traders or farmers would offer for sale the produce of their farms and households, like apricots (including its oil), grapes, almonds, butter, barley, tea cups, stone vessels for cooking, woolen cloth and coarse shawl and the like. They took back, in exchange; cotton cloth and similar goods, tea, gold and silver thread, Yarkandi leather ware and sheep wool etc. From Leh some of this material would find a place towards Lhasa and Yarkand through the regular trade channels. It can safely be said that the Leh–Tibet and Leh–Central Asia trade also provided strong underpinning to the internal commercial intercourse of the entire region. Thus the economies of Ladakh and Baltistan areas were closely interlinked and mutually dependent. Even administratively Skardu was a Tehsil of Ladakh Wazarat then. Some enterprising Baltis would even seek employment further north as well as engage in small business themselves. The tradition has it, that main market in Kargil town then was called 'Balti Bazar' and it was situated below the present day shop-line along the trunk road. While going through the mechanisms of the internal trade in Ladakh, it would be interesting to note the composition and activities of one such trading group. The narrative says, ".... made their expeditions not alone but in groups, together with a few companions from their own and neighbouring villages... even the better off traders did not take servants along to help with the work of the caravan, but the members of the group all pitched in and helped each other....one of a group of anything from six to ten men, with 30 to 40 horses. Along the way they slept in the open, choosing halting places that had enough grass for the horses.... On reaching their destination, the members of the group would fan out, each to the trading partner with whom they probably had a previous association, and did their own business individually."[19]

Ladakh's trade with Tibet has been going on for ages; in fact as far back as one can look. In the past this activity was primarily based on private initiative at the individual levels on both sides and also was not regulated in any manner. There was no involvement of the governments on either side. However, some sort of regulation was imposed on this otherwise free trade by the Treaty of Tingmosgang concluded in 1684 between the two entities, for the first time. Under this arrangement, Ladakh got the monopoly purchasing rights over the shawl wool produced in Tibet; whereas the other side acquired the exclusive right to the brick-tea trade with Ladakh. Whereas almost the whole of raw material of wool

19 *Ibid*, p. 140.

was further exported to the weavers of Kashmir through the Kashmiri traders, who bought this in Leh from the locals. In case of brick-tea, major part the imported quantity was consumed by the local population and only some portion sent to Kashmir. This treaty also formalized the sending of periodical delegations from Leh to Lhasa carrying presents for the Dalai Lama; whom the entire Buddhist population held in high esteem. As the persons, usually comprising high ranking locals, of these religious missions were also allowed to carry merchandise; this acquired a commercial angle over time. The trade practices in due course got well established primarily because the men involved from both sides worked hard and honestly for it; as also provided all possible help to each other in terms of accommodation, transport and resolution of any dispute. These trade relations were further strengthened by the Treaty of 1842 which was made between the Dogra and Tibetan officials. It is also a matter of record that there was no direct commercial linkage amongst Tibet and Central Asia. Therefore, Leh became the focal point of all kinds of goods from Kashmir and Yarkand etc to be dispatched to Tibet. This particular trade received considerable boost for over a century of Dogra rule and even beyond; till the Chinese troops came to Tibet in 1950.

The fact is well recognized that Ladakh has always had a flourishing trade with Western Tibet from times immemorial; particularly from Demchok to Rudok and areas westwards. The two regions became complementary to each other primarily because of the fact that Ladakh being comparatively at lower altitude produced food grains where as the Western Tibet, at a higher plateau was inhabited by nomads whose main occupation was to rear animals primarily goats, sheep, yaks etc. Traditionally, every year just after the Hemis Mela, caravans of Ladakhi traders would set forth east wards carrying all kinds of cereals, including barley and wheat as also dry fruits, spices and other goods imported from Punjab and Yarkand, Sinkiang regions. In return, they would get back Pashmina and other raw wool plus the brick tea for consumption back home. All the transportation was carried mainly through donkeys and sheep. Some traders belonging to lower areas of Nimu and further east would carry their goods on horses also. Normally leaving during May-June; these caravans would return, laden with their goods in the months of September-October.

Seen from a modern day point of view these commercial transactions would certainly fall in the category of 'restrictive trade practices'; but during those days there was no recorded evidence of any complaints in this regard and people of every region appeared to be happy as also satisfied with the system then existing. In fact the whole arrangement was respected as traditions by all parties. The entire gamut of Ladakh- Tibet commercial interaction has been described by a local scholar at Leh as "On arrival to Leh this Pashmina and wool would be sold to Kashmiri traders who would always be waiting for these goods. These transactions were carried either in cash or barter. The important Kashmiri traders of that time were Shahdad and Mam. According to trading treaty the Pashmina and wool was to be sold to Kashmiri traders who would not be allowed to go beyond Leh and who had to buy their wares only from Ladakhi traders; who in turn were allowed to Western Tibet but were prohibited for taking their goods to the markets in Kashmir and beyond...It is also a fact that this was a very paying outing for all the traders who would double their investment... Despite such profits the quantum of trade remained at a particular level primarily because of this being restricted to Ladakhis who were further limited both in number of humans as well as animals. That is why most of the families who indulged in this trade were well off. The trade with Western Tibet and Kashmir also benefited the entire region in a spin-off manner; that is why Ladakh economy has traditionally remained above the subsistence level. Hence the agriculture and nomadic economies were not only complementary to each other but also did comparatively well with mutual support..."[20]

Reminiscences about the commercial activities with the Central Asian region are still vivid with the older generation of Ladakhis; and Tashi Rabgias recalls "On the other hand the trade with Sinkiang was mostly carried out by Yarkandi traders, there were very few Ladakhis. These traders from Sinkiang would bring mostly handicraft items from the entire region, particularly *namdas,* silk, raw silk threads and *charas* etc. laden over horses, camels and donkeys. From this side the trade was mostly dominated by Punjabis, in particular those from Hoshiarpur, few of latter's descendants still have shops in Leh...Although there was hardly any local involvement in this trade but this activity did help the local economy as well, as while passing through Ladakh the locals would provide them hay and feed. Invariably the traders would also take the local

20 Interview with Tashi Rabgias at Leh during September 1998.

animals on hire and would scrupulously and honestly pay the hire charges and would also compensate on the death of the animals… Few well off families would purchase Yarkandi horses for riding but these were only in the realm of luxury."[21]

This third leg of commercial interaction of Ladakh, that is, business with the Central Asian region was certainly much more important than the internal trading activities as also deals with the Tibet side. This was not so only for strategic reasons but also from the monetary point of view, as the turn over here was decidedly of greater significance. Janet Rizvi has calculated the value, in Rupees, of selected commodities from Leh to Yarkand as 14,10,206; 28,55,286; and 22,56,711 in 1912-13, 1917-18 and 1922-23 respectively. The same figures for Yarkand to Leh being 11,82,554; 30,74,635; 22,31,985.[22] Taking into account the value of rupee those days, these numbers do represent considerable market interaction between the two sides. Similarly, comparatively lower statistics both ways in the year 1922 as compared to 1917 tell its own story about disturbances in the region following the Russian revolution.

Although main artery of this market activity remained the Leh – Yarkand axis; traders from different areas used more convenient stages, from their point of view, to reach this path-way at Leh or beyond. For example, the traders from Skardu could also follow the Khapalu-Chorbat-Nubra approach; while those from Kishtwar area found it easier to come via Kishtwar-Padar-Zanskar track. In addition some enterprising people from the Nurpur, Kulu,Lahoul and Spiti region would come through Rohtang Pass-Keylong-Bara Lacha La- Taglang La and Leh path . All the same, from Leh to Yarkand the most important and popular route always remained Leh-Khardung La- Nubra valley-Saser La-Karakoram pass and Yarkand. This was notwithstanding the fact that from Leh there were other two passages to Yarkand which went over Changla Pass as well as followed Digar La- Shyok axis and through Daulat Beig Ouldi (in short called DBO) to the destination. But being relatively longer and fuel, grass and water not being available so abundantly, it did not become popular with the traders in general; except for those in emergency and with few adventurous ones. Otherwise, it was usual for Indian as also Central Asian traders to bring their caravans to Ladakh-Leh in summer

21 *Ibid.*

22 Janet, *op.,cit.* p.295.

and start home ward return journey in the autumn. From the Indian side the goods included cloth of different types, Kashmiri shawls, brocades, spices, indigo, opium, dry fruits, coral, sugar, medicines and the like. The Central Asian merchants carried to Leh things like gold and silver, shawl wool, tea, carpets, felts, *Charas*, leather ware, Chinese tea-cups, raw silk and ponies etc. Most of the people exchanged their goods at Leh with their counterparts; although there are records of some, but very few, adventurous ones making directly to the destination at the other end - generally in the pursuit of higher returns.

Many people have recorded that the otherwise sleepy little town of Leh would be full of activity and people of different kinds, during the summer months, when traders from various sides collected there for rest and recuperation of men and animals; exchange of goods as also spend time in the more salubrious climate. This commercial interaction brought an all-round prosperity; to the local population as well as the persons actually connected with the trade from either side. It has also been observed by some authors of the contemporary scene that Ladakhis benefited from this activity only partially because very few of them carried their own business. Their main income came through acting as pony drivers and porters or suppliers of pack animals and grass as well as feed to the traders. But, there is no denying the fact that all segments of society; merchants as well as the locals stood to derive economic benefits from this cross border commercial interaction in a number of ways. Apart from remunerative advantages, the socio-economic scenario in Ladakh was certainly affected in diverse ways by this sustained interaction. One of the significant outcomes was that a new class of people called 'Arghuns' came into existence. They were the offsprings of Kashmiri or Central Asian Muslim traders who had taken Ladakhi wives on temporary or permanent basis; and thus became almost a part of the local milieu. By and large the Arghuns continued the tradition of trading with Tibet and Central Asia or took up jobs related to this business. They have also, over time, become an integral part of the local society.

Broadly three categories of traders married local girls. By virtue of the circumstances of the trade, some men were obliged to take up their residence in Leh for considerably long periods. There were also merchants, particularly of Kashmiri origin, who traded in goods from Tibet and thus bought and sent Pashmina wool and brick tea to Kashmir. Thirdly, some

Central Asian traders preferred to stay back in Leh owing to the closure of passes or during the periods of political uncertainty in their homeland. Interestingly, according to some scholars, the conjugal relationships of Buddhists and Muslims subtly affected both the systems of Polyandry as well as Polygamy. The Muslim women learnt from their Buddhist counterparts, not to share their husbands with any other lady; similarly the Buddhist females also looked at favorably not to have more than one husbands. However this trend, either way, remained confined mainly to Leh town and probably some nearby villages. The trade activities, over the years, also affected the dress as well as food habits of the locals. All types of cloth, handmade or machine manufactured including Chinese silk and velvet etc; animal skins and various types of head gear influenced the dress sense of the locals – particularly the elite class of Ladakh. Likewise, the consumption of brick tea from Tibet or China became a house hold essential activity. Yarkandi *pulao* – rice cooked with meat and spices in a particular manner – is a luxury cuisine item in the area even today. Some people also claim that the steam dumplings of meat, called *mo-mo* – which is now almost a staple food – originally came from the Central Asian region. The use of jade or porcelain articles, leather based products as also quilted materials made a strong impact on the Ladakhi way of life; as did some forms of music and dance styles. The quantum of this trade also gave impetus to the local weavers to make large quantities of coarse woollen cloth to meet the constant demand for packing of the goods; as these were loaded and dispatched for the final destination. This was also a good way of finding a use for the local coarse wool, which was available in surplus stocks. Villages around Leh, especially those on the merchant trails, took in a big way to growing improved and almost perennial variety of grass and feed. The extensive cultivation of 'Lucerne' and Yarkandi *ol* belong to this category. The farmer class also benefited by leasing out their fields and grasslands to pony drivers to feed their animals on. Above all, of course, was the almost legendary hospitality of Ladakhis to make their guests, including animals, happy and comfortable. The security of the life and safety of their goods was never in any doubt, irrespective of where the traders came from.

More so after the treaty of 1870 was signed between the Maharaja of J&K and the Government of India; the trade with Central Asia received a coordinated boost by the combined efforts of both administrations. This took different forms like Taxes benefits, security and facility to the traders as also effective maintenance of the main track. In connection with Tax structure and benefits; Janet Rizvi records "Srinagar had two centres for Yarkand trade: the Kak Serai near the Idgah, and the serai at Safa Kadal... Safa Kadal Serai was the depot for repacking goods arrived from the plains by wheeled transport, into a form suitable for loading onto horses. The prescribed maximum load for the pack-horses was two and half *maunds*; accordingly the merchandise was made up into bundles of one and quarter *maunds*, to be slung on either side of the pack-saddle. Repackaging also involved examination by the state customs of dutiable goods, which had been sealed at the custom post at Domel on the Punjab-Kashmir border. Goods for the frontier districts, including Ladakh, and for export to Central Asia, were exempt from duty, which was however paid at Safa Kadal and the bundles resealed. On arrival at Kargil with the seals intact, all duties already paid were refunded, even those paid on foreign goods at their port of entry into British India...Consequently, even after taking the cost of transport into account, the general level of prices was lower in Ladakh than in Kashmir. Similarly Yarkandi goods, with the exception of *charas*, though subject to state customs if sold within Jammu and Kashmir, if taken into British India were exempt from state and imperial customs duty... From Srinagar; such goods were sent by wheeled transport down the cart-road to the railhead at Rawalpindi. In the early years of the century this would have been by cart and tonga...."[23]

The internal trade within this region was going on since ages and continued on the same pattern and scale. But, commercial interactions with the Tibetan and Central Asian region were conducted in a much more organized manner from around the middle of nineteenth century. Soon after his armed forays into Ladakh, Baltistan and western Tibet; General Zorawar Singh paid considerable attention to improve this route and make it easy passage for men and animals; thereby impacting positively on the trade links with Tibet. With the entire belt getting politically settled and restoration of peace therein under the Dogra rule; the enhancement in the trade with Central Asian area was but a natural corollary. There was a further boost with the treaty of 1870; as after that the security, facilities for the traders as also maintenance of the main route received considerable attention of the State administration and the Government of India – in addition to the tax incentives. For the security and facilities of the traders there were two large serais each at Leh and Srinagar; which also doubled

23 Janet, *op.,cit,* p. 229.

up as storages. Kargil was another important stop on this route for rest and recuperation. In addition godowns, stables, dak bungalows and rest houses were established at various stages of the route, where the traders received shelter, supplies and forage for the animals at notified rates. Also, villages around a particular stage felt responsible – and in this respect the local administration too played its role as and when required – for supplying pony and coolie transport to travelers at reasonable rates. It has been recorded that the safety of this route was considered to be so effective that in case of unforeseen circumstances; the traders would just leave their goods at a particular place and march ahead. The merchandise was fetched after the climate improved or substitute transport became available. There was never an occasion for any complaint in this regard. The State granaries were also located at Leh and other nodal places where barley was supplied to traders at fair prices.

Continuous efforts were registered by the concerned authorities to make this long and arduous journey as smooth as possible by constant repair and regular maintenance of the route. Right from the beginning in 1870s the State allocated a yearly sum of 2,500 Rupees for the upkeep and repairs of this passage and Serais located enroute. By the end of nineteenth century, this amount was raised to five thousand per annum; which helped in keeping the Srinagar-Central Asian track in a fairly good condition; there by ensuring regular movement of men and merchandise on this route. This was a diligent and deliberate endeavor undertaken by the State Government; the contours of which have been graphically described as, "The Srinagar-Leh route, along which flowed the vast bulk of Ladakh's trade with Punjab as well as with Kashmir, followed roughly the line of today's motor road, except on the approach to the passes, where it could take a steeper and more direct line…From Baltal to Karakoram Pass it had been declared the free highway for trade provided for in the Commercial Treaty of 1870 between the Government of India and the Maharaja of Kashmir. It was maintained and administered by the two commissioners appointed under the terms of the treaty. For the purpose of maintenance, it was divided into sections – Drass to Kargil, Kargil to Khaltse, Khaltse to Leh, Leh to Khardung, Khardung to Panamik, and Panamik up to the Karakoram Pass. Each section was under the care of an overseer, and was serviced by a gang of about 20 men known as *darokh*. During the trading season, they were on the job full time, working even on the Saser-la. The BJC inspected it along its whole length every year. Having travelled up from Srinagar to Leh, he personally toured both the Saser and the Shayok branches of the onward route, right up to the Karakoram pass. This gave rise to a perception that, while the other routes, for example that from Kargil to Skardu, were maintained by the state government, it was the British who were responsible for the upkeep of the Treaty Road."[24] This was again a typical mode of the Raj - to garner the credit for good work; while the expenses were incurred by the local ruler. But there is no doubt that the trade with the Central Asian area did contribute positively to also the well being and prosperity of the entire Ladakh region.

Ladakh Around 1940s

Expressions in the vein of 'cold desert', 'moon land', 'exotic place' and the like have often been used by observers to describe Ladakh. It is in fact all this and much more. How did this area look like around the time of independence or couple of decades before that? All one can say that, historically speaking, not much had changed there till then as compared to a decade, score, fifty or even a hundred years earlier. It was the same cold, arid, isolated place that this land had been for a long, long time. One can attempt to portray this region, may be somewhat reasonably well, as seen and recorded by the contemporary individuals and published material. It would be like looking through a window of time – a prism of sorts.

Hashmat-Ullah Khan, who was Wazir -i-Wazarat of Ladakh from 1911; has recorded this in his book titled "History of Tibet and Great Tibet", at pages 188-190. "The agriculture season is very short in Ladakh. Since most of the regions are located at 10,000 to 15,000 feet high from the sea level. Almost all the agricultural lands are one crop field but the land is fertile, and the crop gets ready within a small time. Though the wind blows, yet there is no rain. Therefore, without irrigation no crop is possible in the valleys. The major agricultural productions are barley and grain. "Grim" is a kind of barley which has no stra, and this is the major food of the Ladakhies. Beside, the Rabi crops are peas, mustard, masoor and baqla. Whereas the Kharif crop are tranba, kangni, and chanba. Among the vegetables the turnip is very famous and is produced in a large number. Moreover, some vegetable and onion, etc., are also produced. The foreigners grow cabbage, karam-sag, cauliflower, turnip, "chaqander", and potatoes. I have grown chilly, bottleguard, maize and other Indian

24 *Ibid*, p. 228.

vegetables for experiment but the local people have no interest to grow these vegetables… As for as fruits are concerned, the people of Nubra and lower Indus valley (Sham) grow walnut, apricot, apple and a limited number of mulberry and grapes, but there is no fruit in the areas of upper Ladakh… There is no forest in this area. The white-lead and willow trees are being planted for domestic and constructional purposes. The people cultivate some types of grass as fodder for the animals. The fuel in Ladakh is very few, except Nubra, where some sorts of trees are grown in the Nallahs and around the hills and the wood is used as a fuel…Salt is procured from Rupsho and Tangtsey lakes but the process has left on nature, and because of bitterness it is not able to use. However, the local people take it for human and animal use, and are a great source of income. If it is extracted tactfully, one can have a very pure salt…Instead of water people use Chhang and those who didn't drink Chhang use tea. The people drink the tea at a large scale, which is salty. Butter is mixed in salt tea… Among the peculiarities of Ladakh is the hot springs. Some springs have the smell of sulpher. Since the springs of Rupsho are situated near the mines of sulpher. Some springs have no smell of sulpher, like that of hot spring of panamik… Some patients take bath there for different disease… The local people have great faith in its effectiveness…"

As mentioned earlier, two Wazarats of Ladakh and Gilgit were created, in 1901, under the orders of the State Council. This fact and other details about the entire area have been mentioned in greater details in Part I of the Report of Census of India – 1931. A relevant portion of which states, "Enclosed by Karakoram on the north and the central range of the Himalayas on the south this division comprises three-fourth of the area of the State but on account of its high altitude and highly mountainous and barren character maintains a population of only 288,584 people giving a density of 5 persons to a square mile. Except Gilgit the ranges in this Illaqa vary from 17,000 to 22,000 ft. and in Ladakh there are vast deserts,… This includes the three separate administrative divisions:

1. Ladakh District — Ladakh, Skardu and Kargil Tehsils.
2. Gilgit District — Gilgit Tehsil.
3. Frontier Illaqas — Hunza, Nagar, Yasin, Chilas, Ishkoman, Kuh-Ghizar, Punial Illaqas included in the Gilgit Agency.

The physical characteristics of the various portions of this country differ very widely and we have almost rainless and therefore dry and barren tracts of Ladakh on the one extreme and Baltistan and Gilgit with their lower hillsides and valleys verdant with orchards and cornfields on the other... The population of Gilgit is constituted of Muslims of the Dard race and this small tract enjoys far better climate and cultivation than Ladakh; producing wheat and other crops as also fruits. The production in Political Illaqas is again of an inferior kind....The Chiefship of the Frontier Illaqas classed under item 3 are in feudatory relations with the State and are under the direct charge of the Political Agent who is an officer of the Government of India...The Frontier Disrticts though shown as a province do not in reality constitute a province under a Governor but each of the districts, *ie*, Gigit and Ladakh is separately controlled by a Wazir-i-Wazarat who is (unlike other Wazirs) directly under the Revenue Minister like the Provincial Governors."

In the Report of the Census of India – 1941, there is no change recorded in relation to the territories mentioned above; except this.... "There is no change in external boundaries during the decade ending 31st December 1940 but there was one important change of administrative boundaries. Reference has already been made to the partition of the old Gilgit District into two separate units – Astore and Gilgit (Leased Area). In the middle of the decade (1934) negotiations were concluded between His Highness the Maharaja Bahadur of Jammu and Kashmir and the Government of India by which the Trans-Indus part of the old Gilgit District was leased to the Government of India for administrative purposes. This area, designated Gilgit (Leased Area), has since been administered on behalf of His Highness' Government by the Government of India's Political Agent at Gilgit...Subject to the changes discussed administrative units remain the same as those shown in the 1931 tables..."

Mentioning about the state of revenue administration in the beginning of 20th century; Tashi Rabgias recalled this in September 1998, "One of the important things done during this period was settlement operations of land. My grandfather who was Numberdar of village Sakti took part and helped in these settlement operations. The land used to be measured with chains of specific length and every village had a map of lands which were called *Lathhas*. It was at that time when the need was felt to have local *Patwaris* but since no one knew how to read and write Urdu, schools were opened, up to the primary level, where people were taught to read and write Urdu. It is said that one of the first Buddhist Patwari was a person called Wachay Sonam Chewang. He was a self made man belonging to an ordinary family but he worked hard and picked up his job well. After functioning for some time as Patwari he also worked as a judicial clerk, *Wasil Waqi Nawis* in the Tehsil office and became an important government functionary in his own right; which incidentally was the highest post held till then by a local person."

The state of education in Ladakh did not receive much governmental attention; it was only towards ending 19th century that there is a reference of a primary school being established at Leh. In 1889, the Moravion missionaries started a missionary school to win over the locals to the Christian faith. Their activities did not succeed much, but it did jolt the state government in starting more primary schools all over the region. The poor state of education, before independence, can be imagined from the fact that the literacy index of the place stood at 19 per thousand people in 1921and it barely moved to 31 in 1941.

The highest educational institutions in the entire region during 1940s were a middle school each at Leh, Kargil and Skardu. Of course there were around fifty primary schools spread all over the place; but considering the huge landmass this number and level, both were woefully inadequate. For supervision of educational activities in this vast tract, a School Inspector was posted with headquarters at Leh. His job was to ensure proper functioning of all the educational institutions in Ladakh and it was incumbent upon him to visit each school at least twice a year. It is recorded that as late as January 1948, when the Pakistani tribal raiders were literally swarming that region, this officer was on tour and inspecting schools around Skardu. While mentioning about the status of education in the pre-independence Ladakh; it is difficult to miss out the name of Shridhar Koul (Dulloo). Fondly called as 'Pandit Dulloo' there, he was long remembered in Ladakh, first as a very committed teacher; then a fine Inspector of Schools. During the 1948 crisis in the region, he was very much in Leh and acted as a guide and philosopher to the local population; all respectable people in and around Leh depended on him for a sage advice. Apart from other qualities of head and heart; he was genuinely interested in the welfare of the region and its people.

In so far as medical facilities in Ladakh are concerned during this period, the same were as inadequate and wanting as the educational services. Leh, Kargil and Skardu had one doctor and one compounder each with meager resources at their disposal; even though the medicines from the dispensary, whatever was available, used to be given free. Notwithstanding the fact that these services were skeletal in nature; the staff was generally well committed. The compounder would not only attend the work in a dispensary but also go to every village around and do the vaccination…Those days the locals in Ladakh hardly depended on the facilities provided by the government for the treatment of diseases. They had a fairly developed indigenous regimen of curing ailments called the 'Amchi' system. This expertise had been traditionally passed down there from father to son, like a family lineage. It was heavily based on local medicinal plants and came from Tibet; where it originated, was nurtured and developed over centuries. Every area in Ladakh had its own Amchi – the medicine man – who learnt his trade from father, an elder Amchi or enrolled in the nearest Amchi School. Some enterprising and well off young men went to Tibet to learn the skills from well known masters as also in some institutions famous for this purpose. The system of payment for Amchi services too was traditional and based on voluntary contributions. People gave what they were able to afford in cash or kind in exchange for the medicines and the services rendered. According to a local expert on this subject – who himself is an eye specialist with M.B.B.S. and M.S. degrees, the first Allopathic doctor from Ladakh – holistic philosophy of the Amchis is described as, "Through the ages, the medical men of the Himalayas have enriched this system of Buddhist medicine by introducing more and more herbal drugs. Their major contributions are the recipes in the field of Buddhist medicine and the use of medicinal plants growing in high altitudes. Such an indigenous medical practice is unique and is followed by the Amchis of this region…In fact, the final court of appeal is the bedside of the patient. The Tibetan medical formulation is the product of the Indian medical practice and the Tibetan art of healing; accumulated experience of centuries of observation and adaptation…Many persons believe that the Tibetan System (Amchi System) of medicine is merely an empirical and symptomatic treatment. But it unfolds its own rationale and scientific basis to someone who delves deep into it…because their common approach is holistic in nature. Their mode of treatment, as they claim, is to create equilibrium between the mind, body and environment rather than treating the diseases separately."[25]

There was, in addition, a veterinary doctor at Leh. His job was not only to treat the local livestock, but also to provide veterinary cover as well as regular inspection of the horses of the passing caravans. After the arrival of each caravan at Leh, when the animals had been unloaded it was the duty of the veterinary doctor to check them; and if anyone was found in injured condition, he would treat the injury as also prescribe for the minimum number days rest so required. This was strictly enforced. If it was determined by the veterinary doctor that a particular horse should not be loaded or moved for any number of days; the owner or the contractor would not dare to flout the orders.

An interesting incident around middle of 1940s has been mentioned by a local, who was then a school boy at Leh. Abdul Ghani Sheikh recalls, "In the period before India gained independence, an English officer who was known as the British Joint Commissioner (BJC) would serve in Ladakh for 2 to 3 months every summer. He supervised the Central Asian trade and kept an eye on Tsarist Russia's activities along the borders… The BJC's journey from Srinagar would take 16 days and ended with a grand event at Leh. Along the route, Union Jacks would be hoisted at villages, where receptions and exhibition polo matches were held to honour the BJC. In the mid-1940s I was a student in the Government Middle School Leh and had presented the BJC, Major Ludlow with a guard of honour in Leh Bazar with a scout's baton. I still remember that banners had been put up in Leh Bazar and shop facades were decorated with colourful frills to welcome Major Ludlow. Officials had travelled to Spituk village to await his arrival. At ten that morning we performed a march past in the bazaar dressed in khaki uniform and red ties with a scout's rope around our waists, a baton on our shoulders and led by a band…After a long wait, the BJC reached Leh…The children sprang to attention and stood upright with their batons. A few minutes later, the BJC and his procession reached the gate of bazaar led by his peons and staff members…Major Ludlow descended down from his horse, dressed smartly in riding pants and long boots. He was surrounded by imposing officials…The event started with soldiers presenting a guard of honour, after which the BJC moved towards

25 Dr. Smanla T. Phuntsog, *Ancient Metria Medica*, Paljor Publications (P) Ltd., New Delhi, 2006, pp- 27 and 28.

the crowd. Next, the children presented a guard of honour with their batons. Major Ludlow acknowledged the salute by taking off his hat…"

Around the first two decades of the twentieth century, three important personalities of Ladakh were born; Kushok Bakula, Sonam Narboo and Rigzin Namgyal Kalon. They were contemporaries and between them provided comprehensive leadership to the Ladakhi people. Whereas Kushok Bakula is credited with leading in spiritual, moral and political matters; Sonam Narboo excelled in the administrative field – and also became a minister of the state government towards end of his career. Kalon Sahib, the third of these personalities, was not only one of the saviors of Leh in the dark days of 1948; he was an effective social guide to his people for more than five decades thereafter without ever accepting a formal political role or office. While mention about the other two would be made elsewhere, some details about the life of Kushok Bakula may be given here. Born in a noble and highly respectable family in 1917; he was a religious scholar, diplomat and political leader – all rolled into one – and lived a full life of 86 years, passing away in 2003. At a very young age of four, he was recognized as the 19th reincarnation of Arhat Bakula by the 13th Dalai Lama and shifted to the Spituk Monastery in Leh; which was to become his home for rest of the life. He received extensive education in Buddhist philosophy and metaphysics for almost fifteen years in Tibet, after which he came back to Leh. He was advised and persuaded by Nehru and Sheikh Abdullah – when they visited Leh in July 1949 – to join politics; and on his agreement, he was made head of the National Conference in Ladakh. But, soon he came in a clash with the Sheikh, by opposing the application of latter's Land Reforms Act to the lands held by the monasteries. These were ultimately granted the requisite exemption. He is also credited with bringing the NEFA type of administration into Ladakh during the 1960s. In the early nineties, Kushok Bakula was appointed as Indian ambassador to Mongolia; where he was greatly respected as a leading Buddhist scholar and an eminent spiritual personality. During his active life of over five decades, he performed various roles as a member of the Jammu and Kashmir Constituent Assembly, MLA, minister in the J&K Government, member of the Lok Sabha, member of the National Minorities Commission and the ambassador of India. To many a people he was a living example of humility; as also a life time dedicated to the betterment of Ladakh and its people.

The diverse facets of life in Ladakh, couple of decades before independence, give a comprehensive picture of the socio-economic milieu of the region. For several reasons, the life in Kargil area – now a separate district – was in some ways different than other parts of Ladakh. Both have been vividly described by people who grew up in those years. About Kargil sector, Munshi Ghulam Hussain – a much travelled person belonging to a respectable family of the area, and born in 1919 – narrated how the living conditions in Kargil were then[26]. He said, "In the pre-1947 years Kargil was almost a closed place, particularly during the summer season, when most of the people would be engaged in agriculture and animal husbandry activities. The efforts would be to grow sufficient food grains and collect other means of livelihood during the six months of summer to survive during the winter months. Life in Kargil during the winter became practically standstill but for family functions and religious ceremonies. However, a number of able-bodied men would go out and venture into as far as Punjab to seek employment. Our people were known as good road builders and made a name for this in the Shimla region. They were so good that contractors would often pay even advance to some of them so that next year they would come and work for the identified employers. Those days means of transport were limited and mostly these people would travel by foot from Kargil, right up to at least Srinagar. Later, with the help of some friendly people from Leh, the Kargil labour started moving on vehicles from Kangan onwards.

"There was also an institution of *Galladars* in major villages of Kargil who would store food grains, mostly derived from the tenants of the big chunks of land. These Galladars would give grains on interest to the needy. The normal interest used to be 20 seers for two maunds in a year. Some of the shopkeepers would also trade in commodities on barter system. For example 250 grams of tea would be taken equal to one maund of grains and like this; most of the time small farmers would be perpetually in debt. In a similar vein, most of the trade in Kargil area used to be on barter system and majority of the shopkeepers were Baltis; they would come from the north or from Srinagar side. That is how the main bazaar in the town came to be known as Balti bazaar. It exists even today below the main road and the shopping area. Those days, it was the hub of commercial activity in Kargil. There were hardly any Kargili shopkeepers. Few of them who ran business establishments were also government employees. There were also

26 Interview with Munshi Ghulam Hussain, in Kargil, in September 1998.

shopkeepers from Punjab, mostly belonging to Hoshiarpur – though couple of Sikh families also conducted business here – these people continue to trade and live in Kargil up to these days[27]. Some of the more enterprising shopkeepers would load their goods on horses and go to important villages like Sankoo as some kind of mobile shops and return with the animals loaded with grains. There were hardly any Yarkandis doing trade in Kargil. The only Yarkandi one would find here, were going or coming from Haj pilgrimage. Their main area of activity was either at Leh or Srinagar and Kargil was at best a place of haltage for them.

"Kargil had only one Primary School where I used to study. It became a High School only after 1947. In the entire Kargil region, before 1947, there was only one other Primary School; and that was in Drass. Even Sankoo did not have any school. Our day would start with salted tea and some roties; afternoon also we would have some roties and one or two ordinary dishes. The same would be menu for dinner too. This was our normal eating though we belonged to one of the affluent families of Kargil. Ordinary families, which were very poor, could only afford black tea and *Sattu*. If a family could eat roties, some vegetable dishes, it would be considered a luxury. In the school at Kargil there were not more than 20-25 students at a time and we were all taught by only one teacher. Like schools of these days we did not have any copy pencils, but would learn basics of reading and writing on slates and wooden *takhties*. The school would normally be in session from 10 a.m. to 3 p.m. with half an hour recess, during which those who could manage would run to their houses and eat something and return. The teacher used to take lot of pains in imparting education; which also included physical punishments to weak students. Some of the boys did small chores at the residence of the teacher and the students of well to do families would contribute vegetables and other necessities to the teacher. These were seen as a natural expression of gratitude and were taken to be a normal practice. After passing my 5th class there was no means to study further in Kargil and for one whole year I used to wander aimlessly in the town. Thereafter arrangements were made for my further education in Srinagar, as my father was a well to do man and could afford it. I set forth for Srinagar with my elder brother and mother. First night we spent at Shamsha Kharboo and the next at Drass. After couple of days more when we reached Kangan; some of my

27 Interestingly, one Sikh boy from Kargil got a preference seat in the Govt Medical College Srinagar, in the late 1990s, for belonging to a Scheduled Tribe area.

mother's relatives were present to receive us. We spent the night there. From Kangan we went in a tonga and the next day reached Srinagar, where my father had a house. There, a tailor was called to stitch clothes for me and after a couple of days I was admitted in a school."

About the orthodoxy of the predominantly Shia population of the area, he said "The influence of Agas (highly respected religious teachers in Kargil region) came to Kargil from Baltistan somewhere around the beginning of 20th century. Before that people of Kargil used to be as fun loving as anywhere else and interested in singing and dancing and other forms of merry making in which both men and women used to indulge. The most important religious personality, of the time, was Aga Mohd. Shah of Shigar who had gone to study in Iraq. On his return he preached and influenced the local population a lot. At that time almost half of Kargil Muslims belonged to a sect called Noor Bakshi; whose religious practices lay somewhere between Shias and Sunnis. It was Aga Mohd. Shah who was responsible for influencing all the Noor Bakshis to become Shias. The Agas had always been a part of the Kargil way of life but their influence was not all pervasive before the advent of 20th century."

On the administration, Munshi Hussain's views were interesting as also informative, "Tehsildar was the senior most officer for administration; he was vested with magisterial powers and was assisted in the maintenance of law and order by a few constables. There was hardly any crime those days. He used to function in Kargil on behalf of Wazir-i-Wazarat who was located during summer months in Leh and winter months in Skardu. He would camp at Kargil for a couple of weeks on both forward and return journeys. Average yearly stay of the Wazir in Kargil, was of the duration of almost two months. Occasionally the British Joint Commissioner would pass through Kargil but only in transit to other destinations. He would hardly stay in Kargil and never showed any interest in the affairs of these people...Administrative offices, whatever few they were, used to be located across Suru River at a place where Army Hospital is these days. It had the Tehsil office and also a grains store apart from other structures. There used to be a temple also in this area. The existing road or we can say a wide track between Leh and Zojila and beyond used to be maintained by the BJC. Maintenance part of this road in Kargil area was the responsibility of two local overseers, one operated from Kargil towards west and the other towards east. Both of them were not qualified in terms of professional training but otherwise were efficient and competent in their job and kept the road well. There was also a small contingent of the State Forces based in Kargil which was part of the unit deployed in Leh and Skardu. Kargil also for them was more of a transit camp than a regular army establishment…There was no telephone system in Kargil before 1947. In fact the telephone exchange came into the town in 1960. But the telegraph line between Srinagar-Kargil-Leh was very effective and if ever it was non-functional for more than 24 hours; somebody would lose his job. Even during the winter it was mandatory to keep this line through. There were some telephone like instruments attached with this line at Kargil, Khaltsi and Leh; but only for their internal use to check the functioning of the telegraph lines and these were not meant for the public. The telegraphic maintenance unit was based in Khaltsi during summer months and at Gumri right in the midst of huge snow pile during the winter months. It was the responsibility of this group of people to ensure that the telegraph lines were functioning even at the height of the winter and amidst blizzards. Similarly, the postal system was very effective, particularly, considering the mode of transportation available during that time. During summer a letter from Srinagar would definitely reach within four days and during winter it would never take more than eight days. Newspapers like Inqlab, Ahsan, Pratap, Milap and also some magazines from Lahore would reach Kargil in five days."

He has also made mention of certain matters of general interest, including, "During the Second World War I left Kargil to join army but found myself in the Air Force. I was temporarily asked to work with the Americans and spent sometime in the Middle-East and for a short while I was near Bahrain. There I got sick and was repatriated to Karachi. In the beginning of 1947 communal violence had started in Karachi. I had also been away from home for a long time and my elder brother had also expired during my absence. All this made me to leave the service and return to Kargil for good…The first radio in Kargil was brought by Kachu Mohd. Ali[28] and then by me on return from the Second World War. These would run on big batteries which would suffice for 2-3 months and could be replaced from Srinagar…I was one of the few people interested in hunting. Those days one could find good *Shikar* in Wakha Nallah near Mulbekh

28 A highly respected man belonging to Pashkum village, near Kargil. He joined the army as a senior non commissioned officer in the Ordnance wing, during the WW II and left this job after the war. In the 1970s, he was a deputy minister in the state government.

and Shanshi Nallah in Panikhar area. While on hunting in Shanshi I could see some rocks resembling marble. There were also rumours that oil deposits existed in the area but nobody had either the means or experience to explore further…Most of the horses belonged to the people in Drass and Karchey area, very few were reared in Kargil as there was hardly any vacant land for grass for the animals. In fact the entire economy of Drass and areas around depended upon the income generated by carrying of goods by these horses. There was hardly any food production in this area. Thus, people in Drass would get their daily necessities from Kargil and live off the earnings of their animals…The Moravian Christian Mission also started its activities in Kargil in 1930. Although they did not construct any church here, they would conduct their prayers in one of the rooms in the building they had erected. However, just before the Pakistani raiders came, these people left Kargil and went towards Manali. No one from Kargil converted to Christianity during this period."

In the early 1930s there were agitations in the valley against the Maharaja's rule and the demand for democratic dispensation rose. This resulted in the State Government appointing the Glancy Commission to suggest ways for better meeting aspirations of the people. Although Ladakh did not participate in these demonstrations; the Glancy Commission report became a harbinger of the first step towards establishment of people's rule. Interestingly, this Commission in its report made two observations and recommendations, concerning Ladakh region under the heading 'Social Reforms in Ladakh'. These were mentioned as, "It has been represented that steps should be taken to restrict the consumption of 'chhang', a mildly intoxicating liquor prepared from 'grim', a kind of barley. It is more than doubtful whether any official action in this direction would meet with anything approaching general approval; it is on record that a move in this direction was made by the authorities some years ago and proved a lamentable failure. Those addicted to the consumption of 'chhang' claim, and with some reason, that in the rigorous climate of Ladakh the use of a mild stimulant is not a luxury but a matter of sheer necessity. The Commission has no recommendation to make in this behalf… It has been suggested that both polyandry and polygamy, which are now prevalent in Ladakh, should be prohibited by law. There appears, however, to be no general feeling in favour of this proposal, and it seems to the Commission that any legislation of the nature suggested would be premature and ill-advised. Official interference in this direction must be deferred until there is reason to believe that it would receive the sanction of local opinion in general."[29] Thereafter *Praja Sabha*, the People's Assembly, was organized in 1934 which also had Ladakhi representation; three of them being Gyalpo Jigmet Dadul, No No Tonyot Shah and Tsewang Rinchin Kalon. In this connection Rigzin Namgyal Kalon said, "Although my father was not very well educated, his younger brother was the first Ladakhi who had entered a college and studied outside Leh. My grandfather also became a member of the *Praja Sabha* when Maharaja Hari Singh instituted the forum. Shri Iyengar was Prime Minister of J&K at that time. He became fond of my grandfather and would occasionally call him to Jammu and Srinagar for consultations. I accompanied my grandfather couple of times at both these places. My grandfather was a very progressive man who did not practice the system of Polyandry then prevalent here and always propagated in the society against it. All male members of the family of my grandfather had their own wives; even the daughters were given their due share in the property. My father and uncle also became members of the *Praja Sabha* during later years."[30]

Rigzin Namgyal Kalon was born on December 9, 1923; therefore the memories of his childhood and early adult life graphically and comprehensively bring alive the existent conditions prevailing in the region in 1930s and 1940s. Kalon Sahib recalled, [31]"Even though my father was not an educated person but he was well versed in the ways of the world and was a very practical man; therefore he wanted me to acquire good education. I did begin to go to school at appropriate age but was very poor in studies. However, may be due to influence of my family the teachers would promote me every year and this way I reached up to sixth class. Life was generally easygoing and comfortable. The children would never get any home work from the schools and whatever reading and writing had to be done; it was completed in the school itself. So there was no class work carried home from the school. Even this little effort at studying I avoided and when my father came to know of this academic disinterest; he was very annoyed. After class six I stopped going to the school any further. Some elders suggested to my father that I should be sent to Srinagar so that I could pursue my studies there. But he flatly refused to do so; as he was

29 Glancy Commission Report, p. 48.

30 Interview with Kalon Sahib in September 1998.

31 *Ibid.*

apprehensive about my safety, having lost his younger brother who died in Srinagar of illness after graduation. This way my formal education came to an end after class sixth.

"I inherited considerable landed property as part of my grandfather's *Jagir* through my father as my uncle had already died in Srinagar. In addition, I also inherited about two thousand kanals in village Saboo which belonged to my grandfather's sister who died without a child of her own. My grandmother, who was the daughter of Leh Lompo[32], also owned a large tract of land which too devolved on me. Thus I came to inherit considerable areas of fertile and fallow land in Leh, Pheyang, Saboo, Khurdung, Nyoma etc. right up to Khaltsi; these also extended as far away as Lanak La and Hot Springs in Aksai Chin area. My possessions, in addition, comprised large herds of livestock of all kinds; including over one thousand goats and sheep, more than fifty horses and around fifteen cows… I used to regularly go to highland pastures in Nyoma and Hot Spring areas along with herds of my cattle as a young man. My last visit was in 1958 to the latter sector. I was very fond of spending some time on my way up as also on return journey in my hut at Lukung on the western edge of Pyangong Lake.

"My father was a very considerate man. After the death of my uncle, he looked after his children and also instructed me to do so. He gave large pieces of land to his nephews which significantly reduced the share of landed property which came under my control. However, I made efforts to expand my inheritance by working hard and also by purchasing land, whenever I could do so out of my savings. Thus, over the years, I came to acquire considerable land in my own right. The house where I live these days is a cluster of different kinds of buildings, some as old as two hundred years with parts also built quite recently. I was born in this house. Till late 1970s we were all staying in this very complex as a joint family and after that my uncle's children moved on their own to other building. But we still maintain cordial relations. We also have a family temple of our own which was a small structure earlier but has now become a building of ample proportions…When I grew up I used to see lot of poverty around me – that was the life of an average family in Ladakh then - although we were regarded as one of the wealthy families of Ladakh. I remember my

32 'Lompo' in Ladakhi means a 'minister'; and when prefixed by the name of a place it indicates a very respectable person - with this title - belonging to that locality.

childhood very vividly. It was a delightful time and we all would go out to graze the cattle which included horses, donkeys as well as sheep and goats. I felt very happy to go to mountains with the flock and spend the whole day with them; riding horses and donkeys, looking after the cattle; eating meals in the open and playing with friends. May be, an abiding interest in this kind of life was the reason I could never develop fondness for books or education and had to leave my studies, quite early... The most enjoyable season during those days was August- September when the crops were gathered and the horses and cattle were let loose from the houses and they would roam around lazily and graze in the lands and pastures. With the fields full of horses, donkeys and other animals; we children had a field day in playing with and riding them. This was not only great fun but also instilled confidence and a spirit of adventure amongst the youngsters who would learn the technique, often the hard way, of handling the beasts. The boys took frequent tossings and injuries as well in their stride, even pain and failures with grit and determination. The weak hearted of course would not enjoy these pleasures. Most of the children had only one set of clothes, which usually consisted of *Pappu* (shoes made of Yak hair), Pyjamas made of *Pattu* (coarse sheep wool) and a shirt of coarse cloth over which, those who could afford, wore a Goncha (Ladakhi long-gown). The children would get this one dress for entire winter and one for summer; everyone would spend the whole season in the same attire. Since everybody would live in the similar way, these things were not considered unhygienic. Once we got admitted in the school, each boy additionally needed one shirt and a pair of white Tennis shoes. This was to be worn on ceremonial occasions to give salute to the Wazir-i-Wazarat and the British Joint Commissioner as there was very small army garrison stationed at Leh. During summer the children used to get Chappals made of old tyres. Fancy foot ware was only meant for brides and bridegrooms. It was only when the traders from Hoshiarpur started coming to Leh and brought different kinds of merchandise with them, including leather shoes, that the people who could afford purchased them and shoes became a part of the dress of wealthy people.

"There were neither much resources available to the children those days nor were many distractions to take their minds away from the daily routine. During the vacations and in the harvesting season, life used to be little more interesting with activities other than studies. One would look forward to crops being gathered and fruits plucked from trees so that we as small children could have our share from the plenty that got around during the short period. Also, one would sneak right on to the horses and donkeys which belonged to traders or to the grazers who had come to sell their sheep in Leh market. Occasionally we would try to steal some wool from fattened sheep. The boys would operate in small groups and whatever they could lay their hands on or procure surreptitiously; would be shared by the entire party thus teaching valuable lessons of sharing, comradeship and sticking together in adversity. During winter we would have two months vacations. Even though the weather used to be extremely harsh and the resources as also clothing limited to the ordinary children; these deprivations were made light by high spirits and ingenuity. Skiing or moving fast on the silvery surface of snow has always fascinated the young ones everywhere. Since those days there was no question of any skiing equipment being available, in fact none of us knew anything about skiing, still the wish to move fast on the snow surface made us to take recourse to local resourcefulness. We would dip the soles of our *Pappus* (shoes) in the water during night so that in the morning a hard crust of ice would be formed at the bottom of these shoes. This would enable us to slip with speed over the snow and ice surface with much happiness and glee. Evenings and nights used to be dark, stark and cold; we would try to keep ourselves warm by burning dry dung and animal droppings. Even lanterns were not available then and the only source of light was a small wick-type of a lamp which could be lit in the houses of the wealthy people who could spare oil or butter for the purpose. There were no cots or *Charpais* for sleeping; everybody would sleep on the floor, where a covering could be managed depending upon resources of the family. There was no question of having any different sets of clothes for sleeping and used to be no pillows. In the summer season, of course, most of the people would sleep on the roofs and there too on the ground. On very few warm nights, the Goncha would be taken off and used as a pillow…The diet was very simple and spartan. The meals of an ordinary person during summer months consisted of Sattu, Paba and butter milk. It was in the winter season that the variety and nutrition in food would increase. During this period Thukpa (a kind of stew), made of a variety of vegetables both fresh as well as dried, with occasional meat pieces used to be prepared along with Paba and Sattu. This would give warmth as well as much required nutritious value to the diet which was so essential during the winter months. The general health of the people would improve during this period. The regular meals as we understand these days comprising cooked dishes and rice etc. were very rare. These, for our region, originated from Yarkand and one could eat such lavish meals only on special events and festivities. However, the availability of meat was not very difficult during the winter, as the owners had to dispose off their sheep and goat which were getting aged. Thousands of sheep used to be sent to Kashmir before the onset of winter and whatever were left within Ladakh, were sold in the local market and thus the meat found its way in the hearths and kitchens of the people.

"Those days there were not many schools in whole of Ladakh; in any case most of them were of Primary level only. The highest educational institution was a Middle School, located in Leh. There was no school for girls and the girls' education was nonexistent in the area. Muslim girls used to be taught to read Quran Sharief at home, whereas Buddhist Association ran a school for Buddhist girls. Teachers of this school were paid out of the donations collected by the Association. In the government schools there were Ladakhi and Kashmiri teachers, of them the Kashmiris were more competent masters. We also had an Amchi School, which taught the Amchi system of medicine. Three of the Amchi students of that time are still practicing medicine in Ladakh and one of them is in Leh.

"There was a tradition that the flock of the entire village would be taken out to the pastures for grazing in the morning and returned in the evening. Instead of members of each household going with the animals, the community had organized a system by which males of every family, including children, would by pre-determined rotation take flock of the whole village for grazing and return with these animals in the evening. I used to eagerly await for my turn as this took me away from the school and I could also enjoy the outdoor life as well as privilege of taking raw milk from goats and cows, in addition to riding horses and donkeys...Even though people were not very particular about their personal hygiene; the community was quite aware to keep the environment clean and collectively acted in a disciplined manner for the general good. Nobody would urinate or defecate on or near a track. Similarly, in a water body or stream one could not even wash his hands as this was considered to make the water dirty. If one had to wash hands or clothes, he would take the water out as washing of any kind in the running stream was considered to pollute and water was to be left clean for drinking purposes. Some people would take this to such an extent that they would prostrate next to the stream and put their mouth directly into the water rather than dipping their hands into it.

"The economy of Leh, other than agricultural activity, mainly depended upon the Central Asian trade from Yarkand to Srinagar, which used to pass via Leh, as also commercial intercourse the other way round. These traders would depend upon the horses provided by the local people. I would also accompany some of these caravans as a young boy up to Khardung on one side and Khaltsi on the other. My father used to tell me that the journey from Yarkand to Leh was very tough as also risky and resulted in the death of a number of horses every year and at times of human beings also. Malnutrition amongst men and beasts was quite common during the arduous journey over the high mountains and barren landscapes. One can imagine the difficulties and risks involved in this travel, from the fact that whereas one could buy a good horse during those days with an amount of rupees ten to twelve; one way journey between Leh and Yarkand would cost a trader up to rupees eighty or even more per horse. There were occasions when none of the animals of a caravan would make it to the other end alive. However, the entire trade on these routes was carried out in a very methodical and professional manner. In particular no businessman or contractor who took responsibility from place A to place B would back off or refuse to honour his commitment, whatever the cost to his person may be. I have never heard of a case where a person broke an agreed contract. Even at times when all the animals of a caravan perished, the individual who had taken the responsibility for carrying goods would buy or hire an entirely new caravan and ensure that goods were delivered at the appointed place. No one ever talked of any dishonest act or theft or litigations in the courts of law. People who used to regularly move between Leh and Yarkand had established their own practices and methods to ensure their survival as well as of their horses by various strategies. One was to stock food for themselves and Dal for horses stored in caches at pre-determined places so that these could be used in times of emergency… There was so much honesty in the entire population that whenever the traders or transport contractors were not able to go to Srinagar or Yarkand due to bad weather or any other reason; they would keep their entire stock in Leh either in somebody's house or right in the open and come and claim it during the working season next year; without taking any receipt or drawing any legal documents just on the trust and honesty of the local population. Never was anything found missing by these traders. Whenever we children while playing went anywhere near these stocks, we were scolded by our elders telling that these things belonged to Yarkandi traders and the trust of the entire community was involved and that we should not do anything which would damage those goods.

"The whole thrifty management and life-style were based on availability of local resources. As hardly anything used to come from outside, therefore life of the people had to be fully sustained locally. Families would weave their own cloth and even make shoes at home; each household would rear goats not only for mutton but also for weaving of rugs as well as keep sheep for taking wool to make clothes and woolen garments. Every domestic establishment, at an average, kept three cows for milk and minimum two to three donkeys for carrying load and produce from one place to another. It was only horses which some households did not have. But other domestic animals were an integral part of the family; without which survival was difficult. It was only the wealthy families which kept horses and Zos (a kind of Yak like bull) which were used for ploughing purposes. The entire community used to work in a cooperative manner. If a farmer did not have his own Zo, he could borrow it from a wealthy neighbor who would not charge for it. Similarly, if additional hands were required during agricultural operations the concerned farmer would only provide meals and refreshment to those who came to help. There was no question of paying money or demanding wages for such assistance. It was the life of a society at peace with itself and an example of existence in harmony. Similar spirit of cooperation and collaboration was evident when somebody wanted to construct his house. The issue of making payments never arose. The concerned person would request for a village gathering and give a feast of *Chhang* and meals and indicate a desire to build a house; whereupon each family and individual would commit for donating labour, timber or any other help that they could afford and like this a new house would be constructed. Every family and the village community had to bank upon themselves for fulfilling their day to day needs and essential requirements. One could not depend on getting anything from outside as there would hardly be any money with an ordinary family to purchase even those things which might be available in the local market. Everything in the shops was very costly as the goods had to be transported over long distances and difficult terrain. Even oil and ghee for cooking had to be locally made by growing oil seeds and converting milk into butter. Also, for long and severe winter fodder, fuel and food grains etc. used to be stocked well in advance and every household maintained sufficient reserves to cater for unforeseen eventualities. All this stocking involved a lot of hard work and planning as well as traversing long distances by human beings and beasts. Fuel and fodder was almost gold for the people and used to be considered an indication of wealth; as apart from feeding one's own animals this could be traded for cash or goods. Almost four-five hundred horses would reach Leh in the shape of a caravan to and from Srinagar and such a large number of animals required fodder which could be sold by those who had sufficient surplus stocks and were well paid for the same. Government stores also used to provide feed, which was generally available at the rate of 20 to 25 seers per rupee. But the fodder had to be procured from the local market; therefore, anybody who could grow surplus fodder was that much richer. The live stock was quite cheap, considering the present day rates. Ranging from two to ten rupees; was the cost of one goat, sheep, donkey, cow, yak or horse. The animals also provided much needed soil nutrition in the form of manure, as no chemical fertilizers were available then. Droppings of animals were carefully collected and converted into manure. The cows normally remained at one place and horses were used for riding as well as carriage of goods. These could also be given on hire to the caravan and transport contractors. Sheep and goat were normally sent to highland pastures during summer and kept at various locations during winter. All my Yaks were stationed at a place called Digger as these animals could only be kept at higher altitude. This land was part of the *Jagir* of Leh-Lompo which came into the inheritance of my grandmother.

"In Ladakh of those days there were peculiar traditions of repaying the debt as well as debt relief to those who had fallen on bad days. These also reflect and underline the basic philosophy of community living and spirit of interdependence in a society at peace with itself. If somebody owned a person 25 *Khals* of food grains (equivalent to 10 Kgs.) and he could not afford to pay back then in front of the village community he had to present one string of rope to the lender and this act of humility and submission was considered to be adequate compensation to clear him of his liabilities. Similarly for a debt up to 1000 *Khals* that person had to pay either a carpet or an Ox to a Gompa to clear off his liability. This was accepted by the entire society. Of course in the bargain the affected person did lose his stature and self respect in front of his village and peers and this deterrence was considered strong enough measure by the elders who had put this practice into operation. This way the poor and those who had fallen on bad days did get an opportunity to stand on their own feet again and re-build their and their families lives. There were similar types of conditions and traditions for different kinds of debts after fulfilling which the person could start his life all over again and was considered to be worthy of giving another loan. This way a healthy balance was maintained in the society and equilibrium of equality and opportunity was ensured. However, where the village community was of the opinion that the borrower had sufficient amount of land available and due to lack of effort he was not able to repay the loan; an appropriate part of the land was given on mortgage to the lender for a pre-determined number of years so that he could recover, by cultivation, his dues after which the land was restored to the original owner.

"As a part of the defence strategy, the Maharaja had distributed pieces of land at important locations of ingress to Kalons and Lompos. These included Hot Springs, Hunder, and important villages along Nubra River so that these trusted officials and high families had to send their men and cattle to these far-flung areas; keep the local population at peace as also get the information about state of affairs of outlying areas. This method worked well for the security of the State; as also provided useful information and feedback in addition to keeping everybody under due check…From early in my childhood I learnt to go to the highland pastures and manage large flocks; first from my grandfather and then from my father. I have spent considerable number of years in the Aksai Chin area. In that sector, before Independence some British officers used to go there for survey and preparing maps; they would invariably hire our horses and clear the dues. Once, because of lack of water 75 of our horses died. No payment was made for these losses. My grandfather had petitioned before the Wazir-i-Wazarat about the loss of this large number of horses, but he was informally advised that the British officer who had taken these horses on hire was a Lt. Col. in the British Army, an important dignitary, and therefore nothing should be brought in black and white against him and it would not be advisable for the local respectable people to come in conflict with the British. We realized the importance of keeping the British on the right side when, sometimes in the early 1940s, my entire flock along with three attendants in the Aksai Chin area was captured by the men of Chiang Kai-shek – then the ruler of China – and in spite of our requests as also the efforts of Wazir-i-Wazarat we could not get them back. Then the British Joint Commissioner was approached; and since we maintained cordial relations with him, he promised to help. Within fifteen days our entire flock along with two men returned, the third person died of illness on his way back. It transpired that the BJC had taken up the matter through telegraph with his counterpart across the border in the Chinese administration. Even those days of primitive communication facilities, administrative channels at certain levels were fast and effective.

"The administration in Ladakh was headed by Wazir-i-Wazarat who had all the executive as well as judicial powers, including awarding of death sentences. He was assisted by other administrative and police officers to run the administration on behalf of the Maharaja. Whenever he or another important officer, like Tehsildar, went on tours, their programme would be intimated in advance and they would move in camps. The Nazir was required to make all arrangements of boarding and lodging for which the requisite money was paid by the concerned officer. They never lived off the local population. Whatever food grains, chickens, eggs, milk and fuel was procured for the visiting officer's camp was paid for. Of course one cannot rule out a case here and there when the Nazir or some lower functionary would draw the amount for this purpose from the government treasury and not pay to the people who rendered the services. But whenever such a person was caught by the officer he was invariably punished and, therefore, the cases of non-payment were few and far between. The Wazir-i-Wazarat used to keep his headquarters for four summer months in Leh and for six months of winter would shift it to Skardu. Since the route to Skardu passed through Kargil, he along with his entourage would camp in Kargil for one month each on his way to as also on his return from Skardu. Both at Leh and Kargil the local administration was run by a Tehsildar and a Naib Tehsildar. The Naib Tehsildar also enjoyed the powers of a Kotwal (SHO) and had services of 5-6 policemen at his disposal. As I grew up I did not find these policemen wearing any uniform but they could be distinguished from an ordinary person only by the wide leather belt with a copper plate they wore as policemen. Later around late 1930s they started putting on *Khakhi* uniform and one of them got one stripe and the senior most got the rank of Head Constable with three stripes. It was only around 1946 that a regular Sub-Inspector was posted in Leh and the functions of Kotwal were transferred from the Naib Tehsildar to the SI. Till then the Naib Tehsildar was assisted by a Naib Kotwal who was a senior person but he exclusively looked after the police functions; as the Naib Tehsildar would be busy in his revenue administration duties. Justice was fair and quick. The administration was so effective that from Damchok to Nubra –

almost the entire east west axis – the whole vast area was taken care of by six village Kotwals, who were responsible for maintenance of peace and public order as well as detection of crime. There was hardly a case which remained undetected or unresolved.

"Of course there was a system of *Begari* but that had been integrated into the administrative set up and even in begari certain method was expected to be followed and government functionaries were required to take recourse to begar system only within these norms. For example a chaprasi was only entitled to take free service of one person from one village to another who was supposed to carry his personal belongings; and from that village to the next one another individual was to be arranged by the Numberdar for travel to the subsequent village. If the chaprasi asked for more than one person's services or demanded use of a horse without payment, he was deemed to have violated the norms and let himself open for disciplinary action. For begar, the services could only be used from one village to another and not from one stage to the next. The facility of horses for individuals from one stage to another could only be obtained on payment. At every stage there were at least ten horses maintained for use by government officers, travelers, traders and postal services; though on payment.

"The population of Leh region those days was around forty thousand with almost same number of people living in the Kargil area; the Skardu sector was more densely populated with around one lakh souls. Both Leh and Skardu had land record offices (called *Muhafiz Khana* in the revenue parlance). There was none at Kargil and the land records of Kargil used to be kept at Leh. There were 8-10 Patwaris each in Leh and Kargil with much larger number in Skardu. Departmental Stores existed at Kargil, Leh, Gia and Panamik where government food grains and stocks were kept including the feed for animals; these were mainly used by traders. The whole external trade was conducted under the British over lordship; the State officers did not have any authority to check the goods that were carried from one place to another – as these routes were technically leased out to the British by the State Government. The British Joint Commissioner would every year go to Yarkand as part of his duties. The British Resident used to pay visit once in 10-12 years. He was received with great pomp and ceremony and considerable time and resources were spent in preparing for his visit. The Resident would give presents to important and respectable locals. My grandfather who was also a *Zaildar* would receive a silver wrist watch and people with lower status would get table clocks as presents during his tour.

"In Nubra Valley there were always apprehensions of flood during the summer months, due to the melting of glaciers in the higher reaches, and elaborate arrangements used to be put in place, constantly monitoring the threat of floods. This was given such an importance that whenever British Joint Commissioner would go on tour to Nubra he would personally check the level of river at Hundar. This, at an average, he would do twice during the summer months every year. Whenever there was threat of flood, special care used to be taken and a post would be established at Khalsar. Two people were put on duty and their job was to take levels both during the day as well as night. At Khalsar there was a pile of dry cow dung as also dry shrubs and in case the water rose to dangerous level during night then this post was required to light the fire, so that this could be seen at a distance – near Khardung La – and a similar pile of fire was arranged to be lit there so that people at Leh could know about the danger within few minutes of water rising at Khalsar. From Leh the information could be instantly transferred on the telegraph line to Srinagar and beyond. If the water level crossed the danger mark during the day time then the pile of cow dung was lit so that a large ball of smoke signal could be raised, which was seen at the next point. The same drill was repeated here for transmission of warning right up to Leh and there from to other regions. This was probably to ensure that the warning could travel through fast means to the plain areas of Punjab where such information could be used for timely action to minimize the flood damages. This is how an effective system was put on ground and made operational; even though the means of communication prevailing then were quite primitive...Similarly, in case there was any threat to life of the community or danger to the State then any government official could put the details on a piece of paper, enclose it in an envelope and that envelop could be wrapped around a stick with a red flag on top. This stick, with the red flag, could be given to any horse rider or a person moving on foot. It was incumbent on this man to deliver the same to next village through the fastest means; and this way the communication reached Leh, with speed. No charges were required to be paid for carrying such messages and these were never stopped at any place en-route even during the night...The system of information and intelligence was very efficiently organized and meticulously followed right down to the village level. At every village, a respectable person was designated as Village Kotwal, which was an honorary appointment. He would report every incident of importance or arrival of any person in the village to the Numberdar – a nominated headman of the area. A Numberdar covered up to 8-10 villages. These reports originated on a printed format which was in Bodhi language. Numberdar, in turn, would send his compiled report to the Tehsildar. Apart from the reports of all new happenings, regular fortnightly, monthly and six monthly reports were also made by the village Kotwal to Numberdar and by Numberdar to Tehsildar in proper format. Thus the administration kept track of all the happenings on regular basis; even daily if required. These reports also included the good work and the misdeeds of touring officers as well as performance of local officers posted in the area.

"The journey from Leh to Srinagar was then covered in 21 stages. On every stage there used to be a Dak Bunglow where government officials and important persons could stay. Normal charges for each horse between one stage to another was one rupee and rent for the single night in a Dak Bunglow was twelve *annas*. The whole system was under the supervision of British Joint Commissioner; who enjoyed the highest order of precedence in the region. He would also appoint contractors on yearly basis for every stage. These contractors would provide fodder, firewood, chickens, eggs, etc. at rates determined in contract; this list was displayed in every Dak Bunglow. Rest of the food material was expected to be arranged by the traveler himself. The first stage from Leh was Nimoo and last Kangan. After Drass the stages were Machoi, Gumri and then across Zojila at Baltal. After Baltal the next Dak Bunglow was at Sonamarg followed by Gund and then Kangan. Normally horses used to be taken on hire from one stage to another and at every stage horses were generally changed. In case of important people, like my father and grandfather, they used to take their own horses as well as hire some enroute right up to Drass. Nobody carried own horses from Drass into the Valley as keeping an eye on them was difficult, therefore, all private horses were left at Drass in the care of the locals – on payment - and collected on return. Since there was large pasture land in and around Drass, one found that the animals were generally healthy when they were collected on the return journey. Travel on horses and ponies during those days had its own charm...Because of smaller distances that could be covered then in one day; the interdependence of people and communities was inevitable and in fact considerable, giving rise to its own social dynamics. In order to remain mobile, people had to establish and maintain cordial relations almost at every village. Whether one was going towards Srinagar or Skardu or Yarkand; each frequent traveler kept contacts and retained friendships virtually in every village along the way. Whenever a person or a caravan reached a particular village they had relations with, few households would welcome them, give a hot cup of tea and arrange for the night stay as well as provide food and fodder. In turn the visitors would hire their animals for the next stage. On reciprocal basis similar hospitality would be extended to those households when they came to Leh. Since the stay at major places like Skardu, Kargil and Drass was usually extended; one had to keep more cordial and better relations with the people at these locations. The caravans of big traders would be large ones; at times exceeding one thousand horses. Usually such sizable number of animals carried the loads of Hoshiarpuri traders or came from Manali side with the stores of British functionaries. The goods of latter category could not be inspected by officials of the State Government. However, on two occasions when their horses fell off a cliff and the contents got scattered; word spread among the people that once it contained rifle cartridges and the second time opium.

"At the age of fourteen I went to Srinagar for the first time, in the year 1937. Since it was beginning of summer and the snow had not fully melted at Zojila, I was fascinated to see such a huge pile of snow which one had never seen in Leh. On the steep descent in the gorge across Zojila, what struck me first were the trees growing on the mountains. I had not seen so many trees at one place. This amazement grew further as I entered into the Valley and noticed walnut and apple trees. It was a journey full of surprises and eager expectations of a young mind open to an entirely new set of circumstances and life style. Till then, for me Leh was the biggest and most advanced place in the world and here it was an entirely different scenario. At Kangan, I saw a *tonga* for the first time which was carrying 4-5 people as also load; something that was quite unimaginable back home. Then on the way, I also saw a motor car with canvas top and wheels. This was a most amazing sight and a bit scary too. I also came in contact with an important Pashmina shawl merchant named Ahmad Ullah Shahdad. We were staying in Kaksarai at Srinagar and my father wanted me to collect something from Shahdad; who sent me back in his car – which was a big luxury for me. I also saw the busses of N.D. Radhakrishan Company going from Srinagar to Rawalpindi and Lahore. Later; once I attended Dussehra in Srinagar and saw the Maharaja come from his palace in a motorcade up to the old palaces on the right bank of Jehlum. From there he rode on horseback in full uniform right to the ground near Maggarmal Bagh area; a place where presently Iqbal park is located. There important State functionaries, including my father as a member of the Praja Sabha, would offer *Nazrana* before the Dussehra proceedings began...I also remember an interesting incident when I saw a traffic constable for the first time. From the footpath I was watching this man standing right in the middle of the road with vehicles going past him at considerable speed and I thought this man would get crushed. I kept watching him for good over one hour, left the place thinking that the person must be lucky that none of the vehicles hit him; and also wondered how long his luck would hold on.

"Some of the trade followed practices which were discriminatory to the Ladakhis. For example, we could not deal in Pashmina for which specific persons were authorized and only they could conduct business in this commodity. The local producers or traders were not allowed to sell Pashmina directly to Kashmiri businessmen and this would have to go through the middle man who would have his own commission. It was a system which was quite unfair as well as loaded against the owners of the flock. However, some enterprising people like me would cross frontiers of the State and buy things as far as Rudok under the Tibetan administration and then trade in the local market. Since we could not buy Pashmina which was produced in large quantity in Changthang; we would go further and buy Toosh from Tibetans at the rate of one rupee for two seers and sell it to Kashmiri traders at a profit of multiple times... Changthang was full of vast stretches of grassland and almost all flock of Leh would move during summer to these pastures where animals would fatten themselves. Few intrepid people would also gather surplus fodder and sell to Yarkandi caravans. One gunny bag full of dry fodder would generally fetch from Yarkandi traders one Namda and four *annas* which effectively made the cost of this fodder at one rupee per bag.

"One can imagine the comparative cost increase in goods from the fact that for one rupee almost 20 seers of Sattu would be available at Leh whereas, same commodity in Western Tibet would sell at the rate of two seers per rupee and if you went further east it would be one rupee per seer and at the same location a sheep may be available for the similar amount. Therefore, we would also prefer to carry 16 to 18 seers Sattu on each sheep; sell the Sattu there and on return feed ourselves on the meat of sheep only. Also on journey back we would buy large flock of sheep at one rupee each. Enroute this herd would live off the grass in the pastures and with little investment on the additional pack one could sell these at the rate of rupees two each at Leh. On one particular trip I bought 1000 sheep and made a neat profit of one thousand rupees; which was a very handsome amount during those days. However, all this required a lot of hard physical work, deprivation and certain amount of risk. There was always a lurking chance of disease and malnutrition during the travel as well as of losing investment if the flock got into some trouble. One also had to take care of some dacoits who occasionally made their presence felt; particularly along the far off borders. For this some of the traders, including me would carry weapons. Since getting a firearm license was almost impossible those days, we would carry weapons unauthorized and surreptitiously. As the danger only existed beyond Changthang; we made it a practice to take weapons from Chushool onwards and hide them in pre-determined places during the return journey hoping to find these during the next trip. Later on, I was the only person in Ladakh area who was able to get a weapon license. We would also use firearms at times to shoot small birds and enjoyed this as a game as well as a delicious addition to the meals.

"The way trade used to be carried on between different parties would surprise anybody these days. Almost everybody was illiterate and in that area nothing was recorded in black and white. As the leader of my group I would invariably go in advance during the day, select a campsite, collect dung and fire wood to prepare tea for the main party and if by chance met my counterpart from the other direction the two of us would start chatting, even without knowing the name, place of residence and other particulars of each other. The talks would proceed to business opportunities of mutual benefit. The commodities to be exchanged, the quantities and rates as also details of the terms would be settled. The place and time would also be fixed where goods and money would be traded next year; in addition to the current trade discussion. Due to difficult communication and long distances a margin of plus minus five days was understood to be available to each party. After that, a delay of each day was to be compensated by the defaulting party at pre-determined rates or conditions. The deal having struck to the mutual satisfaction and without the presence of independent witness; both picked up a blade of grass or a dry twig and jointly broke it signifying that if any party breached his part of the contract then the God would break him like a dry twig or the blade of grass. It was most satisfying as well as amazing that never there was a single case of any person going back on his deal or contract arrived at in this manner. That was the level of confidence and character which existed then as compared to people of these days going back even on the written and well defined agreements... For reaching Kailash one had to go via Damchok. From Damchok the journey took to Tashigong; it is seven-eight days travel which is almost on a flat land with hardly any incline. The route from Leh to Kailash is the easiest trek to this holy place and if it is opened for regular pilgrimage, it will be a great boon to Hindu devotees as well as Ladakh tourism industry.

"Most of the Gompas owned substantial tracts of land attached to them. Whenever religious ceremony was performed by the monks in a household, the head of the family presented the Gompa with cash or kind, food grains and other things. There was also the custom of giving away part of one's land in lieu of performance of religious rites. That is how some of the Gompas came to acquire considerable chunks of land. Like Hemis Gompa, the largest and most famous one in Ladakh, had almost 18,000 Kanals of land attached to it spread all over the Ladakh region. Most of the Gompas maintained food stocks and food stores for their own use as well as in times of natural calamity. During 1940s a famine struck Ladakh and the people could survive on the food grains made available through the government stores as well as stocks maintained by the Gompas which gave grains to the local population. I recall the Rezong Gompa had about thousand *Khals* of food grains in its stores and it is said that these stocks were up to 100 years old. Since the food grains were required for feeding the local people around, these were distributed and people consumed it without any adverse effect and the entire stocks of the Gompa were thus used gainfully. Almost in every household there used to be a tradition to put the food grains in the store during a particular ceremony and unless these were required for dire emergency more stocks were put in next year. Thus at any given time every family unit had a certain quantity of food grains available going up to 10-20, fifty or even hundred years old.

"Postal system which was conceived and organized by the British was a very efficient one. Between Srinagar and Leh the *dak* was expected to reach in four days, where as normal travel would take over twenty one stages. After every four miles the department had established a post manned by two persons who were paid regularly by the Postal Department authorities and they worked as runners. Each one carried a large staff with trinkets which would make sound while travelling so that the person carrying *dak* on the run or walking very fast would get clear path as he was supposed to cover the requisite distance within the specified time. If someone was not fit enough to do so, he was relieved of the service. To keep an appropriate control on these posts a number of Jamadars were appointed. There were two Jamadars between Leh and Kargil; with one responsible up to Khaltsi and another from there to Kargil. They would supervise the functioning and proper delivery of postal articles in all the areas and keep a track of the time taken in delivering the *dak* from one post to another. Even a delay of one hour was taken adverse notice of. There was much talked about story about a British Joint Commissioner becoming unhappy because official communications from Srinagar reached him late 'by full four hours'. The postal supervisors were constantly on move on their horses; checking adequacy of the movement of the *dak* and also ensure that it was continuously mobile as per schedule and the postal bundles were never stationary at any place. Even during the height of winter this system ensured that the post runners continued operating across Zojila as per their appointed schedule of movement. The only concession that was made during snow and blizzard period was that instead of four days, the delay could be of maximum up to two days; but in no circumstances the *dak* was expected to take more than six days between Srinagar and Leh. During the winter season the staff at Drass was increased up to 25 persons. The tickets on the envelopes were those of Queen Victoria and the King Emperor as the State did not have its own postal system, and thus no J&K stamps existed. The whole of Ladakh had only one regular post office and that was at Leh. Same efficiency and promptness was ensured in matters of telegrams also. Transmission of telegrams between Leh and Srinagar was very prompt, almost instantaneous. The rate, if I recall correctly, was one *anna* per word. The telegraph system had started even before I was born. However, before 1947 there was no public telephone facility here. The first telephone line was laid between Leh and Khaltsi after 1947 and for a few years that was the only telephone link in the entire Ladakh region.

"The system of Posts and Telegraphs was so efficiently managed and strictly monitored that every one well understood that no excuses were accepted and therefore the employees of the postal department were always alert as well as duty conscious. There was also a category of 'four *anna* telegrams'. By paying four *annas* per word the telegrams could be sent from Leh to anywhere, including far off places like Lhasa. These telegrams took priority over all the traffic from origination to destination point but these, even after having made requisite payment, were to be authorized by the British Joint Commissioner or Wazir-i-Wazarat himself. In 1946 when my eldest son Wangdus was born, my father was in Lhasa and I wanted to inform him about this; it was then that the local Post Master told me about this type of telegrams. I made the requisite payment and after getting the permission from Wazir-iWazarat he transmitted the telegram to my father in Lhasa. Later, on returning home he confirmed that the message was received by him on the same day. That was the efficiency of the service during those days even when the system in existence was almost primitive.

"People, particularly traders, used to cover long distances in those days without the help of charts or maps. For the persons who understood complexities of such travels, it was neither unusual nor surprising to see the head of a caravan riding a donkey when he could very well afford to be on a horse back instead. This was not out of any lack of means or poverty. The reason for such a practice lied in the fact that amongst men and animals donkey is the best navigator. Ladakh and also some regions beyond, being bereft of major landmarks, authentic direction finding and navigation was a big issue with caravans and groups of people on move. There had been reported instances when, inexperienced people, after a nights good sleep, would set off the next morning in the wrong direction and come to a grief. Therefore, as a matter of abundant caution; the seasoned travelers, which included trading caravans, took two elementary precautions. They always slept with their heads towards the direction of onward journey so that the next day after getting ready the entire group set off in the right alignment. Riding a donkey was also a part of this carefulness. Because, uncannily the donkey would always head towards the correct direction, the next morning. The routes were either memorized or handed down from one generation to other through names of important villages. Where the distance between two villages was extremely large; then by visible signs existing on the ground like rock formations or a cluster of stones and similar things. At the border, boundaries were demarcated by visible markings on rocks and specially erected stone structures by the respective governments. It was a tradition to touch the ground with one's forehead before leaving the boundary, walk nine steps with back towards the other territory; then turn and resume the journey. On return also on entering own area the custom of touching the ground with forehead was repeated. This respect to and knowledge of territory and ground had stood the test of time and from generation to generation served the people without fail. In those olden days when individuals and even households did not have written records; it was this understanding of the ground situation which helped the community to avoid disputes between individuals and villages."[33]

It would be interesting to mention an engaging case study to show how the State Government was sensitive to issues relating to maintenance of public peace and order; in a far off area like Ladakh in those gone by days when communication systems were rudimentary as also primitive in nature. In 1932 which was a leap year – the month of February had 29 days – it took just 13 days for a proposal of the Wazir-i-Wazarat Ladakh to have a telephone connection with Kargil and Skardu; to get final approval of the Maharaja. This period also included the ruler having seen the concerned file once in between. The matter originated in a telegram dated February 26, 1932 from Wazir-i-Wazarat Ladakh – camp Skardu – to the Prime Minister, saying "…propose phone connection be arranged immediately on all the three Tehsil stations enabling District Magistrate to know day to day happenings…" This telegram was put up to the Maharaja for his information three days later, as also seeking permission for taking up the matter with Superintendent Telegraphs "…as to the feasibility and cost of putting up a telephone line between Leh and Skardu…" On getting the requisite approval; a communication was addressed to the Superintendent Telegraphs and Telephones, on the same day, to do the needful. That officer responded with a detailed proposal and cost estimates vide his letter No. 1509/C dated 3rd March 1932.

Based on the material available, the Prime Minister put up a comprehensive proposal to the Maharaja on 10 March. This document included, "The Wazir of Leh reported on 26th February 1932…that telephones might be installed at Skardu, Kargil and Ladakh to enable him to keep in touch with daily events at those places…The journey from Leh to Skardu takes about 16 days and it is therefore considered essential to have the quickest possible means of communication, especially in these days of political agitation…telephone communication between Leh and Skardu is not practicable on the existing wires. If new wires are required to be erected, the cost will be prohibitive. Telephone communication between Skardu and Kargil, and Kargil and Leh can, however, be arranged on the existing wires with special types of telephones at a cost of Rs.

33 *Ibid.*

1397/- but this too can be done after the Zojila pass opens…it seems necessary, in the interest of administration, that the Wazir-i-Wazarat who is the District Magistrate also, should remain in constant touch with every movement in the District. It was at one time proposed to erect wireless stations on the frontier but it is doubtful whether in the present financial stringency it would be possible to undertake such a big work immediately. If His Highness approves special telephones may be installed at Kargil, Skardu and Leh as proposed by the Superintendent Telegraphs at a cost of Rs. 1397/-; the funds for the purpose being provided in the Telegraph Department Budget of the current year. Submitted for commands."

These papers were returned the same day by Maharaja Hari Singh, with orders, "Sanctioned as recommended." This episode throws considerable light on the prevailing general situation in the region; as also gives a glimpse of the mechanics of decision making process in important matters.

Ladakh, as also the general condition of the people of this region, remained practically unchanged for centuries till the partition of India in August 1947. So also was the case with its principal town of Leh. An illustration of life there has been graphically described by Knights, in his book, and it would be in order to quote him, "Leh, conveniently situated as it is about half-way between the markets of India and those of Central Asia, has become the terminus for the caravans from both regions. In the summer, traders arrive at Leh from every part of India, and from Turkestan, Tibet, Siberia, and the remotest districts of Central Asia. Here the goods and produce of the south are exchanged for those of the north. It is seldom that a caravan from India goes north of Leh, or that one from Central Asia proceeds south of it. The merchants, who have been travelling for months along the difficult roads from either direction, meet here and dispose off their loads, to a great extent by barter; but before they commence the long, weary homeward journey, they rest here for a month or two, so that the bazaar and the environs of the city are thronged with camels, yaks and other beasts of burden, as well as with men from all corners of Asia. At this time there is such a motley collection of types and various costumes, and such a babel of different languages, as it would not be easy to find elsewhere. Savage Tartars in sheepskins, and other outlandish men, jostle with the elegant Hindoo merchant from the cities of Central India… Leh in September is, indeed, one of the busiest and most crowded of cities, and the storekeepers and farmers who have to supply this multitude must make a very good profit for the time. Leh is therefore a very cosmopolitan city, even in the dead season; for there are resident merchants and others of various races and creeds. Small as is the permanent population, at least four languages are in common use here – Hindostani, Tibetan, Turki and Kashmiri – while several others are spoken. Six religions have their followers in Leh… The people are fairly tolerant of each other's beliefs, and intermarriages in families of rival creeds are not infrequent."[34]

Many people have wondered, sometimes aloud, as to how the main road in Leh bazaar is so wide. The fact is that this central market place also doubled up as the local polo ground whenever the resident population or a high dignitary so decided in the olden days; especially before independence. Now, of course, a separate place has come up for this purpose. Those days it was a normal thing to play in the bazaar and people were informed of the coming contest by the playing of local drums and instruments' – particularly a local version of *shehnai* like thing called *surnai.* During the game all shops were closed and people watched the contest, with keen interest, from the road side, balconies and the roof-tops. The players were all astride puny looking but sturdy ponies. In the local lore, Zanskari horses (which were ponies in fact) were supposed to be the most sturdy and fittest lot for this game. Polo has always been a favorite game in Ladakh; with people cheering enthusiastically every time a goal is scored as also letting out a collective sigh of disappointment over the missing of such a chance. Sometimes one can see old, black and white, photographs – and even slides – of a game of polo in progress in the main bazaar of Leh.

The interaction between Muslims and Buddhists of Ladakh has traditionally been cordial and of friendly co-existence. The Muslim traders finding this place peaceful and tolerant; some of them settled here and few of them married local Buddhist ladies, which are the main reasons as to how Muslim population came into existence in and around Leh. There have been two main factors responsible for this phenomenon; one is that the Muslims came here as traders and not as conquerors and the other being the fact that Ladakhi rulers have traditionally been very tolerant and large hearted. Even in the times of Singhe Namgial, over three hundred years ago, the Muslims were given place in Leh to build a mosque. It is true

34 Knight, *op., cit,* pp. 177-178.

that since the olden times, because of the tolerating attitude of the rulers of Ladakh and Ladakhi population, there was never a conflict between the Muslims and the Buddhists and the two communities have always lived in harmony. The advent of Christianity in the region began with the opening of Moravian Mission towards the second half of nineteenth century. However, it did not make a perceptible change in the milieu of Ladakh. According to a local scholar at Leh, "The Christian missionaries were not able to make a dent in Ladakh and hardly any family converted to Christianity. The story of an important family joining this fold has a background. One of its elders had a dispute with the King and felt that the latter had done injustice to him; so out of sheer vengeance he converted to Christianity. Later, the missionaries also started picking up poor and bright students, gave them good education and helped them. Few were even sent out for higher studies; even then hardly any of these students converted. Since the number of Christians was very small and the missionaries had a lot of influence with the British; they were able to get the local Christians good jobs in the government and hence this small community is generally better off. However, the presence of Christians in Ladakh region is not only restricted to Leh town but there also the figure has remained very limited."[35]

Some facets of life in Ladakh then, has been expansively described by an author as, "Nature is never unkind to mankind. Seeing the adverse climate combined with high altitude and comparative poverty one may be lead to think at first glance that human life as such must be suffering a lot in this land. But very soon one sheds this belief away when going a little deeper one sees the ways in which nature has helped not only the human beings but also the animal life in this land. The people actually look happier and more contended than at many other places of the world. Few people look ill or poor in health. Red cheeks and smiling faces are a common sight...The method of irrigation in Ladakh is peculiar but nonetheless well suited to the country which is mountainous to the extreme. While the stream high up in the distant mountain might supply an unending source of water, the ingenuity, the patient labour and the dogged perseverance which make the water available to the fields miles away are supplied by the local people. One cannot but marvel at the ingenuity and the natural engineering skill of the people of Ladakh if one sees how even along the most precipitous cliffs, which seem almost inaccessible except to the most

35 Interview with Tashi Rabgias at Leh in September 1998.

skillful amongst the mountaineers, the cooperative effort of the resourceful farmers has succeeded in building these canals. Every body in this remote region of the world seems to have an abundant faith in the goodness of human nature. It is easy for a man to go to the bazaar and get a few things which he needs urgently and tell the shopkeeper that the money will be paid subsequently. It is also absolutely safe to give a rupee or two to the fisherman or the butcher on the understanding that the next day he must send to one's house a fish or some meat. People trust each other and have complete faith in each other's bonafides. It is a common occurrence in the bazaar that the shop is kept open when the shopkeeper is away for his lunch or on some personal work. People, whether they run a shop or dwell in a house, pay very little attention to security because of their abiding faith in the goodness of their neighbours and in the trust-worthiness of the strangers."[36]

36 Rajendra Nath, *Strategic Ladakh*, Vij Books India Pvt Ltd, New Delhi, 2016, pp. 73, 90 and 70.

CHAPTER III

Barely Saved (Pak Ingress in 1947-48)

General Picture in Ladakh – Troops and Preparedness

It was in the month of August 1947 that India gained independence and the Dominion of Pakistan came into existence. At that time; general picture of the resources available for defence and security of the entire frontier region of the State was not encouraging. All infantry soldiers of the state forces, numbering not more than six Battalions, were deployed along the long borders of Jammu and Valley; and this too was quite thinly spread on the ground and not tactically grouped in the real military sense. Of this meagre force level, there was hardly anything that could be spared for the Ladakh region; except for the existing troops in the sector. Starting from the north; Gilgit Agency was already under the control of the British and there were no forces of the State army in that region. This landmass was thus effectively under the security cover of the locally raised militia called Gilgit Scouts; a paramilitary outfit comprising Muslim men of this area. Therefore, the State Government's responsibility for security and consequently the regular positioning of forces did not go beyond Bunji, located about fifty kilometers short of Gilgit on the road to Srinagar. One regular unit, the 6th J&K Infantry was located in the entire Ladakh; with the following deployment:-

(i) Battalion less two companies at Bunji; under the command of Lt. Col. Abdul Majid Khan.

(ii) Company less platoon at Leh. Major Sher Jung Thapa being the Company Commander.

(iii) Two platoons at Kargil; under Capt. Ganga Singh.

(iv) Company less platoon at Skardu; under the command of Capt. Nek Alam.

This unit, "headquartered at Bunji, had recently relieved 5 JAK. The composition of 6 JAK at the time was 50 *per cent* Sikh, 50 *per cent* Muslim. The Sikh element of the battalion, recently formed, was weakened by a substantial number of recruits not yet proficient in weaponry.... The battalion was responsible for the security of the northern frontier of the state, exclusive of the Gilgit Agency, between Bunji and Leh."[1] As if this low level of troop deployment was not inadequate enough; the situation became further worse for Kargil and Leh when, because of the fast deteriorating situation, Major Sher Jung Thapa was asked to move to Skardu for its defence and he reached there on December 3, 1947. He collected all possible force from Leh and Kargil for this assignment; leaving behind only an administrative set up at Kargil and one platoon at Leh. This meant that in that sector not more than one section each could be deployed at Nubra, Khaltsi and Leh; an extremely unsatisfactory state of affairs. Things became still more difficult when the presence of some infiltrators was noticed in the Nubra Valley in January 1948. By that time Gilgit had fallen in Pakistani hands and Lt. Col. Abdul Majid Khan imprisoned by the rebels. His unit, the 6 JAK, practically ceased to exist as an entity. The Muslim troops, half of the battalion, had been effectively subverted and joined the other side with the rebels. Of the rest, the Sikh soldiers at Bunji were either killed or captured. Only operational elements of this force were the small contingents at Leh, Kargil and the men who were with Sher Jung Thapa at Skardu. Also, after the apprehension of Lt. Col. Majid Khan became public; Thapa was entrusted to command the remnants of this unit with the rank of a Lt. Col.

By the beginning of 1948, with the whole of Gilgit Agency in Pakistani hands; the situation in Skardu sector began fast deteriorating; especially for the administration and the minority community. The ground conditions there have been graphically described by Shridhar Kaul, an Inspector of Schools then, who was on an official tour in the interiors of this area. Pandit Dullo, as he was affectionately called by the people of Ladakh - as also remembered as such in the later decades by the local men of that area - became almost a legendary figure during the crisis at Leh

1 Major-General D.K. Palit, VrC, *Jammu and Kashmir Arms,* Palit & Dutt Publishers, Dehra Dun, 1972, p. 226.

in 1947-48; being a sort of their friend, guide and philosopher. He was first posted in Ladakh in 1939 as an Education Officer to spread literacy there; and continued to stay and work for uplifting the local population for more than a decade. This in itself was unique, considering that the man was an outsider and did not belong to the region. During the last month of 1947, in the Skardu belt, he has recorded, "At Shigar with its considerable Sikh population, panic among this foreign element in a hostile native population was even more pronounced. I went about the middle of December to Shigar from Skardu on an official tour, found the atmosphere surcharged with rumours of a sensational variety. Mr. Wazir Ahmed, a local teacher seemed to know more about the coming storm than he cared to reveal. It was not difficult to perceive from his carefully guarded words that Pakistan was expected to plant her flag in Baltistan before long… On the eve of my departure from Shigar, I was told in confidence by Mohd. Akbar Khan, Headmaster of a local school, that a catastrophe of gigantic proportions seemed eminent and that I had better hurry back to a zone of safety. He even went so far as to say that if anything happened by the time I reached Skardu from Shigar, he should be informed instantly so that he might escort me to safety. Nothing, however, happened by the time I reached Skardu and, thence to Khaplu. Here also rumours poured in thick and fast… I left Khaplu for Kargil in the first week of January 1948. Here too, a frightful crop of ominous rumours greeted my arrival. One of the rumours had it that a Gilgit force was already within rifle-shot of Skardu. Friends tried to persuade me to abandon my tour programme and to make for Kargil with forced marches. Not believing, however, that things had really come to such a pass, I refused to be swayed by these well meant exhortations. The tour programme was adhered to according to plan and I reached Kargil about the middle of January."[2]

In Kargil, with its predominant Shia Muslim population, the general atmosphere and feelings amongst local people was not of hostility towards the existing dispensation; but they were collectively watching the unfolding events with a sense of fatal resignation. In Leh, on the other hand, there was a sense of acute consternation about the happenings around; including a worrisome dilemma about the safety and honour of the people. Also, the community as a whole was much more organized there. The general mood and conditions there have been portrayed by Rigzin Namgyal Kalon

2 Shridhar Kaul and H.N. Kaul, *Ladakh Through the Ages,* Indus Publishing Company, New Delhi, 1992, pp. 168 and 169.

as, "Nearing the Independence, political and community activity in our region picked up, spearheaded by Ladakh Buddhist Association (LBA). My father was the President of the LBA and they would hold fortnightly meetings to assess latest political developments within the State and rest of the country, as were becoming known through radio, telegrams and other means. After Independence, these consultations became even more frequent and the LBA would meet almost every week. Some people started toying with the idea that independence meant freedom of choice and therefore Ladakhis should decide about their own future. Whether they should remain part of the existing dispensation or try to be with China or Tibet…Those days a Kashmiri Pandit officer – Dulloo – was posted as Inspector of Schools here. He was a highly respected man and his words carried considerable weight. When the elders consulted him he advised them against any such move and forcefully reiterated in unequivocal terms that the Ladakhi people must remain with the State and the rest of the country, and this should be clearly and loudly conveyed to all concerned… By this time names of Pandit Jawahar Lal Nehru and Govind Bhallav Pant had become known in Ladakh. Gopalaswamy Iyanger who was the Prime Minister of the State earlier and was now a member of the Indian Cabinet was also known to Ladakhis and enjoyed their confidence, therefore, a number of telegrams were sent to all the three, informing them of the loyalty and support of the entire Ladakh region. We received due replies conveying us that Maj. Gen. Thimayya had already been sent to Kashmir to take care of the developing military situation and we should establish contact with him and Sheikh Mohd. Abdullah… Towards the end of 1947 when the situation started turning bad in the entire Gilgit region, Major Sher Jung Thapa was commanding the Leh garrison with around one hundred troops. Under orders from the higher army authorities, he left for Skardu taking almost eighty men with him which left only about three sections worth of soldiers for the entire sector. This number was grossly inadequate for the town as well as area around it. After some time we received a telegram from Major Thapa asking for three local guides to help him in Skardu area and who could be trusted by him. In the meeting with locals, it was decided to prepare and send 15 persons to work for him. Donations were collected for these people to be able to undertake a journey and meet expenses till they reached Skardu; but before this group could depart from Leh, information was received that Skardu had been surrounded by the raiders and it would not be possible for anyone to get into the fort. Therefore, this idea was dropped.

"Since troops available for the defence of Leh were grossly inadequate and almost negligible; telegrams were sent to Sheikh Abdullah to dispatch more forces, which though appeared a remote possibility due to closure of Zojila. A request was also made to him to authorize local recruitment for the defence of the area. Telegraphic instructions from Srinagar authorized raising and training of National Guards and for that the mobilization started. On the first day, there were only 20 volunteers, including myself, which number was very insufficient. My father then used his influence and enjoined that one able-bodied person from each household must become part of this new force. On the second day, we had a gathering of almost 200 volunteers. Training started in right earnest under the guidance and supervision of the State Forces' detachment. The daily routine was long and tough, which started early in the morning and carried on till six in the evening."[3]

In this frontier region, ominous developments had started taking place from the middle of 1947 itself. It adversely affected Gilgit, Skardu, Kargil, Drass and Zanskar areas sequentially. These also laid bare the designs of the Pakistani government and its supporters; foremost being the British who undisputedly were then the colonial and 'paramount' power in the Indian sub-continent. The contemporary British interests have been succinctly described in a well researched book as, "However, the two areas of the state that Britain had absolutely marked out for Pakistan – one in the context of Britain's world strategy and the other to ensure Pakistan's security – were successfully kept out of Indian control and so they remain even after more than fifty-five years. These were the Northern Areas of the state along the Chinese and Soviet frontiers and the strip of territory in the west with a common border with Pakistani Punjab. The Northern Areas consisted of the Gilgit Agency, with its dependencies of Hunza and Nagar and the principalities of Swat and Chitral at the northern end of the Durand line, the de facto boundary between Pakistan and Afghanistan. Lying to the north and east of the NWFP, the Gilgit Agency stretched to the Chinese province of Sinkiang and only a narrow strip of Afghan territory separated it from the Soviet Union. It was of no less strategic importance in British calculations than the NWFP, which Mountbatten had worked so assiduously to place in Pakistan's hands... the British expectation was that northern Kashmir would remain under their influence either as a part of an

3 Interview with Rigzin Namgyal Kalon in September 1998.

independent state or as a part of Pakistan."[4] The sixty-year lease of Gilgit Agency, which came into being in 1935, from J&K state to the British Indian government, would have become redundant on the lapse of British paramountcy in the Indian sub-continent on 15 August 1947.

Further, this book goes on to mention, "Fifteen days before independence, i.e., on 1 August 1947, the Gilgit lease was receded by Delhi to the Maharaja of J&K and Lieutenant-Colonel Roger Bacon, the British political agent, handed over the area to Brigadier Ghansara Singh, the newly arrived state's governor sent from Srinagar. According to V.P. Menon, 'the Kashmir authorities did not have the resources, including financial, to hold Gilgit which was cut off from Srinagar during winters… In view of the lapse of paramountcy, the retrocession was probably inevitable; but the fact remains that no sooner was Gilgit handed over to the Maharaja than it came under the mercy of Pakistan (through the NWFP)'"[5]. Brig. Ghansara Singh, as one of the senior most officers of the state forces, was especially picked up by Maharaja Hari Singh for this job for his experience and soldierly qualities. It is on record that to take over this assignment; Ghansara Singh flew to Gigit on 30th July along with Maj. Gen. Scott, Chief of Staff of the State Force. Gen. Scott, on his return gave his report to the Maharaja, which included the decision of the two British officers of the Gilgit Scouts, Major W.A. Brown and his Second-in-Command, Capt. A.S. Matheison, to opt for Pakistan. Having been informed of their determination to serve Pakistan, the Maharaja did not take the logical step of dispensing away with the services of these officers. Not only this lapse; but to make matters worse for the new governor, Brig Ghansara Singh was sent to Gilgit all by himself; under the premise that the lower administrative staff already posted there would automatically change its loyalties from the British to the State. That, of course, did not happen and the employees in Gilgit continued to operate as if they were still a part of the North West Frontier Administration, as earlier. To make matters worse the new head of the administration was not delegated with requisite legal, financial and administrative powers. Also, in anticipation of the transfer, the Political Agent had exhausted all stocks of essential commodities before handing over charge of the Agency. The only quick and reliable system of communication with Srinagar was a lonely wireless

4 Narendra Singh Sarila, *The Untold Story of India's Partition,* Harper Collins *Publishers* India, New Delhi, 2005, pp. 330 and 331.

5 *Ibid*, p. 332.

set in Gilgit; but that too was controlled by Peshawar. Thus, shorn of a credible official backing, lacking in the stocks of essential commodities and doubtful of the loyalty of the only force present there – 600 strong contingent of Gilgit Scouts raised by the British in 1913 for defence of the Agency – Gilgit and the new governor were almost doomed from the beginning. So much so that, "Brown and Matheison agreed that if the Maharaja did accede to India, they, with the help of the Scouts, would stage a coup d'état and hand it over to Pakistan. Details of the operation were planned and the code word fixed for putting it into operation was Datta Khel"[6]. The British went a step further and posted Lt. Col. Bacon, on transfer from Gilgit, as Political Agent Khyber with headquarters at Peshawar. This ensured complete coordination between Gilgit Scouts and authorities in Peshawar. The only silver lining was the support of local Rajahs and Mirs to this reversion from British to the J&K government. But there too, Pakistani agents were busy in systematically subverting the local population as also petty rulers of the region; with positive results. Brig. Ghansara Singh carried on his onerous responsibility quite manfully through the months of August, September and almost the entire of October.

The situation in rest of the state, particularly in Valley, started deteriorating fast with Pakistani raiders' crossing over the state borders, in ten large columns, on 22 October 1947. Four days later, Maharaja Hari Singh acceded J&K State with India. In Gilgit, however, the first move was made by the new governor on 30th October when he ordered Lt. Col. Abdul Majid Khan to come to Gilgit with as large force as possible. The latter, being ill at his headquarters at Bunji, was unable to move to Gilgit himself but in good faith dispatched Captains Hassan Khan and Ishan Ali with D company of his battalion; the maximum force he could spare at that time. These officers reached Gilgit in the morning of 31st October and treacherously joined with Major Brown and his Scouts. Further sequence of events there has been graphically described as, "The coup d'état took place on 31st October 1947… By next morning the Governor who offered personal resistance had been taken into custody. Apart from Brown, other leaders of the coup were Lt. Haider Khan and Sub- Major Babar Khan (He was an uncle of Mir of Nagar and had married the sister of the Mir of Hunza) of the Scouts. The Muslim company earlier sent by Col. Majid

6 Lt. Gen. Vijay Madan, *Jammu and Kashmir Operations, 1947-48: The Other Version*, USI Journal July-September 1992, p. 311. In fact, the author strongly feels that in all probability this task was spelt out by the Political department of the British.

Khan to Gilgit, on the requisition of the Governor, also joined the rebels. The Sikh company in Bunji was attacked, while their route of withdrawal was blocked at Astore by Capt. Matheison. They were either killed or taken prisoners. A provisional government was formed of which the leaders were Major Brown, Capt. Ehsan Ali, Capt. Mohammad Khan, Capt. Sayeed, Lt. Haider and Sub-Major Babar Khan. Interestingly, no local Raja or any member of the public was included in this set up. Major Brown held a formal flag hoisting ceremony on 3rd November in the lines of the Gilgit Scouts… The purpose and intention of Major Brown's actions become even more clear from his post take-over exertions. He stoutly resisted attempts of the local Liberation Front, aiming for complete independence, and sent messages to the premier of NWFP as also to Roger Bacon, the political agent at Khyber, asking for the immediate appointment of an authority from Pakistan. A third message was sent to Peshawar on 13th November. On the 16th, Khan Sahib Mohammad Alam of Provincial Civil Service of NWFP arrived on Gilgit air strip and took over as the political agent. Regular air service between Peshawar and Gilgit was started which brought in a steady flow of Pakistani civil and military officials. By the end of November, Pakistan was in complete control of the administration of the Gilgit region. Thus Gilgit was lost to Pakistan, practically given to her on a platter. This opened up the way for subsequent Pakistani incursions into Ladakh, Gurez and Tilel valleys, Zojila and the capture of Skardu."[7]

Since the J&K State acceded to India on October 26, 1947 and the events in Gilgit took place after that; whole nation has to accept the responsibility of all that happened there; particularly beyond the said date. The tragedy of Gilgit would forever remain a blemish on the names of contemporary Indian political and military leaderships. Undoubtedly, taking that region back from Pakistan was not an easy military venture; though it certainly was possible to make an attempt through the Gurez valley and over the Deosai plains. However, there is no evidence available of even planning of such an undertaking by India. Records of that time do make it amply clear that no offensive was ever envisaged by India to regain Gilgit. It is also equally certain that the matter was never raised in any cabinet or Joint Defence Committee meetings in New Delhi. The British complicity in this affair, even at the highest levels in London, becomes amply clear as, "…Nor did the King in England frown upon the coup. An

7 Dr. Sudhir S. Bloeria, *The Battles of Zojila, 1948*, Har-Anand Publications Pvt Ltd, New Delhi, 1997, pp. 59 and 60.

entry in the 1948 *London Gazette* reads: 'The King has been graciously pleased on the occasion of the celebration of His Majesty's Birthday to give orders for the following appointments to the Most Exalted Order of the British Empire: "Brown, Major (Acting) William Alexander, Special List (ex- Indian Army)".' The above mentioned *Military Bulletin*, which cites the above award, thereafter states: 'No further details are available from official sources for what might have been recorded as a somewhat equivocal award.'..."[8]

After the fall of Gilgit and Bunji, loss of two companies and imprisonment of Lt. Col. Majid Khan in Gilgit, the Second-in-Command Major Sher Jung Thapa, based at Leh took over the reins of the 6th Battalion. Thapa, whose inspiring leadership was to create history at Skardu; belonged to an illustrious military family. His grandfather Subedar Balkishan Thapa, Sardar Bahadur, OBI, IDSM, and his father, Honorary Captain Arjan Thapa, had also served the Indian Army with distinction. The troops now available in the remainder of his unit were one Muslim Company less platoon in Skardu with one platoon of this Company located at Kargil. At Leh there was one Sikh Company less one platoon which was positioned in Kargil. The State Army Headquarters ordered Thapa to move to Skardu immediately with one platoon from Leh and one from Kargil. He left Leh with a small body of troops on 23rd November, collected the nominated soldiers from Kargil and thus with two Sikh platoons reached Skardu on 3rd December 1947. This small force comprised of 2 officers, 2 JCOs and 75 men, including three operators of the only wireless set available with the unit. On conducting a detailed recce of Skardu area, Major Thapa found that his garrison of four platoons was too insufficient to undertake any meaningful defence of the area. He observed that the town was situated in a small valley through which the Indus river flowed; on edge of the town met the Shigar river from North into the larger stream of Indus. The Skardu valley was dominated by a hill feature 2700 meters high, the base of which was 5 kms in circumference. The highest part of this mountain was called Point 8853 – which in fact indicated its altitude in feet. Skardu fort, the mainstay of Thapa's defences, was halfway up the eastern slope and hidden from the peak by an intervening knoll. After detailed study of the lay of the land and other related factors; Thapa decided to locate a strong post 32 kilometres down the river from Skardu – at a place called Tsari. Of a total of four platoons, he put Capt. Nek Alam

8 Sarila, *Op. Cit.*, p. 334.

with a Muslim platoon on the right bank of the river and a Sikh platoon with Captain Krishan Singh on the left bank. His idea was to have enough warning of any intruders well in advance. Thapa also sent messages to Srinagar requesting immediate reinforcements if Skardu was to be saved.

Although by this time the Indian Army had arrived in strength in the Valley, their priority was to drive out the hostiles from there. The responsibility of providing help to Skardu garrison continued with the State Force. After collecting all available men in Srinagar cantonment; a force of one company plus was organized under the command of Capt. Prabhat Singh, assisted by two other officers; Lt. Ajit Singh and Lt. Bhagat Singh. This column left Srinagar on 13th January 1948 in the peak of winter. After trekking through deep snow and reaching Sonamarg, this force was split into three groups, one under each officer, to cross the Zojila separately due to limited accommodation enroute. By sheer grit, determination and endurance these soldiers crossed Zojila in the foul and extremely cold weather. This force collected at Kargil on 1st of February and five days later the march to Skardu was resumed; again in small columns but this time due to tactical reasons. The first group, under Capt. Prabhat Singh reached Skardu on tenth of February and that was just in time. Unknown to the Skardu garrison, the hostiles had attacked two forward platoons deployed at Tsari on the night of 9/10 February. In the attack on this position, the Muslim platoon joined hands with the attackers; the Sikh soldiers either died fighting or were killed after being captured, including Captain Krishan Singh. After overrunning Tsari the hostiles went on to Skardu and launched attack on the main defensive position there on the early morning of 11th February with a force of 600 men, made up of tribals, Chitralis and about 80 deserters of the State Force. This attacking group was led by Major Ehsan Ali, Capt. Mohammad Khan and Lt. Babar Khan – recently promoted from Subedar Major. They were equipped with rifles, 2 inch and 3 inch Mortars. This was the first of many assaults on the Fort in the course of next six months. The Skardu garrison, having just been reinforced by Capt. Prabhat Singh and his troops, put up a spirited fight lasting nearly six hours. The attacking body was forced to retreat, leaving behind ten dead and one wounded – taken prisoner, some arms and ammunition. Before withdrawing, however, these people killed the non-Muslims, including Wazir Wazarat Amar Nath, and ransacked a major part of Skardu town, which was outside the defensive parameters and therefore open to such depredations. Casualties of the defenders were seven soldiers killed; along with one officer and fifteen other ranks wounded. The three Muslim troopers, who manned the wireless set, also deserted their posts. Thapa was well versed with operation of this set and hence took charge of it himself. This departure of hostiles facilitated the second batch of Lt. Ajit Singh and 70 men to reach Skardu on the 13th safely. The third group of the same strength entered the Fort on 15th February, raising the number of Thapa's force to 285. Still, the size of this group was much too inadequate to undertake any meaningful defence of Skardu garrison; which now also included 229 non-Muslim refugees, 19 Muslim refugees and 22 Muslim civil prisoners. On the night of 14/15 February, the hostiles occupied the hill feature called Point 8853, followed by other features of tactical importance to the defensive position at the Fort.

The Siege of Skardu had begun

Lt. Col. Thapa continued with his exertions to negate efforts of the enemy to breach his defences and also, simultaneously, kept on requesting his superiors for more supplies and manpower; keeping them informed of a situation fast becoming critical in Skardu. He also suggested a tactical withdrawal to Kargil so as to present a much stronger and compact front. The supplies and ammunition stocks of Skardu were running low and also getting depleted further with each passing day. It was certainly a small garrison in an isolated position, only trying to defend itself, and not capable of either harassing the enemy or threatening his flank. It was also not in a position to deny any hostile movement towards East by the enemy. On the other side, it was much easier to provide relief in terms of men and material from Srinagar to Kargil. From the tactical point of view too; a credible force based astride Kargil, such as Skardu troops, could become a thorn in the extended line of communication of the enemy as also threaten its flank. However, this sensible proposal was not accepted by headquarters JAK DIV, then looking after operations in the state; and the Skardu garrison continued a gallant defence against heavy and ever mounting odds.

"With Skardu garrison in dire straits, the State Force Headquarters made a desperate bid to despatch relief. The commander of Kashmir Brigade, Brig. Faqir Singh was ordered to proceed to Skardu with whatever force could be mustered. He left, on 16th February 1948, at the head of a column of a weak company of assorted troops with two MMGs and two 2 inch Mortars. In the traditions of the British days, an officer of the Indian Army Maj. Victor Coutts of 6th Battalion the Rajputana Rifles, was attached with Brig. Faqir Singh. This column reached Kargil on 1st March. After a few days rest and making arrangements for porters and animals, it commenced march towards Skardu on 8th March. On 17th March the troops left Gol, on the last stage to Skardu. Enroute, at the gorge of Thurgo the column, moving without tactically securing the flanking heights, was effectively ambushed by the hostiles. The column fell back in confusion after suffering heavy casualties of 26 men killed, 7 missing and 18 wounded. Heavy baggage, MMG, substantial arms and ammunition were also looted by the hostiles. Brig. Faqir Singh too was injured and he left for Srinagar after handing command of the remainder of the force to Maj. Coutts at Kargil. The misfortune of this column, which had almost succeeded in reaching Skardu, was that Brig. Faqir Singh as well as Maj. Coutts did not employ the elementary tactics and field crafts so essential for any force operating in an area believed to be under enemy control. They were also not getting along well with each other. Having badly mauled the relieving force, the hostiles mounted a well prepared attack on Skardu garrison on 28th March. It was beaten back by the defenders. Another determined attempt on 7th April too was effectively foiled. During these two engagements, each lasting over four days, the Skardu troops stuck to their defences against a much larger force and very heavy odds."[9]

Yet another attempt was made to send reinforcements from Srinagar to the beleaguered Skardu. This time, learning from past mistakes, a much larger force was put in operation. It consisted of two companies of 7th J&K Infantry, located at Srinagar and the entire 5th J&K Infantry battalion, moved from Jammu. The two companies of 7th battalion, being already at Srinagar, were despatched immediately to Kargil, reaching there by the first week of April. These were put under the command of Maj. Coutts and his group ordered to move forward. Of the 5th J&K Infantry, three companies were airlifted to Srinagar and the fourth one was moved by road from Jammu. On 3rd April the first batch of this unit left under the command of Lt. Col. Sampuran Bachan Singh of 1 Sikh of Indian Army. In the third batch of this big column came commanding officer of this unit, with one company, Lt. Col. Kripal Singh; the tail moved in the last group. This force, though a large contingent for Ladakh area, was very widely spread in a tactically unsound manner. This huge dispersal was a sure recipe for a disaster; to the bad luck of the doughty defenders at Skardu.

9 Bloeria, *Op. Cit.*, pp. 67 and 68.

For instance, on 14th April, while Major Coutts' party was 14 kilometres beyond Bagicha – on way to their final destination of Skardu – the first batch from Srinagar was just entering Kargil. The second group was near Drass, the third at Matayan; fourth and fifth batches were at Gumri. The sixth group of this force was just leaving Srinagar. As if this huge dispersal was not bad enough in itself; in any military or tactical sense. Matters were made worse by a palpable friction between the two Lt. Cols who accompanied this force – Sampuran Bachan Singh and Kripal Singh; Maj. Coutts was not without blame himself. There is enough evidence to suggest that he did not have the inclination to fight. On top of it came the vacillating attitude of the immediate higher formation of Headquarters 163 Infantry Brigade. By the time the latter sorted out the command and control mess, it was too late. Big scattering of this relieving force - very credible otherwise - and personal squabbles amongst the three senior officers were the two major factors responsible for the tragedy which befell this last, and undoubtedly a huge effort to relieve Skardu. The raiders' commander and troops, realizing actual strength of the relief column; lack of command and control therein, as also scattering of this large body; hit it simultaneously at a number of places. This made the relieving force utterly ineffective and also ensured its piece-meal destruction. Of this big column, only around 150 persons could ultimately make it back to Sonamarg and safety by the beginning of June; the rest perished.

"Thus ended in a fiasco, the last effort by the Indian troops to relieve the beleaguered garrison of Skardu. The mission failed not because of shortage of manpower or paucity of arms, ammunition or equipment. The resources were more than adequate. Dispersal of forces, absence of a tactical approach, confusion in command and control, uninspiring leadership and less than competent handling by the Commander of 163 Infantry Brigade, were the factors responsible for the misery and calamity which befell this force."[10]

So far three attempts had been made, during the last four months, by the Indian forces to reinforce the beleaguered Skardu garrison. Of these the troops led by Captain Parbhat Singh were able reach the destination in the second week of February; after which the enemy effectively tightened siege of the Fort there. The subsequent two relief columns headed by Brig. Faqir Singh and Lt. Col. Kripal Singh were badly mauled by the raiders'

10 Bloeria, *Op. Cit.*, p. 70.

ambush between Kargil and Skardu. The Pakistani commander(s) must have reckoned that with the approaching summer, Indian efforts to relieve Skardu and conduct operations beyond it to Gilgit and further north; would certainly increase. Therefore, for them the primary task appeared to deny this opportunity to the Indians; and this could only be achieved by dominating the line of communications from Srinagar to Kargil as effectively as possible. The total force available to the Pakistanis, for this purpose, was of 800 men. With this limited resource their commander made and ventured on an audacious plan. With two recent successes under its belt, the initiative was already with the enemy; and as the events unfolded, even the luck seemed to favour them. The planning and conduct of this bold offensive has been described as, "The line of communications from Srinagar to Skardu, ran parallel to the battle-front. To deny this tenuous line, the enemy had 800 in the Skardu sector. Of these, 200 were left to besiege Skardu. The remaining were to be utilised as a right hook from Sonamarg to Kargil. The operation was to be carried out from their base at Chilam Chowki:-

a) A force of 250 men were to cross the Burzil pass, occupy Gurais, then cross the Rajdiangan pass and demonstrate against Bandipur. This was to be a feint attack.

b) Now termed as the first column, of two platoons, they were to advance from Gurais via the Tilel valley and Baodab, turn South and strike the line of communications near Gund.

c) The Second column, also of two platoons was to accompany the first up to Baodab, then keep going East by the Kaobal Gali, move down the Muski 'nala' and strike near Pindras.

d) The Third and Fourth columns were to set out together, climb up onto Deosai and then go down the Shingo valley to Gultari. From Gultari, the Third column of 100 men was to march to Dras and capture the same. The Fourth column of 250 men was to advance down the Shingo river and capture Kargil.

All columns were to strike their objectives on the same day; 10 May 1948. Their movement schedule had been planned with this date in mind. In accordance with their programme, the columns moved out on staggered dates. The feint attack against Bandipur was carried out on 28 April. The main force, or the Third and Fourth columns moved out from Chilam Chowki at 0100 hours 1 May. Each raider carried one week's rations and 150 rounds of ammunition. Porters and sledges carried a reserve stock of 10 days rations and ammunition."[11]

In simpler terms the Pakistani force of 800 men was split into four groups with separate tasks. One batch of 200 was to remain in Skardu and effectively maintain siege of the Fort; another force of 250 was to split into smaller units and strike at different places between Bandipur and Sonamarg; in addition also to occupy the whole of Gurais valley. The third group of 100 was given the target of capturing Dras, where as the last batch of 250 was assigned to attack and capture Kargil and thence forth move a splinter group to occupy Zanskar. On the due date of 10 May; the entire enemy force struck simultaneously on different locations across a large frontage; achieving its respective targets and completely surprising the Indian troops. In addition these men also attacked and badly mangled batches of troops of Lt. Col. Kripal Singh's column strung along the Dras – Kargil – Skardu axis. But, a weak company of 5 J&K Infantry under Capt. Kashmir Singh held on at Dras till the end of May; even though surrounded by the raiders on 10th May. A company plus of the same unit, under the command of Capt. Rachpal Singh was at Machoi – between Dras and Zojila. Kashmir Singh held on for almost a month. Thereafter, with his supplies and ammunition almost exhausted, he and his troops slipped out of Dras on 6th June in an effort to join forces with their sister garrison at Machoi. A major engagement with raider forces at Pindras ensued in which Capt. Kashmir Singh, all his JCOs and majority of soldiers got killed. Some were captured also. Only very few could make it to Machoi. Thus Dras fell into the enemy hands. Between the attacking troops and Zojila, was now only a company plus of 5 J&K Infantry deployed around Machoi and one company of 1 Patiala, recently sent up, dug in at Gumri. The danger to the Valley from the east appeared quite real, at least for the next few months till the Indian troops cleared the entire Gurais sector of the Pakistanis as also took up effective defensive positions along Zojila and literally pinned down the enemy there.

---

11 Lt. Gen. M.S. Shergill (Retd), *A Hero Forgotten – Brigadier Sher Jung Thapa, MVC*, USI Journal, July-September 2007, New Delhi, pp. 431 and 432.

The brave and bold defenders of Skardu were still holding on

The Pakistani offensive on and around Kargil is mentioned in greater details as, "The main attack on Kargil was completely successful. First the raiders crept up to a section of Gorkha troops guarding the Kharal bridge across the Shingo river, less than 16 km from Kargil. Not one man out of this group was allowed to escape and warn the garrison of Kargil. Then the raiders attacked Kargil. The garrison outnumbered and taken by surprise, could offer no effective opposition. The raiders had sneaked around and occupied positions on the hill behind the town, and their 3-inch mortars played havoc with the defenders running to their positions. The fight was soon over; the garrison scattered and escaped by batches, some up the Indus towards Leh, others up the Suru to Pahalgam."[12] Similarly, the military situation after the occupation of Dras by the Pakistanis has been described by Indian record keepers in these words, "With Dras already gone, offensive operations by 1 Patiala lost their main purpose. It was still desirable to hold the positions beyond the Zoji La, to facilitate the advance to Dras and Kargil expected later. So 1 Patiala and platoons of 5 Kashmir Infantry maintained their picquets, the forward most of which was about 5 km beyond Machoi, some others being around Gumri, and on Pt. 15305 overlooking the Zoji La… On 25 June 1948, Headquarters 1 Patiala moved up from Sonamarg to Baltal…. By the end of June 1948, the hostiles were concentrated in the Zoji La sector in a strength of about two battalions. They kept up a continual fire against the Indian posts, so that from 2 July all the supplies and ammunition which had to be taken to the forward posts were conveyed only during the hours of darkness… But, General Thimayya's hands were full with important operations in other sectors. Tithwal and Gurais had been recently recaptured, and active operations were going on in Punch, which had also been placed under 19 Division from 3 July. He could ill afford to commit more troops beyond Zoji La…. Acting on the information then available, he decided to pull back his force from Machoi to Zoji La, where the situation could be stabilised without committing more troops. When the time came to recapture Dras and Kargil, he probably thought it would not be very difficult to advance from Zoji La and reoccupy Gumri and Machoi. Orders were received by 1 Patiala on evening of 6 July to withdraw from the forward positions, hold

12 S.N. Prasad and Dharam Pal, ed, *History of Operation in Jammu and Kashmir (1947-48)*, History Divison, Ministry of Defence, Government of India, New Delhi, 1987, p. 295.

Zoji La in strength and to remove all threat to the line of communication behind Zoji La. The troops pulled out from Machoi and Gumri on 7 July, abandoning with regret the posts where they had fought so long and so well against tremendous odds."[13]

With Dras and Kargil in the enemy hands, the traditional route to Leh and Skardu was closed for the Indian forces and Pakistanis could now, patiently deal with the defenders of Skardu and plan to bag up the entire left over portion of Ladakh, right up to Leh and beyond. This way the raiders looked forward to obtaining wealth and women of 'Buddhist' region of Leh area without much serious fight. At least that is what these people thought at that time. Leh was caught, in the middle of a pincer movement of hostile forces advancing from two different directions of Nubra and up the Indus valley from the Khaltsi area. More details about the grim and decisive struggle there; at a later stage. An appraisal of the Pakistani forces at this point of time; would reveal that mid-June represented the high tide of Pakistani successes in the Northern Sector. With only about two battalion of troops and in a period of around eight months; the invaders had been able to occupy a vast and strategic region from Gilgit to Nubra and from Karakoram to the Zojila and Gurais. As a result of these manoeuvres, the line of communications to Leh was cut, and Kashmir valley itself was surrounded from the north and east also. The Pakistani commanders' plan of four column strike at Gund, Pindras, Dras and Kargil has been rightly described, by Indian historians, as "a brilliant and daring stroke."[14] Looking back, one can say that the middle of June represented the high mark of Pakistan's successes in this sector also. Then by the month end, advance towards Leh was checked effectively, Gurais and Tilel valleys were recaptured by Indian troops and Zojila area was secured by the defences and presence of 1 Patiala Battalion there. The entire Pakistani force operating in this sector comprised Gilgit Scouts, Chitral Scouts, deserters of the State Forces, tribals and stiffeners from the Pakistani Army; in the form of officers, men and heavy weaponary. It goes to the credit of their commanders that such disparate elements were welded together effectively in pursuance of defined objectives of much strategic importance. The commanders realized the fighting potential and combat qualities of their men. They were hardy, war-like, mountain people, used to hit and run type of warfare since ages. This tribal strength

13 *Ibid*, pp. 298 – 300.

14 *Ibid*, p. 293.

of guerrilla operations was successfully exploited by their officers who were themselves, decidedly, good military commanders and also led their men well.

On the other hand, it is also a fact that the Pakistani forces there were operating under certain favourable conditions which put them in an advantageous position as compared to their adversary. The control over Gilgit gave them a head start. Their campaign started with a great prize and high morale. Their line of communication was also shorter and more secure. The troops were used to moving light and hence were more mobile. Most of them, being locals, had no problem of acclimatization in these oxygen deficient heights. In addition, large quantities of arms, ammunition, equipment and supplies fell into their hands in Gilgit, handed over by defectors of 6th J&K Infantry; as also looted from the two relief columns of Brig. Faqir Singh and Lt. Col. Kripal Singh. At the same time they were also fighting under some constraints, mainly being, lack of administrative support as available to a regular army unit as also operating without any air support whereas the other side – as seen by them – enjoyed complete air superiority. It is also a fact that although the raiders attained highly successful results by undertaking the type of operations which suited them; they were not able to achieve any breakthrough where the opponent put up resistance from well prepared defensive positions. The tiny group of defenders of Dras refused to give in their positions for almost a month till they ran short of food and ammunition. Skardu too held on in the face of repeated assaults by forces far superior in numbers – for six long months. This saga of grit and valour needs to be told in some details.

The siege of Skardu was effectively laid by the middle of February 1948 and continued relentlessly thereafter, but Thapa and his inspired men refused to give in. As the bulk of enemy troops in the sector were taken away and deployed in delivering strikes in Gurais sector as also between Sonamarg and Kargil; Thapa's force had pressure taken off them from the middle of April to the beginning of July. But, by this time ammunition and food stocks of the defenders became dangerously low and Thapa had to resort to rationing; 250 grams of wheat flour and 30 grams of Dal per day for every person – a very low diet indeed. Every bullet issued to the defenders was carefully counted. Slowly the attackers started closing in the periphery of the siege on the garrison and reducing it in size to just about less than one and half kilometres in length and half a kilometre in breadth. Thapa's repeated requests to JAK Force headquarters to have supplies air dropped also did not materialise, and this made matters worse for the defenders. On June 17, Lt. Col. Shahzada Mata-ul-Mulk, son of Mehtar of Chitral and commander of Pakistani forces in Skardu, sent a letter to Thapa asking him to surrender. The latter refused to give in and the siege continued. "On 7 August, the Tempests appeared overhead again. They attacked the enemy positions and dropped two containers for the garrison. But the situation did not materially change for Thapa and his garrison. On August 9, for the first time, Pakistanis used 3.7 inches Howitzers. The shelling was resumed on August 12, though it was directed mostly on one picket. Within a short period of shelling, the picket itself came under attack by a strong force of 200 men. Thapa's men fought like wounded tigers. Their ammunition ran out. Thapa sent them the last ammunition box available with the garrison. The momentum of the assault carried the attackers to the edge of the bunkers, where hand-to-hand fighting ensued. This lasted for four hours. Finally, the attack was repulsed and enemy retreated leaving behind a number of their dead around the perimeter of the picket. This battle proved to be the last success of the Garrison. A quick stock-taking of the ammunition revealed that the garrison was left with just 10 rounds of ammunition per rifleman. The veterans now realized that the game was up… When the morning of August 14 arrived, Lt. Col. Thapa was left with 4 officers, 1 JCO and 35 Other Ranks. The refugees huddled themselves in a corner. That day Skardu capitulated….The Muslims were led away and many among non-Muslims were murdered in cold blood. Same fate was met by the males among the refugees. The women were saved to serve an expected purpose. Capt. Ganga Singh, the Adjutant of the Battalion, was tied to the ground and shot. The only survivors were Lt. Col. Thapa and his orderly, Sepoy Kalyan Singh."[15]

Despite being outnumbered and also against very heavy odds; Thapa repulsed repeated attempts of the enemy to storm his position and held on with dogged determination for six long months, surrendering in the end only after exhausting his food supplies and ammunition. All military historians of India are unanimous in their condemnation of the treatment given out to the prisoners of Skardu, both military as well as civilians, by the Pakistanis. Commenting on one aspect of this sad episode, a perceptive

15 Col. Tej Kumar Tikoo (Retd), *1947-48 Indo-Pak War: Fall of Gilgit and Siege and Fall of Skardu*, Vivekananda International Foundation, New Delhi, Occasional Paper. July 2013, p. 16 and 17.

observer has mentioned, “The only survivors were Lieutenant Colonel Thapa and his Sikh orderly, Sepoy Kalyan Singh. The moot question remains, why? General Sir Douglas Gracey, KCB, KCIE, CBE, MC had assumed the appointment of Commander –in –Chief of the Pakistan Army in February 1948….He had been apprised of the happenings and in particular the defiant stand taken by the garrison of Skardu. He was also informed that this garrison was commanded by a Lieutenant Colonel Sher Jung Thapa….Doubtlessly his reflections would have taken him back a quarter of a century to 1924 when he was the Adjutant of the 151 Gorkha Rifles Regimental Centre and he had played hockey against a young lad at Dharamshala whom he had encouraged to work hard and seek a future in the armed forces. Lieutenant Colonel Thapa was that young man he had befriended…With the fall of Skardu now imminent, strict orders would emanate, that Lieutenant Colonel Thapa is to be extended all courtesies of war and his person is not to be harmed. No one dare disobey an order from the Commander-in-Chief. Fate thus intervened and gave to Lieutenant Colonel Thapa a reprieve from what would have been certain death at the hands of the raiders. It was ‘kismet’….What will live on forever, is the heroic stand at Skardu which was possible because of one man alone, Lieutenant Colonel Sher Jung Thapa. Whether it was in siting his weapons, fortifying his bunkers and defences and most importantly, rallying his command to surmount every conceivable hardship; that his majestic personality shone like a radiant star. The siege of Skardu will always be linked to Lieutenant Colonel Thapa and sheer will to go on despite all odds.”[16]

After the war ended on 1 January 1949, Thapa returned from Pakistan to a warm welcome and rejoined his duty. He rose in the army hierarchy to become a Brigadier, before retiring from service in 1961. Thapa was also decorated with a richly deserved Maha Vir Chakra for his celebrated stand at Skardu. His citation, partly read, “… On 14 August Skardu capitulated. This brought an end to the six months old heroic defence of Skardu. Throughout this siege, Lt. Col. Thapa displayed outstanding leadership and conspicuous gallantry in the face of the enemy.” However, what he did in Skardu would never be adequately covered in any citation. Such deeds, in fact, cannot be measured by any yardstick, even that of gallantry. These belong to the realm of traditions. Thapa added yet another chapter to the glorious traditions of the Indian Army.

16 Lt. Gen. M.S. Shergill (Retd), *Op. Cit.*, pp. 437, 438 and 439.

Geographically as also militarily it was but natural that the operations in the eastern half of the Northern Area revolved around the town of Leh; as the important people there provided leadership to the entire Ladakh region. It can also be presumed that war came as bewilderment to this isolated region and essentially peace-loving people. It was equally true that before moving out for the defence of Skardu in the last week of November 1947, Lt. Col. Thapa had left behind only one platoon at Leh. This force level meant that only little more than thirty men were available for the defence of the town as well as the huge area around it. Therefore, only one section each could be deployed at Khaltsi, Nubra and Leh. This was a very unsatisfactory arrangement and practically the entire region was left without any credible defensive shield; and this naturally agitated the local Buddhist population and their leaders no end. Since the troops available for the defence of Leh were grossly inadequate and almost negligible, telegrams were sent to Sheikh Mohammed Abdullah who was heading the Emergency Government in Srinagar, to send more forces – which appeared a remote possibility due to the closure of Zojila. In addition, a request was also made to him to authorize local recruitment for the defence of the area; with the existing small force acting as a nucleus. The prevailing local condition has been described as, "The fall of Gilgit had caused widespread panic and consternation among the Buddhists of Ladakh....The great peril brought by the coup in Gilgit so alarmingly within the bounds of imminent possibilities, roused the Buddhist population to consider plans for the defence of Leh and the part they could play in that defence. Their deliberations gravitated to one point: they should move the Emergency Government at Srinagar to bring into being a body of National Guards at Leh which could form the nucleus of a local resistance movement and aid regular troops in stemming the tide of the threatened invasion... The orders sanctioning the scheme were communicated to the Wazir and the President Young Men's Buddhist Association who had made the proposal on behalf of the Buddhist population."[17] On receiving these telegraphic instructions from Srinagar, mobilisation of locals for the purpose started. On the first day there were only twenty volunteers; which was a very low number. Then the local elders stepped in and enjoined that one able bodied person from each household should become part of this new force. On the second day the number of local participants rose to a respectable figure of 200 volunteers. Their training started in right earnest under the guidance

17 Kaul, *Op. Cit.*, p. 169.

and supervision of the State Forces detachment. Thus a people's army was getting ready for defence of their homes and hearths.

Back in Srinagar and beyond; the Indian military planners were quick to grasp that the strategic advantage had gone in favour of Pakistan in this region by its occupation of Gilgit. That, with Gilgit providing a firm base; it would enable Pakistan to operate unchallenged in the entire Gilgit – Skardu – Nubra axes and thus it would be in a position to consolidate control over the entire Ladakh region. The only way to stop this disaster from taking place and saving Leh, was to strengthen its defences; for which more force was an absolute necessity. This could only be done through the land route – and it was middle of the winter of 1947-48; also there was no landing strip in the entire Ladakh region, under the control of Indian forces. The only Indian military formation then operating in the Kashmir valley was a brigade strong – 161 Infantry Brigade headed by Brig. L.P. Sen. It was indeed a tricky situation. The trail of subsequent events has been aptly described as, "161 Inf. Bde. had picked up wireless intercepts emanating from Gilgit area, indicating increased activity of "Operation Sledge". This operation was planned in Pakistan Army Headquarters and launched from Gilgit in mid-February 1948, for the capture of Leh. The force employed was a strong contingent of Gilgit Scouts, defectors from State forces and tribals. On 3rd March, the Skardu garrison reported by signal that about five hundred men and two hundred porters had arrived from the direction of Gilgit, and had set off in an easterly direction, towards Kargil. "Operation Sledge" was now under way. To meet the impending threat to Leh, HQ 161 Inf. Bde. arranged to despatch a strong platoon of Lahaul- Spiti soldiers of 2 Dogra, under the command of Maj. Prithi Chand and Capt. Khushal Chand. This small but well-knit body of troops, closely followed by two platoons of the State force under Capt. Badri Singh, left Srinagar on 16th February and after hazardous crossing over Zojila, reached Leh on 12th March 1948. Some extra arms and ammunition was also sent with the troops. The task given to Maj. Prithi Chand and his force was to beef up the defences of Leh and to raise, organize and train local militias. The three platoons of the State force were also put under the command of Maj. Prithi Chand."[18] The timely arrival of these two groups of soldiers infused new hope in the hearts of the defenders of Leh and perceptibly raised their otherwise sagging morale. Immediately on arrival Maj. Prithi Chand set about his task with professional zeal and personal

18 Bloeria, *Op, Cit,.* p.66.

commitment. The programme of training the locals was also taken up in right earnest. By 15th April, 300 Ladakhi Home Guards were trained to form the 7th Battalion of Jammu and Kashmir Militia with Prithi Chand as its first Commanding Officer. This was a significant event and notable improvement in an otherwise bleak scenario; but the region was still in the throes of unseen problems and speculative gloomy future.

It is a matter of record that Maj. Prithi Chand and Capt. Khushal Chand were first cousins; as also they and their whole group – which belonged to the Lahul and Spiti area adjacent to Ladakh – had volunteered for this hazardous task. This adventurous body of troops, forty in number, included two Nursing Orderlies, three wireless operators as also Subedar Bhim Chand, a maternal uncle of the officer cousins.[19] Ladakh would forever be grateful to the gallant deeds of this wonderful band of soldiers; and a large part of the credit for this region being a part of India today goes to this intrepid group. For showing conspicuous bravery and exceptional qualities of leadership; Prithi Chand and Khushal Chand were each awarded with Maha Vir Chakra; and Bhim Chand was also decorated with a well deserved Bar to Vir Chakra. However, all this was after the war finished; but at that time Maj. Prithi Chand and his troops coming to Leh has been graphically described as, "Maj. Prithi Chand and his small band of Lahulis were the first Indian Army personnel to enter Ladakh after J&K State had formally acceded to India....momentous event took place on March 13 when Prithi Chand lowered down the British flag and hosted the Indian tri-colour. A public meeting was organised for formal hoisting. At 1100 hours, a large crowd gathered outside the British Residency building, known as Karzo Palace. The Lamas prayed and played their cymbals, drums and Tibetan horns for worship as per Buddhist traditions. The Lahulis and the soldiers of the J&K State Force stationed at Leh presented arms and the Union Jack was lowered. The national flag was then ceremoniously hoisted and the national anthem sung, as people cheered...The soldiers again presented arms and the local band played jubilantly...He exhorted them to come forth and join hands with the regular soldiers in defending their motherland. When he asked the people to raise their hands if they would like to join the volunteer force, the first person to raise his hand and

19 The composition of this detachment has been variedly mentioned as 2 officers, one JCO and 18 other ranks by Maj. Brahm Singh; whereas S.N. Prasad puts this strength as 2officers, 1JCO and 13 other ranks. However, it would be more accurate to accept the figure of 40 troops as noted by Sen who was then Commanding 161 Inf. Bde. He has given this number in his book, *Slender was the Thread.*

offer his services as a volunteer for training and service on the front was a school boy of seventeen. He was Chewang Rinchen.[20] Many hesitated probably because of the in-born abhorrence of violence; but very soon a large number of young Nubrans volunteered to join Rinchen – who was a great inspiration - in this patriotic cause."[21]

Prithi Chand also utilised this opportunity to give a 'pep talk' to the assembled gathering of Ladakhis; knowing very well that his utterances will spread far and wide by word of the mouth. He first invoked the blessings of Lord Buddha and then told the audience that he and his colleagues had come there to stay and defend the locals; as also secure their Gompas and 'Chortens' against any attempt to desecrate or harm them by the enemy raiders and troops. He assured them that very soon the airfield at Leh would be ready and this would ensure a constant stream of troops and supplies for the defence and benefit of the entire region. Hailing from the adjacent Lahaul-Spiti area, Prithi Chand and his people had a natural affinity for the locals – the Thakurs of his area and the royal family of Ladakh also had a history of marital relations – they all considered themselves to be a part of the extended family of Ladakhis. This feeling of mutual respect and harmony was a great source of satisfaction and encouragement to both sides. On the days of rest and relaxation, which were few indeed, he would feel comfortable in the local attire. His activities during the first couple of months have been described in official history as, "Major Prithi Chand, the new commander of Leh garrison, sent out a small detachment across the Ladakh Range to the Shyok valley, and began patrolling down the Shyok and Indus valleys. In April, the raiders were nowhere in evidence, and the patrols went up to Biagdangdo on the Shyok and to Dah and Yogma Hanu in the Indus valley, without finding any trace of them. The main route through Mulbekh and Lamayuru was still safe, because Kargil was in Indian hands; but the raiders could try to reach Leh either up the Shyok valley or over the Chorbat La. Their non-appearance at Biagdangdo and Yogma Hanu was, therefore, a relief for Leh garrison, although it was realised that it was only a temporary immunity and that things might be

20 Then a lad of seventeen years, who had just passed his middle class examination from a local school; he was to become the most famous of Ladakhi veterans. Late, Lt. Col. C. Rinchen,(Retd) MVC and Bar, SM. He was awarded MVC in 1948 and 1971 as also Sena Medal in 1962.

21 Dr. Virendra Verma, *A Legend In His Own Time* (Col. Chewang Rinchen), Young India Publications, Dehradun, 1998, pp. 27 and 28.

very different once summer came, and Chorbat La opened, probably about 10 May. Defensive preparations, therefore, continued briskly at Leh. The runways at the landing ground were lengthened and improved. The training of the militia proceeded apace... More arms and equipment were asked for from Srinagar..."[22]

With the beginning of summer, the planning and preparations for offensive operations by the Indian forces was now taken up in hand with requisite seriousness; as the next six months of good weather were going to prove crucial. This also included reorganisation of command and control structure in J&K. Till then the Headquarters JAK Force, commanded by Maj. Gen. Kalwant Singh was responsible for operations in the whole of J&K State. He left on 1st May 1948 to take charge of his new posting as CGS at the Army Headquarters in New Delhi. In view of the huge territory and to ensure more effective control and coordination it was decided to form two separate divisions; called Jammu Div based in Jammu and Sri Div with headquarters in Srinagar and Tactical HQ located in Baramula, as Poonch was included in the area of responsibility of Sri Div – though later in August 1948 Poonch was brought under the command of Jammu Div. Both these formations were put directly under the Western Command. The general dividing line between these two Divisions was the Pir Panjal Range. The command of Jammu and Sri Divisions was given to Maj. Gen Atma Singh and Maj. Gen. K.S. Thimayya, DSO, respectively. In addition, to take care of the long line of communications as also military stocking of this vast area, a separate L of C Sub Area was created under the command of Brig. Jai Singh, based in Banihal. It was expected that with these changes, requisite push and increased momentum would be provided to the offensive potential of Indian troops based in the State.

The situation of relative peace and quiet in the Leh sector was to change rapidly in the beginning of May, which also coincided with the onset of summers. It was reported that some raiders had collected and were hiding in a *Nullah* near Biagdangdo village on the Shyok valley. That route was much easier for them to follow since any enemy group could enter Nubra (or the Shyok valley there) easily from Skardu and proceed eastwards without meeting any opposition; there being no defenders between Skardu and Biagdangdo while the Rajas of Shigar and Khapalu were actively helping the Pakistanis. Also, with the fall of Kargil as well

22 Prasad, *Op.Cit.*, p. 328.

as the new strategy of the Pakistanis in by-passing Skardu and denying the Indians the land route across Zojila – things in Ladakh sector began turning adversely. The line of communications of Leh garrison was cut off and raiders could march on the town from different directions. They could come through the Shyok valley and over Khardung La or could follow up the Indus valley either directly or via Bod Kharbu. Thus, Leh was vulnerable from many directions; from the north, west and also south. The defence of Leh was weak and number of troops present there woefully inadequate. The only land route open for any kind of reinforcement lay through the 400 kilometres long mountainous route from the Manali side; which in fact was very time consuming. Time was of great essence for Leh and the people of the region. The only other possibility of providing quick relief to this beleaguered area was to rush troops and supplies by air. That is where the importance of making a workable landing strip near Leh came; and work on this crucial project was being done at a feverish pitch.

Sonam Narboo[23], a young and energetic Ladakhi engineer – who had been trained in England - had accompanied Maj. Prithi Chand's column to Leh as a guide. In the hind sight, one can term this as an act of providence; because as soon as he arrived, he seriously set about constructing a make-shift airfield in the outskirts of Leh town. For this he was officially sanctioned a grant of Rupees Thirteen thousand; as also he was helped in the task by a trained local overseer called Babu Dorje. In addition, sufficient number of labour was available at hand and on this score, Narboo faced no problems. The people from villages on both sides of Leh – from Pheyang to Chhachoot – were mobilised. In fact they were more than willing to help; such was the spirit prevailing in the area at that time. A 2300 yards runway was made ready for landing by the first week of April 1948. HQ 163 Inf. Bde, then looking after the Ladakh sector was informed accordingly. The wireless message dated 6th April from "Narboo Engineer to HQ 163 Inf. Bde." read as, "2300 yds. long runway serviceable (.) Remainder 500 yds

23 He was one of those rare persons who become legends in their own lifetime. Sonam Narboo also enjoyed the distinction of being the first Ladakhi engineer. He rose to the rank of a Superintending Engineer in the Public Works Department of J&K State; before joining the Border Roads Organization as a Chief Engineer. In his eventful career, he was associated with a number of important projects. He considered the survey and construction of Kargil-Leh road as his proudest achievement. He was also Development Commissioner of Ladakh for some time. Shri Narboo became the Works Minister in the Cabinet of Sheikh Mohhamad Abdullah in 1975 and remained in that position till his death in 1980.

need enormous cutting and filling which will be done if found necessary on landing (.) Small Igloo hut can be constructed out of savings out of thirteen thousand grant already sanctioned for landing ground (.) Send planes immediately (.) Weather most favourable between early morning and noon." However, the sanction for construction of Igloo hut for guards was not received in time and Sonam Narboo deposited Rs. 2109 into the Treasury as savings. Also, a month and half more was to pass before the first plane made a historic landing in Leh. In the intervening period the situation was fast deteriorating on different sides in the region; with the town of Leh feeling increasingly strangulated.

The Pakistanis had sent a small party from Kargil on the same day they occupied it, that is, on 10th May itself. This party encountered one of the JAK patrols near Khaltsi and, after a short engagement, lost three dead. On May 14, the garrison at Nubra was attacked – the first major action in the Shyok valley. The battle lasted for a day and a night before the enemy eventually withdrew. The Indian casualties were one killed and one wounded. The situation appeared to be completely in favour of the raiders. On 22nd May the vital bridge at Khaltsi was assaulted, with supporting fire from medium machine guns and mortars. Anticipating such a move by the enemy, as this bridge was the only crossing point on the fast flowing Indus river, Maj. Prithi Chand had already deployed a body of troops under Capt. Khushal Chand to defend it. This weak detachment proved no match for the enemy; and was heavily outnumbered and outgunned. Khushal Chand finding himself in much disadvantageous position; denied the access of this bridge to the enemy by setting it ablaze. It was a desperate situation and response of the defenders was equally reckless. It is on record that during the time Khushal Chand was engaged in dousing planks of the bridge with kerosene and setting it afire, Naik Bir Singh kept the enemy engaged by accurate and devastating fire. This brave soldier was mortally wounded in this engagement and was later awarded a Vir Chakra (Posthumous). The action at Khaltsi denied this axis to the raiders for days together and thus secured valuable time for Leh garrison; at the same time it enabled the defenders to fall back, almost intact, on the main positions. By this time; it was reported that the raiders numbering 500 and stiffened by some regular Pakistani troops as also armed with MMGs, Mortars and automatic weapons were seen in the Dah-Hanu area. Simultaneously, in the Nubra valley a small body of troops, helped by a group of highly motivated and trained locals, under the command of Bhim Chand was fighting a desperate holding battle with the raiders. This band of committed fighters, of which the most famous has been Chewang Rinchen, kept the enemy at bay for weeks together and did not allow them to come anywhere near Leh from the north side. But, the threat was palpable all the same and therefore people there rightly felt endangered from three sides. The small body of troops already present there and the people of Leh – though some of them had become trained by now in handling of few firearms – could not be expected to hold on for long in the face of a multi-pronged and determined enemy assault. The landing strip had been made ready but expected relief by air was nowhere in sight; in spite of Maj. Prithi Chand sending urgent wireless requests to Headquarters Sri Div for immediate reinforcements by air. The locals, headed by Ladakh Buddhist Association, also addressed various telegrams to political leaders based in Srinagar and New Delhi for urgent succor by air.

With the situation becoming more serious by the day for Leh and people around; Maj. Gen. Thimayya in his Tactical Headquarters at Baramula, realized that the only way left to send reinforcements to the beleaguered Leh was by air; more particularly now that the landing strip there had been made ready. But the problem was that the fleet of transport planes with the Indian Air Force only consisted of aging Dakotas. Flying these war-worn Dakotas fitted with old engines, was quite hazardous; including the risk of ice forming on the wings of planes while over the mountains at such heights. An additional difficulty was the unpressurised chambers of these aircrafts. Only one person could be of help in this critical situation, Thimayya thought, and that man was the local air force commander Mehar Singh, affectionately called ‘Baba’ by his friends and admirers. He was an ace pilot himself, having proved his worth in the Burma sector during the World War Two; where Thimayya had also served well. Both of them had registered distinguished performances in their respective fields and were decorated with the prestigious award of DSO – a very rare feat by Indian commanders then. He invited ‘Baba’ Mehar Singh from Srinagar to Baramula for a one to one chat. Both decorated soldiers settled down at Thimayya’s Tactical Headquarters; on the bank of river Jhelum and under the blossoming cherry trees. Thimayya had organized a very tasty fare of Strawberry and cream for his guest; but both also had an equally serious business at hand – and that was how to send urgent aid to Leh by air. The two men discussed various options back and forth and at the end of this meeting they had agreed to a mutually acceptable way to help out the virtually trapped garrison and people of Leh. It was put into action a couple of days later.

Further details of this successful, but highly hazardous mission, have been described as, "The desperate situation required a desperate remedy. No air force officer really knew whether one of their old Dakotas could fly across the mighty Himalayas and land at the improvised strip at Leh. The gallant Air Officer Commanding, No. 1 (Ops) Group, Air Commodore Mehar Singh, DSO, therefore, decided to find out the answer himself, by piloting a Dakota to Leh. The equally gallant Divisional Commander decided to accompany him. It was a leap in the dark, but the distinguished pilot's skill and courage were rewarded by a successful flight and safe landing at Leh on 24 May. The achievement gave a tremendous fillip to the morale of the troops and civilians at Leh, proving as it did that they were not fighting cut off and forlorn, beyond the reach of help. Major-General Thimayya saw the situation, talked to the troops and left by the same plane with Air Commodore Mehar Singh, promising to send reinforcements within a day or two. The defending troops resumed fighting with renewed hope."[24] Describing the almost magical effect of the same landing, from a local point of view Kalon Sahib recalled, "The first plane when it landed at Leh presented a sight which I have never been able to forget. The landing strip was bumpy and dusty and, therefore, when the wheels hit the ground it kicked a lot of dust and shortly after touching down the plane got engulfed in a pall of dust which, to all of us watching the landing with awe and curiosity appeared to have swallowed the big white bird. The population of almost the entire Leh town was on rooftops watching this spectacle as the plane had circled a couple of times before landing. As the dust settled we had an unforgettable sight of a Dakota plane standing in front of our eyes. I was Commandant of the National guards. All respectable of the town, including my father, were there to welcome the visitors who in fact were our saviours. A grand reception was given to the party. Amongst the welcoming party were also Pandit Dulloo (Pandit Shridhar Kaul), our mentor, guide and philosopher during those difficult days...It was a great day for Ladakh. Suddenly, people who had not even seen a vehicle were presented with the sight of an aircraft landing in front of their eyes. There was a total commotion and bewilderment amongst the local people who thronged around the plane. Some of the men were seen offering grass and 'Chhang'; thinking it was a big horse which having flown all the way from

24 Prasad, *Op. Cit.*, p. 330.

Srinagar must be tired requiring refreshments. The landing of the plane opened a new vista for the defence of Ladakh. In fact but for this landing it is doubtful if Leh could have withstood the onslaught of the invaders…On landing, Maj. Gen. Thimayya asked Major Prithi Chand about how many additional troops were required immediately for the defence of Leh and areas around and his answer was one company."[25]

At this point of time; even though the raiders still remained where they were and Leh was not yet threatened perceptibly, but the situation could only be termed as gloomy there. When no reinforcements arrived, two days later, on 26 May, panic reappeared once again in Leh. On learning that the promised relief may not be coming in the next few days; Major Prithi Chand decided to defend Leh with all his might and proposed to the Sri Div that he be allowed to pull back the detachment of regular troops, including Subedar Bhim Chand, from Nubra and concentrate to defend Leh itself. It was a sound military proposal; though it involved leaving the defence of entire Nubra region in the hands of local volunteers – even though some of them had by now received rudimentary training in handling of few weapons. Prithi Chand was somewhat assured about this sector on two counts. Past couple of months had given him enough confidence in the ability of Chewang Rinchen and his colleagues to effectively deal with the raiders; and secondly any enemy ingress from that side – if at all it took place – would have meant an extended line of communication and supply over difficult terrain for the invading troops. This could be successfully disrupted by the locals; at least over a long distance east of Biangdagdo as the entire area was inhabited by the Buddhists. In addition he sent a strongly worded wireless message to Sri Division expressing resentment over not sending the promised help in time. The locals also sent similar telegrams to political authorities in Srinagar and General Thimayya. Two days after the plan was sent to them, on 28 May, Headquarters Sri Div accorded permission to the Leh garrison for withdrawal of troops from the Nubra sector for the close defence of Leh. Reinforcements were promised at the earliest once again. Simultaneously another development took place which would have far-reaching consequences on the situation in Ladakh over the next six months. In the official history, this has been described as, "On the same day, 28 May, a column left Ferozepur for Manali, to march to Leh over the mountains. This column was commanded by Major Hari

25 Interview with Rigzin Namgyal Kalon in September 1998.

Chand[26]and was composed of men of D company of 2/8 Gorkha Rifles. Its strength was 2 officers, 4 Gorkha officers and 151 Gorkha Other Ranks, with a section of 3-inch mortars, and a Signal detachment, and also carried 600 rifles, and 60,000 rounds of SAA for the militia and other troops at Leh. This body of troops came up to Manali by vehicles and thereafter proceeded ahead on foot. This marching column, however, could not reach Leh for several weeks, and all hopes were pinned on the flight of the company of 2/4 Gorkha Rifles….It took off at last on the morning of 31 May. The flight consisted of 6 Dakota planes…. But bad weather over the Himalayan range compelled the planes to turn back after flying half way through to their destination. The Gorkhas waited impatiently at the Srinagar airfield and again boarded the planes before dawn on 1 June. The perilous flight was thrilling but uneventful, and all the planes landed at Leh without a mishap."[27] This company of 2/4 GR was commanded by Lt. Kaul and comprised 2 JCOs, 4 NCOs and 77 Other Ranks. It also brought along one thousand rifles and ammunition for the local militia. Since there was no regular Quarter Guard to keep the weapons; therefore these were stored in the nearest house next to the airfield and the entire ordnance was stacked on the ground with a local militia guard mounted, round the clock, for its safety.

Also, soon after landing; the Gorkha Company was rushed to the 'front' and situation was stabilized around Saspol village 39 Kms from Leh. For the time being Leh was saved, just by the proverbial skin of the teeth. With the arrival of new Gorkha troops of 2/4 GR; the Leh garrison felt emboldened and strong enough to be on the controlled offensive for the first time. Both in the Leh as well as in the Nubra sectors, the Pakistani forces were pushed back and by end of the June; the forward positions were secured near Biagdangdo in the Nubra valley and around Dumkhar – little downstream of Khaltsi – along the Indus valley.

Prithi Chand was a professional soldier and in that capacity he would have known, at least broadly, as to how completely the troops under Thimayya were engaged in various operations in the Valley and it was not possible for him to spare more than this much strength; even one company may not have been easy for him to part with. But the locals in Leh were only concerned about safety of the people and defence of their vulnerable

26 Hari Chand was to become a house-hold name in the region for decades to come.

27 Prasad, *Op. Cit.*, pp. 331 and 332.

area; and rightly so. Consequently, there was some misunderstanding on this count; and Kalon Sahib vividly remembered, "We also received information that the raiders in strength of almost a Brigade were advancing towards Leh. Therefore, only one company of troops would hardly be able to defend Leh town itself, leave aside the vast area around it. Then the question arose during the discussions with the local leaders as to why more troops had not arrived. At that time someone remembered that Major Prithi Chand had asked for only one company. My father was told that Prithi Chand had deliberately done so as if he had asked for a Battalion; he would have lost command to the CO of the incoming unit, in respect of all the troops that were functioning in the region. This he took to be very selfish of Prithi Chand and got so annoyed that he practically dragged Pandit Dulloo along with him and went to Maj. Prithi Chand and had a heated argument with him. Both of them almost came to blows. My father accused Prithi Chand of being selfish and vain and having put the defence of Leh and security of the lives and property of local population at grave risk for his own personal ego and ambition. The latter vehemently denied this charge; however, my father was neither convinced nor satisfied and stormed out of the meeting. Later, that evening respectable locals of the area were assembled to take stock of the serious situation that had arisen due to the impending threat by such a large number of raiders. A petition was drafted by Pandit Dulloo and he was urged to represent the people of the area and take the petition to New Delhi via Manali and Kulu. All arrangements, including horses, ration, money and helpers etc. were made for this journey. Dulloo was accompanied by Sonam Wangyal, who later became MLA and a Minister of State in J&K and who was his cook at that time. The party left next day for Delhi. On reaching there, Dulloo was able to meet Shri Iyanger (then a Minister in the Central Government) who knew conditions of the State very well. Iyanger understood the delicacy of the situation; promised to speak with people in authority and assured of all the help from the Government of India to the people of Ladakh. This effort also, no doubt, supported in committing more troops and resources to our region."[28] It needs to be placed on record that the verbal spat between the two important people in that region did not have any adverse effect on the future performance of either of them; for which the credit must go to both of them.

28 Rigzin Namgyal Kalon. *Op. Cit.*

An appraisal of Pakistani forces by ending June would indicate that, except in the Northern Areas, these were on the defensive in all sectors. In Jammu region, Rajouri had been recaptured, Naushera virtually cleared and serious efforts were afoot to establish an effective link-up with the beleaguered garrison at Poonch. In the Kashmir valley, Handwara had been cleared in the early months of summer; followed by Tangdhar and Tithwal. In fact, at one stage Muzaffarabad was seriously threatened from this sector. If they were provided with couple of battalions more; the Indian troops could have made a successful bid for this town itself. Gurez and Tilel valleys were also cleared of Pakistanis. The latter were fighting defensive battles in all sectors; except in the Ladakh region and therefore it stood to logic that the raiders would make even more determined efforts to push the advantage in this region. Here too, 1 Patiala had reached Zojila and made its presence felt by spirited deployment and aggressive operations. The military planners at higher levels and the defenders of Leh had to be prepared and contend with renewed enemy efforts to advance further again in this belt. It was also a fact that the motivation to the hostile elements was provided by a heady mixture of the excitement of combat and aroused religious fanaticism. In addition, they were employed in the kind of warfare that the tribes excelled in; guerilla raids and battles of attrition – of course added with promised and perceived rewards. On the other side the raiders had to contend with the steely determination of the Leh garrison as well as the fact that local Buddhists were fighting not only for their homes and hearths but for very existence of the race itself. Also their resources had perceptibly increased in the immediate past with more help on the way. An existentialist struggle was developing in these Himalayan heights between the marauding hordes and the defenders of Leh – both military men and inspired civilians population.

The military planners at Headquarters Sri Division had started preparing about the administrative arrangements for the existing and expected forces at Leh for the next one year; and it was important that in addition to meeting the current demand of rations and stores adequate buffer stocks were created and maintained at Leh. For this purpose, a proposal was mooted by them to the Western Command recommending the establishment of an Advanced Supply Base at Manali which was the motor-head then. Adequate number of porters and ponies were proposed to be located and organized there so that supply stocks may move smoothly towards Leh. Since time was of essence, it was emphasized to make this route operational for supplies as early as possible. It was then the only alternative available to keep the things going at Leh; that was already under considerable pressure. The other land artery, over Zojila and passing through Kargil, was already blocked by enemy troops and to maintain such a large body by air was also not a practical option due to frequent spells of bad weather in these mountains as also taking into account the heavy commitment of available Dakotas of the air force in other sectors. The troops at Leh were already feeling the pinch of shortages; it was thus desirable to organize and operationalise the first supply column from Manali as soon as possible. This task was taken in hand and successfully carried on – though with considerable difficulty – over the next few months; before the high passes enroute got blocked due to heavy snow fall. However, back at Leh; the town was still not out of danger. As apprehended and feared by the defenders; a large body of raiders, approximately six hundred strong and supported by automatic weapons and mortars, attacked the forward posts of troops near Dumkhar on the Indus valley. The defending forces fought well and inflicted heavy casualties on the enemy; but were heavily outnumbered and had to fall back over twenty kilometers behind at Nurla. In addition, the ammunition stocks at Leh were also dwindling and urgent replenishment by air was again requested. The raiders pressed forward this advantage by attacking the 2/4 GR posts at different places in the following days. Even though the broad front held; danger to the main positions at Leh was becoming palpable unless more troops were made available there immediately. Gen. Thimayya could not have spared more forces as his hands were tied with ongoing and planned operation in other sectors of the Valley, including the breakthrough at Zojila. Fortunately, at this critical point of time, Major Hari Chand was making good progress with his forces of D company of 2/8 GR heading for Leh from Manali side; having left their base at Ferozepur to towards the end of May. These people left the vehicle transport at Manali and put their baggage, stores and supplies on mules and porters and left for the mountainous region ahead on way to Leh. Passing through the town of Keylong and crossing over the high Baralacha La (Pass), Hari Chand and his troops reached Leh on 7th July 1948; and just in time. They were immediately sent to strengthen the forward positions around Nurla area in general; being held by the boys of 2/4 GR company there. Then on 10th July, this combined strength of two Gorkha companies was attacked from behind and over the mountains and overwhelmed by a far greater force of enemy in terms of men as well as fire power. Also the main concern of the two company commanders was rightly the defence of Leh over everything else. "So the men of 2/4 Gorkha Rifles and 2/8 Gorkha Rifles fell back rapidly, leaving behind them two 3-inch mortars and some ammunition and loosing 7 men killed and 5 wounded. The raiders were estimated to have suffered 70 casualties, but the Gorkhas for some time ceased to be an operational force. They straggled into Leh in parties of two and three, and were not reassembled till several days later. Several officers, including Major Hari Chand, were missing and were supposed to be dead till they reappeared at Leh."[29] After surviving this setback to his person and the troops; Hari Chand acquired the reputation of being invincible in the whole of Ladakh region. People in general believed that nothing could kill this man and that he was capable of meeting any situation successfully.

Buoyed by this success, the raiders pushed along both sides of the Indus river; along the left bank these people could easily reach up to opposite Nimoo, as there were no troops or defensive positions on that side of the river in this area. They had to stop at this place; at the confluence of Zanskar and Indus rivers. This was for two reasons; one being that it was not easy to cross the fast flowing streams of either Zanskar or Indus at this point without a bridge – which did not exist – or without proper equipment for going across such gushing waters and the raiders did not have any such gear or material. The second reason for the raiders to stop their advance at this point was that the defenders of Leh had prepared and manned a strong defensive position in the village of Gia; across the Zanskar river so that no enemy could go beyond this position unchallenged. On the right bank of Indus the raiders could, at this point of time, only come as far as Nimoo because the withdrawing Gorkhas were engaging them in at multiple locations and this was also acting as a dampener on the raiders' advance. All the same, the general atmosphere at Leh was one of gloom and despondency with calls for help to meet this serious situation going up from Maj. Prithi Chand through army channels to Gen. Thimayya in Sri Div; as also messages of assistance emanating from civilian respectables to the political leaderships in the State as well as the Center. On the army side, Gen. Thimayya was helpless. He had no troops to spare from the heavy fighting going on in Poonch, Tithwal and Kanzalwan areas. But he was certainly taken aback at the sudden deterioration in the situation; reiterating once again that Leh be held at all cost, with the available resources. Kalon Sahib vividly remembers this bleak time, and also an

29 Prasad, *Op. Sit.*, p.334.

interesting incident which he mentioned as, "Maj. Prithi Chand along with bulk of his troops was physically manning defensive positions outside Leh. Even I was planning to leave Leh when the time came and I intended to take one LMG along with one Havildar and some National Guards to give some fight to the Pakistanis and then go to Darbuk via Diger. As we were discussing our options, in an assembled group, we found two sons of the Lompo of Nimoo amongst us. They were on their ponies and had come to Leh to get their belongings as they were studying in the school. These youngsters came to me and handed over a letter. And they also mentioned that some Indian troops were still around the place; which information raised our morale. Since I could not read well myself, the Gorkha Havildar who was little better in this, went through the letter and said that this was from Hari Chand mentioning that he and his boys were near Nimoo but were short of rations and they don't want to enter the village as this would alert the Pakistanis. It was further mentioned in the letter that the troops were hungry and needed to be fed early. We were happy to know that our forces were still holding on much beyond Leh...Even though there was a substantial amount of rations stocked in the Fort, we did not have men who could cook except for a few National Guards. I asked them to make as many *Rotis* as they could and also kill a goat and start preparing mutton for our soldiers at Nimoo. In the meantime, I was told that one Muslim Baker had lit his Tandoor and had prepared lot of *Rotis* in anticipation of the Pakistani troops coming from the other side, as welcome offer to them. I put my guards on the Tandoor and also collected whatever he had cooked after making payment for the same. The entire quantity of *Rotis* and meat was sent on the horse back, accompanied by the two youngsters to Maj. Hari Chand and his troops. He was so grateful that he never tired of mentioning this incident to me for years to come."[30]

Back at the Headquarters Sri Div the atmosphere was somber; as they could neither send extra troops to Leh and also due to bad weather the air supply was hampered. At the same time negative tactical developments could not be accepted beyond a point. On 16th July it ordered the Leh garrison commander to hold the town and the airfield to "the last man and the last round." Maj. Prithi Chand replied these instructions in the affirmative adding that he intended to call troops from Nubra to defend Leh. Two days later, on the 18th, a party of raiders reached as near as Taru, only about 13 kilometers from Leh as the crow flies. On 23rd July the

30 Rigzin Namgyal Kalon, *Op. Cit.*

detachment from Nubra reached Leh; it consisted of a platoon of Sikhs, 68 State Forces troops and 47 men of the militia. With their coming the defence of Leh was further strengthened. The raiders were finally halted and the position stabilized around Taru. That was the nearest to Leh that the Pakistanis were able to reach. It would be interesting to go through the comments, by a Pakistani author, about the military situation around this point of time; as this would give indications of the picture as seen from the other side. This version says, "By July 16, Lt. Babar established his HQs at Nimoo, a few miles short of Leh. Then he sent out small parties who climbed the overlooking hills around Leh and established picquets.... Despite being so advantageously placed, Lt. Babar failed to seize initiative and did not attack the Leh HQs which were somewhat thinly held at the moment."[31] But, the pressure on the defenders remained with their stocks of ammunition and supplies running progressively low and no help from Srinagar in sight.

The defence of Leh had been organized well and in a very professional manner. The outer parameter – nearest to the enemy – started from the right bank of Indus in line with Pheyang, over the Pheyang hillock and on to the hill beyond the present Corps Headquarters and extending right up to the Khardung La ridge. This defensive perimeter also included one post across the Indus at Gia, about which mention has already been made. The second ring of positions were dug and kept ready, though not manned, few kilometers behind the outer perimeter. The third set of fall back positions was based on the very out skirts of Leh. Even though the defenders had been able to hold on to their farthest positions astride Pheyang; still this arrangement clearly indicates their will and determination to fight till the very end.

Airborne supplies and reinforcements were expected at Leh on 19th July, but the bad weather intervened. For the next few weeks also an extended spell of foul conditions prevailed forcing a number of air cancellations. This increased the hardship of troops who had been fighting without any respite or relief for an extended period. The fighting continued and engagements with raiders took place regularly around the village of Taru – their farthest point of ingress. For some inexplicable reasons the main body of Pakistani troops remained at Nimoo; probably expecting

31 Lt. Col. (Retd) Sikandar Khan Baloch, *Gilgit and Baltistan,* Sang-e-Meel Publications, Lahore, 2004, p. 241.

more reinforcements to arrive from their rear before attempting another serious push to Leh town. This situation of stalemate remained for the first half of August. Then with the fall of Skardu on 14th August; the alarm bells started ringing afresh in Leh. It was expected, and rightly so, that with this development the Pakistani forces released from the siege of Skardu would now be available for bolstering their ranks in Nimoo; and then from there the enemy push to Leh would be a matter of time. There was a discernible new impetus in the military and civilian requests for the earliest help to save the situation from going out of hand. From 15 August onwards the weather improved and with that the air flights to Leh became more regular; bringing in the badly needed arms, ammunition and supplies. Four days later a senior staff officer from the Sri Div landed at Leh airfield and gave the good news of the garrison being strengthened by arrival of the whole battalion of 2/8 GR, whose D company, under Maj. Hari Chand, was already operating in Ladakh from the beginning of July. This unit, commanded by Lt. Col. H.S. Parab, left Ferozepur and concentrated at Pathankot – then the railhead – on 18th August. From there Lt. Col. Parab with his headquarters, A company and section of 3-inch mortars left for Srinagar by road. The other two companies of this battalion, B and C companies, departed Pathankot for Manali on the vehicles and from there started marching on foot to Leh. These reached the destination on 18th September. With their arrival the defending forces at Leh had a virtual strength of two battalions worth of troops; which number consisted of the whole of 2/8 GR, one company of 2/4 GR, State Forces troops, Maj. Prithi Chand's boys and the local militia. These were fully backed by the local people. Leh could now breathe easily. But, quite a bit had taken place during the previous one month.

On 19th August, Lt. Col. Parab reached Srinagar where he was briefed about the situation in Ladakh and the task ahead for him, personally by Maj. Gen. Thimayya. The latter told Parab that he was to defend Leh 'at any cost'. He was also appointed the Military Governor of Ladakh and clothed with the requisite extraordinary powers. This important document was signed by Bakshi Ghulam Mohammad, the then Deputy Prime Minister of the State, who was also in charge of the Home Department; and read as, "In the interest of Public Security and to ensure co-ordination between the Civil and Military authorities Col. H.S. Parab of 2/8 Gurkhas is appointed administrator for the District of Ladakh until further orders. He shall have complete control over the civil administration, both executive and judicial in that District. He shall also exercise all the civil revenue and criminal powers which the Wazir-i-Wazarat, Ladakh, has heretofore been exercising. It is further ordered that no appeal shall lie to the High Court from or against any order, sentence or decree passed by him under any law for the time being in force...."[32] Thus briefed personally by the Sri Div Commander and also armed with special powers by the State Government, Lt. Col. Parab, along with his A company and supporting elements, landed in Leh on 23 August 1948. The weather that day was good and all the troops were able to reach together, by a series of Dakota flights. On landing there he found the civil administration virtually defunct and general conditions very unsatisfactory. In addition, people had started hoarding food grains and the situation was further complicated by the arrival of refugees in large numbers; in general confusion and panic prevailed in the town. According to a published account[33], he made the following appointments to help him in day to day administration of the area:

a) Sh. Chetan Phunsog, Tehsildar, Leh – Administrative Member.

b) Sh. Rigzin Namgial Lompo – Defence Member.

c) Sh. Chewang Rinchen, the Kalon of Nubra – Supply Member.

d) Sh. Kunzag Dorje – Political Member.

e) Sh. Stanzin Dorje Kaga – Transport Member.

Kalon Sahib has given a slightly different version of these developments. According to him, "Lt. Col. Parab straight came to the town on landing and in the gathering of locals and respectables announced that he was imposing Martial Law in the entire region. He issued a decree assuming all the civil, judicial and military powers for the entire Ladakh region. He appointed my father (Chewang Rigzin Kalon) as the Defence Minister. The Britisher who had stayed back was made in charge of Health and Aksha Khoja as Minister in charge of arms and weapons. Tuntun Shah was made the Labour Minister. Every able-bodied person was instructed to carry some weapon whether it was a rifle, sword or a knife. Lt. Col. Parab also encouraged recruitment of local Muslims into the National Guards. His efforts were supplemented by the exertions of Abdul Shah,

32 Govt. Order No. 16/H-48 Dated 29th July 1948. It was published in The Jammu & Kashmir Government Gazette on 24th August 1948.

33 Dr. Virendra Verma, *Op. Cit.*, p. 40.

to affect a breakthrough at Zojila; followed by the proposed link-up with Leh. It does go to his credit that Lt. Col. Parab moved on all these five aspects quite resolutely and with effect. With the concentration of the 2/8 GR, over the next one month, the defensive positions were systematically prepared and completed; making Leh a very safe place.

For almost next three months a kind of stalemate prevailed in the military situation, with the operational fronts in Leh and Nubra remaining more or less static. The occupation of Leh town remained a dream for the raiders as they could not penetrate the defensive line beyond Taru; notwithstanding a number of armed clashes between the two sides as these mostly remained ineffective and desultory in nature. Though, towards the end of August the raiders made a significant attempt to turn the left flank of the defensive arc that was put around the Leh town. This was done when the attacking troops tried to cross the Zanskar river, from the left bank of Indus – opposite Nimoo at a place called Choksi. It was quite a determined attempt where Pakistani troops were supported with one 3-inch mortar, one 2-inch mortar, one MMG and two LMGs. Fairly heavy fighting took place for two days, but all efforts to cross the Zanskar river were beaten back by the defenders; which were also helped by the reinforcements sent from Leh. After this, the raiders fell back at their main position in and around Nimoo. However, Lt. Col. Parab and his colleagues were working very earnestly, including, "A rope bridge was thrown across the Indus near Taru to connect the Chilling positions with the main front. Performed entirely by manual labour, this was no small feat. A rationing system for civil population was also established. Plentiful stocks of rations, ammunition and stores were collected...The front line positions near Taru were strengthened and tactical position was stabilized. At the same time, it was decided to form a guerilla band under Major Hari Chand for operating behind the enemy lines. Guerilla tactics offered tremendous possibilities in the sparsely populated, mountainous, thinly-held areas of Ladakh. The local population was also sympathetic to the Indian troops, and since the raiders were in very small numbers compared to the area occupied by them, deep penetration behind their lines was expected to be relatively safe as well as profitable."[36]

This is where the legend of Hari Chand was born in Ladakh area. With the arrival of Lt. Col. Parab and his troops, the security of Leh

36 Prasad, *Op. Cit.*, p.340.

town was no more the main priority of the defenders – that having been adequately taken care of – now was the turn of the Indian soldiers to take on the offensive. As their number *vis a vis* the enemy was not in the ratio as propounded in the classical offensive operations; it was felt better to resort to unconventional methods to strike at the raiders forces. Based on this concept a special commando type of group of around fifty soldiers was organized in the first week of September 1948; under the command and guidance of Maj. Hari Chand. He had especially hand-picked these men from the Gorkha soldiers, State Forces men as also few locals of the trained National Guards; men who were hardy, could climb high mountains with ease, withstand extreme cold temperatures and also have the capacity to move swiftly on empty stomach, if required. Special care was taken about their clothing, arms, ammunition and explosives. For the next over two months 'Major Hari Chand's Commandos'; as this bunch of people came to be called, operated almost freely and effectively behind the enemy lines with great effect and also creating considerable confusion amongst the raiders. Two of their exploits are worth mentioning; the strike at Basgo and the ambush at Lamayuru. These need to be recounted in greater details. The former was also the first strike of this small force. These people started from Leh in the morning of 6th September and reached their destination of Nimoo village after an exhausting and concealed march of two and half days. They had intended to target the raiders' headquarters which was located in that village. But, on reaching periphery of the settlement, this group learnt from the locals that a big gun, probably a 3.7-inch Howitzer, had been brought up by the raiders and it was located at Basgo – a village about six kilometers downstream the Indus from Nimoo. Maj. Hari Chand decided that this was a better target to hit than the enemy nerve-centre at Nimoo. Accordingly, the daytime of 9th September was spent in hiding behind the hilltop above the Nimoo Dak Bunglow – the raiders' headquarters - and early next morning located the house where this piece of artillery was lying. "After some difficulties, the guerillas reached the house just as the dawn was breaking…The 3.7-inch Howitzer was destroyed by bursting a grenade in its barrel and by smashing the smaller parts on the rocks. Thus, ended the story of the big gun which the raiders claimed had been captured at Skardu, and which they were going to use against Leh. With their mission completed, the commandos disappeared from the scene. They went deeper behind the enemy lines to baffle their pursuers, and finally crossed over to the Shyok valley by the Nila Pass on 12 September. The platoon returned to Leh on 15 September, tired but triumphant."[37] Encouraged by the success of this first venture Hari Chand and his gallant band launched a number of other fruitful operations. A very effective blow was delivered by this group to the enemy by crossing Zanskar river, in the Chilling area, on 28 October; going up to Lamayuru and there ambushing a pack of twenty ponies carrying supplies for the raiders. The escort of this pack, numbering 20 raiders, was killed to the last man; the arms and ammunition destroyed and the captured clothing distributed amongst the happy villagers. The commando party returned to Leh by the same route. This was to be one of the last actions by the group; as soon enough the link-up with Leh by the advancing Indian troops from Zojila would be established.

It is reasonable to believe that the Pakistanis thought these operations were being carried by the Indian army troops against them, as no retribution of the locals was reported. But all the same these raids did succeed in spreading fear amongst the raiders who till then had thought that they were the masters of this craft on unconventional warfare. Suddenly they found themselves at the receiving end. And it adversely affected their morale as well as freedom of operations. They became defensive both in mind as well as in action. They also started bothering about the security of their rear areas as well as lines of communications which had been no problem to them till then. Particularly the operation in Lamayuru across the Indus, which baffled the Pakistanis no end, was carried out by crossing the river on inflated skins, a traditional method followed by the locals to cross streams. For this, an expert was especially called from Nubra. This strike had a considerable negative effect on the raiders by sending a clear message that they were nowhere safe from being hit by the defenders. Kalon Sahib had this to recall about Major Hari Chand, "Out of the soldiers who fought in Ladakh during that period, the name of legendary Hari Chand stands out. To us he was almost like a god. Apart from being an outstanding leader of men in the battlefield, he was an able administrator and a very fine human being. He never considered the status of his rank while fighting. At times he would lead as small a group as 4-5 soldiers on a short and quick raid. His daring exploits of sneaking behind and conducting raid at the enemy camp at Nimoo created utter confusion among them as also inflicted a number of causalities; in addition to destroying a big gun. He distinguished himself by his fearlessness and brave exploits. He was present at every trouble spot and at every place where he could find some opportunity to exploit

37 Prasad, *op. Cit.*, p. 341.

the situation in his favour and therefore operated in a wide arc ranging from left bank of Indus to right across Khardung La into Nubra valley. He acquired a reputation of invincibility and it was believed in Ladakh that no bullet could hit Hari Chand. For us one Hari Chand was more than one infantry battalion."[38]

Time to survey the scene at Nubra; an area mainly drained by the Shyok river which is half way through joined by the Nubra river originating from the famous Siachin glacier. Here for the first few months of 1948 summer a series of grim battles were waged mainly by the locals, armed by the army, who fought valiantly and successfully against the Pakistani raiders and ultimately got better of them.

The serious threat to Leh was not only up the Indus valley, though this was certainly the easier route for the raiders. The other axis from Skardu to Leh was entering the Shyok valley, near Skardu, then going upstream and intrude into Nubra area at Biagdangdo. Up to this village the population was of Muslim origin and hence considered sympathetic to the Pakistani troops. From this point upstream – and to the east – started the Nubra valley and Buddhist population. The danger to Leh from this side existed over the Khardung La Pass in the north. This peril of enemy 'pincer movement' materialized after the middle of May; when the Pakistani commanders decided to bye-pass Skardu and move ahead to Kargil, Dras and Zojila. Advance to Leh from up the Indus and Shyok rivers was a part of these plans. However, by this time Maj. Prithi Chand had reached Leh and started the training of locals in right earnest, teaching them the basics of handling the weapons. Rinchen, a celebrated name later, was one of the first ones to join this "peoples' army". He hailed from Nubra; and many Nubrans also joined him in due course. This group in Leh was called National Guards and in Nubra the local name for them was Nubra Guards. Both these entities were later merged to form 7 J&K Militia Battalion. The first initiative from Leh was in the form of sending a small group of troops and trained locals in the beginning of May. These people carried two LMGs and 10 rifles with them; this was in addition to the 8 rifles already available in Nubra. They hurriedly trained 200 of the local volunteers. By this time Pakistanis had come right up to the river across the present airfield at Partapur. The number of weapons with the locals was many times less than the number of volunteers and for every

38 Rigzin Namgyal Kalon, *Op. Cit.*

single rifle four persons were prepared so that in case of death of one, the same weapon could be utilized by the second, third and the fourth person. Such was the spirit amongst the local population. Few sharp exchanges took place with the invaders, at this place, in which the Pakistanis received good drubbing and were forced to retreat. Thus Nubra was saved, in this first onslaught, by action of the volunteers, their timely training with weapons received from Leh. This victory also greatly helped in raising the morale of the local population.

It certainly is a matter of great credit to the locals of Nubra, so ably lead by Rinchen, that almost by themselves they held the raiders at bay for over three long months – from middle of May to the end of August; when after the arrival of Lt. Col. Parab in Leh, some troops could be spared for this area. Maj. Prithi Chand recalled that difficult time as, "Due to enemy pressure at Taru front in the Indus valley, I had to withdraw the State Force and Subedar Bhim Chand from Nubra valley to reinforce the Taru front... Rianchen with his Nubra volunteers with only 28 rifles was left there to defend the valley. Rinchen took defensive position at Skuru and stopped the enemy advance. He surprised the enemy by his deception tactics and made the enemy believe that there were regular Indian soldiers in large number in the Nubra valley. He and his party patrolled north and south banks of Shyok river to stop enemy advance...It was in August 1948 that I sent a company of 2/8 GR to Nubra to reinforce Rinchen's party...This young bold Rinchen and his men thus saved Nubra valley from enemy advance for about two months."[39] The locals, under his guidance, also took to offensive to keep the raiders off balance. In one notable case, Rinchen led a small group and after marching for ten days, attacked a Pakistani post across the Chumik La on 10th June. The raiders were completely taken by surprise and ran in confusion, leaving behind few dead bodies as also some arms and ammunition. The attackers also had another advantage of rolling down from a higher position on the mountain. After this attack, another post of the hostiles was also ransacked and Pakistanis pushed back to Biagdangdo. His biographer has mentioned the *modus operandi* of this bold and energetic group as, "Chewang Rinchen had only twenty-eight trained Nubrans with him but he made out that not less than a company was deployed there against the raiders. To mislead the enemy as to the number of men actually deployed and their firing power, Rinchen carried out raids from different points and directions. Another deception device

39 Dr. Virendra Verma, *Op. Cit.*, pp. 50 and 51.

employed was to burn fires at different places with a view to creating a sense of extensive deployment of the forces. His plans succeeded well and the enemy forces were so disheartened that they avoided open clashes and kept away."[40] The entire Nubra valley people stood like a solid rock behind this young man; fighting bravely for their land and its people. Maj. Prithi Chand came to Diskit, the headquarters of Nubra valley, and while addressing a gathering of people there announced that Rinchen had been appointed as a Jemadar (the present day Naib Subedar in the army) in the Indian army. His first uniform was the dress of a JCO of 2/8 GR given on loan. He was the first person to be directly recruited as a JCO in the army; and that too at such a young age. He was also decorated with a well deserved gallantry award of Maha Vir Chakra. The MVC citation, giving some details of important actions in Nubra, records "Rinchen, then a student, left the school and joined the Nubra Guards. He organized the Ladakhis into a useful force. Meanwhile, the situation in Ladakh sector grew more serious. The 7 J&K Militia was then holding Shyok valley axis of the enemy advance on Ladakh. It beat back the enemy attack on Kharu on 28 and 29 August 1948 and again humbled him on 16 September at Kharu Nala. The JCO played a decisive role in these defensive actions. In September 1948, he was detailed to capture 'Lama House', an enemy position to the west of Shyok river. It was an extremely difficult task involving 4 days' march through a treacherous terrain and a 5200 meters high mountain feature. He occupied the objective, inflicted heavy casualties on the enemy and captured 3 rifles. On 15 December 1948, crossing over high snow drifts, he led a fierce attack on a higher hill feature near Biagdangdo village. In this assault the JCO and his band of 50 Ladakhi guerillas walked through snow for 3 days and forced the enemy to withdraw…Jemadar Rinchen was awarded Maha Vir Chakra for exemplary courage, leadership and initiative in the most adverse conditions…" It needs to be mentioned for record that the saga of Rinchen did continue further. He was decorated with a Sena Medal in 1962 operations against the Chinese; and then again with another MVC – this time as Maj. Rinchen – in the 1971 war with Pakistan.

Behind Rinchen stood the entire population of Nubra valley. Some of the other people who deserve to be mentioned in this regard include the Numberdar of Tiggar, Abbakar of Hunder, Rigzin Namgyal of the same village, Tundup of village Diskit as well as Sonam Wangyal who was

40 *Ibid.* p. 37.

Zaildar of the area. The heroic story of Nubra people would be incomplete without the mention of an incident, which happened in the beginning of the conflict and was recalled by Rigzin Namgyal Kalon in September 1998. He then remembered, "It may be worthwhile to mention about the exploits of one Lama, whose name I am forgetting as he was always known as 'Lama'. The story of his adventures began in a Gompa in Nubra which was overrun by Pakistanis. The religious place was destroyed, the Lama was captured and abused by Pakistanis and used as a porter for carrying arms and ammunition for their forward march. After reaching the edge of a fast flowing *nallah* the Pakistani detachment stopped for rest. On this side of the rivulet were some of our fighters. Somehow the Lama managed to cross the fast flowing current along with some ammunition and told the Havildar this side that during the night when Pakistanis are asleep they should either cross over or give him a rifle with ammunition so that he could shoot them. However, our boys had still not gathered enough courage and they refused the offer; may be either because of the gushing water or could be they were scared of the Pakistanis. They also did not part with a rifle which in any case was in a short supply, but agreed to give a grenade to the Lama and also taught him how to use it. Then they tied a rope to the waist of the Lama and he crossed the stream; secured the rope with a rock on the other end and stealthily walked towards the sleeping Pakistanis on the other side. After sometime, the people on this side heard an explosion and little later saw the Lama returning with the help of the rope. To their utter surprise and joy they found him carrying three rifles and he said he had finished at least 4 Pakistanis, who were sleeping, by exploding the grenade in their midst. This incident raised the spirit and morale as well as confidence of our boys in Nubra and made them believe that each one of them could get better of the enemy. In a way, Lama provided the much needed spark to ignite the spirit of the local youth in Nubra valley. He then renounced the Lamahood and joined the Nubra Guards; and ultimately became a soldier in J&K Militia." Such stories indicate the efficacy of people's struggle against the raiders; which they waged very effectively and ultimately getting better of the adversary. Here the defenders became strong and bold enough to take the offensive into the enemy ranks and began clearing and reoccupying villages and heights around from September onwards; although the progress was slow and rate of advance quite sluggish. This part has been mentioned in the official history as, "In the Shyok valley to the north, the militia and Indian troops kept their advance, and recaptured Biagdangdo and Malachka on

27 November. The advance slowed after that against stiffening resistance. The route became progressively worse, and supplies were getting scarce…Finally, the Shyok valley column was halted about 8 km west of Biagdangdo about the end of November."[41] When cease-fire was declared a month later; this became the dividing line on ground.

Back in Leh sector; the people there were not yet aware of the strenuous efforts being made by the Indian troops to break through Pakistani defences atop Zojila and affect a link-up. The former were busy with basically two objectives in mind; to build up the stocking at Leh for the long winter ahead as also to further shore up defences of the town. The first issue was of feeding and clothing of troops under Lt. Col. Parab; which now reached up to two battalions in numbers. There was his own unit in full strength, the 2/8 GR; in addition he had to cater for the requirements of a company of 2/4 GR, the State Forces troops and the trained locals formed into 7 J&K Militia. The land route over Zojila was not available, being under Pakistani control and Air lifting was not possible due to non-availability of sorties and unpredictable weather. The only alternative was to build up stocks by using the Leh – Manali track; and this too crossed over four high passes and hence liable to get blocked anytime after the first week of October due to heavy snow fall on the mountains enroute. Therefore the Leh garrison tried to build up as much provisions and supplies as possible through this accessible window and also in the short time at their disposal. For this all available ponies and porters were pressed into service from both ends; including two large supply columns code named 'Chapati' and 'Chawal'. In addition, smaller groups were also pressed into service. The reserve stocks at Leh started building up and by October the situation was much improved and almost comfortable. The Dakotas, of course, continued to fly to Leh – depending upon the availability and good weather – bringing urgently needed supplies and evacuating casualties and sick back to Srinagar. Ending October, two 4.2-inch mortars were also airlifted to Leh. These heavy weapons proved very useful for the Leh garrison in destroying strong enemy positions and also bringing destruction in his ranks whenever required.

During the winter, Zojila and mountains around were presumed to get closed because of heavy snowfall. In the resultant situation, it was expected that the Pakistani troops becoming spare there, would attempt

41 Prasad, *Op. Cit.*, p. 345.

to attack Leh once again. Parab and his people were not aware of the Indian plans in the Zojila sector. So while the feverish activity was in full swing to build up stocks for the winter; the defenders of Leh were equally concerned about upgrading their preparations for ensuring safety of the town from any fresh offensive attempt. The situation from the north, that is, Khardung La and Nubra was quite satisfactory; along the main axis up the Indus valley, the position almost stabilized around Taru. In addition, with the induction of heavy mortars the firepower of Indian troops had further enhanced. It was the left flank of the defensive perimeter – at the confluence of Indus and Zanskar rivers, more particularly on the right bank of Zanskar river – resting on the village Gia that needed further strengthening. This was to ensure that the raiders were denied any opportunity to outflank the defensive perimeter from this side. For converting Gia into a stronghold, the preparations started with redoubled efforts and seriousness. As a part of these exertions a body of troops and trained locals was assigned to prepare and man a major defensive position here. Trenches were dug; shell proof bunkers made and manned during the month of October. In addition about 200 able bodied men of the village and area around were also trained in the use and handling of fire arms. However, as the subsequent events proved, no action was to take place in this area as entirely different things were happening at Zojila. A major breakthrough was achieved there on 1st November 1948, when Indian tanks and troops smashed through the Pakistani defences astride Zojila and beyond; followed by subsequent gains and advance.

The accomplishment at Zojila followed months of painstaking preparations and probing actions. This also included the construction of a tank able road from Baltal to Zojila top; commonly called 'Thangaraju Road'. Name of this eight kilometer road was a befitting tribute to a selfless, modest and dynamic officer, Major M.A. Thangaraju, under whose inspiring command this road was made. Notwithstanding the fact that the last few hundred meters were literally hewed right under the Pakistani troops' observations and therefore the work on this stretch was carried out during the night hours. This was also the highest battlefield in the world, where tanks had been used. The Indian operation at Zojila has been mentioned as, "The dawn of 1st November broke with an overcast sky, dense fog and snow falling on the pass accompanied by strong winds lashing the narrow defile…The tanks groaned forward at 10.30 hours, synchronizing with the first volley of shells bursting on the hostile positions ahead and on the slopes on both sides. The falling snow and poor visibility made the tank commanders and the drivers to keep their hatches open as they could not see anything through the periscopes...By 1400 hours, the enemy had withdrawn and left the Gumri basin...The appearance of tanks over Zojila with clattering tracks, blazing guns, and destroying the bunkers, must have come as a shock to the unsuspecting hostiles on the other side of the pass. That they were completely taken aback was confirmed from the wireless intercepts."[42] It would also be interesting to read about this breakthrough, as seen and described from the other side, "...Visibility was extremely poor. The biting cold confined the men to their bunkers where they sat hugged together wrapped in their blankets. Then suddenly the grinding sounds of machines right in the centre of the defile aroused their curiosity which next moment turned into anxiety when a volley of shells landed on their positions in all directions. The enemy had come once more. Before they realized as to what the situation was, their forward most platoons had been rendered ineffective, the enemy had driven a wedge between them... When mist cleared; came a wave of bombers which started unremitting bombing and strafing. Being caught up in such desperate situation; the Scouts opened up with their small arms on tanks. The results were obvious. By opening fire, they disclosed their positions which were now engaged one by one by the enemy tanks...The Scouts withdrew only when they had exhausted their ammunition. Trudging through the snow covered mountains; they reached Dras on the third day in a shaken state of mind. Physically, most of them had been rendered disabled due to frost bite and snow blindness. In that battle, one 3.7-inch Howitzer was abandoned to the enemy. The disabled and exhausted Scouts were unable to carry this gun when they could hardly drag their feet."[43]

Taking the tanks up to that height where no armour in the world had gone earlier; as also building up a new motor able track from Baltal to Zojila were certainly unique feats for the Indian army. The shock effect itself, of seeing the tanks amidst them, was enormous for the Pakistani troops. This was graphically described by Maj. Gen. Thimayya – who was then commanding the Sri Div – as, "The enemy was completely surprised. When the tanks entered Zojila the soaring walls echoed and re-echoed the roar of the motors, magnifying the sound many times. This part of the world had never heard anything like this. The tanks shot out the enemy

42 Bloeria, *Op. Cit.,* pp. 154, 155 and 156.

43 Lt. Col. (Retd) Sikandar Khan Baloch, *Op. Cit.,* pp. 263 and 264.

high pickets while our infantry mopped up the slopes. The tanks could not blast out the deeply dug bunkers, but the unexpected sight and the sound of armour terrorized the tribesmen. They fled in panic."[44] The army formation responsible for achieving this breakthrough at Zojila was 77 Para Brigade, commanded by Brig. K.L. Atal. This brigade had three battle hardened battalions under its command; which included 1 Patiala (now 15 Punjab), 1/5 GR and 4 Rajput. They were also very ably supported by the tanks and armoured cars of 7 Cavalry. The further advance of 77 Para Brigade towards Kargil was cautiously slow; as it had to contend with considerable enemy resistance – particularly around Pandras area - and also secure the important heights astride the line of advance. In spite of these stumbling impediments, the 77 Para Brigade was able to establish a firm grip on Machoi-Matayan belt, on the 2nd November. The next important objective of reaching and securing Dras was achieved on 15th November. Finally, the Indian forces entered Kargil on the 23rd.

Following the major Indian success in the Zojila sector and anticipating general retreat of the Pakistani troops; Headquarters Sri Div issued orders to Lt. Col. Parab on 8th November to advance, keep in contact with the enemy and pursue the raiders to Khaltsi and beyond down the Indus valley; also simultaneously try to effect a connect with troops of 77 Para Brigade on the Khaltsi – Kargil axis. Parab and his troops began offensive operations around the tenth; but the Pakistani troops located in the Taru – Nimoo offered stiff resistance for over a week. It was only around 19th November that these raider forces broke contact and embarked on a general retreat in this sector. The Indian troops closely followed in a virtual hot pursuit. After securing the Saspol village very next day, these troops literally chased the fleeing enemy down the Indus valley. Concurrently, Major Hari Chand, with his commandos and a small force, crossed over to the left bank of Indus, at Alchi bridge near Saspol, and evicted the raiders from Chilling area – driving them all the way to beyond Lamayuru. Thus, by the 20th November Parab's forces had reached Khaltsi and also the area up to Lamayuru and beyond was cleared. On that day, Headquarters Sri Div ordered for a link up at Kargil between 77 Para Brigade and Leh Brigade (even though the troops under command of Parab were around two battalions he was being referred to as Commander Leh Brigade; this ruse was to basically deceive the other

44 Humphry Evans, *Thimayya of India – A Soldier's Life,* Harcourt Brace and Co, New York, 1960, p. 261.

side). Khaltsi was securely occupied by the advancing troops from Leh, two days later on 22nd November; to the happiness and relief of the local inhabitants of the entire area. From here, two companies were detailed to follow the retreating raiders and, if feasible, occupy Marol – a strategically important objective located near the confluence of Indus and Suru rivers - as it controlled the routes from Skardu to Leh as well as to Kargil. It was a natural target of acquisition by any military commander operating in that area. One detachment and commandos left Khaltsi with Lt. Col Parab, over Lamayuru towards Kargil to meet elements of 77 Para Brigade; while the remainder of the force made Khaltsi into a firm base and consolidated the area around. Finally, the link up with Kargil was established at 6.30 pm on 24th November 1948. The 1/5 GR War Diary entry for 24th November records, "Lt. Col. H.S. Parab, Maj. Hari Chand of 2/8 GR, Second Lt. S.K. Kaul of 2/4 GR who had all grown big beards together with a small guerilla party mounted on ponies reached Kargil. The link-up had been completed…" The Leh garrison could now heave a sigh of relief; as the Leh town was decidedly out of danger; in fact just about saved in time

A number of efforts to capture the strategic objective of Marol could not succeed; by both the advancing troops from Leh side down the Indus valley; as well as by the men of 77 Para Brigade mounting the offensive from Kargil direction. These attempts were neutralized by stubborn resistance put up there by the Pakistani forces. Marol was a very prized objective for both sides and when the cease-fire was declared, it had eluded the Indian troops. When all fighting stopped in J&K with the declaration of cease-fire on 1st January 1949; the territory under the Indian control, in Ladakh region, included roughly the line connecting Biagdando in Nubra, Batalik- Gargardo in the Indus valley and little north of Kargil. In fact at the time of cease-fire the hostiles were very much present, not only in Marol but also in the close proximity of Kargil town, the nearest point being a hill feature called 13620; this being the altitude in feet of the highest point of the mountain. From the top of this feature the Dras-Kargil road was in visual contact and could be effectively engaged by the MMG fire by the Pakistani post located there. It was only during the December 1971 operations that the Indian forces occupied this crucial post and hence were able to secure Kargil; after a lapse of 23 years.

It would be interestingly educative to go through the relevant excerpts of the MVC citations of the three heroes of these battles in Ladakh; Maj.

Prithi Chand, Maj. Khushal Chand and Maj. Hari Chand. Some excerpts of the MVC citation of this outstanding soldier – Prithi Chand - read as, "... By May 1948, the enemy there had overrun most of Baltistan and Kargil. He was advancing on Leh along the Indus and Nubra valleys. Major Prithi Chand contained the enemy advance by adopting guerilla tactics. Covering a front extending over many hundred kilometers, he organized raids and ambushes on the enemy. He underwent extreme physical strain to make his presence felt everywhere. One day he was seen in the Indus valley and the next day in the Nubra valley. He and his men lived mostly on 'sattu' (grain powder). With very little ammunition he kept the enemy at bay, until reinforcement arrived by air...This brave officer and his men greatly contributed to the defence of Ladakh. Throughout these operations Major Prithi Chand displayed exceptional leadership, courage and bravery..." More than thirty years later, the assessment of an aging Prithi Chand by a senior army officer is also interesting and worth quoting. He recollected as, "Incidentally, in 1981, when I was the GOC, Punjab, Haryana and HP Area, I called upon Col Prithi Chand at Kullu where he had settled down post retirement. He had set up a lovely orchard and had a serene prayer room in his house. Well into his old age, he remained ever so humble about his achievements."[45]

Major Khushal Chand, a cousin of Prithi Chand and junior to him in service, was a soldier of great eminence endowed with steely determination, immense courage and enormous grit. His unparallel feat of crossing over the daunting Zojila pass under most inhospitable conditions in the month of February 1948, along with a small band of very highly motivated troops all the way from Srinagar to Leh, is by itself worthy of historical record. His personal bravery and the exploits of soldiers under his command over the next 9 months truly belong to the realm of high military traditions. The valiant troops under the inspired leadership of Maj. Khushal Chand, with wholehearted support of the local population, kept in check the large force of Pakistani invaders from entering Leh, till help arrived. He was also awarded a well deserved MVC, parts of citation of which read as, "...Major Khushal Chand , with one platoon of J&K State Force and about twenty local militia, delayed the enemy advance on Leh along the Indus valley for four months. He skilfully applied guerilla tactics to fight a numerically superior enemy. By his mobile tactics he gave an exaggerated

45 Maj. Gen. Rajendra Nath (Retd),*Strategic Ladakh,* Vij Books India Pvt Ltd, New Delhi, 2016, p. 168.

impression of his strength to the enemy. On one occasion he held the Khaltsi bridge for 24 hours with just one sepoy. In the night, the sepoy kept on firing on the opposite bank, while Major Khushal Chand crawled down to the bridge and set it on fire. This delayed the enemy advance by another one week. The absence of communication facility added to his problems. He had to make frequent visits to Leh to keep the commander informed about his activities. Throughout these operations, Major Khushal Chand fought without adequate rations, weapons and ammunition. He led his small band of men to success with great vigour and skill in adverse weather conditions..."

The third member of this trio of brave officers, Maj. Hari Chand, became a living legend in Ladakh during those critical days. He fought the enemy with great gusto, imagination and heroism; and was also decorated with Maha Vir Chakra. His MVC citation, in segments, reads as "...Another column left Manali for Leh under the command of Major Hari Chand. General Cariappa had himself selected Major Hari Chand for this task. Major Hari Chand's column entered Leh on 7 July 1948, after a long and hazardous journey. He soon deployed his men in defensive positions to meet the enemy onslaught. He also led numerous attacks on the enemy positions and his line of communication. By 18 July, the enemy had reached Taru, about 13 km from Leh and mounted repeated attacks on Indian positions. On one occasion troops holding the defences became panicky and withdrew from their posts. But Major Hari Chand hung on to his post for three days with a platoon. This prevented the enemy from consolidating his gains and gave Indian troops time to reorganise their defences. If he had not held on to this position firmly, Leh would have certainly been lost to the enemy. In September 1948, Major Hari Chand led a guerrilla party of 35 men over a height of 5200 meters and treaded 96 km to raid a village and destroy the enemy gun located there...In October 1948, Major Hari Chand led another guerrilla party to harass the enemy lines of communication. In this raid, he killed the escort of an enemy convoy and captured arms, ammunition and other supplies. Throughout these operations Major Hari Chand displayed leadership, courage and gallantry of a very high order..."

Lt. Col. H.S. Parab was commander of all the Indian troops in the Leh and Nubra sectors; in addition, the state government had also appointed him as the Military Governor of Ladakh with requisite powers delegated to him. He has at times been criticised for being too cautious and exhibiting lack of dash. He was certainly a conventional and careful commander; who must have always remembered that the primary task given to him by Maj. Gen. Thimayya was to defend Leh at any cost. This he did to the best of his ability and deployed any additional resources that he got, for the safety and security of Leh. To be fair to him; he managed this key assignment competently and with success. In addition, highly commended military leaders like Hari Chand and Chewang Rinchen also functioned under his overall command. However, in the official account of the J&K Operations, a comprehensive analysis of his achievements has been made as, "Colonel Parab had nearly two battalions of troops under his command...Still, he was unable to overcome the few hundred enemy troops opposing him. It is possible that he was deliberately holding his hand, so as to keep the raiders in Ladakh well away from the Zojila area, where crucial operations were in progress; but no documentary evidence appears to show this...Colonel Parab was cautious in his moves and more thorough in his defensive preparations. Time was in his favour, and his problem of recapturing Khaltsi, Mulbekh etc. was in the end solved by the advance of 77 Para Bde from Zoji La to Kargil. In the pursuit from Taru westward in November, Colonel Parab was shown at his best, and his careful planning was rewarded by the smooth rapidity of advance up to Khaltsi."[46]

The cease-fire was declared on 1st January 1949. Without going into details of the military situation on the ground, as also 'ifs' and 'buts' of this step; the fact remains that all operations came to a halt on and from that day.

After Pakistani forces overran Kargil on 10th May 1948; a detachment of their troops moved on to Zanskar, to occupy that region. This small group of raiders made village Padam as their headquarters; which was over ten days' march away from Kargil. For the next six months they terrorised and troubled the local peace-loving people of the area, no end. After the Indian break-through at Zoji La, followed by further successes culminating in the link-up with Leh forces; the Pakistani troops hurriedly withdrew to Marol and further north from the entire Kargil and Leh sectors. In this haste, they seemed to have forgotten about the small body of troops in Padam. No military account of that time mentions about them.

46 Prasad, *Op. Cit.*, pp. 343 and 346.

Even the official history of this war, commissioned by Defence Ministry of India, does not make a reference to this group. Few details about them were narrated by Kalon Sahib; who recounted the events of those days as, "Sometime in the month of January 1949, after the declaration of cease-fire; one day I received a message in Khaltsi that some raiders were still operating in Zanskar area and that after the cease-fire no action was to be taken against them and they were to be returned to Pakistan. For that they had to first surrender to the Indian troops which required the presence of a local magistrate. Since I was performing this duty also; I was asked by Lt. Col. Parab to quickly move to Rangdum. I reached Leh and carried with me one policeman and the Labour Officer. Enroute, one company of the army was tasked to accompany me to Rangdum Gompa. Since a day had been fixed for this; we had to travel the long distance quickly. Our party made it to Khaltsi in one day and reached Kargil the next evening. From there we set forth for Rangdum. There were eight Pakistani troops, who were present there, which included one Captain – Murtaza -, one Havildar and six soldiers. I had been given a letter written by Pakistani authorities; presumably advising these men to surrender. While the area had been effectively cordoned by our troops, it was further reinforced by one Gorkha company which had come along with me from Kargil. Since the Pakistani defences had not been overrun; I carried the letter with me along with a white flag and went to meet the Pakistanis all by myself. There were eight soldiers and over thirty civilians, fully armed with considerable stocks of ammunition and rations. I told them that ceasefire had been declared and it would be in their interest to lay down their arms and as a local magistrate I assured them safe passage to their territory. It was decided that they would come out and have necessary formalities made next morning.

"On the subsequent day, a meeting took place in more or less normal atmosphere. Whereas the Pakistani troops had agreed to peacefully go over to their territory, the question of other 32 persons created heated exchange; as they were all local Muslims who had been recruited by these Pakistanis. The local Buddhist leaders vehemently insisted that since these persons had decided to throw their lot with Pakistanis and had come into their true colours, therefore they should go back along with other soldiers to Pakistan. Otherwise, if they were left behind it would disturb the existing atmosphere of communal harmony and the local Buddhists who had a majority of ninety percent in Zanskar area, could not assure the safety of the Muslim population. Minus these people who had supported

Pakistanis; they said they would ensure complete safety of the local Muslim population which were concentrated around Padam village. Pakistani Captain Murtaza on the other hand said that he could take his locally recruited youth along with him to Pakistan but in return he must be assured of the safety of the Muslim population of Zanskar who, according to him, were in the dander of reprisal particularly from the local Ladakhi youth of the National Guards. After considerable discussions it was decided that the locally recruited men would accompany Capt. Murtaza and party and Zanskar would be vacated of all our troops, including National Guards and a small detachment of Gorkha troops, around ten persons, would be left at Padam to look after the security and also to maintain peace and public order. Thus, the thirty two youth left Zanskar along with Capt. Murtaza; all Pakistani soldiers were also allowed to carry their personal weapons. Rest of the arms and ammunition were put into bags covered by cloth and sealed by me as the local magistrate and these were handed over to the army representative for being taken to Kargil."[47]

When the ceasefire was declared on 1st January 1949; the Indian forces in Ladakh region were on the offensive. They had successfully broken through at Zoji La; occupied Dras and Kargil as also effected link-up with the troops in Leh by chasing the raiders down the Indus valley. The advancing Gorkhas of 2/8 GR were able to recapture the villages of Dumkhar, Sukurbachan and Dah-Hanu, all inhabited by Buddhist population, without much opposition. However, their advance was abruptly brought to a halt about five kilometres short of Marol where the Pakistanis had prepared and occupied strong defensive positions on both sides of the river. This was the farthest; the Indian forces could reclaim the lost territory down the Indus valley. Capture of Marol, so important an objective, eluded the Indian troops. Their progress further north in the Shyok valley was also not very successful and the raiders were pushed back only across village Biagdangdo. The important village of Turtuk[48] remained with the other side. Hence when the ceasefire came around, even though Dras-Kargil and Leh had been cleared of the Pak forces and secured, much of the Northern Areas, including the strategically important

47 Rigzin Namgyal Kalon, *Op. Cit.*

48 This was captured by Indian troops in December 1971; thanks to the offensive operations carried out in this sector by Major Chewang Rinchen. He was awarded the second MVC for this military feat.

Skardu and Gilgit regions, remained and continued to remain till date in the hands of Pakistani forces.

Ladakh, as people understand the region these days, and particularly Leh as well as the areas around escaped the depredations of Pakistani forces and the tribal raiders; due to the exertion of the Indian troops as also remarkable support extended by the local population. The entire people there rose like one man and stood solidly behind Indian forces. It was indeed a peoples' war, in the way locals participated fully in all activities of the troops; ranging from the defensive preparations to the offensive operations. The locals' engagement was indeed spectacular; which effectively began with able bodied young men getting trained in handling of the arms when such means were made available, as also an appeal to this end outlined by Major Prithi Chand and his colleagues. The locals responded to his call magnificently. The National Guards, particularly so in the Nubra valley, were purely a people's army. Other than arms and ammunition, no resources were forthcoming from the government side. Transportation, clothing, rations, etc. were all procured and managed locally either by the volunteers themselves or by the community. None of these combatants were paid any salary, nor was any claimed. The requisite money, whenever required, was also obtained locally on contributory basis from well off families as well as Gompas. Buddhist Association had made an appeal to all Gompas to open their granaries and contribute for feeding the troops of the National Guards. They were also liberally helped by the well to do members of the community. The ladies too pitched in their efforts by carrying rations from one place to another on ponies and sheep. Even when Lt. Col. Parab took charge of the situation and sanctioned rupee one per head for the local National Guards and Nubra Guards; still lot of logistical support continued to come from the local population. There were occasions when the villagers catered to the requirements of the 'guerrilla' forces as they were generally out of the army supply lines and in need of rations. However, payments were made when the troops specifically asked for sheep or goats. Sometimes, the local population would prepare 'Paba' and send it to the needy soldiers. The locals would also pool their resources and make available some quantity of local 'Arrack' with which these troops could keep themselves warm. Like this, through a unique cooperative effort of mutually supportive defence and administrative actions the troops of the Indian army and the locals presented credible and effective defensive ring around Leh and in Nubra; and later on extended this to launch offensive against the enemy. Almost the entire population, particularly the leaders and *Numberdars,* actively participated in this great endeavour. Remembering those eventful and nostalgic times, Kalon Sahib recollected, "It is not possible to name everyone who did exceptionally well but some of the names that I can recall were; Skalzang Rinchen of Shey, Thinless – Shey Lompo, Paljor, Numberdar of Igoo, Numberdar of Gia, another name which comes to mind is of Tundup Sonam who is currently Naib Tehsildar of Leh; Zaildar of Timisgam, Zaildar of Lamayuru, Zaildar of Saspol named Ishey Lompo, Zaildar of Nimoo- Rigzin, Ishey Phunsog from Skara, Sonam Wangyal, P.T. Wangyal and Sonam Khalsar etc. were amongst those notable persons who did good work. All these local leaders provided the nucleus around which the entire population rose as one to face the common danger. To keep this unique collective effort going; stood like rock the Buddhist Association which was run by leaders who were respected by the community through the length and breadth of Ladakh. In a situation where do or die were the common refrain and the decision of the Buddhist Association was the ultimate law; the fact that everyone accepted the decision of this body provided further strength to the singular effort made by the local population as a collective body."[49]

After the declaration of ceasefire, normal life started returning to Leh and other notable places of Ladakh, like Disket, Khaltsi, Kargil, Dras etc. The Leh town and its people were able to escape the depredations and humiliation of being an occupied place. In this respect they were luckier than the people of village Taru and the belt west of it down the Indus valley; as also the inhabitants of the Kargil region, that is, the areas of Zoji La, Dras, Kargil and Zanskar. Also the myth that the Buddhists, being peace loving and pacifist people, may not make good soldiers was exploded as they acted in combat like seasoned, brave and bold fighters. In the end, suffice to say that Ladakh region – the present Leh and Kargil districts – was saved; though barely.

49 Rigzin Namgyal Kalon, *Op. Cit.*

Chapter IV

The Forsaken (Dark) Period (1949-1962)

A young Captain of the Indian army, who visited Leh and areas around, for the first time in 1950, has recorded this account as his impressions about the territory, "Situated in the remote regions of the Himalayan ranges, forming the crest of India's crown, surrounded by lofty mountain mastiffs, the mighty majestic heights of whose peaks few men have reached to, watered by the perennial springs of the Indus, Shyok and Nubra, inhabited by people whose noble nature and simplicity are paralleled only by their humble living and spiritual thinking, once a centre of the Central Asian trade, paradise of game-hunters and mountaineers, and the melting pot of Chinese, Pakistani and Indian relationships – such is strategic Ladakh."[1]

This period, of thirteen years between 1949 and 1962, in the long history of Ladakh has really been a span of neglect from the political, economic, administrative and even military points of view. Even though outwardly the place looked as serene as before; but it had now become a part of a very large entity called India; with its entire multifarious splendor including a large area and equally burgeoning population. Ladakh had just emerged out of a long drawn and disastrous war, though not unscathed but fortunately saved, but the threat of renewed hostilities remained hanging. The Great Game was certainly going on around this region; played mainly by the major world-powers; in this region specifically by the Americans, the British and the Russians. In this background it was not surprising to find few rumors and even some conspiracy theories doing rounds of the place. Ladakh; as a region as also respectable persons of the area were trying to

1 Maj. Gen. Rajendra Nath, PVSM (Retd), *Strategic Ladakh*, Vij Books India Pvt Ltd., New Delhi, 2016, p.1.

find their respective places under the sun, in the new and emerging order in India – a huge country whose part they had now become.

The army troops in the Indian part of this frontier area comprised the soldiers of 77 Para Brigade; mainly strung along the Dras–Kargil axis and Lt. Col. Parab and his forces of about two battalions strong in Leh and Nubra areas. By the time a breakthrough was achieved in Zojila, link up established with Leh and efforts made to capture Marol – it was almost end of December, with quite a bit of snow fall in the higher regions. There was no question of de-induction of these forces at that point of time and this lot had to stay back and spend the harsh winter in Ladakh itself; for which preparations were made as effective as possible. For example, by 21st December 1948, the supply position at different locations was found to be as follows:

Dras : Supplies for 68 days for 3000 troops.

Kargil : Stocks for 23 days for 3000 troops.

Leh : Stocks for 17 days for 1200 troops.

The balance supplies required for the winter months had to be procured locally or transported by air.[2] However, as soon as the summer set in, all these units left one by one. Though one Brigade worth of troops was located in the Dras – Kargil belt; as some mischief from Pakistan was still not ruled out and this much strength was considered a minimum requirement to meet any unforeseen eventuality. All the same, Leh region – specifically the Indus and Nubra valleys - were completely denuded of any regular, Indian army, forces. In the whole of this vast region only one infantry battalion, the 7 J&K Militia was kept in Leh. That too, perhaps because back then the J&K Militia was not yet a part of the Indian army and this outfit was considered to be a state unit as it was paid for out of the J&K revenues. This unit comprised four companies; of which two were of Kashmiri Muslims and the other two companies consisted of the local Ladakhi Buddhists. As there were no regular barracks in Leh, these troops were located in the small fort at Leh, which was constructed by General Zorawar Singh in the 1830s when he first occupied the town (this place is still in existence). Their officers had occupied another big and beautiful

2 S.N. Prasad, *History of Operations in Jammu and Kashmir, 1947-48*, (History Division, Ministry of Defence, Government of India),Thomson Press, New Delhi, 1987, p. 365.

building, not far away from this site, which was once the nerve centre of the British Joint Commissioner. This place, which now houses a Corps Headquarters Mess, was then serving as the officers living accommodation and Mess of 7 J&K Militia. There was only one jeep in the entire Leh region which was meant for the use of only the Commanding Officer of this Militia unit. There were no regular roads in Leh area at that time, only tracks. But, with some deft manoeuvring the jeeps could operate on these rough paths also. The same was the condition between the town and airfield; as these two points were also connected by a mud track which was meant for use of ponies and camels but the jeep could also be driven upon it.

Not only the regular units of the Indian army practically vacated the entire Indus and Nubra valleys; no effort was made by either the state or the central governments to improve the infrastructure in the entire Ladakh area. This was in stark contrast with the exertions of the Chinese. They were wide awake and busy in their long term plans, while the Indians were literally sleeping. The Chinese border outpost near Damchok, for example, was manned by their regular soldiers. On the other side, the Indian post at Damchok was manned by some constables of the J&K police. Same was the position in the northern part of Ladakh. The Chinese had a regular post just north of the Karakoram Pass; whereas India just did not have any presence in the entire sector. The 7 J&K Militia troops; the only army unit in the region was mostly facing the Pakistanis in the northwestern sector. It appeared that the authorities did not perceive any threat from the Chinese side in the north as also from the east. What gross miscalculations, as events over the next decade would prove. More spiritless and confused actions from the Indian side would follow before the country finally woke up to the real threat from this big neighbor.

During this period, the early 1950s, the missionary activities there have been described by an outside observer as, "There was the well kept Moravian Mission, headed by the gracious Dr. and Mrs. Driver, from the UK; they extended medical care inclusive of medicines to the poor. Being missionaries, they were very dedicated and tried their best to spread Christianity while extending medical care. The couple was however not popular in spite of their medical care as they remained aloof from the masses and maintained a distance. They were replaced in 1953 or so by a Swiss couple, Dr and Mrs. Vittoz, they mixed well with the population and were certainly more popular but they were also unable to spread Christianity."[3]

Just after the hostilities ceased, during the summer of 1949, one person named Ganderbali, was sent by the state government as the first civilian Administrator of Ladakh; though there was no structured hierarchy of the local civilian set up existing at that time. Ganderbali asked Kalon sahib to work as his Tehsildar on a fixed pay. The latter declined to accept this generous offer saying that he had taken active part in the local affairs, including defence of the town and areas around, and generally managed affairs of the region only as a call of duty and not with the intention of making a profession out of it. His priority was to look after the property, lands and livestock as also manage the family affairs. The first regular and qualified Tehsildar in Leh was posted around 1954. His name was Pushkar Nath Kaul; who incidentally rose to become Chief Secretary of J&K later. Slowly, and over the next few years, the civilian administrative structures stabilized and took effective roots in the Ladkah district; which then comprised two Tehsils of Leh and Kargil; with Nubra being one of the Niabats – with its headquarters at village Diskit - of Leh Tehsil. Also, Ladakh district formally became a part of the Kashmir Division of J&K; Jammu being the other administrative Division of the State. However, Ladakh continued to be a neglected part of the state set-up and was invariably treated more as a far outpost than an important part of the system. The local people understood this disregard and indifference well; raising their voices against it periodically. At this point of time, however, the local population was more keen to pick up pieces of their collectively disturbed existence and get on with the new realities of life that they were now facing; particularly after the dark and desolate year of 1948.

Being essentially a law abiding people, the Ladakhis were less interested in the administrative set up and hierarchies; but eagerly looking forward to revive the economy which had been so rudely shaken and badly shattered. The life in Ladakh generally revolved around agriculture and pastoral activities – produce from the small pieces of productive land and income from as also use of animals domesticated by each family. Thus, the economy was largely based on primitive lines and hence not much affected by the cross-currents of modern civilization. Every family was almost self-contained, and whatever little help was required outside the family; the

3 Rajendra Nath, *Op. Cit.*, pp. 155 and 156.

same was readily available in the village, like the odd jobs to be done by carpenters or black-smiths. In that sense every village, if not each family, could be taken as an economic unit. The requirements of individuals, families and the society, at large, were quite limited and this was one of the main reasons for the people there to be leading a happy and contended life in spite of a very harsh climate, limited agricultural season as also small land holdings. Still, as a group, the economic life of these simple people depended quite heavily on the Central Asian trade; of which Leh town was practically a central point, and similarly the trade connections, on the eastern side, with Tibet provided considerable collective benefits to the Ladakhi society. After the events of 1948, the trade on both these sides dropped down to a trickle and became totally closed in the mid-fifties. This brought about three pronged distress to the entire community. The sources of ready and homely supplies of special kinds of goods dried up. At the same time the workload for the cattle reared by the locals also reduced very considerably; as these animals were employed in large numbers by the caravans traversing these trade routes. Thirdly, the sizeable quantity of surplus grass and fodder consumed by the animals of the caravans also got heavily reduced and this too impacted adversely on the local economy. All these negative developments originated with the rise of the Chinese Communist party and spread of its tentacles in Xinjiang (then called Sinkiang); as also tightening of the Russian grip over its southern possessions; the Central Asian region. Simultaneously, the Chinese had started choking the Tibetan area, starting from Lhasa and moving westwards. All these happenings added to the travails of the general public in Ladakh. It was commonly believed that of all these sources, the most important for the local economy was the trade route to and from Sinkiang; in which both Indian and Central Asian businessmen participated. Ladakh was practically being bottled up. Virtually forgotten by the J&K state government as also by the central administration in New Delhi; and squeezed by the Central Asian and Tibetan regimes, the community in Ladakh came under considerable distress and faced economic hardships. It was practically left to fend for itself. It is a collective tribute to the resilience of the people and their remarkable capacity to live off the limited resources available that they not only survived these difficult years; but also managed to retain their proverbial simplicity and a natural smile on their happy faces.

About the important trade route on the Sinkiang axis, an eye witness account of 1952, narrates this gloomy tale as, "The Chinese authorities welcomed them as they helped in trade between India and China. Many of them had married local women also though they were Muslims while the Indian traders from Punjab were either Hindus or Sikhs. They had purchased houses and shops also in Xinjiang particularly in the districts of Yarkand and Kashgarh of Sinkiang (Xinjiang). However, the Chinese authorities suddenly decided in 1952 that there would be no trade between Ladakh and Xinjiang and that all Indian traders from Xinjiang would have to leave Xinjiang immediately. Consequently, the Chinese Government ordered the Indian traders to wind up their businesses and to do so within a week at the most. The Indian traders, therefore, lost not only their houses and shops but all their belongings and wealth also as they were allowed to take minimum luggage only. The Indian trade commissioner in Xinjiang was posted in Urumachi, Capital of Xinjiang province and tried to help the Indian traders in Xinjiang but all his efforts failed. He was also ordered to leave Xinjiang at short notice. His request to travel along with the Indian traders to Ladakh was also turned down. He had to go back to Shanghai and then travel to India via the sea route…I met the expelled Indian traders at Leh in Ladakh in the local bazaar and later talked to them in the Sarai in Leh. A few traders told me that they had to sell all their goods as well as belongings in their houses at the minimum possible price, as they were permitted to carry limited stock only. Each trader was allowed to take back only stocks which could be carried by one camel while he was allowed to take one horse for travelling back to India via Ladakh…most of the traders I met had lost heavily and were certainly not backed by the Central Government adequately."[4]

It was around this time only that other traditional trade routes, to and from Leh, also got closed for one reason or the other. This proved to be a bad hit economically to the people of Ladakh collectively; as their centuries long and well established trade practices towards the regions of north and west lay now denied to them. The only alternative left for them was to depend on the business transactions, with the rest of India – generally in south and easterly directions. But, here the infrastructure, trade practices as also dealings and contacts had not yet been developed. That certainly was a hard period for the local population of Ladakh. Under those trying circumstances, only the smiling visages, joyful countenances

4 Rajendra Nath, *Op. Cit.*, pp. 151 and 152.

and egalitarianism as also contended community life based on the village as a basic and functional economic unit; helped the society. Nineteen fifties, few years before and after that – roughly about fifteen years – were certainly a troublesome period for the Ladakhis. The quality of life was not high; but peace prevailed in the region. The existing social and economic system ensured that both rich and poor shared and cared for each other; by and large people were happy and contended. There was joy in the air in spite of hardships caused by loss of centuries old, traditional business and the absence of any kind of luxury. The remarkable social balance in the community was a big plus factor during that period and ensured collective equanimity during back-breaking hard work of summer months and a long as well as bleak winter season.

When the military danger to Ladakh was finally averted towards the end of 1948, followed by the declaration of ceasefire; the local population started feeling the need for meeting and explaining their plight and position to the highest authority in New Delhi. The earliest opportunity came their way in the beginning of summer of next year when these people could reach their destination from Leh via Manali. This important event has been described in the first person as, "In fact, the first ever deputation from Ladakh headed by Mr. Chewang Rigzin Kalon[5], President Buddhist Association, Ladakh, called on Pandit Jawaharlal Nehru, the Prime Minister of India, on May 4, 1949 and presented a Memorandum to him which pleaded that Ladakh should not be bound by the decision of any plebiscite that might be held to decide Kashmir's accession. The Memorandum said, 'Ladakh is not prepared to go to Pakistan whatever the result of the plebiscite may be.' ... The Memorandum concluded with an appeal, 'We seek the bosom of that gracious mother (India) to receive more nutriment for growth to our full stature in every way. She has given us what we prize above all other things – our religion and culture. The Ashoka Wheel on her flag, symbol of goodwill for all humanity and her concern for her cultural children, call us irresistibly. Will the great mother refuse to take to her arms one of her weakest and most forlorn and depressed children – a child whom filial love impels to respond to the call?'[6] I happened to accompany this delegation to the Prime Minister's house at Teen Murti. While the Prime Minister shared the concern of the deputationists in principle, regarding Central

5 Father of Rigzin Namgyal Kalon (Kalon Sahib).

6 This paragraph is also quoted by Thupstan Chhewang, the MP from Ladakh, in his article at page 22 of the *Border Affairs* in its issue of April- June 2013.

take-over of Ladakh, he observed that the Kashmir issue was before the Security Council, it would be inadvisable to take any constitutional or administrative action which might weaken India's stand on the issue. The delegation did not, therefore, press its demand for a 'Union Territory Status' for Ladakh in national interest and on the Prime Minister's assurance that their grievances would be looked into and redressed."[7]

Just about a fortnight thereafter, another delegation from Ladakh, this time led by Kushok Bakula – a well known and highly venerated Lama of Ladakh, who was the head of the Spituk Monastery near Leh as also a reincarnated monk, generally referred to as Rinpochey – called on the Prime Minister on 20th May 1949. This group also, more or less, emphasized the same broad points raised and discussed by the earlier delegation. It might indeed appear odd or incongruous that two separate deputations, one headed by the President of L.B.A., and the other led by Kushok Bakula, waited on the Prime Minister of India in New Delhi, in a span of a fortnight and apprised him of their general conditions as also requested for early remedial measures; more or less on the similar lines. That this was done during the beginning of summer of 1949, when coming to New Delhi from Leh over a very difficult route; was all the more amazing. However, a dispassionate and objective analysis of the prevailing situation would indicate that the region had just emerged out of an unprecedented crisis which had shaken the Ladakhi beliefs, systems and way of life to the core. In this year of turmoil, where the entire people stood like a rock and also actively participated in the defence efforts; the L.B.A. and the younger generation had played a remarkably outstanding role which in all respects was much more noteworthy than the participation of clergy or religious elements during that critical period. In a way, therefore, these developments represented the contours of a struggle for primacy in the region; between the 'traditionalists' represented by the Rinpochey Kushok Bakula and the 'modernist' faction led then by the L.B.A. For the next few decades, this internecine struggle in the Ladakhi society would shape the local responses and the contours of its exertions against the State Government and at times with the Central regime itself; in addition to the internal churning, as also longing for joining the emerging mainstream

7 Shridhar Kaul and H.N. Kaul, *Ladakh Through Ages*, Indus Publishing Co., New Delhi, 1992, pp. 184 and 185. In this case, Shridhar Kaul – the then Inspector of Schools there and also well known in Ladakh as Pandit Dulloo – had accompanied the said delegation.

in all respects. The many future years saw an interesting phenomenon of one section gaining ascendency over the other; as also sometimes both coming together on a common platform. However, way back in 1949 and immediately thereafter, Kushok Bakula certainly gained an upper hand in this tussle. It is also interesting to note that demand of the Ladakh Buddhists for a direct rule by the Central government; as also declaration of the region as a Union Territory (U.T.) was raised for the first time way back in May 1949.

Urged by both these delegations, as also their pleadings for an early visit, Pandit Jawahar Lal Nehru landed at Leh, in the month of July the same year, for a four day trip of the region. He was also accompanied by the Prime Minister of J&K, Sheikh Mohammad Abdullah. In addition to meeting representatives of different sections of society; he also undertook an exhaustive review of the prevailing situation in Ladakh, including political, economic, military and administrative requirements of the region. Orders issued by the visitors and policy contours finalized were implemented over the coming years. An important initiative was to persuade Kushok Bakula to take on political responsibilities in addition to his religious duties. Also, one of the promises made in the Leh public meeting by Shri Nehru was redeemed within ten months. As assured, the sacred relics of Lord Buddha's two principal disciples - Sarriputta and Maha Mogallanna – were flown to Leh in May 1950. After exposition for four days in Leh, the relics were taken to many other places, in the Indus valley, including Hemis Gompa. This step was greatly appreciated by the local population; as also further strengthened its bonds with the rest of India.

The July 1949 visit was certainly a very productive and useful trip by the two VIPs, which considerably helped in the mainstreaming of this far-flung region of the state. A part of this has been comprehensively described by 'Pandit Dulloo' as, "It was, therefore, providential that Pandit Nehru during his visit to Leh in July 1949, along with Sheikh Abdullah, picked up Kushok Bakula for political leadership of Ladakh. Kushok Bakula eventually took over as President of the Leh unit of the National Conference and represented the Ladakhis in the Legislative Assembly for a decade and half and dominated the Ladakh political scene… Circumstances forced him into the forefront of a long-drawn struggle with the state authorities, a struggle, which ended temporarily with the exit of the government headed by Sheikh Abdullah in August 1953."[8] Thus, Kushok Bakula appeared to have been picked up by the providence to lead the Ladakhis not only in religious matters but also in political affairs. In the latter role he had to stand, at times, in a confrontationist role against the state government; something which Sheikh Abdullah and his colleagues did not like. The very first such occasion came in 1950. That is the year when J&K enacted the most revolutionary land reforms statute, attempted anywhere in the country till then. This enactment was called Big Landed Estates Abolition Act (B.L.E.A.), whereby the proprietary rights in land in excess of the ceiling limit of 182 Kanals - 9.21 Hectares – were expropriated by the state without any compensation. The land so acquired was transferred to the actual tillers. Only orchards were kept out of the purview of this Act. Notwithstanding positive intentions of the lawmakers to benefit the very disadvantaged sections of the society; this law created two majors problems in Ladakh region – where only 21 holdings were found to be beyond the prescribed ceiling. Obviously, the figure of 182 Kanals was relevant to the prevailing conditions in the Valley and not in Ladakh where soil fertility was much lower than anywhere else in the state; more particularly the Valley. Connected with this was also the question of tracts where local people had planted good number of trees for fuel and housing purposes. Such land pieces also did not get the exemptions, applied to the 'orchards' in other parts of the state. Secondly, the Gompas which traditionally held large tracts of land spread all over the region were also not exempted from the provisions of the Act; which thus applied very much to the land holdings of the Gompas, in excess of the prescribed limit. This hit at the very roots of the Buddhists' social and religious life and beliefs. The local Buddhists; as a part of religious ceremonies, on special occasions as also on personal volitions gave pieces of their lands to the Gompas of their choice. For example, Hemis Gompa had lands in its name all over Ladakh region, down the Shyok, Nubra and Indus valleys as also other areas. Same was the case with other Gompas. In turn these Gompas fed and educated a large number of 'Lamas' and 'Chomos'; in addition to opening their granaries in the times of dire needs of the society. These were, in fact, inextricably linked with the religious, social and economic life of the local residents. The Gompa Association as also the local peasantry rose in unison against the provisions of BLEA Act and demanded special concessions to Ladakh; in the least asking for

8 Shridhar Kaul, *Op. Cit.*, p. 186.

exemption of the Gompa lands from its provisions. Kushok Bakula, at the head of a delegation, met J&K Prime Minister Sheikh Abdullah with their request; who refused to alter the legal provisions and, in the end, promised that the Constituent Assembly of the state would take a final decision in this regard. Not satisfied with this attitude, the Kushok and his people approached Jawahar Lal Nehru in sheer desperation. It was only on the intervention of the Prime Minister of India that an executive order was issued by the state government keeping the Gompa lands out of the B.L.E.A. stipulations and ceilings. The main Act was still not amended and these along with other related issues were given to a Committee for detailed examination and suitable recommendations.

The J&K government appointed a Committee in February 1953, to look into various aspects of the operation of BLEA Act. It was headed by Mr. Justice Janki Nath Wazir, Chief Justice of J&K High Court. Before giving its recommendations, this Committee toured various places in the state including "Leh and went up to Hemis, 22 miles away from Leh."

The final Report of the Committee, particularly in respect of Ladakh, makes an interesting reading. It is under the heading "Working of Land Reforms in Ladakh District". The four relevant paragraphs are quoted as follows:-

> "65. *Gardens – Exemption from Abolition Act* – While the Committee was in Ladakh the proprietors appeared before the Committee in large numbers and they were unanimous on this point that the unit of 182 *Kanals* was not sufficient for their requirements taking into consideration the productivity of the land and the inferiority of land in that *Ilaqa*.... They had, with great difficulty, planted trees of willow and poplar for the purpose of fuel and timber. They have not been allowed to retain these gardens because not growing fruit trees they did not come under the definition of orchards.
>
> 66...
>
> 67. The Committee proposes that *bedzars* and *safedzars* and gardens having trees in Ladakh District should be allowed to remain with the proprietors in addition to the prescribed units.
>
> 68. *Gumpa lands – Exemption from Abolition Act.* – In Ladakh it was represented to the Committee by the tenants as well as the proprietors

that the lands which are attached to the religious institutions of theirs called *Gumpas* should be excluded from the operation of the Abolition Act. It was rather surprising that the tenants who were likely to gain by the operation of the Act on the lands attached to the *Gumpas* have unanimously desired that these lands should remain attached to the *Gumpas* and be free from the operation of the Abolition Act. It was specially enquired from them why they were in favour of retention of the land with the *Gumpas*. Their reply was that the lands which were attached to the *Gumpas* were cultivated by the tenants and they had to pay only ¼ th of the produce to the *Gumpas.* The *Gumpas* share of produce was utilized for educational, religious and charitable purposes and for feeding the poor and the needy and, therefore, they would like that the *Gumpas* should not be divested of these lands. It would hurt their religious feelings in case the Act was made operative on these *Gumpa* lands.

69. The Committee was told that on their representation the operation of the Act had been suspended for the time being by an executive order of the Government yet the demand of the public at large was that the exemption of the *Gumpas* from the operation of the Act should be incorporated in the Act itself. This suggestion is commended to the Government for favourable consideration."[9]

Thus the requisite and happy outcome of the BLEA, was finally ensured as requested for by the people of Ladakh, collectively. It was the acceptance of a very genuine demand of the local population by the State Government. This one positive act considerably assuaged the feelings of the people there. All the same resentment of the local population of the entire Ladakh region was not only palpable; it was increasing, over time, on all counts. The army had practically vacated the entire district, keeping virtually a nominal level of deployment against the Pakistani forces and their expected misadventures. The much more perceptible threat from the Chinese side was not yet comprehended, in spite of provocative actions by them. The Central government appeared to have forgotten about this far-flung area in its priority and urgency to concentrate on and build up facilities in the core areas of the country. The J&K government did attempt to make some positive changes in the lives of the people there but the

9 Report of the Inquiry Committee Appointed to Examine the Working of Land Reforms, ETC. 1953 A.D. Published by the Jammu and Kashmir Government and printed at the Ranbir Government Press, Jammu. pp. ii, 30 and 31.

benefit of such exertions were obviously limited to the interest taken by the employees in the local welfare. The immediate concern of the public servants, most of who in the middle and higher levels were in any case from the Valley, was to see that their tenure in Ladakh got over somehow; and not the local good. Some progress, though, was made in the fields of Health and Education but the headway was much slower than other parts of the state. The death rate in Ladakh, for example, which was 10 per thousand in 1951, came down to 6.43 in 1961. All the same, neglect of the region, particularly in the decade of the fifties was palpable. One of the primary reasons for this indifference was low level of employment in the government of the local people. According to a perceptive observer, "Even though the Buddhists were in a majority in the entire district, their representation in the total of services was hardly 27 % while even in Leh Tehsil where they formed about 90 % of the population, their representation was hardly 43 %. In Kargil Tehsil, where the Buddhists formed about 25 % of the population, they were practically unrepresented, viz. 3 constables, 1 girdawar and 2 peons being all they came in for in that Tehsil."[10]

There were also other grievances of the local population like the genuine need for improving the roads and other means of communications in Ladakh; lack of rehabilitation of a number of refugees from Zanskar who had moved to the adjoining Kullu area during Pakistani occupation of Zanskar in 1948, and were now living in abject conditions. There were also complaints of lack of interest by the state administration to give a fillip to the local language of Bhoti (Bodhi); as also its forceful assertions to the propagation of Urdu instead. A related issue was the indifferent attitude of the Government towards providing facilities to the Ladakhi students who wished to pursue higher studies; even though this number was very small. For example, the first boy of the district, who opted for medical studies; T. Smanla hailed from Timisgam village of the middle Indus valley; and he was allotted a seat in the far away Medical College in Dibrugarh, Assam. At the heart of these complaints, which were multiplying, was the lack of a sense of sympathy and compassion for the problems faced by people of this far flung region. This process of neglect prompted the local M.L.A. to bitterly complain in the Legislature. "…reminded me of what Kushok Bakula, as a legislator, had told the State Assembly in May 1952. Kushok Bakula had then lambasted the Government for not making even a token provision about Ladakh in the State Budget. He pointed out: "Read the

10 Shridhar Kaul, *Op. Cit.,* p. 190.

statement from one end to the other, you will not find Ladakh mentioned even once much less will you find a reference to its economic and other needs which are urgent and pressing and cry for urgent attention and fulfillment."[11] It was indeed a difficult time for the people of Ladakh and their representatives.

The Delhi Agreement of July 1952 was seen as a concession for the demand of greater autonomy of Kashmir; and consequently it was no wonder that greater devolution of powers was expected and demanded by the Ladakh region. These yearnings were outlined by Kushok Bakula in a Press statement on 15th January, 1953, which said "I am no enemy of Kashmir. In fact, Ladakh wants to have the closest ties with Kashmir. But if freedom is good for Kashmir, it is good for Ladakh also. We want to have an effective voice in the administration of our area and we want a relentless, remorseless and ruthless war to be carried on against poverty, ignorance and disease in Ladakh. That is the long and short of the matter. I do not want to pull any wool over the eyes of the State authorities and let there be no misunderstanding in any quarter about our aims and objectives." It was indeed a difficult situation; and so were the extra efforts, made by different leading personalities in Ladakh, to be heard in the right circles. The most basic problem continued to be the lack of road connectivity of various urban centers of Ladakh with rest of the state and the country.

Even though the army cut a makeshift road in a record time between Baltal and Zoji La and performed the unique feat of taking tanks to the highest battlefield at Zojila top; on 1st November 1948; the access to Kargil was made traffic worthy for mechanical transport only a couple of years later. This was then thought to be sufficient, at least from the military point of view, to effectively meet any threat from Pakistan side. It is a sad commentary on the misplaced national priorities that the road link between Kargil and Leh was to take place after another long gap of more than a decade. As no threat was perceived in the early fifties from the Chinese, in spite of their machinations and intentions to the contrary, Leh was not thought to be strategically important from the army perspective. Therefore the road linkage to that place could wait. The entire expanse continued to be steeped in neglect, poverty and virtual abandonment. A visitor to Leh in the mid 1950 reported that even though that place had the distinction of being one of the highest inhabited locations in the world;

11 Thupstan Chewang, *Op. Cit.*, p. 23.

the settlement at Leh comprised only a couple of hundred homes mostly made up of mud bricks walls and local timber roof tops; with decorative frontages in some structures. The town was dominated by the fort and monastery; silhouetted against the mountainous ranges to the West. His amazed observations include, "...and where else in the world is Polo played within the confines of the village high street and market-square?... Presumably, goals are scored, between the heaped up cairns of stones set up at either end of the market square".

Ladakh is one of those rare places where people had seen the aircraft before either the train or the vehicles. Small motor transport in the form of Jeep, that also a very limited number and exclusively for the use of defence forces, made its appearance around Leh few years after the Independence. These too were brought, in dismantled conditions and in pieces, by the aircrafts. A graphic account of seeing the train for the first time has been expressed, by the scion of a prominent family, as "It was around 1957 that one of my acquaintances dropped in home. He had recently been to Delhi and was, naturally, full of stories about different things and places that he saw – some of which we had only heard about. One of these, which intrigued me, was his claim of having seen and also sat in a train. After considerable time and description when he was not able to satisfy me as to what exactly a train is like; out of understandable exasperation – understandable now that is – he said that a train is just like the house we live in; it has a place to sit, a place to sleep and also a real bathroom. The whole thing intrigued me so much that next summer when I had a chance to go to Srinagar, I decided to see a train myself. So from there I boarded a N.D. Radhakrishan bus, the best one available those days. It was a post office red vehicle, with the word MAIL painted on both sides; which took me to Pathankot with a night halt enroute at Batote. I straight away headed for the Railway station there, as Pathankot was then the rail-head for the entire J&K state. That is where I saw the train for the first time. It was an awe inspiring and magnificent sight for me; the huge black smoke-belching engine plus a long line of bogies standing and moving on the iron tracks. But, frankly also, I was disappointed to find that it could go up and down on the rails only and there was no 'house like' structure in it; as my young mind had anticipated in its fancy. Like it generally happens; the imagination was more elaborately colorful than the real thing. I thought train was something which could – by magic – move the whole house from one place to another. In a peculiar sort of way, I found my journey all the way from Srinagar, not very fulfilling."[12]

Up to 1947, the trade regulations of the state stipulated that Pashmina and Shahtoosh wool could only be sold to the nominated Kashmiri dealers, by the producers or Ladakhi traders. In that sense it was a highly restrictive trade practice. After the independence, these controls were removed and technically the locals could deal with anyone who offered better bargain. However, benefit to the native population was only short lived as right from the beginning of 1950, the Trans border trade started slowing down – because of a myriad factors – and almost came to stand still by the mid fifties. So much so that Ladakh and western Tibet; which had been traditionally interdependent, were forced by the fast changing circumstances to find their own ways of sustenance and survival. Lot of upheavals were taking place in the entire area north of Ladakh; due to the communists coming to power in China and also the growing Russian influence in the Central Asian region. Notwithstanding the upheavals in these Central Asian states, these developments affected Ladakh only to the extent of the Kazakh exodus from Sinkiang (Xinjiang). These people professed Muslim religion and the first group of Kazakhs migrated to the Sinkiang area after armed clash with the Soviet troops in the 1920. The second wave of these immigrants entered Sinkiang following the Kazakhstan famine during 1932-33. In the aftermath of communist regime taking control of China and consequent advance of the Chinese Red army into this province; a body of Kazakhs fled from Sinkiang to Tibet. These migratory Kazakhs were generally nomadic and also somewhat violent in nature; and they came in conflict with the Tibetan forces as well as war-like local groupings, which looked at this movement with suspicion. Following the clashes in Tibet and determined to preserve their way of life, including tribal customs and Islam; a group decided to head towards Kashmir via Ladakh. It has been estimated that of the four hundred families that fled China – Sinkiang – about three hundred and fifty arrived at Srinagar. Their stay and journey through Leh was described by a local observer as, "...a number of them along with their horses and families migrated to this side. Each one came at least on two horses with one carrying arms and ammunitions. In certain cases complete families moved. Three to four hundred of such people, in my estimation, came from Sinkiang. Some of them carried good quantity of gold with them. They came in and around Leh, sold their goods and

12 Conversation with Col. Wangdus (Retd), on 18th November 2018.

even gold to make their living. Gold was exchanged freely for goods and eatables. These people had such a large flock of horses and animals and were in need of day to day articles that they resorted to distress sale while in Leh and also on move. They were also talented horsemen and would enthrall the local population with their horsemanship and different activities with the horses… Those days there were only 70-80 State Forces troops in Leh, which were commanded by Major Abdul Majid. He sent a word to this group that he was also a Muslim officer of the State forces and even though the troops available with him were less in numbers than the visitors; if they created any problem or tried the path of confrontation then the entire might of the J&K State would deal with them in a ruthless manner. After exchange of messages and personal meetings, these people deposited their weapons in the State Armoury. I recall around a hundred horses load of weapons were surrendered by these people. Thus, with the presence of mind and tactful handling by Major Majeed Leh was saved, otherwise these armed men could have looted the place and created problems before the State forces from Srinagar could arrive."[13]

During that desolate period Ladakh was provided a kind of collective leadership by three people, working independently; in different fields of life; and this certainly was a good fortune of the region. In military matters, this did have a crucial importance in those days, the leadership mantle fell on the shoulders of Chewang Rinchen; on social issues and matters affecting normal life of the public the leading and headship responsibility devolved on Rigzin Namgyal Kalon; whereas the guidance and charisma of Kushok Bakula became invaluable to the public in respect of political and religious aspects. About the first two persons, much has been mentioned in the earlier parts and more will follow at the later stage; reference has also been made about Kushok Bakula joining the National Conference, becoming the first Legislator from Ladakh as also his strong opposition to the application of BLEA Act to the lands in possession of the Gompas. In this stand, as the subsequent events unfolded, he did have the last word and scored a notable victory. In the religious role, he was not only head of the Spituk monastery, but also had the exalted status of a reincarnate Lama – called Rinpochey in the local parlance. The term Rinpochey means 'precious one' in Ladakhi; which in practical terms stands for a reincarnated Lama. This is widely perceived in the region as a form of rebirth consistent with the Karmic view of existence; a belief heavily loaded with religious

13 Interview with Rigzin Namgyal Kalon in September 1998.

connotations. Some of the important monasteries in Ladakh are headed by Rinpocheys; which include the Hemis, Spituk, Thiksay and Phyang Gompas. It is widely believed and also expected that an incarnated Lama, before his demise, would leave enough clues to help the concerned people to locate his successor without much difficulty. Such indications include some of his daily routine things, favorite hymns, details of a recent dream and the like. The young children, whose parents lay claim of their son being a Rinpochey, are then put through an elaborate process of scrutiny by a Gompa Committee constituted by the head Lama. This group includes senior Lamas of the Rinpochey's past life; who examine the child. If he selects the right articles from the Rinpochey's earlier life and also replies the right answers to various religious questions; then this Committee recommends him as the new Rinpochey. This recommendation is treated as the final determination; but the verdict is still taken as tentative. The details of the new born Rinpochey and the Committee's judgment are then sent to His Holiness the Dalai Lama for final confirmation. After the receipt of his validation; the child is formally recognized as a Rinpochey without any doubt. The same procedure in its entirety was followed in the case of Kushok Bakula, who was born on 27th May 1917. But, his duties and involvement in the lives of Ladakhis was not merely limited to showing the path of religious rectitude; destiny had also put on his shoulders the responsibility of providing political guidance to them. This role made him to accept the offer to join the National Conference; become its local district head and also first MLA of the region.

Within a couple of years his disappointment with the Sheikh Abdullah regime was palpable; not because of any personality clash but he sincerely felt that the state government was not showing enough understanding and sympathy for the development of Ladakh. The circumstances in the state took a turn to see the end of the rule of Sheikh Abdullah; and Bakshi Ghulam Mohammad became the next Prime Minister of J&K in August 1953. The Bakshi assured a fair deal to Ladakh region, in his set up and it created a positive impact on the collective psyche of the people of this sensitive and neglected area. In the beginning of November that year he was inducted in the State's Council of Ministers as a Deputy Minister in charge of Ladakh Affairs. By this act, the Bakshi virtually brought back the Ladakhis firmly in the fold of the state and their emotional attachment with it grew further. Kushok Bakula assumed his new office with lot of expectations, that are obvious from the press statement he issued on 9th

November and which included, "…Monks, as a rule, had no time for politics. I break this century-old tradition only because I have the interests of Ladakh at heart – the interests which were ignored by the previous regime." A fortnight later he repeated similar sentiments, though in a different way, in a public meeting at Leh, where he reiterated that after taking the charge as a Minister, he had become the peoples' servant and guide in the real sense.

The description of overall functioning and different activities in the region at that time has been narrated as, "The Ladakh Affairs department, which was thus created and headed by Kushok Bakula, started looking after the developmental and other activities of the district. The Department raised problems with the ministers whose Departments were represented in Ladakh and even to the Prime Minister, when necessary… The Deputy Minister for Ladakh Affairs convened frequent meetings of the District officers and pursued their problems with the concerned Departments. No powers were, however, vested in him for effecting changes in the administration or creation of posts or allocation of funds. All the same, in the face of these limitations, he tried to make the best of the situation. However, while there was an appreciable change of heart on the part of the Bakshi Government towards Ladakh during its first few years, the remaining period was not characterized by absolute harmony and understanding…. yet Kushok Bakula felt that with the sympathetic attitude of Kashmir's Prime Minister and the unremitting solicitude of the Prime Minister of India for Ladakh's prosperity and advancement, the region would usher into prosperity before long… They were thus unhappy with the Bakshi regime which, they felt, also treated them as a mere cultural entity and not a political reality… Kushok Bakula's direct rapport with Pandit Nehru irked Bakshi more than anything else and, who did not make any secret of it through his unrestrained and indiscriminate outbursts."[14] In the early sixties, there was another change at the state level and the government was headed by G. M Sadiq, who also recognized the importance of the Rinpochey and elevated him to the status of a Minister of State in his cabinet. However, by then, Kushok Bakula had been involved in the affairs of Ladakh region for almost a decade and half; his political domination of the region was no more absolute and unchallenged. New forces and faces had started emerging in the area and he thought of enlarging his field of activities by becoming a member of the Lok Sabha. After this; particularly

14 Shridhar Kaul, *Op. Cit.,* pp. 214, 215 and 218.

after the Chinese aggression in 1962, Kushok Bakula took more interest in national and international affairs than the local matters. His finest and most productive period came when he was made Indian Ambassador to Mongolia, in 1990 for almost ten years. He worked tirelessly for bringing the people of Mongolia and India even closer; as also provided theological and doctrinaire under pinning to the religious revival in that vast region. People literally revered him for his religious knowledge and his high status as a Buddhist monk. He is still fondly remembered there as an "Ambassador – Teacher". Kushok Bakula breathed his last on 4th November 2003. Over the last many decades of his life, he evolved as a Buddhist Monk, of a very high order, as well as a successful politician both at the State and Central levels. With his long list of achievements, it is no wonder that he has always been held in high esteem in Ladakh.

Reverting back to the decade of the fifties, when Kushok Bakula held sway over the entire belt. His training as a high priest and later the evolution as a political personality gave him a unique insight into national and international affairs; more particularly the happenings which affected Ladakh region and the areas around. He was specifically wary of the Chinese intentions. In 1955 the Government of India sent him to Lhasa, at the head of a delegation to coordinate with the Government of Tibet, the programmes about the 2500th Buddha Jayanti celebrations which were to take place in India the next year. He was also to request the Dalai Lama and Panchen Lama to participate in these events. "He spent over six months in Tibet and on his return to New Delhi, informed Nehru about the grim situation facing Tibet. His warning was ignored with consequences which are only too well known."[15] Similar observations have been made by a Captain of the army, who was sent to Ladakh by the Army Headquarters on a special mission. He met Kushok Bakula in 1953 and has recorded, "In one of his discussions with me, he was frank and said he did not trust the Chinese at all. According to his judgement, the Chinese would one day ensure that Buddhism as practiced in Tibet was finished off and the same fate would be of Ladakh in case the Chinese captured Ladakh too. Whenever I asked him as to why the Chinese would attack Ladakh, considering that both nations wanted and advocated close relations, he would become pensive. He would only say that it is not wise to take things for granted, for nations changed their views and policies as per their changing interests. His oft stated views were to welcome peace but to be

15 Sonam Wangchuk Shakspo, *Border Affairs,* New Delhi, April – June 2018, p. 10.

simultaneously alert and to have a certain degree of preparation always for any eventuality. I found such statements profound for a Buddhist Monk in an isolated region such as Ladakh. He was a wise saint and leader and I wish he had given this advice to the Indian leaders more vociferously in the 1950s."[16]

On the balance; it is a fact that Ladakh did not develop with the speed as also to its potential in the decade of the fifties. In fact growth activities were almost non-existent during that period. But this was not due to any lack of effort on the part of Kushok Bakula. Even his critics would not accuse him of that. He certainly led a very fruitful life in the later six decades of his existence. In that period he served as a member of the J&K Constituent assembly, MLA, Minister in the J&K Government, member of the Lok Sabha, member of the Minorities Commission and Ambassador of India to Mongolia. In each of these diverse roles – which incidentally were not in line with his basic training as a high Buddhist monk - he served with distinction and registered a notable performance. Humility always remained central to his persona; even though he reached great heights as a religious scholar, political leader and a diplomat. Essentially, Kushok Bakula Rinpochey was a modest person who strove hard for the welfare of his disadvantaged people and development of his desolate, far flung region – almost forgotten – in the first one and half decades after independence.

After the J&K State acceded to the Indian Union in October 1947, followed by the military operations for over next one year against the Pakistani forces; the Ladakh Wazarat only left with Leh and Kargil Tehsils, was constituted into the Ladakh district and the head of the district administrations was designated as Deputy Commissioner, like other parts of the State. This system notwithstanding; the entire area was first governed by Lt. Col. Parab as the Military Governor from August 1948. Parab was replaced, next summer, by Gandarbali who functioned as an Administrator of the region. Thereafter, as in other districts of the State, regular established hierarchies took over – albeit in phases – the regulatory and supervisory functions of the whole belt. It is generally believed that the first regular Tehsildar of Leh was Pushkar Nath Kaul; who was followed by Kanshi Nath Raina. It did take couple of years, though, for the entire administrative structure to fully establish itself. The earliest records of this time, available with the State Archives, pertains to a Govt. Gazette

16 Rajendra Nath, *Op. Cit.*, p. 156.

notification dated 7 August 1952 indicating that Mr. J. Dechan took over as the Deputy Commissioner Ladakh from Pt. Kashi Nath Kaul on 5th Har, 2009 (corresponding with second half of June 1952). Three months later, the Finance Department of the State Government delegated the powers of Income Tax Officer, to Shri Dechan for the entire Ladakh district. This was followed by an order of the High Court of Judicature, Jammu and Kashmir, of 5th March 1953 (published in the Government Gazette dated 19 March 1953), "…investing following officers with powers to hear civil suits the value of which has been shown against each name…:-

1. Mr. Dechan, Deputy Commissioner Leh …… Up to Rs. 3,000/-
2. Mr. Jagan Nath Sumbli, Tehsildar Leh………Up to Rs. 1,000/-
3. Mr. Mohd. Shafi., Tehsildar Kargil ………Up to Rs. 1,000/- …"

Thus, it becomes quite apparent that the various functionaries of the district administration were adequately clothed with regulatory and supervisory powers; but the delegations and responsibilities in respect of the developmental activities – which in fact were the crying need of the entire region – were nowhere to be seen or noticed in the district hierarchy. It was simply missing; and this is what was sorely felt wanting in the area. Another heavy dose of, such controlling mechanisms, was administered vide notification dated 8th November 1956 (this was published in the J&K Gazette on 22nd November 1956). This order stipulated, "…no person shall enter into any place in the Frontier District of Ladakh from any place in the State outside that District nor shall any person for the time being in the Frontier District of Ladakh proceed to a destination outside the said District except under the authority of a written permit granted by…." The competent authority, under this order, was IGP Kashmir and SP Leh for residents of the State; whereas other persons and foreigners were to be given such permits by the Government of India or their authorized officers. Thus, an effective permit system was introduced for entry and exit to and from Ladakh. This applied also to the Government employees posted in the region. This 'permit' order remained in operation till the entire Ladakh was opened for tourism in July 1974 – after a gap of eighteen years. The feelings of the local population can well be imagined that the people who were keenly looking forward to an era of progress and enlightenment were instead faced with harsher regulatory restrictions. Such measures gave rise to general discontentment and unhappiness amongst the locals and demand grew ever louder for posting of outsider officers who were better acquainted with the contours of developmental activities. This made the State Government to ask the Centre identifying such people and lending their services for Ladakh area. Thus was paved the way for some of the notable Indian Frontier Administrative Service (IFAS) officers to work in Ladakh. The first one was K.A.A. Raja, who was posted as Development Commissioner, Ladakh; with headquarters at Leh. A write up about him mentions, "...He had served in the Indian Army as a Lt. Col...keeping in view his excellent services in Army, he was soon after taken into Indian Frontier Administrative Service and posted to the NEFA region. When the said officer did considerable work for the development of that area, he was requisitioned by the J&K State Government and called for posting in Ladakh region to work as Development Commissioner for the development of Leh and its surroundings and far off remote areas like Nubra, Changthang and similar backward tracts. He served in Ladakh in 1959 and 1960. In Nubra and Nyoma he had started construction of an airport each at village Thoise and Chushul respectively. To complete these two major works and for the construction of roads, to these areas and other allied works, Shri Raja requisitioned for the posting of two other IFAS officers at the rank of Assistant Commissioner, who were Shri K.D. Menon and Shri Barua. These two officers had earlier served under Raja in NEFA. These officers worked there for some years performing good job for the development of these areas... They are still fondly remembered by the people of Ladakh for the services rendered, good relations with the defence personnel and excellent behavior with the locals..."[17]

Talking about these times, the late fifties and early sixties, a highly respected local recalls, "The Ladakh administration was reorganized with the posting of one Assistant Commissioner at Nyoma and one Assistant Commissioner at Nubra... Col. Raja was strict disciplinarian and had a very high sense of justice. He was particularly kind to the ordinary citizens. Once Sonam Wangyal (he had established himself as a local leader by then) slapped another person, who went and complained to Col. Raja. After inquiring into the incident and finding that the complaint was based on facts, Raja insisted that Sonam Wangyal offers public apology to

17 Unfortunately, author of this note is not known. Another article about the IFAS makes this candid statement, "The fact remains that these officers who decided to sacrifice their careers to join the IFAS were all remarkable personalities and still today, even though the cadre does not exist anymore, they should be role models for young IAS / IPS officers.

the victim failing which he threatened to shoot the perpetrator of crime. Since Raja used to carry his revolver all the times on his person, his orders were carried out immediately and public apology was tendered... The Government of India also deputed another very good officer named Sir Datar Singh[18], who used to monitor the developmental works of Ladakh from the Home Ministry in New Delhi. Datar Singh would periodically visit Ladakh and because of his active interest and dynamism, the developments in the region picked up. He was particularly helpful in providing funds and material which enabled timely construction of road link to Kargil and from there to the Valley. Most of the officers, particularly senior functionaries, were then dedicated and honest men who in spite of lack of resources tried their best for this region..."[19]

It is a fact that forceful exertions of a few officers did result in visible acceleration of developmental activities in the region. This was certainly to the delight of the local populace and opinion leaders. In Ladakh this productive period came to be known as the 'NEFA type of administration' – as the experiment was first tried in NEFA, the eastern most part of the country. But, it started in Ladakh region quite late, in 1959, and did not last even five years. This dispensation was abandoned during the regime of G.M. Sadiq. Could be that the entire scheme of IFAS was one of the favorite ideas of Pandit Nehru and after his demise in May 1964, the administrative echelons not well disposed of towards the IFAS got an upper hand and this whole group got amalgamated with the IAS. But, it did fire the imagination of Ladakhis who collectively drew the conclusion that progress could be achieved by a few development oriented and dynamic officers at the top. Not that no forward movement was made in the area during the fifties; but the pace of such activities was slow and much below the local expectations. As compared to the almost complete neglect during the Sheikh Abdullah government; this belt did receive some attention in the regime of Bakshi. During the second Five Year Plan – 1956-61, expenditure to the tune of 86.65 lakhs was made in Ladakh out of the 'Plan' sector. This figure got increased to 147.36 lakhs in the third Plan which corresponded with 1961-66 period. The State Government outlined sixteen different development schemes which were taken in hand during this span

18 He was an ICS officer, and then posted as a Deputy Secretary in the Union Home Ministry. Simultaneously, he also functioned as an Advisor for Development Affairs to Bakshi Gh. Mohd., the Prime Minister of J&K.

19 Rigzin Namgyal Kalon, *Op. Cit.*,

of time; most important being the road connection between Kargil and Leh. These small projects, though appreciable in themselves, fell much short of the local expectations of this vast and backward region. No major agricultural, industrial or power generation project was taken in hand in the whole district, during the ten years of nearly complete dominance of Bakshi's authority. The people in Ladakh, were hence unhappy, more so towards the end of his tenure. Things also did not improve much during the next regime of Sadiq; even though he upgraded the status of Kushok Bakula to that of a Minister of State.

The period of fifties can thus be categorized as a time of general disappointment and despondence for the entire Ladakh region. This was notwithstanding some efforts made by Dr. Karan Singh as the then Sadar-i-Riyasat, or Head of the J&K State, to get Leh linked by road with Manali; a step which would have been widely welcomed by the people of both these regions. This endeavor has been described by a scholar as, "In 1954, Yuvraj Karan Singh made a strong plea for constructing the Leh-Manali road via the Rohtang pass so as to link it with the mainland. He pleaded that Ladakh had been part of the Jammu and Kashmir State for more than a century and during the past seven years it had been part of India. The people there had a great affection for India and were loyal to it but in view of the developments in Tibet, it was important that these ties were strengthened. 'Until now the authorities in Tibet have not shown too much interest in Ladakh, but there is no guarantee that this attitude will continue indefinitely, and after consolidation in Tibet it will be too optimistic to believe that Ladakh will escape an undue share of attention. Our information, meager as it is, shows that the Chinese are fast completing the road linking Lhasa with Peking thousands of miles away, and are also engaged in constructing a network of roads within Tibet.' The Prime Minister was attracted to the proposal but expressed constraints in taking it up though he promised to look into the matter further. Soon after this exchange of letters, the survey of the Leh-Manali road was taken up in right earnest but as later events proved; it was too late to be of any help during the Indo- Sino conflict."[20] Thus, even this attempt did not produce any positive results or a bright spot for the area. Seen from any angle, it was a dark and bleak scenario.

20 Harbans Singh, *Karan Singh – J&K 1949-1967*, Brahaspati Publication, New Delhi, 2018, p. 243.

An account of what it was like living and maturing in Ladakh during this difficult, and almost gloomy, period follows. The next few pages, written specifically for this book, give a graphic account of a growing child in a village – Nimoo – near Leh; in the 1950s. The narrative encompasses general conditions of the area; his trips to and from Leh on foot or Pony for acquiring education in the High School there. Also, how in those days it took weeks for the matriculation result to be known to the student and couple of weeks more waiting for the weather to become favourable so that he could undertake an air journey from Leh to Srinagar – the only alternative then was to traverse this distance on foot – to pursue College studies. No wonder only the brilliant and very determined students could make it. The author of this piece, Shri Chewang Phunsog, is the first Ladakhi to join the prestigious Indian Administrative Service. This he did in 1972, after a stint of teaching assignment in the Regional Engineering College, Srinagar. He was allotted to the J&K cadre; where he served illustriously and with distinction for over next three decades; rising to become Chief Secretary of the state. He recollects,"...I belonged to the generation of Ladakhis who received a college education in different subjects and came to occupy some of the key positions in the State administration at different levels. By the time children of my age were in the secondary school, a sizeable number of the government jobs in the district of Ladakh had come to be occupied by college-educated locals. They were a source of inspiration to my contemporaries for going in for higher education rather than settling in life with jobs then readily available for local people who had passed out from the elementary schools. In the isolated economy of Ladakh, based entirely on subsistence farming, education of children was a luxury. Only the few relatively prosperous families could afford to send all the children to school even though, by the middle of the 20th century, a village of average size did invariably have a primary school inside it and a middle school within ten kilometres of distance. Children, both male and female, were constrained early in their childhood by starting with baby sitting of younger siblings and other joint-family younger relatives. In a situation where children of all age groups were forced by circumstances to contribute to family chores without exception, formal education was looked upon as something peripheral or something of a luxury, with the result that the educational standards in the region had remained abysmally low until recently. I was born in October, 1947 in Nimoo village, one of the medium-sized and relatively progressive villages of Ladakh then comprising 60 land-owning major families subject to various socio-economic obligations (prescribed by the village council) and half that number of splinter families free from these obligations. Situated on the ancient highway from Leh, the headquarters of Ladakh district, to Srinagar, the summer capital of J&K State, it constituted the first 'prao' (a day's halt) from Leh to Srinagar being only 30 kilometres for travellers to halt for the night. For providing shelter to government officials travelling on this route, a decent dak bungalow with full board and lodging facilities was available before it was made a part of the government school complex of the village after a motorable road linked Nimoo village to Leh town in 1958.

"During my childhood, agricultural and pastoral activities constituted 90% of Ladakhi economy. Despite single-crop subsistence farming in an extremely harsh agro-climate, Ladakh enjoyed a self-reliant economy thanks to the prevailing practice of minimization of wastes through total recycling. No one suffered from hunger or lack of shelter even though life was one of extreme frugality and parsimony. After the summer drudgery, Ladakhis would have an abundance of spare time in winter to enjoy social life. Despite the unending household chores and pastoral and craft activities, they enjoyed plenty of leisure in winter months which rejuvenated their physical strength for going again through the following summer's drudgery. Farming and major social obligations relating to events like a death or a birth in the family were carried out through cooperatives of a dozen or so families by pooling means of production and human capital. This system not only lent the economy immense efficiency in utilizing scarce resources but also provided enormous emotional and social security. Everyone in Ladakh of those days wore white or maroon-dyed woollen cloaks with a sash, tall sheepskin-lined hats and tie-dye topped shoes, made of Yak or Dzo down with curled up toe fronts and cow-hide soles - all made at home. Women also wore a goatskin back cover which served the dual purpose of protection from cold and abrasion from heavy backloads carried every day in wicker baskets as daily household chore. All these were produced within the family. To be self-reliant in production of consumer durables, there was a fine system of bartering services. Those who had none or one or two of the skills paid for consumer durables through their unskilled labour or surplus food grains.

"In Ladakh of those days, there was no industry worth the name producing consumer durables or construction materials. Few families were self-sufficient in crafts and skills such as carpentry, spinning, weaving, tailoring, sewing, shoe and cap making, healthcare, masonry, pottery etc. although many households had some of these skills available within the family. As mentioned earlier, families lacking skills in any of these areas were required to barter available skills for skills not available in the family. In my family, between great grandfather, grandfather, father and woman members, all skills were available except, cap-making, medical care and pottery. These three unavailable skills had to be either bartered for or purchased outright. My family had originally decided to train me as an Amchi, the practitioner of the Tibetan system of medicine., but on the insistence of one of the two primary school teachers in the village who was a cousin of my father's, the family had abandoned the idea and decided to carry me through modern education. After I was admitted to the village primary school, therefore, the family did not feel the necessity of imparting to me any local skill or craft; I was allowed to prosecute studies without any diversion except ordinary household chores required of me under work pressure in the family.

"In whole of Ladakh, summer months were then reserved for agricultural and pastoral activities to the total exclusion of festivities and major social and religious obligations. Only death-related social obligations would be observed as being inevitable. Winter was the season for festivities and story-telling by the elders. Losar, the Tibetan New Year, was celebrated every year in the eleventh month of the calendar ever since one of the kings of Ladakh decided to advance New Year celebrations by two months to go to war with the neighbouring Baltistan, fearing that many of the soldiers and officers might not return from war. In my village, the fourteen day celebration of Losar commenced with observance of the birth day of Je Tsonkhapa, the Tibetan Buddhist reformer, on the 25th day of the tenth month of Tibetan lunar calendar and end with the destruction of the effigies of evil on the ninth of the following month. Losar was an event looked forward to by one and all, particularly children who would invariably receive a set or two of new clothes and get the best of culinary stuffs to eat every day for the duration of the festivity. In Nimoo village, the celebrations with music and dance would last for nine consecutive days. Every family would have slaughtered three or four sheep or goats and some a yak or a bull to see them through the Losar days and the following winter months. There were not many Buddhists who would slaughter animals themselves. Therefore, many families would hire Muslims to do the job for them, if any, in the village. In my family, our own servant was one of the two Buddhists in Nimoo village who would kill animals for a consideration. The consideration almost always used to be in kind which could be a kilogram of the choicest meat plus the heart or some other eatable organ of the slaughtered animal. Since elderly Buddhists normally did not associate themselves with the slaughtering process, although they did not mind eating and relishing meat, one of my annual chores used to be assisting our servant in slaughtering three or four sheep or goats every year. My job was to keep the head of the animal pressed to the ground by its horns, or beard (in case of a billy-goat), so that he could without effort slash the throat. I could not bear to hear the bleating of the animal or see its body and limbs twitch, so I used to keep my ears plugged and eyes shut until the cry and spasms of the animal came to a complete halt. All this happened mechanically without effort after the first time or second time clumsiness.

"The proper Losar would start with the villagers witnessing a horse/pony race, not a competition but a show, within view of the cairn symbolizing the protector deity of Nimoo village, 'Chomarde', including target-shooting by the horse riders with stones, on the 1st of the eleventh month followed by nine days of folk dances at the traditional venue, Ghozhing. I would invariably be one of the riders on one of our two ponies, 'Kachung' (named after the white spot on its forehead). As a part of the festival, one person each from two families by turn was made 'Lama Dzugi' wearing loose cloaks and turbans in the Kashmiri style. The tradition of playing Lama Dzugi had remained from the ancient times when Jogis or Yogis (Hindu wandering mendicants) from northern India, particularly from Kashmir, came to Ladakh every year for treating Ladakhis to pantomimic expressions, yoga-asanas and rhymic poetry or rhapsody, receiving in return wool and other gifts from Ladakhi families. Lama Dzugis were treated to sumptuous dinners and lunches by village households by turn, during the nine day Losar celebrations, at the end of which they were anointed with a paste of barley farina (in the Hindu fashion) on their forehead and a huge garland of unspun wool on their head which they carried to their families back home. At the end of the feast in each family, the two Dzugis symbolically exorcised evil spirits from the family by taking out their effigy to be discarded at a cross-road for dying. In the evening, the Lama Dzugis would join the village folks at the dancing venue to participate in folk dances and preside over the evening's festivities. Every evening, there would be folk dances for several hours invariably going on till midnight. Children would learn dancing by bringing up the rear of the dancing queues in which the dancers would be arranged. On the last day of Losar, the two Lama Dzugis would take a massive effigy each, made of barley farina, of likely misfortune befalling the village in the following year, away from the venue of celebration and destroy and consign it to flames at the outskirts of the village. Then they proceeded to the village stream to cleanse themselves by having three dips in a pool of icy cold water of the stream, after breaking the ice on the surface, and running absolutely naked for about hundred meters after every dip to cleanse themselves of any defilement. Then they were wiped dry and wrapped in the warmest of fur cloaks in front of a bonfire and treated to a couple of stiff pegs of arrack spirit. Interestingly, there never has been any instance of a Lama Dzugi catching pneumonia or even flu thanks to the extra care that went into reviving their body temperature promptly after their three ice-cold-water dips and hundred-meter naked sprints.

"The beginning of the twentieth century had marked the advent of modern education in Ladakh. The first primary school for modern education was opened in Ladakh region by the Moravian Mission in Leh in 1889 CE. This was followed by the first primary school opened by the State government in the town in 1893. The first middle school, the first high school and the first higher secondary school in Leh and Kargil were opened, respectively, in 1925, 1945 and 1970. Then it took another two and a half decades to open a college each in Leh and Kargil. Consequent to the opening of a large number of elementary schools and two high schools, a generation of youths fluent in Hindustani languages (Urdu and later Hindi as well) and reasonably proficient in English language had provided the initial crop of modern-educated and formally trained teachers, doctors, engineers, white-collared workers and other technical hands to man the positions available in the region of Ladakh, in the second half of the 20th century. Such positions were earlier almost entirely manned by persons deputed from the Kashmir valley.

"In the ordinary course, a village in Ladakh would then be totally oblivious of national and state events and politics. Local politics was limited to voting for a candidate in the State Assembly elections after every five years. However, one major event in the State politics, I recall, had become a subject of household discussions even in a remote region like Ladakh. It was the dismissal of the State's first Prime Minister, Sheikh Mohammad Abdullah, in August, 1953. This event was marked by the Chinese Cultural Revolution style replacement of a slogan, painted on the façade of the school building in Urdu, which said, 'Long live Sher-i-Kashmir' with the slogan which said, 'Long live Khalid-e-Kashmir'. Sher-i-Kashmir was the epithet of Sheikh Mohammad Abdullah, the dismissed Prime Minister and Khalid-e-Kashmir that of Bakshi Ghulam Mohammad, the succeeding Prime Minister. At that time, I did not understand the import of this change. But, when I started reading the history of Kashmir later in life, I realized how vicissitudes of key political figures impacted common man's sycophantic sense even in an area as remote as Nimoo village in Ladakh and as insignificant an institution as a primary school of the village. Barring this, the villagers, and the students of the village school being no exception, seemed during those days blissfully oblivious of political and other happenings outside the village; not to speak of outside the Ladakh region. Ladakhi political landscape was then dominated by one leader of State stature, Kushok Bakula, the head Lama of Spituk Monastery. He was a member of the J&K National Conference led by Sheikh Mohammad Abdullah and had represented Ladakh constituency in the State Constituent Assembly. In social and political matters, few in Ladakh of those days would join issues with him without being scoffed at by his ardent followers. Politically, there was an aura of infallibility about him, at least during those days.

"After passing out from the village primary school, I was sent to Leh, the headquarters of Ladakh District, for secondary education. High School, Leh was one of the only two high schools in whole of Ladakh region. The other was in Kargil; the only other town in Ladakh about 220 kilometres from Leh towards Kashmir. I was sent off by my family again with the usual rituals involved in someone going on an important journey or expedition. Since there was no motor transport in the region in the 1950s, I and my father had to traverse the distance of 30 km on horseback. My family owned two horses, or rather ponies. As in the case of every important event in a Ladakhi family's life; this journey was also to be performed on an auspicious day ascertained from the Lotho, the year's astrological forecasts. The auspicious day fell on a day neither of the horses was available. Therefore, I was made to commence the journey symbolically on that day by taking seven steps from our gate in the direction of the destination as a part, so to say, of the Ladakhi 'rites de passage'. This journey could then be deemed to have commenced on that day, to be completed on the day a horse became available. Thus, the actual journey was performed on a day one of the two horses became available. On the day of journey, my first to Leh town, I was experiencing a mixed feeling of apprehension and excitement and anxiously looked forward to getting to this unfamiliar place; a wonderland for a village boy. Going to Leh for the first time, I was draped in a newly stitched 'goncha' robe made of homespun sheep wool yarn, dyed deep maroon, with collar and exposed front edges piped with silver lace; a new home-made yak wool pair of shoes with thikma (tie-dyed) top and cattle-hide sole, a first time western style haircut and a new sheepskin-lined Ladakhi cylindrical cap. On the day of journey, the two of us stayed overnight with a relative's family in Leh. One of my six aunts was married in that family.

"The next day, I was presented to the wardens of the boarding house of High School Leh as my family had planned to put me up in the high school boarding house. There were two wardens in the hostel both of whom were Kashmiri Pandits named Pran Nath and Mohan Lal. On seeing me, one of them, the lanky but charismatic Pran Nath, shouted in a jovial mood at no one in particular, 'Array, this fellow looks like the image of Thakar Bhagwan in the Barbarshah temple in Srinagar!' Since then, I was nick-named 'Bhagwan' and most students and many of my teachers called me, much to my discomfiture, by that name. Only close friends and strangers refrained from addressing me by it sensing that I disliked it. In the hostel, we lived in dormitories, half a dozen to a dorm. Food was served from the kitchen of a common mess. The inmates were required to fetch their meals from the kitchen themselves on an aluminium plate and eat in their rooms as there was no common dining hall. When the food was ready, the cook's helper would blow a whistle at which the mostly hungry boarders would rush to form a queue outside the kitchen. Since it was first-come-first-served, the hostel inmates would zoom to the kitchen to occupy the first few places in the queue and pre-empt the best parts of the steaming dishes. For the evening meal of my first day in the hostel, I was rushing to the kitchen alone with an empty aluminium plate in my hand when I ran into the only bully of the hostel who was apparently awaiting my emergence from our dorm. He was leaning against a pillar of the veranda in the fashion a real bully does. He had a small folding knife, like a Swiss Army Knife, in his hand. Pressing the sharp end of the knife into my belly, taking care to see that the force was not strong enough for penetration, he addressed me in Urdu, 'huzoor dekha!' meaning something like 'Great man, do you see!' Although the gentle poking of knife into my belly was only to scare me and not meant to hurt, I nearly fainted imagining the glinting knife blade sinking deep into my belly. Grinning at my condition and warning me by saying, 'don't forget this', the bully let me pass to join the queue. I was told later by one of my roommates, already in the queue, that I looked scared out of my wits. The bully also happened to be a student of the sixth standard and belonged to the same section. In course of time, the bully and I became good friends for four years of our schooling together. He dropped out after four years of high school to look after his family business.

"In the High School, I was one of about two dozen students of the sixth standard section-A. As per the State's policy, students were introduced to the English language for the first time in sixth standard starting with learning of the alphabet followed by word and sentence formation. There was a choice between the State's official language, Urdu and the national official language, Hindi. Both English and Hindi or Urdu were compulsory up to the tenth standard. There was also a choice between Bodhi in Tibetan script and Arabic. Buddhist students invariably chose Bodhi in which Ladakhi language is written. Muslims, except for a few, chose Arabic. Although I, like everyone else, had studied Urdu in the primary school in Nimoo, which was compulsory there, I chose Hindi for the secondary schooling and was introduced to the Devanagari script for the first time in the sixth standard. As a spoken language and idiomatically, Hindi and Urdu are the same except that the former has many Sanskrit words and the latter abounds in Persian words. The medium of instructions for subjects other than languages was Urdu throughout high schooling except science (physics and chemistry) subject which was taught in English medium during the last two years of high schooling.

"During the first two years of high school, I fell in bad company. I started smoking cigarette and playing cards sometimes with my ration and pocket money as petty stakes. The card games we generally played with petty stakes were Sweep/Seep, Trump or Rummy. I also felt home sick and frequently skipped classes, sometimes for days on end, to go home in Nimoo. The result was that in the seventh standard, my name was struck off from the school register for unauthorized absence for more than fifteen days at a stretch. It took many pleadings and recommendation of the local Member of Legislative Assembly to have me readmitted to the class without losing a year. All in all, during the first two years of secondary schooling, I was non-serious even from the Ladakhi standard of those days. I barely managed to scrape through the annual exams of sixth and seventh standards. Students like me would do some serious studies a fortnight before the exams and manage to pass them with marks close to the minimum for pass which was 33%. Come eighth standard; which had its final examination conducted by the J&K State Board of School Education, I, even to my own surprise, saw a transformation in my attitude towards studies. I passed the eighth exams with a second division and was placed third in my class of about three dozen. This was a shot in the arm and since then there was no looking back. In the ninth and tenth standards, I found myself competing with four others for the top three positions in the class. I was particularly good at English language and mathematics.

"As I mentioned earlier, those days there was no public motor transport in Ladakh even though some of the villages including Nimoo, in the areas surrounding Leh and Kargil towns, were connected with motor able roads. In the whole of Ladakh District, with a geographical area of about 59,000 sq. kms, there were only half a dozen Willys Jeeps in the district garages belonging to government departments including one used exclusively by the Deputy Commissioner, the head of the district administration. There were also a few Jeeps and Jongas (6-cylinder jeep-like vehicle of Japanese make) belonging to the Indian Army, the Indo-Tibetan Border Force (ITBF of the Intelligence Bureau) and the Indo-Tibetan Border Police (ITBP) that plied on the un-tarred interior roads. Students of High School Leh from Nimoo and other nearby villages had to foot the distance between Leh and their villages whenever they went home on weekends or holidays. Only on some of such trips they would be able to ride horses if their families owned one or hitch-hike in one of the departmental vehicles if the driver felt inclined to give a lift. Ration was transported mostly on donkey back. The journey on foot of 30 kms between Leh and Nimoo would take something between 6 and 7 hours. For youngsters, these were quite tiring and would sometimes take more than seven hours. On some occasions, when we started our on-foot journeys late in the day, we were constrained to halt somewhere in the way for the night in a make-shift shelter. On such trips we often went without food for the night.

"The plateau of Ladakh Kongka falls between Leh and Nimoo village. On the near end of the plateau about four kilometres from the village, there was a human figure-like impression in a huge boulder believed to be that of Lama Guru, the revered figure in a legend that was passed down from generation to generation in Nimoo and villages around. The legend went like this. Lama Guru, on his way from Ladakh to Tibet, was once confronted by a demon at Changla pass, east of Leh en route to Tibet. Lama Guru backed away from this formidable adversary by retracing his journey towards Nimoo. When he was about to enter the two-kilometre gorge that served as eastern gateway to the village, the demon hurled at him a huge boulder, the size of a yak, from behind, but it missed his target. Sensing that his adversary was closing in on him, the Guru hid himself in a huge boulder which miraculously offered a life-size cavity on its far side. The demon moved forward towards Nimoo without noticing the Guru's hide-out. Then, Lama Guru followed him from behind surreptitiously, overpowered the latter in the gorge, numbed his senses, shore off his matted hair (ralpa) and hurled it in the air (which formed the present Ralpa hill east of Nimoo) and secured the demon's unconscious body to the bottom of Indus with nine chains so as to keep the people of Ladakh out of harm's way. It was also believed that on the site of this encounter, water sprang out to form the present Stemdel Chhumik (auspicious spring). During my childhood, we would be told by the village elders that the demon was still alive secured to the bed of Indus and sometimes opened his mouth so that water flowed through his gullet making a roaring sound which we sometimes heard from the river during nights. In our childhood, we would, on our way on foot from Nimoo to Leh or vice versa, invariably lie prostrate with our heads right under the Guru's impression to seek his blessings and more often than not doze off to sound sleep to be woken up by someone travelling on the same route. Nobody knew for sure who Lama Guru really was, but I used to conjecture that Lama Guru was Guru Padma Sambhava, the Buddhist Tantric genius, who was instrumental in firmly establishing Vajrayana Buddhism in Tibet which later spread to Ladakh. Some people, however, believed that 'Lama Sguru' was the name of the stone impression and not 'Lama Guru'. Sguru in Ladakhi means 'bent' and referred to the crookedness of the impression of human figure in the boulder. Whatever the factual position, in the early 1980s, the holy stone impression of Lama Guru was claimed by the Sikhs as being connected to Guru Nanak Dev, the founder of Sikhism, who they thought used Ladakh as route for his visit to Tibet. Relating Guru Nanak to Lama

Guru, the Sikhs constructed a huge Gurudwara enshrining the Lama Guru, along with the usual free langar (kitchen) in the Sikh tradition, under the name and style 'Gurudwara Patthar Sahib'. For this faith transformation, they enlisted support of the then tallest Ladakhi political and spiritual figure, Kushok Bakula Rinpoche. Rinpoche's support to the Sikhs' claim calmed the feeble protests of local people against passing of this unique stone formation from the local Buddhist community; who had held this unique stone in reverence for centuries, on to the Sikh community which chanced upon the legend only in the year 1980. The site with the stone has by now become one of the holiest sites for the followers of Sikhism and a pilgrimage centre for Sikhs from far and wide. Alongside, the legend around the stone impression has grown manifold; now as a part of Sikhism.

"Travellers riding animals would generally bypass Lama Guru. On one of my journeys from Nimoo to Leh, when I was in my seventh standard and 12 years of age, I was travelling on the back of one of our two horses. I was all alone on this journey. Now and then, I came across a traveller or two going in the opposite direction. At a place called Gufuks on the highway about twelve kilometres short of Leh, where the road ran for a kilometre parallel to Indus River about 20 meters north of it, I ran into a pack of wolves that was returning to the mountain apparently after drinking water from the river. The wolves, numbering about a dozen (I did not have the sense of ascertaining it), appearing from behind a 'Mani wall' lining the right side of the track, remained motionless with cocked ears at the sight of a potential prey carrying a diminutive human figure on its back. The horse instinctively backed off by a few steps and let out a few loud snorts that typically ensued from a combination of fear and determination to face a challenge squarely. I had heard from elders that wolves are generally scared of the biped humans, but they cannot see a human being on the back of a horse. I had also heard people say that taller the human being greater is the fear that he inspires among wolves. So, instinct drove me to jump off the horse to register human entry on the scene. Then I quickly raised the whip handle as high as I possibly could, with the monkey cap I was wearing atop it, to let me appear taller than I actually was. Then, an instinct told me to blow a whistle. So, with the pincer of the thumb and fore finger of my free hand pressed against my upturned tongue, which I had learnt not very long ago from my elder sister, I let out as long and shrill a whistle as I possibly could under the obtaining circumstances. The dreaded predatory canines, bête noire of the pastoral folks of Ladakh, were so overtaken by terror, struck by the shrillness of my whistle and tallness of my figure, that they galloped towards the mountain for their dear life, leaving in their trail a cloud of dust and what seemed to me to be a steaming fresh wolf-shit. I might have been equally terrorized that I discovered a wet pair of trousers on me when I regained control of my situation.

It was late afternoon and there were no sign of human beings in any direction. I was so shaken as to have no nerve to continue the rest of my journey to Leh, the destination, still a dozen kilometers ahead. Therefore, I chose to ride off at right angle to the highway to nearby Phey village, about a kilometer and a half downstream of Indus from the incident spot. The horse, already charged with pumped up adrenaline, consequent to his encounter with predators, took me to the village in record time. My eldest sister was married to a family in that village. Later in the evening, the episode of the day was narrated by me to the joint family of my sister's in-laws to their huge amusement and praise from the elders of what they called my 'courage and presence of mind'. Only two grown up children were noticed giggling out of disbelief. Rest of the family was read by me as entirely convinced and impressed. I thought it was best to limit the episode to bravery; the wet trousers part was excluded from my narrative. Little did I realize that someday I would be faithfully recording this incident in the manner I have done here.

"On another of my journeys from Nimoo to Leh after the summer vacation of fifteen days, I was accompanied by my grandfather. We had a donkey carrying my ration for the remaining months of the academic year. I had a pair of brand new all-leather shoes on - the second pair ever of leather shoes in my life until then. The first pair was bought by my father in Srinagar, Kashmir when he was on his way to Tibet via Srinagar and Kalimpong in West Bengal. He had sent these with a monk returning from Srinagar to Ladakh by air. That was three years ago. This second pair was purchased in Leh for 25 rupees, then a royal sum. Leather shoes in Ladakh of those days were a luxury. Every one, male or female, put on local, home-made shoes of yak wool top and cattle-hide sole. Since my leather shoes were brand new, I was impelled to walking in the sandy tracks most of the time barefoot to save the shoes from what I thought abnormal wear and tear. Therefore, the pair was tagged to a bag carrying barley farina on the back of the donkey. When we reached Leh, we found that one of the pair was missing – it had fallen off somewhere on the way. I had to go without shoes for the next two days till an old pair of yak wool shoes were fetched from home in Nimoo. The left-over single shoe was kept in safe custody in the hope that someday someone, who might have found the lost one, would return it. Two years later, we did trace the lost shoe to a family in Phey village who had also preserved it in the hope of finding the other of the pair. By then I had outgrown the shoes and these were given to my younger brother. The leather shoes bought a year later in replacement for the lost pair of leather shoes were a pair in the style of the tough army ammunition boots, two sizes too big for me. I put on these only in the following three winters with thick woollen socks.

"I passed the 8th standard annual exams in 1960 in the second division. It was looked upon as a 'very good' performance from the standards of those days in Ladakh. None of my classmates had managed to secure a first division. The examination was conducted by the State Board of Secondary Education for the first time in Leh that year. The examiner was airlifted to Leh from Srinagar. Under a special dispensation for Ladakh, in view of the difficulty experienced by the State government in deputing teachers and other government employees to Ladakh from other parts of the State, middle (8th standard) pass candidates were eligible to be appointed as primary school teachers, clerks and other low ranking officials in government departments, subject to the prescribed minimum age. The region then had scarcity of even middle pass candidates of the eligible age who were also willing to be appointed to government jobs. Cases of minor children passing eighth standard faking their birth certificates to land government jobs were not uncommon. Therefore, when I passed the eighth standard at the age of thirteen, there was a debate in the family as to whether I should continue my studies further or become a school teacher and augment the family cash income on a regular basis. There were strong arguments both for and against. The main argument of the family for discontinuing further studies was the gross shortage of working hands in the family. My being the eldest son was an added argument in favour of discontinuing my studies to be groomed for the role of the family mainstay. My own argument for discontinuing further studies was to have the privilege of being the first salaried hand in the family with a secured pensionable government job. Argument in favour of my continuing studies beyond 8th standard was based on my demonstrated aptitude and potential for higher studies, particularly in mathematics and science which could lead me ultimately to the job of an engineer or doctor, the two jobs in the government most coveted in the State then. Finally, it was decided that I should continue with my schooling in the expectation that someday the decision would be vindicated by a high-salaried, dignified government job such as that of a doctor, an engineer or a college teacher. Since then, I felt myself under obligation to receive a meaningful education suiting my potential and disposition. By the time I passed out of the high school; my folk were convinced that I was destined to have a university degree involving science. By then, physics was my favourite subject.

"Those days, analytical learning was almost entirely unknown in the schooling system of the entire State not to speak of a place like Ladakh. The examination system encouraged rote learning even in the language subjects. At the end of ten years of schooling, I, like most Ladakhi students, was conscious of the fact that we had learnt none of the four languages we were taught in school to a reasonable degree of proficiency. I had studied Bodhi for eight years, Urdu, Hindi and English for five years each. At the end of my high school, I had not succeeded in having sound grounding in any of these languages. Language is the most important part of one's elementary school curriculum; it being the vehicle on which people could ride to various destinations of life. The syntactic, semantic and idiomatic nuances of a language can be best acquired in one's formative years or one fails to acquire the requisite proficiency and spontaneity. Therefore, rote learning in language subjects is particularly harmful. One may require committing to memory poems to be recited or phrases to be quoted, but one should not have been required to rote-learn what is required to be understood for setting a framework for sophisticated thinking. The schooling system in the country in general and an isolated region like Ladakh in particular seems even now to have preparation of individuals for a better livelihood in life as the sole objective. Preparing an individual for a good livelihood is no doubt an important objective of school education, but even a more significant objective than that is the all-round development of mind and personality. School education is not merely about coaching children for passing exams or getting degrees; it is about shaping human character so that the schools are enabled to send complete products out into society not only to negotiate the rough-and-tumble of life but also to make contributions to advancement of society. School education has been rightly likened by someone to chiseling rocks into diamonds. The famous Irish poet William Butler Yeats has aptly said that 'education is not the filling of a pail; it is the lighting of a fire'. Acquiring a reasonably good proficiency in the medium of instructions in one's school education is, therefore, crucial for fully harnessing one's potential in life. Sophisticated thinking needs sophisticated vocabulary; but schools in our time lacked the facility and atmosphere to equip students with this crucial wherewithal. In my case, I have all along remained conscious of an inadequacy in my personality in that respect.

"In the Ladakh of my childhood, there was no atmosphere for ensuring systematic teaching and learning in any school. Students were left to fend for themselves. Only at the approach of annual examinations, they began to exercise some self-discipline and open their text books systematically. There was no system of periodical tests in class to keep students on their toes as is in vogue these days. A few students who could afford would take private tuition for a couple of months in the run up to the annual exams. I had appeared in the matriculation examination with a serious preparation of about two months and private tuition for that duration for the main subjects. In private tuition also, the emphasis was on mugging up important questions expected to be asked during the year which, as a matter of routine, excluded the questions asked during the previous two years. My private tutor, the Accounts Officer in the office of Deputy Commissioner Leh, selected two dozen important questions in each subject that could possibly appear in the question paper of the year and asked me to mug up their answers from the text book as best as I could. On an average, half a dozen of these appeared in each question paper. The accent was on just passing the exam as there was no competition whatsoever in elementary education in Ladakh. Getting first or second class marks, not to speak of the first few ranks, was rarely a consideration in preparation for exams. In the last three years of high school, although I was among the top few students in ranking in annual exams in my class, I was only an average student from the State's standards.

"The Matriculation Examinations in Ladakh district (Leh and Kargil Tehsils) were held every year in May. The results were announced within a couple of months subject to exigencies, that is, by the middle of July. In Kashmir, of which Ladakh was a part in matters of academic schedule and time table, the Matriculation exams were held in March so that admission to colleges for the Pre-University Course (PUC) could start sometime in the month of June. In Ladakh, these exams were held two months later in

May due to logistics problem. After writing the matriculation exams held in May, 1962, I had about two months to while away before results. During this waiting period, I decided to go herding livestock in the highland summer pasture known as 'phoo' in Ladakhi, owned by the villagers in common. June was then the month to put out livestock to alpine pasture. Phoos in Ladakh are lush green alpine pastures in stark contrast to the bare earth in the Himalayan rain shadow of most parts of Ladakh. Phoo of Nimoo village, at heights ranging from 12,000 feet to 17,000 feet from sea level, was about 20 kms upstream of the glacial stream feeding the village. The pastures constitute the catchments of the perennial stream of the village which originates from the glacier-fed Nimoo Tso (Lake) at a height of 16,500 feet from sea level. So, I took eight donkeys and four calves to Nimoo phoo for grazing in pastures at about 16,000' from sea level. The donkeys were needed to be taken to Changthang sometime towards the end of July or first half of August every year as pack animals to bring merchandise goods like wool, pashmina and butter. Livestock like yaks, dzos (male hybrid of yak and cow) and horses/ponies needed no herding in phoo as they could collectively fend for themselves against common predators. Two each of our horses and dzos were let free on the mountain slopes along with those of other villagers. Two of our dzomos (female hybrid of yak and cow) and one cow had already calved and were in milk. These, along with their three newly born calves, one pregnant cow and two barren cows, were entrusted to a neighbour's herder to milk and herd along with theirs. These milch cattle were taken every day to the pasture by two families by turn. Taking livestock to alpine pastures served the twin objectives of keeping them from the green cultivated fields in the village and at the same time fattening them on the lush green alpine grasses. In the alpine phoos, during the short summer months, wild succulent plants proliferated like wild fire with the thawing of frozen surfaces. These helped fatten the generally famished livestock of Ladakh beyond recognition within weeks to see them through the next harsh winter when they were required to live on nutrient-deficient crop residues. Animals taken to alpine pastures were brought down to the village in autumn only after harvest to first munch on the stubbles of the harvested fields before they were required to be stall-fed with crop residues and dry alfalfa (of the Lucerne family) fodder.

"As mentioned earlier, there was no college in Ladakh until 1994. For college education, high school graduates were required to go to

Srinagar in Kashmir. I took responsibility of herding our donkeys and calves with the understanding that my younger brother would come to relieve me when my matriculation results were declared and I would be needed to rush to Srinagar for college admission. I had asked my family to keep checking about the matriculation results after about six weeks of my departure to phoo and send my relief in time for me to go for college admission should I pass. It was estimated that I could spend about a month and a half herding livestock in phoo before the matriculation results were declared and I would be required to prepare for a flight to Srinagar for college admission. There were no road transport facilities for Kashmir from Leh part of Ladakh even though Leh was connected to Srinagar by a rough jeepable road by then. Earlier, my family had eventually decided to carry me through college education for a university degree. My father was doing a small trading business in wool, pashmina (cashmere), shahtoosh (antelope down) and sheep and goats (meat on hoof) for cash income, for which he would go all the way to Changthang (Western Tibet) during August-September every year to purchase merchandise goods and some livestock partly in cash and partly by barter and bring these to Leh to sell to local or Kashmiri traders for a profit. The barter items from our side included barley farina, wheat flour and dried apricot from our own farm, and tea, rice and other merchandise goods purchased from Kashmir or Kargil town of Ladakh (located half way to Kashmir). It was estimated that the profit would be enough to see me through college education after setting aside the cash requirement for buying the basic merchandise goods required for the family. Ladakhi students in colleges of Kashmir were entitled without exception to a scholarship of 50 rupees per month for the academic year of nine months without which most Ladakhi families, mine included, could not think of sending their children to college in Kashmir. The entire Ladakh region then did not produce enough matriculates to justify the opening of a degree college in the region. As mentioned earlier, a degree college was opened in Leh only in the year 1994 i.e. thirty two years after we passed out from High School, Leh or Kargil. Earlier, in 1970, the only two high schools in Leh and Kargil had been upgraded to higher secondary level to enable desirous high school graduates to prosecute pre-university education.

"At phoo, I and my three fellow herders would take our charges every morning to the lush green slopes of the mountain from the animal pens attached to our makeshift camp at the foot of the mountain and bring them back safe in the evening. To ward off predators at night, when the herders were asleep, two or three fires would be kept smoldering along the fence of the animal pens throughout the night. As mentioned earlier, large and tough animals like yaks, dzos and horses/ponies did not need herding and were let free for grazing on the mountain slopes day and night. They only needed to be visited occasionally to ensure that they did not stray away to pastures of neighbouring villages. Their close-knit herds could effectively ward off the common predators of Ladakh - wolf (shankoo), wild dog (fara), lynxs (eie) and snow leopard (schhan). Of these, snow leopard is the only predator that can now and then prey on yaks, dzos and ponies; particularly the old and infirm among them. For me personally, a few weeks in the wilderness of phoo was a thrilling as well as energizing experience. Herders of milch cattle lived close by in cave-like stone hutments of dry stone masonry, called pooloos, without a door but with two holes opposite the door at different levels for cross ventilation. The only timber used was two joists to hold heavy stone slabs for roofing. Almost every family of Nimoo had one pooloo in phoo used as dwelling for their milch cattle herders during three months of the summer season. Herders like me not tending milch cattle lived in open, makeshift enclosures both for humans and their animal charges, with a partition to separate humans from animals. These were located about 200 meters away from the cluster of milch cattle herders' pooloos, taking us closer to wilderness. Listening occasionally to the whistling of marmots close by, barley farina as the staple food, burtse shrubs and dried animal dungs as cooking and heating fuel, and lots of milk and milk products supplied free by milch-cattle herding families - tending cows, dzomos and dimos in milk- by turn every morning, it was indeed great fun doing this part of the family chores - perhaps only for a change.

"At night, we slept in beds invariably comprising our ration bags as pillows, donkey back pads as mattresses and two goncha robes doubling as blankets. Then, listening to the occasional howling of wolves and looking at the starry blue sky, we would doze off to deep slumber lasting till the crack of dawn. Due to the rarified atmosphere of alpine Ladakh, the Milky Way in Ladakh appears as if a giant painter has run a stroke of brush, soaked in a diluted white paint, across the blue sky. The animals in our charge would go to sleep as well at night and stir to wakefulness in the morning almost in rhythm with ours. As mentioned before, we would keep a few fires smoldering through the night to keep predators at bay. Each day would be like all the others, with no targets to be achieved and no benchmarks to be respected. The only preoccupation was to take our charges to the highland pastures in the morning and bring them back safe from predators in the evening. I was the only herder who could read and write and knew basics of mathematics. I would read a book or a story during the day and narrate the stories to my fellow herders in the evening and they would listen in rapt attention. This would now and then be supplemented by the hilarious dirty (non-vegetarian) jokes by 'granduncle Sangrup', the oldest among us, to make the days lighter and less monotonous. I don't know about the others, but I found the carefree monotony immensely rejuvenating and enjoyable. Looking at the sky at night in the rarefied atmosphere of Ladakh is a spiritual experience making one realize how insignificant we all are in front of the vastness of deep heavens, representing the infinite universe, and the grandeur and magnificence of the Himalayan mountain massif around us. For me, it was also reminiscent of my early childhood days when it was very common for us during summer to sleep on our flat roof-top, under the sky canopy. Under the guidance of elders, children used to learn counting and rudimentary arithmetic looking at stars and their constellations. Looking at the starry sky at night from the vantage alpine site in Ladakh heightened my wonderment of the universe further. From then, I developed an interest in physics as a means to unravel the mysteries of nature; and took a vow to pursue higher studies, through university, in physics as major.

"While herding livestock on the mountain slopes, I sometimes saw an aero-plane fly to and from Srinagar and Leh which sight almost always pumped adrenalin up my system at the thought of soon being in the beauteous Kashmir for college education. Now and then, I would dream of Kashmir even though I was yet to see the famed Valley. The images were ones I had heard from others who had seen the place. Close to two months herding cattle had elapsed, but there was no sign of the promised reliever for me. I could not imagine having failed in the matriculation exams; I was quite confident that I had done well enough to pass the exams. So I suspected that the results had been inordinately delayed for some reason or my folk had been unduly careless in ascertaining the position as promised. A few days more of delay made me restless. It was already past mid-July. So I decided to go home and ascertain the position myself. Requesting the fellow herders to look after my charge as well, for which my family would do a turn later, I started footing down the distance of 20 kilometers to home in Nimoo village. In the village, the members of my family had no information whatever about the exam results. In fact, they had not made any effort at all to find out the position by going to Leh and kept waiting for some word from Leh. Therefore, I went to Leh to find out the position personally. To my utter astonishment, the results had been declared three weeks back. I had passed with a second division with 53% marks and got the third position in my class of three dozen in the school. Considering all aspects of the prevailing circumstances, such performance could be considered as reasonably good. None of those passed from High School Leh had a first division which required 60% marks. About a third of the three dozen classmates had been declared passed. Of them, five had since left for Srinagar for college admission which had commenced sometime in June and since closed even for matriculates from Ladakh. I was already late for admission by a month and a half. Therefore, I rushed back to Nimoo to collect my baggage and say goodbye to my folk and got back to Leh the next day to take the earliest Indian Airlines flight in the hope that admission would be given as a special case.

"On my departure from the village for flying to Srinagar for college, I was given 600 rupees to cover my travel and all initial expenses. I had handled such a huge amount for the first time. Therefore, the currency notes were secured in a pocket sewed to my underwear. Six hundred rupees was then a royal sum and considered adequate to meet my air travel and other expenses such as college uniform, hostel and tuition fees, bedding, books and stationery and other necessities of college life for a few months. There was another classmate, Sangay Dorjay of Shay village placed in a similar situation as me. The two of us purchased air tickets in the only available air service operated by the Indian Airlines Corporation, for the following week i.e., for 28th July, 1962. It cost me 92 rupees, the largest outgo from my allowance of 600 rupees. Although Leh, as already mentioned, had already been connected with Srinagar with a motorable road by then, there was no public transport or taxi plying between Leh in Ladakh and Srinagar in Kashmir. A bi-weekly air transport was the only means available to get to Srinagar or anywhere outside the region or else one had to foot the distance up to Kargil, 190 kms from Nimoo, and catch a bus from there to Srinagar. A journey from Nimoo or Leh to Kargil even on horseback would take no less than six days. Since a Dakota plane carried about thirty five passengers, a bi-weekly flight between Leh and Srinagar was considered enough for available passengers of those days. The flight scheduled for 28th

July was cancelled due to bad weather en route. Since Dakota flew very low, it needed high visibility for the entire route along the Ladakh Range. The flight was rescheduled for the following day, cancelled again for the same reason. Like this, the flight was cancelled continuously for 21 days due only to inclement weather en-route. Every day, the booked passengers had to travel the 5 km distance between the airfield and Leh town with baggage on their back as there was no public transport even in Leh town. The scheduled flight was operated successfully on the 22nd day from the date of booking and I and my friend reached Srinagar on 18th August, a good two months late for college admission which had since been closed. The compulsory long wait of 21 days for the flight to Srinagar to operate had also made a big hole in my allowance of 600 as every day I and Sangay Dorjay returned to Leh after the flight cancellation, we went straight to Himalaya restaurant in the Leh bazaar for a sumptuous lunch in the hope that the flight would operate the following day. Thus, on August 18, 1962, I set off on a long journey in life, with my youthful spirit taking flight, for the time being, like a kite cut from its string in a lightly breezy sky, unsure of the next lap (getting admission in the college) being successful. I and Sangay were allowed to stay in the Sri Pratap College hostel pending a decision on our request for admission to the college, doubling up with two of our friends who had already got college admission. The following working day, we were taken to the Principal of Sri Pratap College by one of our seniors to explain the reason for our inordinate delay in seeking admission. Somehow, in the heart of hearts, I was sure that I would get admission for a science course which was my sincere desire.

"After listening to our explanation for the inordinate delay in seeking admission and taking into consideration the fact that very few students from Ladakh sought college admission every year (there were only seven from Leh region of Ladakh that year and even less from Kargil region), the authorities of Sri Pratap College in Srinagar decided to admit both me and Sangay Dorjay in the middle of the session as an exception, after we gave word to work hard to catch up with our classmates in the remaining period of the academic session. I opted for non-medical science which included physics, chemistry and mathematics and Sangay Dorjay chose arts with political science as major. Both classes had already covered a third of their syllabi and we had missed the preliminary chapters necessary to pick up the basic concepts - particularly important for math and science subjects. Consequently, I remained totally at sea in these subjects as it was difficult to benefit from the remaining instructions. Three and a quarter months later, the college in Kashmir closed for winter vacation after completing the syllabi. As per the standing time table, the final exams were slated for the following March, immediately after winter vacation of two and a half months. Science students were required to do a minimum of one dozen experiments each in physics and chemistry personally to be eligible to sit for the final exams. I had hardly done half that number in both subjects by the time the college closed for winter vacation. I was nonetheless allowed to sit for the final examination of the pre-university class keeping in view the waiver already granted for my mid-term admission as a special case. In the final exams, I not only managed to pass, but also secured marks high enough to earn me a seat in the engineering college in the following session.

"Such were the difficulties the Ladakhi youth desirous of going through college education had to endure."

In somewhat similar vein, Dr. Phunsog T. Smanla M.B.B.S., M.D.; the first doctor and the first medical specialist from Ladakh region, recalls his younger days in the area as, "I was born in 1938 in the village of Timisgam for which a road runs for few kilometres from Nurla – some distance away from Khaltsi on the Khaltsi-Leh part of the road from Srinagar to Leh. It is an old village and our whole area is called 'Sham Ilaqa'; which in the local language means 'lower land' and includes the entire belt from Nimoo to Dah-Hanu; that is, the whole Indus Valley downwards of Leh. I distinctly remember, as a child in my village, seeing the first aircraft heading for Leh on 24th May 1948. What I saw and perceived, thrilled me no end; a big white bird streaking towards the Leh side on emerging from behind the mountains of Fatu La and Lamayuru. Only the next day, village elders excitedly spoke about the first aircraft having landed in Leh and that we would soon be rid of the dreaded and hated Pakistani armed men who had occupied our area. Of course they talked in hushed voices… Looking back at my childhood, I recollect that our area used to supply dry fruits, Sattu, tea, spices etc. to the Changthang region; and get butter, cheese, wool and Pashmina in return. Salt used to come from the Pangong Lake generally; the better quality of it from the lake's farthest extremities which is now under the Chinese occupation. Salt from Tsokar Lake was considered inferior. Sometimes, 'rock salt' was procured from the Skardu side also…. The animals were very important part of the village life and generally every family owned a number of Donkeys, Yaks and Zos; only well to do households also kept few horses. Having a horse was considered a status symbol. Our whole belt had a good number of horses and donkeys for carrying load. These animals; laden with goods and escorted by village men, would generally leave in the month of May and return by November; to spend the winter months in comparatively more suitable and moderate climate. Also back home the availability of fodder was ensured by the individual household members left behind...Those days the entire trade was based on reciprocity and barter system.

"People were generally not wealthy; but everyone lived happily and with a sense of contentment. There was lot of interdependence and the community - though in a state of 'dignified poverty' - led a peaceful and merry existence. Labour charges were paid in kind, in the village. Generally people would work till late at night, sitting around a bush fire and then warm ash; singing folk songs, chanting and recounting mythological stories. Both rich and poor would benefit from this orderly system; there was hardly any difference and everyone had a place of respect. The children were certainly unaware of the concept of poverty... Food habits were frugal and also simple. Sattu and local black-tea was generally consumed a lot. Yak meat, dried and powdered; mixed with Sattu was considered a delicacy... Every village had an Amchi; the community used to support that family as also provide raw material for preparing the medicines. Amchi, in turn, would examine the patients free of cost and also not charge for the medicines given. Amchi family was generally respected a lot in the village.

"Most houses in the village were large and spacious and, particularly the ones belonging to better off families, had designated rooms for specific purposes. For example, every house had a 'summer room' on the top floor and 'winter room' right at the bottom. There were separate rooms for keeping firewood, dry fodder (Bhoosa), a pooja room and also a separate space for keeping eatables, dry fruits and stores. So, generally a normal house consisted of 5-6 rooms. Few families boasted of a separate room for making 'Chhang'. Also, well to do people had an exclusive guest-room and/or sitting room; which were well lit. Every household, generally, kept six months stock in reserve. This was done as a matter of abundant caution and also based on the past experience.... All houses were built by the collective effort of the village people; with neighbours helping in all possible ways which included making arrangements for the 'beams' for roofs and 'Talboos' for ceilings. Poor people of the village would assist in the construction work by providing free labour… A typical system of mutual support and help, which is unique to the area of Leh, is called "Phaspun" (literally meaning 'parental brotherhood/friendship'). It is a small group of people belonging to, at an average, five to ten families. These are organised on purely voluntary basis and often stay in place for generations. All individuals of a 'phaspun' take care of arrangements required to be made in case of a happy or sad occasion; especially like marriage or death, in the family of a fellow member. The normal neighbourhood assistance in such cases is over and above the exertions of 'phaspun' persons. The family 'Deity' of all 'phaspun' members is the same.

"After passing my matriculation from the Government High School, Leh; I cleared the Intermediate examination from S.P. College, Srinagar, with medical subjects. Thereafter, in 1957, I got a MBBS seat in the Government Medical College at Dibrugarh – Assam. Now, I realize that because no one from Kashmir or Jammu might have liked to go to such a far off place and hence this vacancy was allotted to me. Completing my studies so much distance away from home was indeed very difficult; but this experience also taught me a lot – self reliance being the most important lesson. That is how I became the first Doctor; and later the pioneer medical specialist in Ladakh."[21]

As has been mentioned earlier; the most significant project taken in hand by the State Government in this region was to construct the 208 kilometre road connection between Kargil and Leh. The work on this major scheme was seriously undertaken in 1959; under the overall supervision of Sonam Narboo, who was then holding the rank of a Superintending Engineer in the state PWD. He was a Ladakhi and also a leading engineer of his time; who had successfully built the Leh airfield, way back in May 1948. Sonam Narboo took up this work as a personal challenge and also motivated his whole team to work round the clock and complete the entire project as early as possible. As measured from Leh side, the distance of 97 kilometres between Leh and Khaltsi did not pose much difficulty as the entire stretch was on the right bank of Indus and roughly followed

21 This note is based on interactions with Dr. Smanla on 13th November and 5th December 2018.

the existing track. Similarly, the road between Kargil and Lamayuru was also not a major engineering problem as, by and large, it traversed the prevailing track alignment and the deviations were not technically problematic. Though, this part of the proposed road traversed over two passes; the Namik La which was over eleven thousand feet high and Fatu La – its height being more than 13,000 feet. It was the 29 kilometres stretch between Lamayuru and Khaltsi, which presented significant engineering and professional difficulties. The crossing over of Indus, near Khaltsi, was the least of his problems; even though making of a motorable bridge over this river itself was a demanding job. The real difficulty lay in planning of a vehicle worthy grade which would traverse the distance and heights between Lamayuru located at 11,515 feet and Khaltsi being at 9,800 feet above the MSL. Also, here the traditional track was of no help as the men and animals followed the stiff slopes between the two points. Sonam Narboo ultimately solved this tricky issue by following the contours, for most of the distance, and then taking a motorable plunge on a firmer mountain slope. This part, indeed a remarkable engineering accomplishment, consisted of nineteen U turns. These are famously called "Hangroo Loops." It is a fascinating sight to watch the vehicles of all sizes going up and down the slopes; negotiating these famous curves – the most spectacular part of Kargil- Leh road.

However, engineering problems were not the only difficulties that Sonam Narboo had to contend with. There were other matters also that he had to face and resolve before this road was completed. In the final analysis, this man not only had to struggle against the elements – so natural in Ladakh, and overcome technical difficulties that were inherent in a formidable undertaking of this kind. He was also required to procure and maintain a substantial number of labourers - the working hands; and consequently run kind of camps in barren locations between these points. His problems were further compounded by the fact that a strong faction of the Leh society opposed him and this project. These people spread the word, far and wide, that after completion of this road; motor vehicles would ply on this trunk route rendering a large number of load carrying ponies and donkeys superfluous. Thus, in addition to the adverse effect on the local economy – this group contended – the completion of Kargil to Leh road would also have a negative effect on the local employment potential. A word was sent by these people to all villages of Leh Tehsil urging them not to provide labour to Sonam Narboo. It was yet another manifestation of the then ongoing struggle for supremacy between the traditional elements and the newly emerging educated class. The rights and wrongs of this opposition apart; the fact remains that such a serious obstacle made his job even more difficult. But, Sonam Narboo was a person of resolute determination; and this handicap only enhanced his resolve to complete the job in hand as expeditiously as possible. It is a matter of record that for the timely completion of this project he was successful in obtaining crucial help from two quarters. A significant part of the labour force came from Kargil area; and here Narboo was considerably helped by the influence and directions of Aga Haider of Sankoo – a renowned religious teacher who had great authority and prestige in the Kargil region. Positive directions from him ensured that a good number of people from there worked on this project. Traditionally the Kargil work force has enjoyed the reputation of being good road builders. The Tibetan refugees, then camping in different parts of Ladakh, also helped significantly by providing requisite labour to him. These two factors bolstered his efforts and Sonam Narboo was able to complete the most important part of this project – the Hangroo loops – quite within the stipulated time. It was a great achievement indeed, as this connected Leh with Kargil and Srinagar; as also beyond with rest of the country in the autumn of 1960. The first convoy of Mercedes Benz 'UNIMOG' trucks[22], rolled into Leh town, cheering the local population, on 18th August 1960. It was a big day for the entire people as at least for six months of the summer Leh was linked with a motorable road. From next year a bus service was started, connecting Leh with Kargil and Srinagar. Sonam Narboo had once again made a commendable performance for his people.

Many people believe, and with reasonable justifications, that the Chinese occupation of Tibet as also later their military build up in the Ladakh region, brought this area into prominence. This forgotten belt was thenceforth pitch-forked into a high visible tract. Induction of army formations in a big way as also accelerated building of motarable tracks for connecting different places followed in quick succession; thereby opening the interior and far-off locations of Ladakh. It is also a fact that Indian troops were not able to give good account against the Chinese forces in their armed clashes. Consequently, in the aftermath of 1962

22 These sturdy vehicles, especially made for rough terrain, were owned by GTU (Government Transport Undertaking – a predecessor of the later State Road Transport Corporation – SRTC) of J&K Government.

war, India's standing in the international community took a heavy beating and the political leadership also, collectively, lost credibility within the country. It took many years of concerted efforts and purposeful action to overcome these handicaps and repair the damages. Particularly, the military leadership was jolted into action. However, the Ladakh region – as a whole – did gain in totality out of these unfortunate happenings.

The seeds of Indian humiliation in 1962 were in fact sown twelve years earlier when the Chinese forces occupied Tibet in 1950; after overcoming the feeble resistance offered by the local soldiers. The Chinese army quickly spread over the entire country; more particularly to the western part. This development should have started ringing warning bells for the Indian strategic thinkers and senior forces commanders; which unfortunately did not happen. It was just a matter of simple calculations off the map. The maintenance of a large body of troops that the Chinese had deployed in the western Tibet was quite difficult from Lhasa, keeping the distance in mind, and even much more arduous from the mainland China. The easier alternative was to provide administrative backing to these troops from Xinjiang, through the Aksai Chin area of north-east Ladakh. This is what the Chinese proceeded to do; even though this alternative meant passing through a big chunk of land claimed by India. The whole situation has been comprehensively described as, "The Chinese forces in the Western Tibet had to be supplied with their daily requirements all the way from Lhasa in the East which was over 1200 kilometres away while a road joining Western Tibet from Xinjiang province of China in the north of Ladakh would be only 500 – 600 kilometres long if it could pass through the Aksai Chin area of North Eastern Ladakh. The other alternative available for the Chinese was to build a road along the long Western Tibetan – Ladakh border which meant crossing high mountain ranges along this rather long route...The Aksai Chin region had no population. The Ladakh – Tibetan nomads or shepherds did roam around in the area but there were no permanent huts or villages in this dry region. It had no vegetation or trees either except for small bushes. The Aksai Chin area is a high mountain desert. The construction of road through this area did not pose any major problems..."[23] This is exactly what the Chinese proceeded to do; and in the bargain raised the dispute over Indian claims to the entire Aksai Chin area. India failed to forcefully meet this Chinese challenge head on and feebly reacted very late and also with gross inadequacy.

23 Rajendra Nath, *Op. Cit.*, p. 172.

Interestingly, way back in 1952 some senior officer in the Army Headquarters must have suspected something questionable in all these developments and decided to send a young Captain, working there in the Intelligence wing, on a reconnaissance mission to Lanak La in the Aksai Chin tract. In the words of this officer, "I was asked to find out if there are any Chinese troops in Lanak-La pass area. In addition, I was also instructed to ensure the patrol party should not contact the Chinese troops located in the area. There were other instructions also. The second main task given was to find out if the Chinese were constructing any road from Tibet to Xinjiang located North of Ladakh through Aksai Chin which may be passing through Lanak La...The short cut route passing through Aksai Chin would be less than half of the longer route...But in 1952, nobody in India was thinking of India-China conflict. Our patrol to Lanak La was primarily meant to find out if there were any Chinese troops in that area and secondly whether the Chinese were constructing any road in that area....Incidentally, in the 1962 India China War, the Chinese forces which attacked Ladakh were commanded by the Chinese Army Head Quarters which was also located in Xinjiang region and not in Western Tibet...The J&K Government had no police post or any administrative establishment in Aksai Chin region...there were mule paths which connected Western Tibet and Xinjiang province and these were used by the nomads of Tibet or of Ladakh region...The Aksai Chin area is quite vast and continues till the Kara Koram Range in the north along which the boundary between India and China runs according to our (Indian) claims. The whole of Aksai Chin area can be called a Mountain Desert, according to what our patrol observed during their reconnaissance...The patrol party reached Lanak La area when it was almost end of October 1952... Lanak La being a pass about 18000 feet high was getting heavy snow fall...There was no road at all not only in Lanak La but in any area near about it. The patrol party which went up the pass area in the morning returned in the evening. On its return journey to the Hot spring area from the Lanak La area, we came across Ladakhi / Tibetan shepherds with herds of sheep. According to them, there were no Chinese barracks or huts in the area. The shepherds did say that the Chinese forces seemed to be also similarly reconnoitering the area. The patrol party did not see any huts nor met any personnel whether Ladakhis, Tibetan or Chinese in or around Lanak La area. There was no road in that area either in 1952..."[24]

24 Rajendra Nath, *Op. Cit.,* pp. 170, 171, 172 and 174.

A detailed report was given by this patrol to the Army Headquarters; but for some odd reasons no tangible follow up action seem to have been taken on various possibilities or military scenarios which could have been envisaged in the region. Although, two mutually unrelated things did happen. Sometime later this officer, Capt. Rajendra Nath, was posted in Leh as the Army Headquarters Liaison Officer; a kind of 'eyes and ears' of the military top brass in New Delhi. He had a fruitful stay in the region for about two years. Secondly, the Chinese did build a vehicle worthy road through the Aksai Chin plateau connecting Xinjiang area with its forces in the western Tibet; it appears that this was done not much after the Indian patrol to the Lanak La as mentioned above. Our surveillance on the borders remained almost nonexistent for the next few years – which were to be a crucial neglect. Vast stretches of borders remained unattended and unprotected. It would be interesting to connect this development with the nostalgic journey down the memory lane, by Kalon Sahib who recollected as, "Up to mid fifties our men and flock used to regularly go in the Aksai Chin area for summer pastures and nobody would interfere with them. They would reach the designated places after March. The normal practice was to send one responsible person with eatables, tea leaves and kettles early morning well in advance of the main flock and rest of the caretakers so that when the party reached the destination they would have hot tea and snacks available to refresh themselves. This year, when our man in advance reached Lanak La, he found the Chinese were building a road there. They tried to capture him but he ran away, came straight to Leh after a forced march of 6-7 days and reported the matter to me. I went to meet an army officer whom I knew – called Capt. Rajendra Nath who later became a Major General. I told him the whole story; he said that he would like to have a definite proof before the matter could be referred to the higher authorities and I should go there and take photographs of these activities. I could not find anybody willing to take the risk till one day the Numberdar of Sakti, who had been detained by Tehsildar for non-payment of some revenue dues, sent a desperate message to me. When I went to the Tehsil office I found that he had to deposit rupees 200 /- as arrears of land revenue and, therefore, needed this money to extricate himself. He agreed to go to Aksai Chin area provided this money was made available to him. I went to Capt. Rajendra Nath and asked him for Rs. 300 /- in advance and Rs. 200/- later when the mission was completed, to which he agreed. With some difficulty the Numberdar was taught how to operate a camera. A box camera was procured from the market for Rs. 12 /- and along with a number of films he set forth for Aksai Chin. He took as many photographs as he could manage and deposited the films with the officer. These films were developed by Capt. Rajendra Nath and taken to Delhi giving them a firm proof of the ingress that had taken place in our area by the Chinese and the activities they were carrying on inside our territory."[25]

Whatever may have been the reason; it is a matter of record that after the recce mission of 1952, the next long range patrol to this area was sent four long years later. In 1956, this patrol was led by Major Tugnait which reported that the Chinese had built a road through Aksai Chin. Even after knowing about this flagrant violation; the reactions were too little and too late. India failed to take adequate remedial measures as also misread the Chinese military intentions; in spite of ample proofs to the contrary. Another strategic blunder that India committed was not to use the Air Force for reconnaissance purposes; to find out about the Chinese activities along the borders. This step though was perfectly justified for the simple reason that, not only this region lay far off from the nearest troops available, but also the aircrafts would all along fly and operate within the Indian boundaries; something which was perfectly legitimate. The inexplicable failure to do this has been mystifying and also proved much costly later on. Not only India acquiesced to the Chinese occupation of Tibet; but also failed to secure its traditional interests in the region. For example there is evidence that Menser – mentioned as Mansar in one of the old Census Reports and close to the sacred Mount Kailash, a renowned place of Indian pilgrimage – a cluster of habitations comprising 44 households with 87 males and 73 females (1921 Census) deep inside Changthang in Tibet about 280 kilometres from the Ladakh-Tibet border in Demchok; had been paying tribute to the king of Ladakh even after the annexation of Tibet by China, right till the India-China war in 1962. The revenue that accrued to Ladakh from here included 60 sheep, 20 goats, 6 yaks and 60 sheepskins and silver coins that had gone up from 56 rupees in 1853 to 297 rupees in 1905. The idea of a Ladakhi enclave deep inside Tibet was two- fold – use of the revenue to defray expenses on Ladakh's offerings to the holy Kailash Mountain and alongside to provide transit point for Ladakhi and later Indian traders and pilgrims to Kailash and Mansarover. Maharaja of Jammu had agreed in 1846 to honour the obligations of the 1684 Tingmosgang Treaty. Even the sanctity of this historical tradition was not insisted upon by the Indian Government.

25 Rigzin Namgyal Kalon, *Op. Cit.*

The inexorable march of events continued unabated with Chinese actions becoming increasingly provocative. India reacted by improving communication systems in the peripheral northern areas of Ladakh and sending more troops in this region. But, these measures were a classical case of being too little and too late. The matters took a serious turn in 1959 with the Dalai Lama fleeing his palace at Potala in Lhasa and seeking asylum in India. In the wake of this momentous event, many Tibetan refugees streamed into India; and a number of such people together with their herds came to the Changthang area of Ladakh. This created additional burden on the existing pasture land as also adversely affected the economic life of the locals. To make matters worse, the Chinese attacked India in 1962 and took possession of considerable territory in the north Ladakh. This increased the pressure on pasture tracts further. A rough estimate of the existing conditions indicated ten percent decrease in the grazing resources coupled with 40 percent increase in the livestock pressure. If the matters did not come to a head, leading to a clash between the two people; the credit should go to the hospitality shown by the local Ladakhis as also their centuries old traditional ties with the Tibetans. Equally appreciable was the behaviour of these refugees who not only well understood their dependable position on the locals; but also refrained from doing anything assertive or belligerent. In fact they were, collectively, deferential to the local customs and accommodating to the needs of the natives. They also cooperated with the officials of the administration who were trying for the proper and orderly settlement of Tibetan refugees. It took quite some time for the Tibetan refugees to settle down meaningfully in Ladakh, as in other parts of the country, but at no point of time they became difficult or unwanted for the local population.

It was around 1959 that Indian leaders, particularly Jawaharlal Nehru, started realizing the dangers posed by China as the relations between two countries began deteriorating badly. This was particularly more pointed after the arrival of Dalai Lama in India. The main fault in this unfavourable turn of events was that of India; right from 1950 when it acquiesced to the Chinese occupation of Tibet. But even in 1959, India did not fully realize the dangerous dimensions of the Chinese aggressive policies and it still naively believed that China would not provoke a full scale war with India. It certainly failed to realize the reasons and aims behind the Chinese building a road through Aksai Chin connecting with western Tibet and the strategic importance it had for that country. However, the fact remains that some communications improvements had started taking place in the Ladakh region also in this period. Sonam Narboo was seriously engaged in making the Kargil Leh road. The Border Roads Organization was established in India; charged with the responsibility of making and improving road network in far-flung border areas. This was also the time when military units and formation headquarters started coming to Ladakh region in good numbers. Their inductions and interactions with the local population was to set a new high standard of military and civil cooperation; something that was to dominate the contours if this fruitful relationship in the many decades that followed. It has amply shown the various ways in which army has become an important institution of state to fruitfully impact the everyday life of society in Ladakh; a function which goes far beyond the main role of the military as a war-fighting arm of the nation. This positive nature of interactions, naturally, resulted in the development of good rapport between army and local population. At the same time, it also succeeded in improving the living conditions of Ladakhis, impacting this in diverse ways. The two phenomenons resulted in influencing each other positively and thus further improving things and the overall environs. The army certainly facilitated the transformation of economic landscape of Ladakh by being a major employer of manpower as also a leading consumer of domestic products like vegetables, fruits and fodder. Thus unwittingly China, by its belligerence, helped Ladakh to get a share of development and prominence at the national level. It was no more to remain a forlorn and forgotten region of the nation.

The infrastructural improvements in this region also included undertaking the development of three forward airfields located at Daulat Beg Oldi (DBO), Chushul and Thoise. The north-west Ladakh area, right up to the Kara Koram range, was inhospitable and lacked basic communication facilities; making it difficult to maintain troops there from the administrative bases far in the rear. The journey from one post to another was not only difficult; it also took long time and therefore posed serious problems in the posts becoming 'mutually supportive'. The only way to solve these difficulties, to an extent, was to construct forward airfields. This was attempted at DBO – considering the centrality of the place for a big area around it; also the fact that the post there consisted of more than one hundred people and hence being largest in that sector. As there was no habitation around this place; the airfield was made by levelling the huge open ground nearby using the troops labour and some Engineering Corps efforts. The ends of this airfield were marked by using a large number of empty Jerry cans and some human as also animal skeletons lying around – the latter a grim reminder of the tragedies that used to take place on this difficult trade route decades ago. The first aircraft, a Fairchild Packet – a veritable relic of the Second World War - landed at the DBO airfield on 23rd July 1962. And just in time. Similarly, a landing ground was developed at Chushul by firming up the loose soil of a huge open ground, by using the inter-locking PSPs (Perforated Steel Plates). This was also ready for use in emergency cases by the middle of 1962.

The airfield at Thoise was different than the other two, in a number of ways. The work on this project was stared in the middle of 1960, earlier than the rest. Like the airfield in Leh completed in May 1948; this one was also constructed with the active help of the locals - the entire Nubra valley population. It is a remarkable fact that all the villagers of the area offered their free services for this purpose. The main person behind this unique phenomenon was K.D. Menon, an IFAS officer then posted as Assistant Commissioner Nubra with headquarters at Deskit. He was a part of the legendary Lt. Col. Raja's team in Ladakh. The contribution of Menon in the construction of Thoise airfield was a topic of house hold discussions in the entire Ladakh for decades thereafter. He was the one responsible for mobilisation of the locals of entire Nubra valley. He provided adequate quantity of wheat for making *Chhang* – the local beer – which was distributed free of cost to the volunteers working on this project. The Muslims of Biagdangdo and some other villages, as also those who did not take *Chhang* were served the local salted and butter tea; without any charges. For meeting these expenses a separate quantity of grains was earmarked by Menon; to purchase tea and butter. It is said that the entire construction was done on a high priority basis and people worked at times even during the night hours in the moon light or with the help of petromax light. 26th September 1960 was a red letter day for the entire Nubra; as on that day the first Dakota landed on this airfield. Since then this landing ground has remained functional, till now, of course with technological and other improvements.

The operationalisation of these advanced airfields could only facilitate the administrative and back up efforts to the forces on ground; which had hardly any presence in the outlying areas. India had woefully neglected the northern and western borders of Ladakh; in fact along the entire dividing line with Tibet and China. The continued Chinese perfidy and betrayal literally forced the hands of Indian political leaders and military commanders to act. After the independence; only the police forces were deployed on these borders by India as compared to the Chinese who, right from 1950 onwards, sent army troops to man the border posts. Ultimately, in April 1960, the responsibility of guarding the borders was handed over to the military and for the first time the Indian army was inducted into Ladakh in good numbers. This move also, as later events were to prove, was too little and too late. The Indian response was weak – almost pathetic – in the form of 'Forward Policy'. This pattern of deployment has been described as, "…where Platoon or Section posts were deployed in the forward area so that the Chinese forces could not advance any further without physically attacking them. These small posts were established only to show on the ground that the area belonged to India but the small detachments were in no position to deal with the Chinese attacks because of their meagre strength, which varied from ten to thirty men only to each forward post. These posts had no artillery or mortar support either. Importantly, these posts were not mutually supporting as these were located well apart, about two kilometres or so from each other…India had deployed the 114 Infantry Brigade which consisted of four battalions – 14 J&K Militia, 1/8 GR, 5 Jats and 13 Kumaon. This brigade was stretched to cover a large border area starting from Kara Koram pass in the North to Chushul area in the South, a distance of over 150 kilometres. The 70 Infantry Brigade was deployed south of the 114 Infantry Brigade covering the southern part of Ladakh including the Indus River…"[26] It is a matter of record that the number of such penny packets; the forward posts with very poor defence potential, increased from 13 to 65 from April 1961 to June 1962. The smallest figure was five at Parmodak post; whereas the largest number being 125 at DBO. Thus the Indian forces on the borders were limited to a strength of two brigades at the peak; whereas knowledgeable defence analysts put the required figure at a minimum of two divisions' strong force with adequate administrative and infrastructural support. Hence, both the numbers as also quality were much short of the required level.

Although the evolving events were pointing towards an armed conflict; the Indian policy makers still hoped that China would not attack India. As the coming scenarios unfolded; the Chinese had obviously

26 Rajendra Nath, *Op. Cit.,* p. 197.

outnumbered and out gunned the Indian forces in Ladakh in 1962. By any standard it was a humiliating development for India. By default, so to say, Ladakh region became the beneficiary of the confrontation between India and China; as the former realized the importance of all round progress of this far flung area. The real strength of the region was not in terms of the number of people inhabiting, but the tactical and strategic value of the entire belt; the nation could no longer afford to ignore the vast stretches of land there.

The first India – Pakistan war came to Ladakh and the Frontier region when hostilities began in Gilgit on 31st October 1947. These ended with the cease-fire declaration on 1st January 1949. This armed conflict resulted in the areas of Skardu, Gilgit and beyond in the north, being occupied by Pakistan. The present region of Ladakh, in fact a truncated version of its old self, was also saved from Pak occupation just in time by the Indian forces and the local population working closely together. With the war over; the State and the country literally forgot about Ladakh and it slipped into neglect, economic distress and collective misfortune. The traditional trade routes to western Tibet and Central Asian region were first squeezed and then fully blocked within a few years; resulting in serious dislocation, deprivation and despondency amongst the locals. A society already living on the edge; was badly hit by these material hardships and political inattention. The decade of the 1950s was really a very hard period for the entire region and its people. It was only after 1959 that things started turning positive for Ladakh. In fact this intervening period can legitimately be termed as a 'dark and gloomy' era. No wonder it is said that the Chinese brought unintended benefits to Ladakh region by their negative intentions and aggressive designs.

CHAPTER V

The Awakening (1962-74)

The Chinese Aggression (Oct – Nov 1962)

In the six decades after 1890 A.D., the British postulated three 'lines' as the boundaries between the Indian territories controlled by them and neighboring entities. Interestingly, all three have created problems of international magnitude which are yet to be settled with finality. It is a debatable matter whether this was done consciously, as a part of high diplomacy, or the subsequent difficulties arose in the normal course of events. The first of these stipulations was called Durand Line and it came into existence in 1893; as a boundary between Afghanistan and British India. As the people of Pathan origin live on both sides of Durand Line; Afghanistan has never accepted this as the border with Pakistan – the successor country after the British left the Indian sub-continent in 1947. Also as late as 1992, when Mohammad Najibullah was the ruler in Afghanistan and he was placed in a very difficult situation; with hostile and inimical developments taking place all around him, he appeared desperate to make peace with Pakistan. Even in that precarious condition, he was prepared to accept almost all terms proposed by the latter; except that he refused to recognize Durand Line as the border between Afghanistan and Pakistan. Even the Talibans - widely believed as the creation of Pakistan - have never openly accepted the validity of this demarcation. The second entity called McMahon Line came into existence in 1914 as the boundary demarcation between Tibet and northeast region of India. The Chinese, after militarily occupying Tibet in 1950, steadfastly refused to accept the validity of this delimitation. The less said the better about the third boundary; known as the Radcliffe Line and which was drawn in

July-August 1947, as the demarcation between the Indian and Pakistani portions of Punjab and Bengal provinces of British India. Any reference to it brings back to mind the tragic memories of the large scale carnage and human sufferings which followed in the wake of India's partition. Suffice to say that back then; both countries had expressed dissatisfaction with the award of the Radcliffe Line.

With the advantage of hindsight, it can be said that the Chinese questioning the accepted boundary between Tibet, India and itself; was intended to be a smoke screen to further her military plans in the region. More particularly in the fifties, international postures of the two countries were almost diametrically opposite. Whereas in the Cold War era of the bipolar world; when most of the strong and developed countries were either in the American or Russian camps; India had introduced an element of morality and ethical behavior in the field of international diplomacy. Thus antagonizing both major powers; the Americans being more unhappy and displeased with this stance. In contrast, the Chinese followed a foreign policy which suited its national interests more than the righteous conduct. On the one hand it called the nuclear powers of the world as 'paper tigers' – literally mocking at them; while simultaneously increasing its military muscle. In respect of India; the Chinese prepared for more than a decade before initiating a military clash in 1962 on the northern borders of India. At the doctrinaire level, it is not without purpose that the Chinese strategic community has been fond of quoting more than two thousand years old military and political thinkers of the country; like Sun Tzu and Confucius.

Xinjiang (then Sinkiang) has always been a strategically important region for both militarily strong nations of Russia and China. The discovery of large reserves of important minerals like thorium and uranium in this belt further consolidated the Chinese desire to exert its military and administrative grip over this province. Therefore, it was almost expected that after the overthrow of the Chiang Kai-Shek regime in China; the new communist rulers there would amalgamate this region with the mainland. The occupation and consolidation of Xinjiang was one of the first acts of the new Chinese regime. It is also said that at that time the Chinese political officers were trying hard to evoke anti-Hindu sentiments amongst the Muslim population there; as a deliberate step against the Indians. Seen purely in the strategic light, the Chinese occupation of Tibet was also another face of the same coin; to contain India all along its long northern borders. China's own diplomatic maneuvers towards this end were, unwittingly, helped by the conduct of India's foreign policy.

An astute analyst has comprehensively summed up the contemporary scenario as, "According to many experts, one of the important causes of the India – China war in 1962 was the construction of the road by China in the Aksai Chin Area. China wanted India to accept Aksai Chin as part of Tibet and consequently accept the road constructed by China through the Aksai Chin region as a part of the overall settlement of India China border dispute. This was a unilateral offer in a way by a more powerful nation, more so a nation willing to use military power to suit its objective. But the Indian government could not accept or consider the offer…At the same time, India was not prepared for war at all, logistically, diplomatically or militarily. Because of its non-alignment policy it had no strong country like USA to back it, in the world as we realistically know it, a weaker nation looks for allies… India had no alternative but to try and persuade China to vacate the Aksai Chin region and also accept the McMahon line in the northeastern part of India by peaceful means. Its own oft proclaimed peaceful policy towards all countries; particularly towards China; was based on the premise of a totally ruled out possibility of conflict with China. So India's armed forces were neither mentally prepared for a possible conflict with China nor was any effort made to equip our armed forces with modern weapon systems in case war with China did break out."[1]

In contrast, the Chinese preparations went ahead as per their conceived plans. By 1956, they had constructed the planned road in Aksai Chin; thus connecting Xinjiang belt with the western Tibet; and with this a major military objective of theirs was achieved. Having constructed this road; they systematically proceeded to secure it by positioning tactically sited military posts – mostly in the south of the road - worth almost one division strength of troops; that their commanders estimated would be the force level to ensure safety of this road. Small lateral roads were then developed to connect these forward outposts; thus ensuring regular supplies, mutual support and connectivity with headquarters up the line. Even though India had a forward airfield at Chushul, with its attendant benefits; the Chinese were still better placed in this sector because of a good road network which

1 Maj. Gen. Rajendra Nath, PVSM (Retd.), *Strategic Ladakh,* Vij Books India Pvt Ltd, New Delhi, 2016, pp. 185 and 186.

not only linked with the forward most and outlying posts; but also – at a much higher level – provided a dependable connect with their major bases in Xinjiang area as well as the Rudok base in western Tibet. The Chinese had thus, almost completely, achieved their military objective and that too well in time. Now, the question for them remained of getting their ground position accepted by India either through peaceful means; failing which by an enforced armed clash. Thus while the Chinese continued with peaceful negotiations – and also such exertions at various levels and forums – regarding the border disputes with India; they carried on with full scale preparations for a possible war with India, to settle the outstanding issues. Either way, the intention was to make India accept the ground position as developed by the Chinese. The concepts of 'Panch-Sheel', slogans of 'Hindi-Chini Bhai Bhai' and continued parleys; were just effective ways of smoke screening their increasing military capabilities in the Ladakh region; which had actually started way back in 1950 with the military occupation of Tibet. Since then it was merely a process of consolidation so assiduously conceived and executed by their commanders; who rightly anticipated that they were militarily much stronger than India.

The Indian response, on the other hand, was squarely based on a unidirectional approach of parleys and negotiations. The Indian Defence Minister, Krishna Menon was not only a known anti-US person; he also blindly believed in the Chinese promises of resolving the border issues by peaceful negotiations and not resorting to war with India. The Indian army was consequently not prepared for an armed showdown with the Chinese and to make matters worse, political interference at higher military appointments was also resorted to, based on personal likings. The appointment of General Thapar as Army Chief and promotion of Lt. Gen. B.M. Kaul are just two glaring examples in this category. It is also a matter of record that the Chinese Prime Minister Chou En Lei, during his visit to India in 1960, offered India to accept Aksai Chin as part of Tibet and that China in turn was not averse to recognizing McMahon line in the northeast. The Indian government could not accept this bargain for political and principled reasons as also the growing public pressure against any such move. On one side the Indian army was not prepared for a confrontation with China; on the other the Chinese aggressive intentions were almost becoming clear to the Indian leadership. The ground position in Aksai Chin was a matter of fact and the Chinese ingress could not be denied or suppressed any longer. Indian response was almost desperate

– there is no other way to describe this phenomenon – in the form of the infamous "forward policy". These small posts, ranging from ten to thirty men at an average, were not mutually supporting and bereft of any artillery or mortar cover. These were merely to show the 'flag' on ground; without much fighting potential. This weakness was inherent in the very concept of such deployment. May be the Indian leadership, even at this late stage, was hoping against hope of a negotiated settlement with the Chinese. Apart from the tactical weakness of this concept, there were considerable administrative problems, some of which have been brought out as, "Even as the troops in Ladakh braced themselves for a second winter in October 1960, there was hardly an administrative set up in place and the scanty posts were entirely dependent on air drops. Vast quantities of kerosene was required to keep the life-saving bukharis (oil stoves) burning, hence the IAF was hard pressed to ferry even essential survival supplies, leaving no room for war-like stores. There was hardly any snow clothing, a chronic deficiency of tinned milk (owing to a shortage of foreign exchange) and even cooking staple food like dal was a problem. There were no pressure cookers, without which it is well-nigh impossible to cook food at high altitude…Food supplies and accommodation apart; the other major problem pertained to the evacuation of casualties. There were no field hospitals and with the posts so far apart, any medical emergency could only be met with helicopters that were in very short supply at the time…"[2]

Against the entire Chinese forces strung along this sector; India had deployed only one brigade – the 114 Infantry Brigade – consisting of four battalions of 14 J&K Militia, 5 Jats, 1/8 GR and 13 Kumaon; of which the last was to join only in the beginning of October 1962. Of this strength, which significantly was bereft of an effective artillery support; almost the entire Militia battalion and one company each of 5 Jats and 1/8 GR were stationed along in the shape of 'forward posts' manned by small number of men each. Main defences of 1/8 GR were based on the heights and tactical grounds, both on the north and south of Pangong Tso (lake). 13 Kumaon had one company deployed at the Rezang Ridge; while rest of the battalion had taken up defensive positions in the Chushul area. The 114 Brigade, commanded by Brig. T.N. Raina, was operating directly under the instructions of Headquarters 15 Corps – headed by Lt. Gen. Bikram Singh. 15 Corps in turn was functioning under the HQ Western Command, then led

2 Shiv Kunal Verma, *1962: The War That Wasn't*, Aleph Book Company, New Delhi, 2016, p. 323.

by Lt. Gen. Daulet Singh. All these three commanders were professional soldiers of high caliber who well understood the weakness and limitations of this type of extensive dispersion of forces on the ground. The following is a good example of this evaluation, "There was nothing ambiguous in the assessment of HQ Western Command of 114 Brigade's fighting capability. There were very few troops on the ground, and these too had been dispersed over a massive area. Daulet Singh remained apprehensive about the penny packet deployments in the name of the Forward Policy. In a letter dated 17 August 1962, the general expressed his reservations in writing. 'Our forward posts in Ladakh are nowhere tactically sited, whereas the Chinese everywhere are'. He went on to state categorically that our deployment was dictated by political considerations, and that he would be failing in his duty if he did not draw attention to the size and shape of the potential threat."[3] But, warnings of this nature did not make any impact on the Army Headquarters; which was then functioning completely under the sway of the trio of Menon – Thapar – Kaul. Therefore, till the manifestation of 3 Division and 70 Brigade on the scene, which was in the second half of October 1962; 114 Brigade remained responsible for the whole of Ladakh.

The Chinese, on the other hand, maintained a practical focus on what they wanted to achieve in this sector in particular and their entire borders with India, in general. All their military preparations and diplomatic moves were geared towards this end. It has been mentioned in the book on China by Henry Kissinger that Chairman Mao addressed his top military commanders in October 1962, before operations against India started. In this meeting, he reportedly dwelt on the historical background of Indo-China relations. This proclivity of the Chinese leading men to derive inspiration from deep past events has been interestingly commented upon in an article which appeared in the USI Journal, as, "The singular uniqueness of Chinese leaders lies in invoking strategic principles from millennium old events. No other country can claim to link its ancient classic dictums of strategy to its present statesmanship. This is why; the world often gets China wrong while decoding the minds of its leaders. Even in the recent past, series of incidences that occurred on India's border with China invariably synchronized with important visits. Despang in April 2013 preceded Chinese Prime Minister Li Keqiang visit to India, Demchok-Chumar happened in September 2014 when President Xi was in India and Doklam in June-August coincided with PM Modi's visit to

3 Shiv Kunal Verma, *Op. Cit.*, p. 331.

the USA."[4] In the same briefing, as mentioned above, Mao reportedly said, "China and India were not doomed to perpetual enmity. They could enjoy long period of peace again, but to do so, China had to use force to 'knock' India back to negotiating table."[5] Thus the Chinese concentrated on inflicting defeat on the Indian forces in this region; gaining as much territory as possible in the northern Ladakh and securing the assets created in the Aksai Chin area by tactically moving as much south of the new road as possible. All this they were able to achieve in the months of October – November 1962.

The Chinese offensive in Ladakh was largely based on the following parameters,

- From their point of view, this whole area was divided into four sectors and each was made the responsibility of a self-sustaining and integrated Battle Group. It has been estimated that the total strength of Chinese troops was little more than two divisions worth. These forces had adequate artillery and mortar support also. For a considerable time the Chinese troops had engaged in active patrolling all along the border, thereby gaining a lot of useful information regarding the location and deployment of Indian troops; their patrolling patterns as also other activities along the border. This timely diligence paid handsomely to them, once the hostilities started, as all requisite details were available with the Chinese. It is also interesting to note that none of the forces which attacked in Ladakh were located in western Tibet; all this manpower came from the Xinjiang region – with some of the soldiers being deliberately of Muslim origin. Also, the operational control in Ladakh sector was exercised by the Xinjiang Military Command.

- As a matter of practical strategy, the Chinese were carrying out necessary preparations for war, well over a decade, while talking of peace with India at the same time. Because of this ruse, and other reasons, the Chinese rightly calculated that their army was in a much stronger position in this area than the Indian forces.

4 Maj. Gen. G.G. Dwivedi, *Journal of the United Services Institution of India,* New Delhi, April-June 2018, p. 193.

5 *Ibid.*

They were not only superior in strength, weaponry and equipment; the commanders had also developed new tactics of establishing effective blocks behind the Indian defences, before attacking these troops. Some of these maneuvers were reminiscent of the combat methods employed by the Chinese forces in the Korean War. This sense of military superiority was also the main reason why the Chinese did not use Air force in this war.

- Apart from the main road through the Aksai Chin area, which was reportedly completed during the 1953-1956 period, connecting the Xinjiang area with western Tibet region; the Chinese had also constructed an extensive network of lateral tracks. Each of these paths was vehicle worthy, thereby facilitating the Chinese to easily move troops, equipment and war stores right up to the forward locations. It also helped in switching of forces from one point or area to another place; almost at will. The inability of India to deploy air resources or undertake effective patrolling along the borders; further enabled the Chinese to occupy large tracts in the northern parts of Ladakh and capture big chunks of land in these regions- almost quietly.

The dice was thus heavily loaded in the favour of China; and when the negotiations with India did not produce satisfactory results from the Chinese point of view; its leadership decided to initiate a military showdown for which it had been quietly and assiduously preparing for more than ten years. This course of action was undertaken in the second half of October 1962. The fighting in this region took place for a little over one month; starting on 19th October 1962. The Chinese attack was carried out broadly in three phases. The first part lasted from 19th to 21st October; the second wave of offensive actions took place on 24, 25 and 26th October; while the third phase started almost a month later on 18th November and continued till the 20th. The Chinese declared a unilateral cease-fire on 21st November 1962.

In the first wave of attacks, the Chinese concentrated on neutralizing the small 'forward posts'; position at the DBO and the area north and south of Pangong lake. The beginning of conflict was made by the Chinese, when on 19 October at 11 p.m. they opened up with medium and heavy mortars on the Chandani post and the nearby air-dropping zone. The skirmishes in this sector have been graphically described as, "The

Chinese also targeted the observation posts at Bishan, Pramodak and Jodha, while also firing sporadically at Bijoy, Trikoni, Pakwan and Takkar through the night. Pramodak II (all observation posts are marked as II) was the main target and at dawn, the Chinese, presuming that all the men had been killed in the bombardment, started to close in on the Indian post. Commanded by a Naik, the five Indian soldiers fought tenaciously. All of them were eventually killed, but not before they had exacted a heavy toll on the Chinese. The attacking troops were all Sinkiang Muslims and it is estimated that more than a hundred of them were killed or wounded; after this incident, the Chinese only approached Indian posts when they were convinced that there were no survivors."[6] Also on that day, 20th October, the Chinese surrounded the Daulat Beg Oldi (DBO) post from all sides and tried hard to overrun it; but the post never surrendered and fought back tenaciously. Further to the east lay the dominating features of Rezang and Pangong ranges rising up to a maximum height of 19,750 feet. The defensive positions north and south of Pangong lake were held by 1/8 GR. In this sector an epic clash of arms took place on the morning of 21st October in which the Charlie company commander of this battalion, Major Dhan Singh Thapa, was awarded Param Vir Chakra. This general area was called the Srijap sector and it was considered crucial for the defence of Chushul airfield. The company of Maj. Thapa was located north of the lake and deployed on three posts called; Srijap West, Srijap East and Srijap Jamini. There was also an observation point named Srijap Screen.

His PVC citation provides a vivid and chronological description of this momentous struggle. It mentions, "...one of these outposts named Srijap-1 was held by a platoon of C Company under Major Dhan Singh Thapa when the Chinese attack came on 21 October 1962...At 0600 hours on 21 October 1962, the Chinese opened a barrage of artillery and mortar fire over Srijap-1 post. The shelling continued till 0830 hours and the whole area was set ablaze. Some shells fell on the command post and damaged the wireless set. This put the post out of commission...The Chinese then attacked the outpost in overwhelming numbers. Major Thapa and his men repulsed the attack, inflicting heavy casualties on the enemy. But the Chinese were not dismayed by the defeat. They mounted another attack in greater number after shelling the area with artillery and mortar fire. Major Thapa again rose to the occasion and repulsed the attack, inflicting heavy losses on the enemy. In this attack, he also suffered losses but these could

6 Shiv Kunal Verma, *Op. Cit.*, p. 333.

not weaken his determination. He encouraged his men to be prepared for a third assault, which came after a short while indeed...The third Chinese attack was, however, more powerful and intense. The enemy now came with tanks in support of the infantry. The platoon post was now in a much depleted strength owing to casualties suffered in earlier attacks. But the post held out till the ammunition lasted. When it was finally overrun by the Chinese, Major Thapa jumped out of his trench and killed many intruders in hand-to-hand fighting. He was eventually overpowered and captured..." During the past three days, the intensities of attacks, concentration of troops and weaponry and the tanks being used in support of the infantry; caused a lot of worry to the senior Indian commanders at all levels. Increased efforts started to further shore up the defences around Chushul area.

In the second phase; the Chinese did not mount any significant attacks in this sector, but struck further west and south in the general area of Damchok. This also gave them the opportunity to regroup and reorganize in the area where major and wide spread operations had taken place. Simultaneously, the new move also palpably threatened Leh town from another axis – which was hardly defended. From this time onwards the defence of Leh – in addition to strengthening the Chushul base – became a high priority with the Indian military commanders. By 24 October three positive developments had taken place in the Chushul sector. 13 Kumaon had taken up defensive positions in this area; including occupation of the dominating heights at Rezang La. A Mahar MMG (Medium Machine Gun) Platoon arrived on the scene. Also joining the troops at Chushul; was a battery – of six medium range guns – belonging to the 13 Field Regiment. Next day, on the 25th October, six AN-12 aircrafts taking off from Chandigarh landed on the makeshift airfield at Chushul; one at a time. Every flight was carrying one AMX-13 light tank; these tanks were a part of 20 Lancers – an armoured regiment of the Indian army. The arrival of this component of armour added lot of strength to the defensive capabilities of the Chushul base. But, still the fact remained that the Chinese were also uncomfortably close to this position. Concurrently, almost synchronizing with the positive happenings in Chushul; the defence of Leh was assuming greater importance by the day.

After the first phase offensive was over on 21st October, the Peking (now Beijing) radio announced Chushul as being the next Chinese objective; which was quite expected and logical also. But the Chinese attacks in the second phase of operations – from 24 to 26 October – in the Damchok area, took the Indians by surprise. On a different plane; as an integral and effective part of their psychological warfare, the Chinese succeeded in planting a thought in the Indian mind that Leh also could be a possible target of China. This gave rise to a flurry of activity; all aimed at strong and effective defence of Leh town and the areas around. The Western Command was now faced with the urgent need to provide adequate protection to Leh region. It quickly arranged to send almost a division worth of troops to Ladakh by mainly thinning out deployment on the Pakistan border. On 25th October, Brig. R.S. Grewal, MC, came to Leh with Headquarters 70 Infantry Brigade and took over the responsibility for the defence of Indus valley sector. This Brigade soon effectively dominated the axis of Dungti-Chumathang-Kiari; neutralizing the new Chinese threat. On 26th October Maj. Gen. Budh Singh officially established the Headquarters of 3 Division at Leh. The impressive building at Leh, with scenic surroundings, which once housed the British Joint Commissioner and later were taken over by the 7 J&K Militia battalion; now became nerve centre of the new 3 Div. With the help of 70 Brigade; the 3 Div embarked upon a plan for the defence of Leh; which also included holding all possible routes to the town in strength. Hence, in addition to the Dungti-Chumathang-Kiari region; the Chang La pass area was secured in depth, including positioning of troops in Darbuk and beyond. Thus while 3 Div, with the help of 70 Brigade and some other units, became charged with the task of defending Leh; 114 Brigade at Chushul remained under the direct operational control of 15 Corps, and generally responsible for the northern sector.

The Indian higher commanders, at the level of 15 Corps and Western Command, now had to contend with twin priorities in the Ladakh region; the defence of Leh, in addition to the efficient management of operations against the Chinese. The latter were mostly concentrated in the Chushul sector and along the frontage of 114 Infantry Brigade. On 27 October, the Corps Commander Bikram Singh turned down the request of Brig. Raina for additional troops to further secure defence of Chushul; saying that while he understood and sympathized with his requirements, organizing adequate defence of Leh was a bigger priority. There was also a feverish pitch of activity at the Corps and Command Headquarters; as the staff at both these places wrestled with the logistics demands of raising the 3 Div and 70 Brigade; in addition to the induction of a good number of units to these formations. All this had a high precedence over anything else. Thus, a large number of units were not only required to be inducted into Ladakh area at a short notice; but also their winter stocking had to be ensured well before the Zoji La got closed due to heavy snow; which could happen anytime after the end of November. Finding the adequate number of troops, transport and equipment etc. and their actual movement to the destination kept the staff at these two headquarters busy, almost round the clock, during the three months of October, November and December 1962.

The Chinese, on the other hand, were still holding the cards in their hands in respect of the next move; and looking forward to further consolidate the gains made so far. The targets were still the same; greater security to their assets in the Aksai Chin area and militarily humiliate India to the extent possible. The Chinese intentions on Chushul and areas around were hampered and impeded by the Indian defences at Rezang La. Different parts of the Rezang feature have described as; Point 18300 dominated the pass in the north and another peak in excess of 18,000 feet, towered over it to the east. To the south and to the west there was a drop of around 1,900 feet. The pass itself was situated at an average height of 16,000 feet and its northern shoulder was higher than the southern side. The posts at Rezang La were first made and occupied by 7 J&K Militia in May 1961 and later taken over from them by the men of 1/8 GR. Right from the beginning, these defences were not prepared well; as owing to the hard and rocky terrain no regular trenches or bunkers had been made. In most cases the positions were built of stone sangars with tin roof over head as sort of shelters. The quality of stones in that area was brittle; which tended to splinter when hit by artillery or mortar fire; thereby magnifying the destructive impact of any bombardment there. To make matters worse; the Rezang La positions were also conspicuously isolated in many ways. Its defences were not mutually supported by any other post; also lacked cover by the battalion mortars and support from the brigade artillery. The position did not have a gunner FOO posted with them. Rezang La also had a very rudimentary system of communications with the battalion headquarters; which was not dependable and most of the time messages had to be relayed by an intermediary post. Therefore, in more than one way, Rezang La could be termed as an isolated position and no higher headquarters did anything worthwhile to make it more inclusive with the main defences of the Chushul base. It was under these conditions that the

Charlie (C) company of 13 Kumaon, under the command of Major Shaitan Singh, replaced 1/8 GR troops on 6th of November 1962.

Shaitan Singh's outfit consisted of his Company HQ and number 7, 8 and 9 Platoons. Number seven Platoon was deployed on the left higher ridge; while as 8 Platoon occupied the main pass; whereas No. 9 Platoon was positioned between the two. The company command post was little to the west of 8 Platoon locations. The entire defensive locality was cited to look west in the valley; but unfortunately the platoon positions were not mutually supporting; as also bereft of any mortar or artillery covering fire. The Chinese, on the other hand, had enough time to conduct detailed recce of this position; the pattern of troop deployment, weaknesses of this defended locality and possible approaches to it. They moved four columns, simultaneously, during the evening of 17 November so that these men could climb up the slopes during the dark hours of night and attack in strength, the next early morning; duly backed up by artillery and mortar support. While it was still dark; around 4 a.m. on the 18th, all men of Shaitan Singh's company opened fire on the Chinese in the light of an illuminating flare fired by the company commander – inflicting heavy casualties on them.

The Battle of Rezang La had begun

When the morning light was sufficient; the Chinese opened up the backup fire not only in support of their ground troops engaged in assaulting Rezang La; but also carried out considerable 'softening fire' on the adjoining Indian locations. With clearer visibility, as the morning progressed, the Chinese threw everything in the battle to overcome the resistance at Rezang La and subdue its doughty defenders. It is on record that the attacking force employed fire by 132 mm rockets, 120 mm heavy mortars, 81 and 60 mm medium mortars and 75 and 53 mm RCL guns in a direct firing role. This heavy barrage of fire became even more deadly with splintering of the 'sangar' stones. By 7.30 a.m. the positions of 7 and 8 Platoons were overrun; but few survivors continued to fight.

From this point onwards, the inspiring saga of Rezang La has been described as, "With two of his platoons all but wiped out, Shaitan Singh along with his company havildar major, Phool Singh, and two other men decided to join up with No. 9 Platoon, some 550 meters away. Hardly had they covered quarter of the distance when the company commander was hit in the stomach by an MMG burst. Between them the three men managed to somehow evacuate the mortally wounded officer. At 16,000 feet it required a superhuman effort, yet they managed to get within 800 meters of the unoccupied Rezang La Base Camp. Shaitan Singh was still conscious and coherent. He ordered the men to stop, leave him where he was and return to No. 9 Platoon that was still holding out. Phool Singh and the two men did as they were told. All three of them returned to No. 9 Platoon and were killed shortly afterwards. Major Shaitan Singh remained where his men left him, too weak to move, eventually breathing his last amidst the stony, desolate wilderness. He had done enough to carve not just his own name, but also the names of all the men under his command into the pages of Indian history."[7] His PVC citation also details the Rezang La engagement as, "...Chinese attack on Rezang La came on 18 November in the morning. It was the end of a very cold winter night. The icy winds howling through Rezang La were biting and benumbing. In the dim light of the morning the Chinese were seen advancing through nullahs to attack No. 7 and 8 Platoon positions... At 0500 hours when the visibility improved both platoons opened up on the advancing enemy with rifles, light machine guns, grenades and mortars. The nullahs were littered with dead bodies. The survivors took positions behind boulders and dead bodies. The enemy was not, however, discouraged. He subjected the Indian positions to intense artillery and mortar fire at about 0540 hours. Soon about three hundred and fifty Chinese commenced advance through the nullahs. This time No. 9 Platoon which held fire till the enemy was within 90 meters opened up with all weapons in their possession. Within minutes, the nullahs were again full of dead bodies. Unsuccessful in frontal attack, the enemy, approximately 400 strong, then attacked from the rear of the company position.... When 20 survivors charged the post, about a dozen Kumaonis rushed out of their trenches to engage them in a hand-to-hand combat. Meanwhile, the enemy brought up fresh reinforcements. The encirclement of 7 Platoon was now complete. The platoon, however, fought valiantly till there was no survivor. No. 8 Platoon also fought bravely to the last round.

"Major Singh, the Company Commander, displayed exemplary leadership and courage in the battle of Rezang La. He led his troops most admirably. Unmindful of his personal safety he moved from one platoon to another and encouraged his men to fight. While moving among the posts

7 Shiv Kunal Verma, *Op.Cit.* p. 359.

he was seriously wounded. But he continued to fight along with his men. While he was being evacuated by two other ranks, the Chinese brought heavy machine gun fire on them. Major Singh sensed danger to their lives and ordered them to leave him. The other ranks placed him behind a boulder on the slopes of a hill where he breathed his last. In this action 109[8] Kumaonis out of a total of 123 were killed. The Chinese suffered many more in killed. After the war was over, the body of Major Singh was found at the same place. It was flown to Jodhpur and cremated with full military honours."

Rezang La thus passed into the history as a saga of grit and bravery against very heavy odds.

The next afternoon, 19th November, the Corps Commander Bikram Singh and Brig. Raina met at the Brigade Headquarters in Chushul amidst sporadic shelling. Brushing aside the mild protests of some junior officers; the Corps Commander ordered the brigade headquarters to move further west of Chushul and vacate that base[9]. He was expecting the Chinese to anytime mount an attack on Chushul, through the Spanggur Gap and wanted the 114 Brigade to move, along with all heavy equipment, before that happened. Also, for Bikram Singh, the defence of Leh took priority over all other matters in the battlefield. The Chinese did make a move towards this area but never seriously attacked Chushul. In fact, they did not occupy the important features vacated by the Indian troops in that area.

The Chinese announced a unilateral ceasefire all along India's northern borders on the morning of 21st November. Thus, from that date, ended all military operations also in the Ladakh sector. The Chinese said that they were withdrawing to a line, all along the border, which was under their control on 8 September 1962; and that their forces would vacate areas occupied by then in the subsequent operations. By and large, they carried out this stated position in the eastern sector – the NEFA region – but in the western side, the Ladakh region, the Chinese continued to be in possession of areas important to them. In fact, they established six new posts in this sector; and have effectively resisted all Indian moves to go forward. They still maintain an aggressive posture in Ladakh.

---

8 Some sources, though, put this figure as 114.

9 Ultimately this Brigade Headquarters established itself at Darbuk, further to the west.

In this war, the high gallantry awards included a Param Vir Chakra to Major Dhan Singh Thapa of 1/8 GR and also a Param Vir Chakra to Major Shaitan Singh of 13 Kumaon. The Commander of 114 Infantry Brigade, Brig. T.N. Raina was awarded Mahavir Chakra for displaying "commendable courage, leadership and devotion to duty in handling his brigade". The local military hero, Chewang Rinchen (he had become a Lt. by then), was awarded a Sena Medal for his bravery in the DBO sector. The 1/8 GR was at that time commanded by Lt. Col. Hari Chand; who had become a hero of all Ladakh for his gallant acts in 1948 and was then awarded a MVC. For some odd reasons he did not receive any gallantry award in 1962; his further promotion was also blocked and he subsequently retired in the same rank.

It is a fact that the Indian army, for a variety of reasons, was badly mauled by the Chinese forces all along the northern borders of India. This was true of Ladakh sector also. Here, apart from a number of non defensible 'forward posts'; only two companies – one each from 1/8 GR and 13 Kumaon – were engaged in pitched battle against their adversaries. Both gave a very good account of themselves by sheer grit and valour. At a higher level; only one formation, 114 Infantry Brigade took part in these operations – the 70 Infantry Brigade came up in the later stages of the war and was actually deployed in the Dungti-Chumathang-Kiari axis; but it did not take part in the combat. The overall situation has been well described as, "… In fact only one Company of 5 Jats, the 1/8 GR Battalion and one company of 13 Kumaon Battalion had fought very well in the battles of Ladakh, as these were deployed properly on the battlefield. The platoon and section posts deployed in the north along the large frontage could not possibly and logically have faced the large Chinese forces in Ladakh. The Indian Army needed to have at least two Divisions worth of troops in the large Ladakh region to offer any worthwhile resistance in the 1962 war… The actual fact is that the Indian Army was not really prepared to face the large scale Chinese attack while the Chinese forces were fully prepared for the war… India in Ladakh had deployed about two brigade worth of troops, it had only very limited artillery support. It had only one Artillery Regiment in the Chushul area to support the Indian forward positions. Obviously, it was too inadequate to give the necessary artillery support to the Indian troops deployed along the large border…The Chinese, on the other hand, had deployed a number of artillery regiments, equipped mostly with Mortars. In the hilly terrain mortars are more effective as compared to guns for giving necessary fire support to the infantry units. This was a highly adverse development because the Indian forces could not possibly fight effectively without having proper artillery support. The Chinese obviously out gunned and outnumbered us in Ladakh in 1962."[10]

The history of India is replete with examples of wars and armed clashes where heroic exploits of the victors have been celebrated over the ages and tales of their spirited valour talked about for long. But three battles in this country are remembered for the courage, determination and bravery of the defenders – who were also the losers in each of these encounters. The first engagement in this category is the battle of Haldighati. This was fought on 18th June 1576 between the forces led by Maharana Pratap and the troops of Emperor Akbar under the command of Man Singh – I of Amber (Jaipur). It was a bloody clash of arms in which Maharana Pratap lost; but Haldighati became a symbol of fortitude and daring. Colonel James Todd, in his celebrated book titled 'Annals and Antiquities of Rajasthan', equates the combat at Haldighati with the Battle of Thermopylae. That is followed by another memorable encounter, on 12th September 1897 known as the battle of Saragarhi; where 21 heroic Sikh soldiers – from their small fortress - fought very valiantly against thousands of attacking Pashtun Orakzai tribesman (some estimates put this figure as ten thousand). This happened in the North West Frontier area of the then British India. Each one of the brave Sikhs died fighting; hopelessly outnumbered. Their resolute courage was paid a standing tribute by the entire British Parliament when details of this encounter were read over in that House. The third in this illustrious series is the battle of Rezang La; which happened on 18th November 1962. Here the clash took place between hordes of attacking Chinese and resolute men of the Charlie Company of 13 Kumaon. They were very bravely led by Major Shaitan Singh. Inspiring leadership of this daring and gallant company commander put the nerves of steel in every soldier who fought till the last round and the last breath. These three battles would long inspire the young Indians for generations to come.

The 1962 war was certainly a military disaster for India. Decidedly, the well-established road and air connectivity saved Ladakh from being run over entirely by the People's Liberation Army of China when China launched aggression on India simultaneously in Ladakh and Arunachal Pradesh. In this short war; unprepared India was comprehensively defeated

10 Rajendra Nath, *Op. Cit.,* pp. 201 and 199.

and China annexed a huge chunk of uninhabited area of Ladakh; the Aksai Chin. As for the whole Ladakh region; the 1962 Chinese aggression proved, in a manner of speaking, a boon as it heightened manifold its importance to the country's defences. From then, this hugely neglected and backward region of the country started receiving unprecedented attention of both the Central and State governments; leading to its accelerated development. The result was, as someone rightly put it, 'In a short span of a decade, 'Ladakh moved from Bongbu to Boeing (from donkey to jet-plane as means of transportation)', as a part of independent India. This example may be a slight exaggeration; but it succinctly describes the overall impact of these events on the entire region. The number of AN-12 Transport Aircrafts landings in Leh increased manifold in the subsequent years; followed by civilian planes after January 1979. It is also a fact that unlike in 1948; the local Ladakhis did not take part in this military clash as the entire fighting happened in the uninhabited terrain. But, at the same time, huge areas in the Aksai Chin sector which came under the control of Chinese; were good pasture lands where flocks of animals belonging to the Ladakhis grazed in the summer months. These were henceforth, lost to the locals. This was certainly a severe blow to the people who were trying to recover from the loss of trade channels with the Tibetan region and the Central Asian markets. The situation was further aggravated with the arrival of Tibetan refugees in Ladakh.

As mentioned earlier, there was only one army unit in and around Leh in the early fifties; and that being 7 J&K Militia. From this lowly strength of troops; by the end of 1962, force level in this area included three headquarters of 3 Div, 70 Infantry Brigade and 114 Infantry Brigade. The increased presence of forces meant a large number of fighting and supporting arms units. This provided sizeable direct and indirect monetary benefits to the entire population; which in turn helped the local economy to grow. The main road from Srinagar to Leh was handed over to the Border Roads Organization (BRO) for maintenance and upgrading. The BRO had located a Task Force, commanded by a Lt. Col. in Leh till the eighties. Later this was upgraded to Project Himank under the command of a Brigadier; charged with the responsibility of improving and ensuring an alternative access to Leh via Manali as well as constructing and maintaining a number of important internal roads; in addition to looking after the main Srinagar – Leh artery.

Apart from the induction of army in a big way, following the Chinese aggression in 1962; many new posts, sub units and units of the para military forces – particularly the Indo-Tibetan Border Police (ITBP) also came to be located in the region. This gave rise to considerable amount of building activity all over the area; especially the road construction work was undertaken in a big way with consequent spin-off benefits to the local people and the system.

During this period the Ladakh Scouts also grew in strength as well as reputation.

In this region the Chinese designs did not end with the war of October – November 1962; though sinister this was in its own way. Giving a practical shape to the famous percept of Chanakya – of an enemy's enemy being a friend – the Chinese extended a hand of friendship and cooperation to Pakistan. In the beginning of March 1963, Pakistan ceded to the Chinese a territory of 5,800 square kilometres (virtually 2% of the entire area of the erstwhile princely state of J&K) in the Karakoram sector. The document of the Agreement mentioned that this was done 'pending the settlement of dispute over Kashmir'. The mischief was done and its negative effects, for India, continue to be felt. Not long before this development, the airfield at Gilgit was a threat to the Chinese military base at Kashgar in Xinjiang province; and by virtue of this treaty, the Chinese were practically sitting next door to Gilgit. Over the decades since then; China's own military expansion measures coupled with its active support to Pakistan in the nuclear and missile programmes; have posed a serious threat to the security of India. The Chinese have patiently worked on Pakistan since then and almost fifty years later reached an agreement worth about 50 billion Dollars of infrastructural developments in Pakistan under the China-Pakistan Economic Corridor (CPEC); including setting up of modern facilities at the Gwadar port on the Pakistani coast. Finally, China achieved its historical dream of seeking a warm water port for her western and southern regions. From many angles, this strategic Sino-Pakistan axis – which has a number of times been described as 'higher than mountains and deeper than sea' – poses a huge security challenge to India.

Cooperative Society Comes of Age

As already mentioned; the induction of army in a big way in 1962 provided considerable and many faceted benefits to the local population. The mutual respect and a feeling of interdependence has always been the backbone of the civil – army relationship in this region. These sentiments and the situation around that difficult period was recalled by Kalon Sahib as, "...I have always held the belief that fifty percent of the development of Ladakh has been either due to the presence of the army or driven by the presence of army in a indirect manner. They helped us in the form of construction of roads, providing medical facilities in the far flung areas as well as by buying of local produce through the cooperative societies. Of course the local population has also been very helpful to the army. Thus it has been a mutually dependent relationship with almost a symbiotic connection... During the battle of Chushul in 1962, there was shortage of vegetables for the troops. Butalia[11] who was the Deputy Commissioner asked me if locals could spare some vegetables. When I replied in the affirmative, his next query was how much could be spared. I mentioned a figure of two to three tons; hearing which Butalia became very happy and asked me to procure the same. With the help of other farmers and friends we were able to despatch ten tons of vegetables to Chushul garrison. This was made available free of cost to the army. Farmers in Ladakh have traditionally maintained that help to the defenders of the nation in times of war is not to be charged for, as providing assistance to the army during such a time is the national duty. This episode was, in a way, cursor to the beginning of the constitution of cooperative society for supply of vegetables and related items to the army. Immediately after this; Butalia called a meeting in DC's office and asked us whether we can meet part of army's requirement on sustained basis at least for a specific period in a year. Other modalities regarding rates and transportation etc. were fixed in this meeting. We offered cabbage and turnips for one rupee and potatoes for 12 annas per kg. The Deputy Commissioner was surprised at such low rates...1962-63 was the first year of this cooperative experiment and we supplied vegetables worth ten thousand rupees to the army – a commitment which was successfully carried out and created a confidence in our capacity to deliver what had been promised."[12] A crucial breakthrough and an important beginning had been made; which had a considerable impact on the local economy, as the time progressed.

However, it was not easy for even Kalon Sahib to convince the farmers to cultivate and spare sufficient quantities of vegetables – to start

11 He was an IFAS officer.

12 Interview with Rigzin Namgyal Kalon in September 1998.

with potatoes, cabbages and turnips – for selling to the army; and also to organize a Cooperative Society for doing this business. The main stumbling block in this endeavour lay in the traditions long followed by Ladakhi farmer. Vegetables were neither a major source of diet nor a cash crop in Ladakh. The land there is generally not very fertile and land holdings, at an average quite small. So, wherever the land was irrigated, the traditional farmer of the region grew some vegetables just for the family consumption – a sort of luxury in the matters of diet. Therefore, the vegetable cultivation was more on the 'kitchen garden' pattern; than any thought or purpose of selling the produce in the market. Unlike the Kashmir valley; this place did not have any culture of consumption or trading of dried vegetables for the long and harsh winter season. This was for the simple reason that there were no surplus vegetables in the first place. From this rather bleak background to the stage of locals selling vegetables to the army through a cooperative society – and also to the general public in the markets – lies the ingenuity, perseverance and sustained hard work of the Kalon family. Intricately connected is also the story of 'potatoes' and the Moravian Mission in Leh. This tale goes back to the beginning of twentieth century. At that time the Moravian Mission people were importing potato seeds and bulbs into Leh; as potatoes were not the native vegetable of the region. These Missionaries grew potatoes on a patch of land in their backyard and also distributed a part of the crop to some locals in their contact. Over a period, four families were reported to have converted to Christianity due to this potato influence. This development set the bells ringing in the Buddhist community; and it is believed that after a series of discussions a strategy was evolved to deal with the issue. An influential Lama convened a meeting of locals in the Leh Bazaar (main market) and there in that gathering, confidently mentioned that as per the religious scriptures; the persons eating potatoes are likely to go to hell. This pronouncement had quite an impact on the locals resulting in their not consuming potatoes any more. It is also said that the four families, who had converted on this count, came back to the Buddhist fold.

Kalon Sahib's father – Chewang Rigzin Kalon – was not only an influential person in the entire area; but also a very shrewd, hard working and far sighted man. He watched the whole drama unfold but said nothing about it to either party. The Moravian Mission quietly withdrew this effort; however, the residents continued to grow potatoes for their own use only. Chewang Rigzin Kalon realised the high value of this new vegetable; due to its longer shelf life and considerable nutritional value – so important for a place like Ladakh. He managed to get few bulbs from the Mission – a local story goes that he procured these almost clandestinely through his wife; who was on friendly terms with some of the nuns there. He planted these in the back yard of his house; in a patch surrounded by high walls on all four sides so that none could peep over and see what was inside. When matured; a part of this crop was distributed to few of the relatives. The cycle thus continued. Slowly, over the years, potatoes became a popular crop and were grown by a number of people in Leh and Nubra areas.

Yet, nobody ever thought of selling this or other vegetables as a cash crop. This idea was first mooted by Butalia in 1963. He advised Kalon Sahib to start a cooperative society and provide vegetables to the army; on rates and conditions which would be beneficial to both parties. The troops were generally getting all their 'fresh' rations flown by aircrafts – especially during the long winter months – which was often a cumbersome and delayed process. When these supplies were ferried from Srinagar – during the road open period – it took almost three days; or even longer to reach the final destination; the Cook House. Therefore, procurement of local and fresh vegetables, whatever quantity could be spared, was certainly a good proposition and ensured handsome returns to the locals as well as the final consumers – the troops on ground. Still, most of the locals did not then agree with this suggestion of Kalon Sahib and brushed aside the thought of trading vegetables on a commercial scale with the army. For them, this was something the farmers grew for personal consumption only. Some people even made fun of this idea.

Luckily, Kalon Sahib was convinced of the efficacy of this plan and persisted with the scheme. To start with, he practically became the lone supplier of potatoes and couple of other vegetables to the army. He received the first instalment for his produce; in the form of a cheque of rupees four thousand from the army, in 1963. This he deposited in the local branch of the SBI and requested the Branch Manager to encash the cheque; and give him the entire money in one rupee denomination and not in the notes of larger value. The man, of course, did not have such large amount in the required currency and promised to call back when the next quota of notes arrived from Chandigarh by air. After a few days he called Kalon Sahib to his branch and gave him all this money in crisp one rupee notes – still confused about this queer request. It was a large amount in size and Kalon

Sahib put the entire money in the front lap of his 'Goncha' spread over both his fore-arms. In this very position; holding the entire cash between his arms and in the 'Goncha' he headed towards home. Although, the SBI Branch and his own house both were situated along the same outer edge of Leh town; he deliberately went home traversing a much longer distance and walking through the entire market. Along the way, he told the eager bystanders that all this money he had got from selling vegetables to the army; and that this was a paying as well as a possible proposition. This was his way of giving a live demonstration to the non-believers in this venture. As he had anticipated; the word spread that Kalon Sahib had got such a large amount of money from the army by selling vegetables that he had to carry the cash in his lap instead of putting the same in his pockets. Slowly, more and more locals joined this effort; to the benefit of both parties. This cooperative venture started very modestly; with a business of around ten thousand rupees in 1963, as already mentioned. It grew handsomely over the years[13].

Not that efforts were not made in the Kargil region to apply this model gainfully. Kargil was then a sub-division of Ladakh district with two tehsils of Kargil and Zanskar. The local administration there did make credible exertions, particularly in the summer of 1974, to catch up with the successful model adopted by the Leh farmers. In this respect, the diary of then SDM, Kargil noted on 23rd September 1974 as, "I had a discussion with the District Agriculture Officer Wazir, regarding selling vegetables to the army through Cooperative Marketing Societies. This would involve a massive effort first to persuade the farmers in growing vegetables; as also providing them with necessary inputs and finally organising the Cooperative Marketing Societies so that the middle man is removed and the grower gets maximum return out of his produce". This work continued at a good pace for the next few months and various loose ends were tied up as also preparations made to start the scheme from the next summer. In this respect two significant observations were again recorded by the same officer on 27th December 1974 and these read, "... I got a call from Kalon Sahib, Secretary Cooperative Marketing Society, Leh regarding the details of vegetables that we would be able to supply to the army next year. This person on whom Kargil farmers would be depending on for various marketing services and liaison with the army, seemed to be interested in

13 The four paras above are based on an interaction with Col. Wangdus (Retd), on 8th November 2018. He is the eldest son of Kalon Sahib.

our project of growing vegetables on a commercial scale – and that is a good sign… Had a meeting with some of the local farmers regarding vegetable production programme. With their advice and consent we fixed up targets for supplying various vegetables to the army next year. The start is very modest, a target of 450 quintals only; as I am personally keen to see that we make a cautious but sound beginning. This is certainly a measure to bring prosperity to the local farmers. The whole administration is making concerted efforts to see that they get all help; how much they take advantage of it is yet to be seen." But, efforts to replicate the success of Leh in the Kargil region did not fructify then; and there were primarily two reasons for this. Firstly, the local farmers in Kargil did not appear enthused with this idea and thus denied themselves an opportunity to get the benefits that their counter parts in Leh region were enjoying over the last one decade. The second, and more potent, factor was the absence in Kargil of a forward looking and binding personality like Rigzin Namgyal Kalon in Leh.

Seen in the historical perspective; it was in 1964 that few progressive farmers in Leh – including the Nubra area - with the active help and encouragement of local administration, formally established the first Farmers Cooperative Society to produce and supply vegetables to the army. For the next three decades the rates of various commodities were mutually arrived at during the winter season; in a committee jointly headed by the Deputy Commissioner and the local Divisional Commander, and which also included few concerned army officers and the farmers interests represented by Kalon Sahib and few of his colleagues. In this meeting, apart from the rates; various other items like collection points and transportation arrangements were also deliberated upon and decided. About thirty years later – in the early nineties - with the persistent efforts of the growers and with support of the local commanders; the Ministry of Defence approved the 'Negotiated Contract' system of the army with local registered Farmers Coop Societies. This sanction has been generally renewed every three years since then. This system, which has evolved over many decades, is certainly of considerable benefit to the local farmers, the soldiers and the army, as an organisation, as well.

The farmer in this kind of arrangement is in control of everything from his field to the consumer. He gets what the army pays; elsewhere in the country a farmer gets only about twenty five percent of what a consumer pays for his produce. Because there is a long string of middlemen in the chain from his field to the consumer. The army in Ladakh has been the biggest and most reliable consumer; and the farmer gets of what army pays minus the cost of handling and transportation; which is about 93% of the value for his produce. The local farmers also meet almost half of the fodder requirement of the army. The rest of the fodder, in the form of 'bailed hay' is transported from the plains. A much superior local type of fodder called Alfa-Alfa is given to the army; and that too at half the cost of bailed hay. The business of Ladakhi farmers has been in the range of ten crores by the end of 1990s; through the Cooperative Societies; which have over ten thousand house-hold members. These are huge numbers for the area; and that is the extent of financial advantages to the growers and local economy.

A study undertaken in this context established that around half of the soldiers consume local vegetables of Ladakh. To that extent the soldier is fortunate because he gets to eat pure and organically grown produce which is decidedly much more nutritious and healthier than the commonly grown vegetables in plains of the country. Resultantly, considerable benefits also flow to the man in uniform. The army also is a net gainer, and quite handsomely, in this arrangement. It is able to provide, by local arrangements of procurement, a very healthy food to the *jawans* at almost half of the cost which it would otherwise pay. The local availability of a major chunk of the army requirements of vegetables have resulted in considerable savings for it in terms of transportation charges by road and / or by air; which would otherwise range from Rs. 180 to Rs. 230 per kg. This arrangement has also further cemented the good relations between army and the local population. There have been, of course, occasional incidents of vested interests trying to put obstacles in the course of smooth functioning of this decades old and tried system. The struggle goes on. So far the existing procedures have survived.

Taking an overall perspective of this phenomenon, which is unique in many respects, one finds that the parent organisation of this experiment, The Cooperative Marketing Society, Leh was founded in 1964 with the objective that in the event of future wars there, locally produced food items should be available for the forces to strengthen their logistic support. Over the decades, the Farmers Cooperative Societies have increased in numbers to more than fifteen in various parts of the region. All these have come under an umbrella organisation called the Association of Farmers' Cooperative Marketing Societies of Ladakh. These societies are totally self-reliant and do not get any funds from anywhere to sustain themselves. In fact a document of the parent body, as indicated above, proudly proclaims, "...the Farmers Societies have enabled the Army to save around 11 crores on air and surface transport. In fact the Ladakhi farmers have been the bulwark of national defence and security right from 1948...A Ladakhi farmer can be called a soldier without rations, uniform and pay..."

Although the existing system has been functioning to the satisfaction of concerned parties for decades; improvements can certainly be made in the current arrangements. These include a more remunerative return to the farmers based on a scientific study carried out by an authorized professional group which should ideally include few of the local progressive farmers also. The other useful measure could be the providing of temperature controlled storage facilities to the farmers; so that their produce could be enhanced and also kept fresh over a much longer period. Till the time such steps are implemented; this experiment of selling vegetables and fodder to the army would continue to be a unique feature of civil- army cordial and happy relationship in the entire Ladakh region.

Infrastructural Improvements

During this period the J&K state government was headed by three important personalities; in sequence Bakshi Ghulam Mohammad, G.M. Sadiq and Syed Mir Qasim. This list does not include the short and insignificant tenure of Shamas-ud-Din. For little over a decade, under reference, Ladakh region witnessed an increased level of infrastructural up gradation and developmental activities. This sharper focus on all round improvement, as compared to the earlier period, was partly due to the enhanced importance of Ladakh following the Indo – China war of 1962; as also the result of greater push to growth and expansion activities in rest of the state. Of course, the most important infrastructural project in the entire region was the road connectivity between Srinagar and Leh; which was completed in August 1960; and just in time. Beginning of a substantial push to various governmental activities was made in December 1964, when the Sadiq government appointed a high powered body named as The Ladakh Development Committee, to deliberate on all relevant measures and advise the government regarding the policies and issues affecting good governance and speedy development of Ladakh. This

Committee was established by the Government Order No. 387-C of 1964 dated 14th December 1964. Kushok Bakula was to be Chairman of this body by virtue of being the Minister of State for Ladakh Affairs; and Aga Ibrahim Shah, M.L.C. from Kargil was made as the Vice-Chairman. This Development Committee enjoyed considerable powers and it could summon any Minister, Secretary or head of a Department to attend any of its meetings. This was considered to be necessary as all the departments had their offices in Ladakh and the Committee could function effectively only in coordinated collaboration with them. It was prescribed that the Committee would meet at least twice in a year and that one of its meeting would be held at a suitable place in Ladakh district. Almost two pages of detailed instructions were issued in this government order covering duties, responsibilities and remunerations etc. of this body[14]. The whole exercise appeared to be aimed at involving the Ladakhis in their developmental programmes and then also to function as a monitoring mechanism. A month later G.M. Sadiq, famously said, "…the development of Ladakh has been uppermost in our minds and I take this opportunity to assure the Ladakhis that the government will do everything for their advancement". Some analysts feel that such commitments were really not honoured by the state government and this region remained neglected for quite some time more. To bolster this argument; a reference is made to the official figures according to which during the Fourth Plan period, the outlay for Ladakh was only Rs. 600 lakhs as compared to the total outlay of the state of Rs. 15, 840 lakhs. The difference in two figures is really astounding.

The first meeting of the Ladakh Development Committee, so constituted as mentioned above, was held in Jammu on 7th March 1965 and this body resolved to accord priority to "schemes pertaining to generation of electric power, development of irrigation and expansion of education in Ladakh". Under these over all directions; some of the significant projects and schemes implemented and undertaken during the next decade, include the following;-

- Stakna Hydel Project. In the extremely cold area like Ladakh; any channel carrying water for generation of electricity has to be based on one of the two principles. It must either have a steep

14 This scheme was later amended vide Government Order No. 1278-GD of 1969 dated 26th May, 1969; by making the Chief Minister to head the reconstituted "Ladakh Development Board."

gradient, which should give rise to a self-cleansing velocity in the chute or, in the alternative, the water channel should be very deep so that even while the upper crust of water is frozen, due to very low temperatures outside; a substantial amount of water still reaches the generation point in fluid condition and help generate the requisite power. Since the natural gradient of the source – the Indus River – is very gentle in this sector; it was technically decided to follow the latter alternative and a deep channel was planned there. This single project consumed most of the allocated money and, over the years, resulted in huge time and cost overruns. The same allocations could have been utilized in other sectors, more productively.

- Plans were finalized and work started on the Iqbal Mini Hydel project in Kargil.

- The district headquarters of Leh was electrified in January 1965, with the commissioning of the first diesel-based generating set there. This was followed by the installation of lower capacity of generating sets of similar nature, in Kargil, Nyoma and Drass. These provided electricity for lighting purposes only to the local population of these towns, for four to five hours in the evening. Those days, even this facility was a great improvement.

- The J&K Minerals Corporation Limited was asked to conduct a detailed survey of the mineral potential of this region; as it was believed to be rich in this respect. No investigation report was ever made public or an audit of these efforts was thereafter carried out. But this Corporation did put up a pilot plant at Puga valley to collect Borax from the natural 'geysers' there; which sprouted from the surface due to geo-thermal energy. The exploitation of this source of natural energy held a lot of potential; but no serious efforts to study this phenomenon were made.

- Work on Igoo-Phey irrigation canal in the Leh area was started; with a view to irrigate big stretches of land in this region by the Indus water.

- Work on the development of Khumbathang canal and Farm was taken in hand. The latter was completed but the work on the former was never taken to its logical conclusion and left half way through.

- In the education sector; the number of schools was in the range of 4 High Schools, 7 Middle Schools, 18 Central Schools and 136 Primary Schools. This was the figure in the mid sixties; and constant efforts were made to improve educational facilities in the entire region. There was no college in the entire Ladakh yet; and the local students who studied in the colleges outside were sanctioned special scholarships.
- Two Weaving Centers were set up – one each in Leh and Kargil – to impart training to local people in different crafts of spinning, weaving, carpet making etc. Arrangements were also made to market the production of trainees and workers there.
- Three more CD Blocks were set up at Nubra, Zanskar and Nyoma; raising the number to five which included Leh and Kargil.
- To overcome the chronic difficulty of lack of staff from outside the district and general reluctance of the state employees to get posted to Ladakh; service conditions of such people were made more attractive. Vide SRO – 142 dated 23rd April 1965 the rate of Compensatory Allowance for such employees was pegged at 75 % and 100 %; depending on the remoteness of the place of posting.
- An independent PWD circle was set up in Leh under the charge of a Superintending Engineer, with the powers of Chief Engineer; so that all major technical and administrative issues could be sorted out within the district. He was to work under the overall supervision of the Deputy cum Development Commissioner Ladakh.
- Greater attention was paid to the agricultural activities; which was the mainstay of local population – this effort included providing of improved seeds and other inputs. The agricultural set up in the district was reorganized and placed under the charge of a Deputy Director for the entire region.
- A post of Deputy Director of Sheep and Animal Husbandry was created in the district and all Animal and Sheep farms in Ladakh

were placed under his charge. The government farms in Drass, Khumbathang, Stakna and Chanspa performed especially well.

- All health units in Ladakh were placed under the charge of a Deputy Director Health; for better coordination and functional improvements.

All these measures did prove useful in improving the general condition of the people of the district; and was certainly an up gradation of facilities to the local population; with these steps being more efficacious where the government machinery was more committed. But, this was true only in the sense of making a comparative statement. In absolute terms; the Ladakh region needed much more than what was being attempted. Many representatives of the locals consistently complained that the tempo of various project and schemes, taken in hand, was sluggish and certainly not commensurate with huge needs of the remote and backward area like Ladakh. It was also pointed out that even after years of work; the dream of generating hydro-electric power remained still to be realized. It does go to the credit of some committed persons – both locals as well as non locals – that within the resources available these people tried their best to help the local population. Same is true of the exercising of official powers; both inherent and the delegated ones; at various official levels.

Tibetan Refugees ... and... Employment Opportunities to Locals

During the decade of 1960s and early half of the seventies; two main problems faced the Ladakh region and its people. One pertained to the restricted job opportunities to the men and women of Ladakh, particularly the educated and professionally trained lot. For the locals even this limited level of employment was restricted to lower levels of various government departments. The second difficult issue concerned the settlement of Tibetan refugees in the region. Even though Ladakh covered a very large geographical area, the number of people inhabiting this huge landmass was very small and the fertile land was extremely limited; similarly, the pasture areas were also restricted. This latter problem got further compounded with the Chinese occupation of big tracts in the Aksai Chin belt. With the result that natural resources in this region were just sufficient to support the existing human and cattle population. Any further increase, even in small and limited figures, was bound to upset this delicate natural balance.

The arrival of Tibetan refugees in Leh area, even though not significant in absolute numbers, did pose a difficult and hard dilemma for the locals. On one side was the question of sharing limited resources with the new arrivals and on the other was the natural affinity that the locals had with the Tibetans. The people of Leh region had centuries old religious, trade and political ties with these Tibetans and at the time of their need how could the locals refuse normal hospitality to them and show reluctance to share their scarce means. This was an agonizing predicament indeed.

It would be interesting to observe these two developments through the eyes and experiences of a local person, M. Azim, who joined the State Service at the middle level and spent formative years of his professional life handling these matters. Azim joined the government service as an Inspector in the Cooperatives Department in 1961 and, after induction in the IAS, retired as Deputy Commissioner Kargil in 1999. Azim was born in Shey village, not situated far away from Leh as distances go in that area, in 1939; to a Buddhist mother and a Muslim father. Through his growing years, and even later as an adult, he did not feel any communal bias on the count of inter-faith marriage of his parents. That says a lot about the religious tolerance prevalent in society then. Like other growing children of that time, Azim also completed his primary education in the local school and did his matriculation from the High School at Leh – in 1954. After that he went to Srinagar for further studies and completed graduation in 1959 from S.P. College there. Those days it was quite uncommon for a Ladakhi to have a degree under his belt. This prompted Azim to spend some more time in Srinagar and look for an opening in the government. His patience and persistence paid well and he secured the job of an inspector in the Cooperatives Department in 1961. After the mandatory training period he got a posting in his home town at Leh. His initial acquisition of knowledge about different facets of departmental working was carried out under the watchful eyes and benevolent care of his local boss; the Deputy Registrar Cooperatives, Leh, named P.C. Raju (He later joined the State Cabinet as a MOS in 1977). Raju himself was a simple and straight forward man. His qualities of head and heart profoundly influenced young Azim and shaped up as well as consolidated his responses to different professional situations; in addition to strengthening beliefs in leading a clean life.

In the late summer of 1961, he was asked to report to the Deputy Registrar Cooperatives Kathua for further instructions. On arriving there, the DRC Kathua told him to receive about 600 families of Tibetan Refugees on the J&K border at Lakhanpur for their onward journey to Ladakh. Before moving from Kathua, Azim was advised to organize them in a Cooperative Society. He completed the paper work and the due share of the Refugees was paid by the concerned department of the Government of India. All consumables and eatables for these people were bought and distributed through the medium of the new cooperative society. Azim brought them to Ladakh and there; these people were employed by Sonam Narboo, the then superintending engineer of J&K PWD, to work on the Lamayuru – Saspol sector of the Kargil to Leh road. The Tibetans worked there for almost two years; after which the administration shifted them to the Stakna village. Due to lack of water and cultivable land there, these refugees were again relocated and settled in Choglamsar; situated practically on the outskirts of Leh town. A small canal from Shey to near the airport had been recently built and the land coming under this new irrigation scheme had not yet been allotted to the locals due to differing interests of a couple of local politicians. The district administration then decided to settle the Tibetan Refugees there and provide them with assured water availability and land for agricultural purposes. That was how Choglamsar came to be developed as a focal point of Tibetan settlements in the Ladakh region; in the decades to follow. Sometime later few families of this lot, who were exclusively interested in pastoral vocations; relocated themselves from Choglamsar. These people, along with their cattle, settled around Nyoma village – which was the administrative headquarters of Nyoma Sub-Division. As was bound to happen, there were occasional disputes about pasture lands and grazing rights between them and the original inhabitants. It goes to the credit of the local people, their feelings of tolerance and inherent sympathy for the refugees; as also the sense of understanding and deft handling by the successive Assistant Commissioners Nyoma and his subordinate staff that such issues were never allowed to reach a flash point. The irritant matters were invariably solved to the satisfaction of both parties. Though these were difficult times for the Tibetan Refugees; but a beginning of their rehabilitation in Ladakh had been made; which was further consolidated over the next few years and decades. The local population, area, climate and in fact the whole milieu suited the Tibetans well and they were also happy to be a part of the Ladakhi scene.

In the year 1964, Azim was promoted as a Block Development Officer and posted at Leh. After spending a year there; he was moved to Kargil as

BDO. He was to remain there for the next five years before coming back to Leh as the Headquarters Assistant, to the Deputy Commissioner cum Development Commissioner, Ladakh. By the sheer dint of his hard work and enviable reputation for honesty and integrity he came to be trusted a lot by the DCs and that is how he came to play an important role in the process of recruitment of locals in various posts – particularly the ones which were not readily open to them till then. Not that anybody was against the Ladakhis for getting into higher echelons of the state government; but their chances of selection against more educated and better qualified candidates from Jammu or Kashmir regions; were not very bright. This was indeed an inherent disadvantage suffered by them. With the result that only lower posts like clerks, store keepers, assistants or peons etc. were generally filled by the local youth and higher posts were manned by persons from the other two regions. The situation in this area has been graphically described as, "With the rather premature demise of Mr. G.M. Sadiq, Syed Mir Qasim was sworn in as the Chief Minister of Jammu and Kashmir on December 12, 1971... During the first one and half year's tenure of office of Mr. Qasim, the administration did not stir up itself with regard to the developmental activity in Ladakh... While presiding over a meeting of the Ladakh Development Committee on June 14, 1973 the Chief Minister announced that the government proposed to train Ladakhi boys for jobs of teachers, compounders, stock assistants, overseers, mechanics etc. to enable them to man government posts in Ladakh..."[15] Thus, even the Chief Minister of the state did not visualize the Ladakhis getting recruited in the higher levels of the administrative hierarchy. One man, thereafter, was to make all the difference and that person was Mehmood-ur-Rahman, IAS (JK-1965).

Rahman was posted as Deputy Commissioner Udhampur and doing very well there; till in July 1973 he was sent post-haste as Development cum Deputy Commissioner Ladakh to effectively fill the breach which had developed between his predecessor and local officers. He was to spend a very eventful and satisfying tenure of three and half years there, taking his already well established reputation many notches higher. Also, by virtue of the Single Line administrative set up in Ladakh coupled with remoteness of the area from the state capital(s); this was practically an autonomous assignment. Such a job very well suited his style of functioning and the

15 Shridhar Kaul and H.N. Kaul, *Ladakh Through the Ages,* Indus publishing Company, New Delhi, 1992, pp. 243, 244 and 245.

spirit of positive initiatives. He maintained fruitful contacts with the forces and also developed useful relations with the local notables. The higher posts like Block Development Officers, Assistant Registrar Cooperatives, Assistant Tourist officers, Assistant Information officers were included in the 'state cadre' and a state level selection board charged with the responsibility of making selections against vacant posts in these categories. The DC Ladakh could only make recruitments of the 'divisional cadre' and 'district cadre' posts as he was the chairman of both these selection bodies. Rahman worked on a simple but effective strategy by which he persuaded the state Planning and Ladakh Affairs Departments to slightly reduce the pay grades of these posts, for Ladakh only, so that these could come under the preview of 'divisional cadre'; and hence only local Ladakhis could compete amongst themselves for them. Once this was agreed by the two apex departments; that year's Annual Plan for Ladakh duly reflected these posts. The path was then clear for the local aspirants. It was for the first time during Rahman's tenure that the local youth got recruited to more senior and important positions like BDOs, ARCs, ATOs and AIOs; based on written tests and a very fair and transparent selection process. This was hugely appreciated in the entire region as also by the opinion leaders. Azim, as the Headquarters Assistant to the DC, played a prominent role in the whole process.

The memories of that period are still strongly etched in his mind and Azim recalled, "I was then dealing with all recruitments in the district and Rahman Sahib was kind enough to trust me a lot. For the first time, in the early stage of his tenure, important posts like BDO etc. came under the preview of 'divisional cadre' and therefore only the residents of Ladakh needed to compete amongst themselves for all such jobs; even though the minimum educational standard remained unchanged to being a graduate. At the apex level, three Committees were formed; one to set up written papers, another to evaluate answer sheets and the third to assess the successful candidates in an interview. I was a member in all the three bodies. Strict confidentiality was maintained in all facets of recruitment. We were able to evolve a very fair and transparent procedure of assessment at various stages; and the whole system was appreciated by the candidates as also the public at large. In two – three years time Ladakh made a name for visible and clean selection process. Even though the Deputy Commissioner very competently supervised the overall functioning of the recruitment process; he did not even once interfere in the working of the

Committees… I remember one year my younger brother appeared in the tests for the posts of Assistant Tourist Officer. On this count, I expressed my inability to be a part of the selection committees. While appreciating my stand and position; the DC – Rahman Sahib – insisted that I continue with my work notwithstanding this development. How could I even think of betraying such a level of confidence? Frankly, there was lot of pressure on me from relations and family elders to somehow help my brother. The least I could do, I was told, was to share few questions of the paper with my brother. Those were really difficult days for me; but I withstood my ground firmly in spite of the palpable tensions in the family and my neighborhood. I maintained that, and honestly believe it was the right thing to do, if my brother was to get through the selection process; he should do so on his own merit. Incidentally, he did not pass the written test. I must confess that those were very trying days for me; but never even once in my life I have regretted the decision to do the right thing."[16]

In subsequent years, all the vacant and newly created posts of this nature were filled by Ladakhi candidates. It was not just a matter of satisfying the local aspirations. Of course, this measure amply achieved that; but equally significantly, with so many sons of the soil placed in important positions at the cutting edge levels proved hugely beneficial to the developmental activities in the whole region. These people worked in towns as well as far flung areas with zeal, dedication and pride; in fact Ladakh derived considerable befits from this single positive step.

1971 Operations

The India – Pakistan war of December 1971 which resulted in the formation of Bangladesh as an independent country, was primarily fought in the eastern sector; where Indian army and the IAF conducted forceful military operations. Along western borders of the country, the security forces basically conducted 'defensive operations'; which by and large did not have much significance. However, things were different in the Ladakh region; where both in the Leh as well as Kargil areas the troops went on the offensive and resultantly occupied a part of the enemy controlled territory.

In Kargil sector, the military operations resulted in taking back from Pakistani forces the important hill feature of 13620. The scenario, on the joining of a new Deputy Commissioner in Kargil in June 1998, has been

16 Interaction with Shri Azim in July 2019.

described in the following words, "The DC's residence was a beautiful cottage surrounded by impressive greenery all around. Below the edge of the plateau, the Suru River was flowing noisily and few kilometers of the green cover on the opposite high ground, called Khurbathang, was encircled by towering, bare and bleak mountains. The nearest peak towards the North drew his attention particularly and he asked about it. That top, he was told, was known by its height 13620 feet, and occupied by Pakistani troops since 1948 till it was retaken by the Indian forces during the Indo-Pak war of December 1971. Up to that time it was the nearest enemy post virtually on the very doorsteps of Kargil. The men posted there could visually scan the entire area below them including Kargil town, Baroo and Khurbathang plateaus as well as the Brigade Headquarters. It was a local joke that the Pakistanis at 13620 could very well monitor, through their binoculars, the badminton game being played in the Kargil Brigade Headquarters. The Pakistani presence there was a constant nuisance to the army as well as the local population, right from the day of cease fire on January 1, 1949. It was also a major oddity of the Line of Control (LOC). The Indian forces had cleared this post of Pakistani occupation during the Indo-Pak war in December 1971, and fortunately did not vacate it thereafter. Otherwise, the shelling of last few months by Pakistanis, with the possibility of being so much more accurately directed from this point, would have caused immense damage to Kargil and areas around…"[17]

As a result of these operational maneuvers, few villages were also liberated from the Pakistani occupation. In the Diary of then SDM Kargil, there is an entry dated 16th August 1974, which gives some details of his visit to two of such villages. It records, "Today I had gone to visit villages Hundermoo (Ganderman for the army) and Broke, which were among the liberated ones during 1971 conflict. For reaching there one has to go for five kms on Kargil - Srinagar road, cross the Harka Bahadur bridge and the turn right. After about two kilometers on a jeep able track, the vehicle has to be left and river Drass is crossed on a foot bridge. Ten minutes walk up the slope and Hundermoo is reached…There is remarkable sense of honesty among these people. In 1947 when this area became part of the POK territory; certain persons who were staying on our side lost their lands. When these villages were liberated in 1971; the people there who had been cultivating those unclaimed fields since 1947 and had become

17 Dr. Sudhir S Bloeria, *The Men Who Served Jammu and Kashmir,* Vij Books India (Pvt) Ltd., New Delhi, 2016, p. 220.

virtual owners of these tracts; voluntarily gave back the lands to the original owners. In few instances, the villagers were the tenants of the owners who belonged to Kargil town. In all such cases these tenants, though they were not legally bound to do so, told their erstwhile landowners that they would pay back the 'owners share' in installments…"

In the Leh area; military operations were restricted to the border with POK in the Nubra sector. Here a separate body of troops, called Dhal Force, was organized under the command of Major Chewang Rinchen, MVC and SM (the seventeen year old, brave and young local lad of 1948 had become a Major by then). All his troops were hardy and well acclimatized mountainous soldiers. Rinchen led his boys to important victories in this sector. Based on his practical common sense, intimate knowledge of the area and vast operational experience; he ordered five changes in the dress and man-pack load of the *jawans*. He insisted that all soldiers exchange their ammunition or jungle boots with the Ladakhi *Pabos*; which were light and pretty warm and would protect the feet from frostbite. Some village Headmen were only too happy to give away their Pabos and get ammunition boots in return. He also ordered that the boys would go into the operations wearing Balaclava Cap over their heads instead of the steel helmet. He reckoned that the steel helmet was heavier, made lot of noise when falling on the ground accidently and also had more chances of inflicting frostbite on the head and ears, in the extremely low temperatures. The Balaclava was certainly lighter and warmer. Every soldier, in that area, carried one sleeping bag and two blankets, which meant climbing up the mountains with so much of load. Rinchen told his men to carry one sleeping bag and one blanket between two of them thus considerably reducing the load of troops. His logic was that they were not going to sleep during nights and did not require much bedding for rest during day. The fourth innovation introduced by him related to the water carried by each soldier in his 'water bottle'. This would invariably freeze due to the low temperatures at night. During this period every *jawan* carried water mixed with some rum. This concoction was good enough to quench the thirst; would not freeze in low temperatures and also give warmth during very cold nights. Rinchen also halved the authorized scale of ammunition per person; further reducing load of each soldier. He exhorted the men to depend more on hand grenades and bayonets. These administrative measures and the fact that Chewang Rinchen was himself leading them; filled each one of the soldiers with confidence, commitment and an indomitable will to defeat the enemy.

His biographer has recorded Major Rinchen's achievements as, "From the time that the Dhal Force had started from the Assembly Area at Biagdangdo on December 7 to December 17, when the forces reached Thang/Ridge, it had been almost ceaseless fighting for 10 days. During these 10 days' action, the Dhal Force, under the command of Major Rinchen and comprising exclusively the companies of the Ladakh Scouts and the Nubra Guards, achieved great success...Captured Chulunkha defence complex along with several villages (including the important village of Turtok) covering apprx 800 sq km. This was the largest area captured by any unit on the western/northern front during the 1971 war... Not a single casualty occurred on the Indian side except for a few cases of minor injury and frostbite...Pakistani casualties included 18 killed, 2 JCOs, 40 ORs and 4 Razakars taken prisoners and six wounded who were taken to Leh by a chopper... The entire operation was carried out without artillery and air support and with minimum expenditure of ammunition, using only hand grenades and bayonets. Most of the ammunition expended was that captured from the Pakistani camps... Later, the Ladakh Scouts battalion was granted the Battle Honour of Turtok Operations of war."[18]

Major Rinchen was awarded Bar to Mahavir Chakra for outstanding gallantry and leadership. His citation also mentions, "Major Rinchen was assigned the task of clearing Pakistani fortifications from the Chalunka complex in Partapur sector. His force attacked Chalunka, on 10 December and after heavy fighting captured it the next day at 0700 hrs. In this attack the enemy suffered 14 killed and 7 (including 2 JCOs) prisoners, besides a heavy loss of arms and ammunition. On 11 December he led an advance on Turtok along the banks of Shyok River. Passing through the mountain ridges, the Scouts infiltrated into enemy positions quietly and achieved complete surprise. Turtok fell on 14 December and this broke the back of Pakistani resistance in this sector. Other enemy posts in the area were captured without much resistance. By the cease-fire day, the Scouts had advanced 22 km along the Shyok, with the commanding heights on either side of the valley in their hands. They captured nine enemy positions at very high altitudes and in difficult terrain".

18 Dr. Virendra Verma, *A Legend in His Own Time* (Col. Chewang Rinchen), Young India Publications, Dehradun, 1998, pp. 114 and 115.

Evolution of the District Administration and its Developmental Role

The administrative set up in Ladakh has had a chequered history. Just after the first war with Pakistan in 1947-48; and like other parts of the State, this district was also administered by not very competent people at the top. But, due to the efficacy of the earlier system, things carried on rather smoothly for a few years. In this period, unfortunately, Ladakh almost became a forgotten and much neglected territory by the powers at the state and central levels. However, the area came to acquire greater significance in the wake of aggressive stance of the Chinese government; more so during 1959 and beyond. So it was in this period of disturbed conditions that the people in authority started looking at Ladakh and its needs in an entirely new and also practical manner. This changed attitude resulted in, amongst other things, measures to strengthen administration in this area. Therefore an administrative set up was introduced in Ladakh; based on the experiences of the Government of India in the then NEFA area. In Ladakh and in the J&K state, this structure was called 'NEFA type of administration'. Under this scheme, important posts in Ladakh; like the Deputy cum Development Commissioner of the district, Assistant Commissioners of Kargil, Nyoma and Nubra were manned by the officers of Indian Frontier Administrative Service (IFAS). This experiment worked well on the ground till 1964, when the Sadiq government in the state wound it up; on the argument that Ladakh was an integral part of the Jammu and Kashmir State and should, therefore, be administered on the pattern followed in other parts of the State. It certainly was a specious plea; and also does not distract from the fact that the IFAS had earned a name for itself for efficiency, integrity and practical way of managing things in difficult and far-flung areas - mostly in eastern sector of NEFA; as also for few years in Ladakh where working and living conditions were equally, if not more, tough.

The IFAS, as a separate service, was established by the Central Government in 1956 through a Special Selection Board, headed by a senior officer from the Ministry of External Affairs and including representatives from the Ministries of Home Affairs and Defence; as also along with an expert in tribal affairs. The officers were drawn mostly from the ICS-IAS; IP-IPS and the Indian Army. In a few cases, selected officers from the Assam State Service were also taken in the IFAS. These officers were appointed as Political Officers and Assistant Political Officers in the far-flung and remote areas of the then state of Assam; NEFA, Nagaland etc. and they tried their best to manage a difficult and volatile situation prevailing in the entire belt with the resources available at their disposal. The fact remains that basically, this was an adhoc service and before the IFAS could be consolidated into a regular type of establishment; certain vested interests ensured that during the mid-1960s IFAS officers were 'merged' into the IAS or the IPS. Therefore, within a decade of its coming into being, it ceased to exist as a separate entity. The fact remained that these officers who decided to sacrifice their original careers to join the IFAS were all specially selected and remarkable personalities and even today they should be role models for the young IAS /IPS officers. The efficacy of their work, as also style of functioning, can be well gauged from the fact that even in the last decade of the 20th Century; elderly people in Ladakh very fondly remembered them. Some of these officers like Col. Raja, Col. Butalia, Menon and Barua, to mention a few, became household names in the region.

Few experienced civil servants, even at present, do feel that there is still the need to introduce and organize a kind of special service akin to the IFAS; in which selected in-service officers from different streams are taken for serving and providing effective administration in some of the trouble spots of the country.

After the Ladakh administration was brought at par with other parts of the state; all officers at the top level from Deputy Commissioner to SDMs and Assistant Commissioners came from the state cadre or the state service. Taking into consideration the remoteness of the area and difficult communications; most of the line departments of the state government were not able to exercise effective control or give proper technical guidance to their staff posted in this region. Consequently, they were not averse – if not actually relieved – to delegate most of their administrative functions to the district administration in Ladakh. With time this proclivity percolated to the second level also. That is how slowly the Single Line of administrative working in Ladakh actually developed in practical sense over the years. Two examples in this regard should be sufficient to explain the phenomenon. One pertains to the delegation of powers of the Registrar Cooperative Societies to Development Commissioner, Ladakh. In this, vide SRO-115 dated 29th March 1965; the J&K Government issued a notification which said, ".... The Government hereby confers upon the Development Commissioner Ladakh, all the powers of Registrar under the said Act to be exercised by him within the local limits of his jurisdiction." Similarly, substantial powers were delegated to the Assistant Commissioners of Nubra and Nyoma vide Government Order No. 21-LA of 1971 Dated 25th March, 1971. This order emanated from the Ladakh Affairs Department and read, "It is hereby ordered that the Assistant Commissioner Nyoma and Assistant Commissioner Nubra, will be the Heads of all Government Departments within their territorial jurisdiction, subject to the overall control of the Development Commissioner Ladakh." Around that time only; the SDM Kargil came to be called as the Deputy Development Commissioner and controlled all the departments working under his jurisdiction, in the tehsils of Kargil and Zanskar.

Single Line Administration

Historically, because of its being cut off from the state headquarters for more than six months of the year when the passes at high reaches close in the winters due to heavy snowfall; Ladakh region always enjoyed a different system of administration, especially from the 1960s. The Deputy Commissioner of Ladakh was also concurrently designated as the District Development Commissioner. Apart from his revenue, magisterial and administrative functions; the DDC was responsible for planning and implementing annual plans for the region. This system was though born of necessity; but its impact was much appreciated by the local population. The Deputy Commissioner of Ladakh, located at Leh, was responsible for the vast region in all respects including its development. In fact, when the state government officials went to the Planning Commission at New Delhi for discussion of annual plan, the Deputy Commissioner of Ladakh also accompanied the team for discussion of the development plans of his area. It was a unique arrangement, which worked eminently well. This system was commonly called the Single Line Administration in the administrative circles of the state. When Ladakh was divided into two districts in July 1979, in Leh and Kargil districts, the same administrative system was adopted in both the districts.

Pursuant to the landmark agreement between Sheikh Mohammed Abdullah and Indira Gandhi, the then Prime minister of India, in early 1975, the mantle of state's administration fell on his shoulders. He became Chief Minister of the state in February 1975; though the state assembly was dominated by Congress MLAs. The first ministry of Sheikh Abdullah consisted of only four stalwarts, one each representing Jammu (Devidas Thakur), Kashmir (Mirza Afzal Beg), and Ladakh (Sonam Narboo) regions, with Sheikh Sahib as the head of the administration. They were all men of character and immense ability. Sheikh Abdullah wanted to reduce the distance between the people and the government. It was in this context that the idea of extending the Ladakh model of the district administration to all districts of the state was contemplated. The subject was discussed at different levels, including official also; and finally, in 1977, it was decided by the government that the Single Line Administration would be implemented in all districts of the state – including the district of Ladakh where it was already in existence. The primary objective of introduction of Single Line Administration was to bring people closer to the government. Generally, the state governments are administered at the state level through the ministers of the Cabinet; their respective secretaries and other functionaries down the line. The field-level staff being usually supervised by the respective head of the department who also invariably sat at the state headquarters. Often, the distance between people and the government was too vast; as also the real aspirations of the people often did not reach the right quarters.

With the objective of reducing this gap and bringing the administration closer to the people, in each district, under the Single Line Administration, a District Development Board (DDB) was constituted. The DDB was headed by the Deputy Commissioner who was also concurrently designated as District Development Commissioner (DDC). All MLAs, MLCs and MPs of the district were enlisted as members of the DDB. In addition, the government nominated selected Sarpanches of the district also as members; such Sarpanches were to be rotated from year to year. Having thus ensured that the DDB would have representation of the people of the district through their elected representatives; the DDB was to have the district heads of all departments of the government also as members. With a view to ensure that the district plans were made properly and their implementation done effectively, the status of some district level officials was raised. Thus, for Public Works Department responsible for major chunk of works in the district, the district head was elevated to the level of a Superintending Engineer. The District Development Board was to meet at least four times a year.

The main functions entrusted to the DDB were:-

- Preparation of the annual plan for the district; for all the departments operating in the area. The first draft was made by the concerned district level officer, duly vetted by the DDC.
- Discussion of the annual plan of the district at the state level and also at the level of Planning Commission, New Delhi.
- Approval for the plan for the next year from the Cabinet at the annual DDB meeting with the Cabinet; usually held at the district headquarters.
- Presenting the achievements of the district during the previous year and authorizing expenditure by different departments as per plan by the issue of sanction orders for each department.
- Authorizing diversion of funds within a department or diversion of funds from one department to another; depending upon exigencies. Where interdepartmental changes were proposed, the approval of state government was obtained.
- Overseeing progress of the district plan as also interacting with the local population to ascertain their response.
- Calling meetings of the DDB during the course of the year to monitor implementation of the plan and for getting the inputs of elected representatives.
- Preparation of annual report of the district for the consideration of the DDB in its annual meeting.

The first meeting of the year would be attended by the entire Cabinet, with the Chief Minister in chair; where the DDC presented achievements of the district in diverse fields and then outline proposals for the next year. The annual plan of the district was then discussed in the meeting. All elected representatives and Sarpanches had the opportunity to point out deficiency, if any, and also any omissions concerning their areas. In general, the annual plan meetings of the DDB would take about eight hours; with the entire Cabinet sitting through the meeting and responding to the points raised. Often important issues concerning the district, not covered by the plan, would be authorized to be included with special sanction by the Cabinet. In this manner, the people of the district - through their representatives - and the highest decision making authority of the state came face to face at least once a year.

The greatest merit of the Single Line Administration was to give a sense of involvement to the people in governance. Generally, the DDC would be touring the district constantly, taking stock of the implementation of the plans of different departments and also getting feedback from the local population. This helped the administration to remain abreast of the plan execution and also enhanced the level of satisfaction of general public. Secondly, as soon as the district plan was approved by the Cabinet; the sanction orders for various schemes, under different departments, were released. This enabled timely implementation of the schemes, without having to wait for such authorization to come from either the concerned head of department or the state government. Thirdly, intra transfer of funds from one scheme to another within a department became much easier; even the procedure for inter-departmental changes was made simpler. Thus, all the funds allocated to a district invariably were spent during the course of the year. This was quite in contrast to the earlier situation when a good deal of approved allocations would remain unspent and lapse. As the DDC was responsible for the delivery; his control over the various departments was quite strong and effective. Last but not the least, as the district administration was in direct touch with the population on a regular basis; the felt needs of the people usually got projected at the right time, without any disaffection building up. Overall, the Single Line Administration at the district level became a great success. That the system has survived many years and is practiced even today in the state; after over four decades of its introduction – of course with some modifications over this period – is a testimony to its effectiveness. This formulation has been a significant and notable contribution of Ladakh to other parts of the state.

The concept of Single Line Administration, as borrowed from the Ladakh experience; was introduced in all the districts of the state in 1977. There is an interesting background episode to this development. Before the Indira – Sheikh Accord of 1975 was signed; the latter visited Ladakh in October 1974 for a week. He was shown the development works executed in those formidable heights. Rahman, the DDC Ladakh then, took upon himself the responsibility of driving Sheikh Sahib through the austere mountains, green valleys and rugged terrain for his entire stay of one week there. It appears that after seeing the all-round development of a remote area like Ladakh he got convinced that prosperity of the place and people could be guaranteed only through faster development and by the participation of the public in this respect. Some knowledgeable people believe, and not without reason, that the percept of Single Line Administration at the district level that Sheikh Sahib introduced after coming to power in the state, was largely influenced by what he had seen and experienced in Ladakh during his short stay there. In any case the implementation of this idea in other districts of the state was certainly a big compliment to Ladakh and its administration.

CHAPTER VI

Development Trajectory and Tourism Boom (1974-99)

Ladakh Opened to Tourism in 1974

By the early seventies; Ladakh was more or less firmly set on the path of steady progress. There were many reasons for this happy development. The foremost among these was the fact that this far-flung and remote area was no more a forgotten place by the people at the helm of affairs at the state level. The state government; both at the political as well as administrative levels, was seemingly trying to make a positive impact on the developmental scene in various respects. The visit of the state Chief Minister, Syed Mir Qasim, to Ladakh in mid-1973 was a positive signal to all concerned; even though he had to face demonstrations in Khaltsi and Leh demanding UT status and direct rule by the Centre. At Kargil, he bonded with the local people well – who were predominantly orthodox in nature and belonged to the Shia community; where he told them that being a 'Syed' he may be considered a close kin by them. Though, there was no such show of closeness in Leh; Mir Qasim's visit to that area was certainly not without positive results. He was able to acquaint himself, first hand, with various development issues; as also achievements of his government and the gaps left as well as problems faced by the local population. It was certainly after a long time that the state Chief Minister had come to Ladakh; and to that extent itself, it was a useful gesture.

In the past ten years or so; the district administration had firmly stabilized itself and come to grips with major issues confronting the region. The period of 'NEFA type of administration' was over; as also the few years of experiment of having separate persons as the Deputy Commissioner and Development Commissioner too was an issue of the past. At the beginning of 1970s, Ladakh district administration was headed by one person with the designation of Deputy cum Development Commissioner. Also, over the past few years, the Single Line administrative structure had come to stabilize and was proving quite effective in tackling day to day problems and developmental issues.

The sudden expansion in the deployment of army and para-military forces, following the Chinese aggression, had too come to a logical end. This increase in manpower had provided considerable direct and indirect benefits to the local population and also their economy. In addition; recruitment of the local educated youth as BDOs etc. for the first time had a positive impact on the progress of Ladakh. These people happily manned such posts in the far flung areas where earlier the non local officers, from outside the region, were unwilling to go. This in itself made a lot of difference to the place as well as population. Furthermore, these local persons implemented various schemes of the government with a sense of commitment and dedication; thus providing greater benefits and satisfaction to the people. This period also generally coincided with increasing number of locals acquiring medical and engineering degrees; getting employed in government jobs and being posted back to Ladakh. By the beginning of 1970s, it was quite usual to hear about 'surgeon Narboo' and 'physician Narboo' in Leh town. This was literally an era of pioneering professionals in the region.

Likewise, the political personages in Leh as well as Kargil had matured over the past decades, in their understanding of issues, general outlook and influence over the governmental as well as administrative structures. These were all positive evolutions in the changing environment of the entire area; which certainly seemed poised to grow at a fairly good pace. But, the most significant measure came into force in mid July 1974; which totally changed the scenario in Ladakh and had a considerable positive impact on the local economy then and also in the years and decades to come. This was making most of the Kargil and Leh areas open to tourist traffic. Up to that time everybody, including government employees on official duty, had to obtain a written 'permit' from the designated police authorities in Srinagar for making an entry into Ladakh. Lifting of this permit system, in fact, meant that the district was henceforth open to all people including foreign and inland tourists. Restrictions though remained in place for deep interior areas, called 'inner line' and roughly comprising the Nubra and Nyoma sub-divisions. But, it hardly affected the almost revolutionary impact this decision had on the local economy and the people. Ladakh would never be the same old secluded and forsaken place again.

The Senior Superintendent of Police Leh and SDM Kargil met in Srinagar for the first time in mid-July 1974. The police officer was returning after spending his holidays at home in Bangalore; and the young officer – coming straight from the IAS Academy in Mussoorie – was on his way to join his new place of posting as SDM Kargil. Both had almost together reached the Police Headquarters to get their passes for going to Ladakh; when they were told that the state government had done away with the practice of permits and Ladakh was an open place to travel by anybody. The new policy had come into effect from that very morning. These two officers were among the first ones to take benefit of the new regulations; and they decided to travel together to Kargil the next day. In a sort of celebrations; the Police Chief decided to spend the night halt at Kargil. It was certainly an enjoyable journey for both, in the police officer's 'Jonga'; with stop-overs at Sonamarg, Dras and finally at Kargil. In addition, it was also an educative trip for the young SDM – his first visit to Ladakh.

The very first wave of tourists although in very limited numbers, mostly foreigners, followed almost immediately in the second half of July 1974. The word of Ladakh being open for tourism had seemed to spread and there was no looking back since then. This new policy of the government had happened suddenly and without any preparations at the ground level; either by the administration or by the local people. Both were caught by surprise and did their best to cope up with the new reality in their own ways; with the private enterprise soon gaining an upper hand and not surprisingly, in this endeavor. There was an acute shortage of accommodation for these visitors; not only in small places like Dras, Khaltsi and Saspol; but also in two major town of the area, Kargil and Leh. At both these places the reasonably comfortable rooms existed only in single digits in the government Dak Bungalows. Mercifully, for the area, the tourist arrival was not heavy initially; like only fifty five visitors were recorded to have come from Srinagar in the first fortnight of the region being thrown open for tourism.

In time, Tourist Reception Centers along with reasonable government accommodation and posting of appropriate ranked Tourist Officers was managed at Dras, Kargil, Khaltsi and Leh etc. But, progress in the government sector was tardy and irregular. For example, almost six years later; the District Plan Leh for the year 1980-81 recorded at pages 8 and 22, as "The tourist department has already started construction of tourist bungalows/ cafeteria at Khaltsi, Saspol and Sakti. In addition to this, one Motel with a capacity of 32 double rooms has also been constructed at Leh… On Leh-Kargil road, the tourists stop at Khaltsi for having their meals and tea etc. To provide good refreshment facilities to the tourists it was decided last year to construct a Cafeteria at Khaltsi…" In contrast; the response of the private initiative in this respect was much more prompt and timely. One of the foreigners had mentioned to a local officer that no tourist was looking for five-star facilities in that far flung area; what he or she wanted was only a clean room and a neat bathroom with fresh, washed linen and toiletries. The market savvy part of the people at Leh and Kargil were quick to open small, clean and fairly comfortable hotels and restaurant for these visitors. Between the two towns; Leh being a much more open society, people there certainly derived greater benefit from this opportunity and soon made tourism as one of the important planks for economic betterment of the region. Thus, quite early, Leh became the hub of tourist activity in Ladakh. The visitors also hugely enjoyed witnessing the local traditional sports like archery and polo. Within a couple of years a good number of hotels and restaurants literally mushroomed in the town. These included staying places with five star facilities to boarding and lodging arrangements at affordable price ranges. Loans from the banks, on reasonable terms, further helped such entrepreneurs. Some venturesome persons also opened their houses for 'paying guests'. Eating a locally prepared meal inside a typical Ladakhi kitchen and in a traditional manner; became a big attraction for the tourists. It also brought good money to the concerned people. In a nutshell; the Ladakhis made handsome profits out of the tourism flow in many ways.

Another chapter to the tourism sector in this region was added towards ending January 1979; when the first commercial flight landed at Leh airport. This was a plane belonging to the Indian Airlines; and the Leh people, headed by the local minister Sonam Narboo, gave an unforgettable traditional welcome to the entire crew. Soon, regular commercial flights started to and from Leh; with ever increasing number of aircrafts and companies. This facility was almost a boon to the people of Ladakh; in addition to being an additional attraction to the tourist traffic. Till then, the local people had no alternative but to depend on the courtesy and help of the army to travel between Leh and Chandigarh in the IAF planes; particularly during the winter season. It was a cumbersome process; and quite often also not a happy experience for the civilians to get a seat in the defence aircrafts. Obviously, the army had to first cater for its own priorities and requirements. The civilian aircrafts provided much more convenient mode of travel to the desirous persons and consequently, the traffic on this route soon picked up to the optimum levels.

A glance through the official details of tourist flow in the region makes an interesting reading. It says, "…the table given hereunder reveals year-wise increase in number of tourists who visited Ladakh from 1974 onwards. There has been a remarkable increase in the tourist traffic from 551 in 1974 to 14177 in 1980… At present there are no tourist huts in Ladakh. However, travelers are provided with lodging facilities in rest houses at Dras, Kargil, Mulbek, Bodh-Kharboo, Nubra, Nyoma, Khaltsi, Sankoo and Leh. Single room *Sarais* are being built up on other routes to provide shelter to travellers. Proper facilities for board and lodge are available in the hotels at Kargil and Leh. Necessary information about local transport, board and lodge, recreation and places of interest in the region is provided by Tourist officers at Leh and Kargil…"[1] By the end of the decade of 1990; the number of tourists visiting Ladakh was well over one lakh. This was something really significant.

However, the tourist traffic to Ladakh was not always on the upswing and because of the local disturbed conditions and the worsening law and order situation in the Valley; particularly in the mid eighties and beyond, there were ups and downs in the arrival of tourists. The overall situations and also due to cancellation of flights to and from Leh, adversely affected the tourism sector particularly the foreign traveler. The Ladakh Buddhist Association's movement for Scheduled Tribe status to the Ladakhis and the terrorist activities in Kashmir were the two major factors for this downturn in the mid-eighties and early nineties. According to one estimate, the number of foreigners coming to Ladakh stood over twelve thousand in 1986 and this was drastically reduced to little more than four thousand in

1 Gazetteer of India – Jammu and Kashmir State – Ladakh Region, Gazetteer Department Government of J&K, Srinagar, 1989, p. 187.

1990; as also the total tourists arrival decreased to about half of the earlier number – instead of registering an increase. As the things stabilized in both the regions; more and more people started visiting Ladakh. During the later part of the nineties; a big upswing in the arrival of tourists was registered. From the early 1980s; the Leh – Manali road was being put to use by the military traffic only. Due to political unrest in the Valley; this route was also opened to civilian traffic in 1987 – which meant that the tourists too could make use of this axis to visit Ladakh. This was an additional positive development.

With the opening of this second artery, demands for further relaxation of the 'inner line' restrictions grew steadily from the locals, the tourists' bodies and the state government also. Finally, in 1994 the two famous lakes of Ladakh; namely Pangong Tso and Tso Moriri were opened to tourists. Both these lakes are located at an altitude of around 15,000 feet; and are magnificent water bodies. With this relaxation, practically the entire Changthang region lay open for the tourists and they came to Ladakh, practically in droves; both inland visitors as also the foreigners. In fact there was a steady increase in the number of Indian tourists visiting this fabled land.

The tourism related activities in Ladakh were comprehensively summed up by the veteran journalist and tourism expert, Sat Paul Sanhi (Sattiji to his friend and admirers). Addressing a Ladakh tourism seminar in1998, he emphasized various strengths and positive aspects of this sector and said, "…Ladakh attracts mountaineers from all over the world to attempt to climb difficult high peaks in the high Himalayas. Its brave young men dare to scale great heights. Four of them have climbed the Everest. These brave hearts were: Sonam Wangyal in May 1965; Sonam Paljor in 1984; Tashi Gyapo and Chhiring Punchok in later years. No other district in India has the distinction of having sent 4 persons to the top of Mt. Everest… Ladakh now has a network of roads connecting even remote and border areas. It boasts of world's three highest motorable roads. Across Khardung La (18380 ft.) into Nubra valley and beyond to Siachen; across Thaglang La (17550 ft.) to Manali and across Chang La (17350 ft.) to Pangong Tso and Chushul. Besides road connectivity, Leh has regular air services linking it to Srinagar, Jammu, Chandigarh and New Delhi. Telecommunications has been modernized with latest high-tech systems…Over a 1000 taxicabs in Leh and hundreds of passenger buses cater to needs of residents and tourists. There are nearly 300 hotels and lodges… Interest in Ladakh has been building up steadily. Organizing Ladakh Festival in September was started in 1995 and Sindhu Darshan (Indus River Festival) started in 1997. These attract increasing numbers. Besides this, Gompa Festivals staged at Hemis, Phiyang and Lamayuru also attract large number of tourists."

Trekking is a delightful pastime for tourists in Ladakh. There are many interesting and adventuresome routes for this purpose. The main three trails which have been more frequently traversed are; Rangdum – Lamayuru; Upshi – Sku: Markha; and Darcha (in Himachal Pradesh) – Padam. This adventurous activity has two advantages. It keeps the tourists for a longer period in the area; weeks at a time. Secondly, the economic benefits of tourism do not remain concentrated in towns like Leh; but are more evenly spread in the region, including villages in the hinterland. The district administration had quite early realized the substantial potential of trekking for this land and started sponsoring selected young men to undergo training for this purpose. In this connection one of the Annual Plan document states, "Sixteen locals have also received training in mountaineering at Uttar-Kashi during March-April this year; for being employed as High Altitude porters."[2]

Ladakh is a region of myriad attractions for different people. Its moon-like landscape; fabulous water bodies; exotic wild life; barren high mountains – including the famous Nun-Kun peaks - which are almost a dream for the climbers; exciting treks; as also quaint and remarkable Gompas literally enthrall and spellbound visitors to any place in the area. However, not many persons are aware that Ladakh is also a place which can be proud of its very old rock carvings. Unfortunately, this prehistoric rock art of Ladakh has not found a proper place in the local consciousness or got duly reflected in the tourism related writings. Even research and academic interest in this direction is missing. Most common depictions in these primitive carvings are wild and domesticated animals, heavenly bodies, birds, weapons, religious ceremonies and scripts. Over the decades these rock carvings have suffered considerable damage due to human and also natural factors. A good number of these carvings have now become extinct because of breaking of boulders for construction purposes; road widening and other building activity. A part of the damage is also

2 District Plan, Leh for 1980-81, p. 8.

attributable to stealing by people and tourists who know their worth. Some concerned and well intentioned persons and organizations have developed a 'Heritage Rock Garden' at village Taru, located between Nimoo and Leh on the Kargil-Leh road. Here pieces of rocks bearing these rock carvings have been shifted and are preserved. This has the potential of being developed as a tourist destination. In one publication this Rock Art of Ladakh has been mentioned in good details as, "Ladakh also has one of the least known archaeological treasures, which are Petroglyphs. These are carvings/engravings of figures and symbols on rock surface. These carvings on the rocks may be done through various methods like pecking, chiseling and incising... The authors have discovered large numbers of Petroglyphs in different parts of Ladakh, more commonly around Leh, Sham and Batalik areas. Different subjects depicted in these Petroglyphs are Animals, Birds, Heavenly bodies like sun and moon, Symbols like trident, swastika, masks, circles, palm and various other mystical characters like mythical birds etc. Another interesting set of figures show humans indulging in various activities like hunting, performing rituals, fighting and group dance... There are also figures of demons and spirits. Human figures have also been depicted with various weapons and tools... Some inscriptions have also been recorded mostly in Kharoshti, Tibetan and Chinese."[3]

Any reference to this kind of art brings to mind at least two beautiful specimens of rock sculptures in Ladakh. Both are located on the sides of the Srinagar – Leh road. The first representative symbol is a group of three small stone sculptures, located just outside Dras; and the second one is called Chamba Statue at Mulbek, about 40 kms from Kargil on the Leh road. It has been carved out of an imposing rock standing lonely on the right side of the road. The statue is a male figure with four hands – Kamandal in one, grains in the other, rosary in the third and fourth hand extended in a gesture of giving. The Mulbek Chamba is generally described as, "a 9 meters tall rock sculpture of deep relief of Maitreya, the future Buddha, is the most important in this region. Situated on the right side of the road, He appears to bless every one entering Ladakh. It is supposed to date back to 7th or 8th century. Its execution combines esoteric Shaivite symbolism with early Buddhist art, and in fact this is the largest rock-carved sculpture in Ladakh." Both these carvings, along with sketches, find a mention in

3 SDS Jamwal & TL Thsangspa, *LADAKH,* Ingraphics Publications, Jammu, 2010, pp. 147 and 148.

the famous book titled 'Ladakh' by Alexander Cunninghum published in the 1850s. These are certainly good attractions for the tourists coming to Ladakh by road. Also, a reference to rock carvings and stone sculptures bring to mind the ancient history of this famed land as well as its hoary past; which has so far not been appropriately recorded. Details of Ladakh and its people in the first millennium and even earlier, needs authoritative determination. For example, the colorful men and women of Dah-Hanu area; with their distinct and different features, dress and customs etc. are believed to be remnants' of Alexander's army. But, there is as yet no conclusive historical proof of this.

The tourism sector all over the world has significantly helped the local economy to grow. The administration in Ladakh also realized this fact right in the beginning years of the region being opened for tourism. With a view to help the local people channelize their efforts in the right direction as also to focus governmental efforts on essential matters; the DDC engaged the Planning, Consultancy and Engineering Division of the India Tourism Development Corporation in 1980 to prepare a vision document for development of tourism in the region. This report, which was completed a year later, became a roadmap for further improvements in tourism sector in the whole area. Based on one of its major recommendations; the practice of Annual Tourism Festival was started in Leh. Herein, the celebrated parts of Ladakhi culture, handicrafts, flora and fauna were brought for display at one place towards the end of the season – preferably in the month of September. Folk archery, game of Polo, Ladakhi folk theatre and cultural items were some of the main attractions during this period. In addition, the tourists were treated to local culinary delights – which included dishes of Mo Mo, Thukpa and the famous local drink of *Chhang* – as well as Yak and Bactrian double-humped camel riding. This festival, aimed primarily at extending the short tourist season in Ladakh, also helped in broad basing this sector during the few months of summer season in the region. As a part of the tourism development plans for Ladakh; improvements of connectivity to and financial assistance for restoration and maintenance of monasteries was also made a mainstay of religio-cultural tourism of the entire belt. Assistance from the banks and subsidy under various schemes of the government further helped in the healthy growth of the hospitality sector.

Tourism everywhere has proved to be a powerful engine of economic progress and Ladakh has been no exception to this rule. Though it was opened to tourism in a controlled manner in 1974; the arc of activities and areas accessible to the visitors widened considerably in a matter of little over a decade. As an inevitable result, many noticeable changes have taken place in the lifestyle of the local population. This has not been liked by the orthodox and more traditional elements of the society there; that have been insisting upon the population to resist the so-called invasion of the area by alien cultures and advocating a return to the Ladakhi folk culture. But, the efforts of this segment have not borne much fruits as pulls of the change have been too strong; and also not limited to the tourists' influx. This also includes almost revolutionary advances in the fields of television and telecommunications; embracing the mobile phones and all that this technology stands for. In short, the forces of change have proved to be insurmountable. This is also so because the Ladakhis cannot cut themselves off from the forceful world currents accompanying the tourists influx. Particularly, the Indian veneer over the indigenous way of life has been quite conspicuous. The region has become a meeting ground of two different cultures; Ladakhi and Indian and the best of both seem to have been fused together; in an evolutionary process which took decades to manifest. This is amply exemplified by the ease with which Ladakhis have taken to Hindustani; Indian fine art and music; Indian dress; Indian food habits and general way of living. The resultant can be described as Indo-Ladakhi culture wherein Ladakhi language has become replete with Urdu / Hindi words and Hindustani has become the second language for the younger generation. The local folk theatre has given way to Bollywood films and songs; Ladakhi staples increasingly got replaced by rice and curries of the North Indian varieties. The female and male robes have given way to *Shalwar – Kameez* and shirt-pants and jackets respectively. In short, before Ladakhi society could recover from the momentous changes in the wake of developments in the decades of forties, fifties and sixties; the Indian influence was upon this region, with all its pluses and minuses; and the two have happily mingled harmoniously.

Taking an over-all view; it can be said that the challenge for the policy planners of tourism at the state and local levels of administration is to see that further growth in the sector receives the right direction so that the tourism in Ladakh does not impact the local life adversely and this region does not go the way some small, unique tourist destinations have followed. For this all the stakeholders, including the government agencies, should get together to brain-storm, evolve a clear strategy and work in unison. One factor though stands out clearly; that on the whole, for tourists – both international and domestic – Ladakh has emerged as one of the most attractive tourist destinations. This is a fact and reality of life; the concerned people and agencies would have to manage this relatively new phenomenon as best as they can; keeping constantly in view the local sensitivities, environmental concerns, national security parameters and topographical limitations.

The whole scenario was perceptibly described by Tashi Rabgias, an influential local person from Leh, in 1998 as "…It is much later after seeing the development at accelerated pace in Leh that the people of Kargil, particularly the right thinking ones, have realized that the Leh model of development would also do them good. This realization came more markedly after the tourism was thrown open to Ladakh in 1974 and this impacted the individuals', and the families' capacity to earn much more than in the normal development process in Ladakh so far… Tourism has had a very positive impact on the economy of our region. There used to be talk earlier that with the inflow of foreign tourists the Ladakhis will lose their traditional moorings and also after some time their own identity itself. These misgivings were motivated mostly by the foreigners themselves. In fact some irresponsible tourists even mentioned Ladakh as part of the 'Indian Occupied Kashmir'. This is rubbish. Our identity in nothing but Indian – it possibly cannot be anything else. There can't be two opinions on this issue. The interdependence of army and Ladakhis is an ideal example of the essential Indian-ness of our people. Neither party is doing favour to the other; but in fact performing the national service and individual duty in furtherance of their patriotic sentiments. Our destiny is clearly linked with India's. Of course we are changing and we are modernizing. This is essential for any people who want to live with pride in today's world."[4]

State Government and Local Administration Becoming More Development Oriented Towards Ladakh

Contrary to general belief, the natural calamities that bring grief to parts of the region are neither infrequent nor solely based on the excess or lack of

4 Interview with Shri Tashi Rabgias in September 1998.

snowfall. Covering the period of first forty years after Independence, and as a representative sample, these have been officially recorded as "Ladakh is a cold desert with very little rainfall, but cloud bursts are common which cause considerable damage to life and property. During summer months heavy rainfall in the upper catchment area of river Indus and its tributaries bring with itself enormous quantity of melted snow which floods the rivers and thereby cause erosion of fertile cultivated land. During 1955, untimely snowfall caused famine which adversely affected the people of Zanskar. The famine sufferers were granted a cash relief of Rs. 25,000/-. In 1956, food crops grown on an area of 244 hectares were completely swamped. An amount of Rs. 20,000/- was doled out among the sufferers. In 1957, the entire region was affected by floods resulting in loss of food crops grown on 592 hectares. Besides, the produce of another 127 hectares was also destroyed due to erosion. Relief was granted by government both in cash and kind... Heavy and untimely snowfall in 1958 damaged the crops mainly in Kargil area and government had to grant remission of land revenue...Again in the month of August 1978, the river Indus was in unprecedented spate which created havoc to roads, bridges, canals as well as to the agricultural land. The latest flood that hit Ladakh was that of 16th August, 1979. This flood caused considerable loss of life and property in the region... People of Kargil and Zanskar experience natural calamities in the shape of avalanches and landslides. In the month of March, 1983, at least 40 persons were killed by an avalanche which wiped out many houses and cattle sheds in these areas...In accordance with the magnitude of the calamity, the government grants relief in cash and in kind to the people of the affected areas."[5]

Till April 1969, for about five years, there were two separate administrative heads in this region; the Deputy Commissioner Ladakh and the Development Commissioner of Ladakh. The former was to look after the maintenance of law and order as also take care of the duties of the District Collector; and the latter had the responsibility of developmental activities. Sonam Narboo has been a famous Dev. Commissioner of Ladakh. There were practical difficulties in having two different posts at the apex level and coordination between them – so much more crucial in a far flung area like Ladakh – proved to be difficult and often became a point of personality clash amongst the two officers. Ultimately in 1969; this system of a sort of 'diarchy' was abolished and a single post of Deputy-

5 Gazetteer of India, *Op. Sit.* , p. 151.

cum- Development Commissioner Ladakh, was created by the state government to ensure smooth and efficient administration. The DDC was henceforth to look after both the revenue and developmental functions; and was a class apart from the Deputy Commissioners of other districts of the state. Traditionally, he flew the flag designed and approved by the state government for the Divisional Commissioners of Jammu and Kashmir Divisions. In his work of administration, the DDC was assisted, in the field, by one SDM, two Assistant Commissioners and two Tehsildars; at the Sub-Divisional and Tehsil levels. The two main officers in his setup at Leh were the Assistant Commissioner (HQ) and Headquarters Assistant – a person of the rank of Tehildar. The former coordinated the work of various field agencies and government departments; whereas the latter was a sort of Staff Officer to the DDC and also, usually, his confidante. Whereas, the administration there functioned on the principle of Single Line Administration – meaning that all departments working in Ladakh district happened to operate independently under their own respective district heads but administratively the powers of the HOD rested with the DDC within the limits of his jurisdiction. The revenue set up in Leh area was an interesting structure. It comprised one revenue Tehsil, headed by a Tehsildar based in Leh; who was also generally the Chairman of the local Notified Area Committee (NAC). So, technically the entire Leh belt was one big revenue unit; divided into Niabats, Girdawar circles and Patwar halqas and as such following the traditional hierarchy. At the same time, it had two more senior officers based within that area; called Assistant Commissioner Nyoma, based in Nyoma village and Assistant Commissioner Nubra, with his headquarters at village Diskit in Nubra area. Both the ACs, in fact, were engaged in the liaison work with army and other forces as also coordinating the activities of various field departments, located in their respective sub divisions. They were generally not expected to take care of day to day revenue functions; which were managed by the Tehsildar from Leh. To that extent the Leh area consisted of one Tehsil and two sub divisions.

Whereas the DDC and other senior officers of the district administration, based in Leh, were mostly residing in their recently constructed official accommodation; the Tehsildar Leh had been traditionally staying in almost a century old local structure called ‘Basti Haveli’. Ladakh first became part of Jammu Raj in late 1830s and later a segment of the State of Jammu and Kashmir in 1846; during the reign of Maharaja Gulab Singh.

For considerable time, in the initial period, the region was administered through a nominated head known as 'Thanedar'; who enjoyed both civil and military powers. The first such administrator was Mangal Thanedar – whose name was Mehta Mangal. He was followed by Mehta Basti Ram in the year 1846. Mehta Basti Ram is known in the region for initiating steps to establish minor Cottage Industry and a Sheep / Goat Farm; with a view to provide gainful employment to the local population, as also boosting local economy. He is also credited with raising a big administrative building in Leh town, part of which housed the government granary, while the rest of it was used as a residence of the Thanedar. This structure came to be commonly known after his name, as 'Basti Haveli'. In fact, it was a majestic building in the town with a grand entrance called 'Deodi'. It was a two storey building with a large number of rooms on the first floor, while the ground floor was meant to accommodate servants, cattle and family winter stores; with vast open space to serve as lawn. With the passage of time, when the administrative set up got changed; 'Basti Haveli' came to be reserved as official residence of the Tehisdar Leh. Earlier, a large chunk of adjoining land was also attached with the building to be used as garden. After 1980s; the garden part was converted into residential plots and allotted to various local families; besides reserving some portion for community purposes. Presently, even the old structure has been demolished, although a new building consisting of few rooms has been constructed in its place to be used as residence of the local Tehsildar. However, the entrance (Deodi) part is still intact and attracts many tourists. An officer of the state government, Virender Gupta, who stayed in the Basti Haveli, recalls, "I happened to have occupied the building for a period of more than two years – from August 1975 to October 1977 – when I was posted as Tehsildar Leh. It was a huge complex comprising a large number of compact, spacious and airy rooms; built of local sun dried bricks and deodar wood used in roofs; with some rooms having big deodar logs of full medium size trees. In view of my limited requirements, I – as also my predecessors – had been occupying only two-three rooms, a spacious kitchen with a small glass room; whereas rest of the accommodation on the first floor remained unutilized. For the reason of remaining abandoned for years together, the unutilized rooms had become not worthy of occupation. However, during my tenure of posting there, family of one S. Bhajhan Singh, who happened to be posted as the Headquarter Assistant with the District Development Commissioner Leh, was also accommodated in few rooms in the said complex, after getting them renovated".

In the Kargil area, which was then a Sub-Division, the administrative set up was headed by a S.D.M. He also enjoyed the powers of the Deputy Development Commissioner and in that capacity headed all the departments functioning in his region. It had two revenue Tehsils, the Kargil Tehsil headquartered in Kargil and the Zanskar Tehsil based in Padam. It was an interesting place. Whereas, the entire Zanskar is populated by Buddhists, in Padam village about 40 percent of the residents were Muslims. The population of Padam, according to 1981 census, was 139 persons. In the Kargil tehsil, considerable agricultural and horticulture activity took place; whereas in Zanskar the main wealth and occupation of the locals was the rearing of cattle.

Right from the beginning; the people of Kargil felt that they were neglected by various administrations whereas Leh region cornered a major part of the resources. This perceived sense of discrimination gave rise to persistent demands of remedial measures including a separate district for Kargil. The state government did partially consider this clamor and upgraded, at first, the SDM post to that of Additional Deputy Commissioner in 1978. But this measure did not satisfy the local people and the demand was ultimately conceded when Ladakh district was bifurcated, on 1st July 1979 between two districts of Kargil and Leh; and two DDCs were appointed in these districts. The jurisdiction of the erstwhile DDC Ladakh was, therefore, shrunk to Leh Tehsil with two sub-divisions. There was, no doubt an increasingly vociferous demand for such a measure; and it also remained a fact that this region always received less attention from the DDC Leh and his staff; who were based far away in Leh. But the step also came under sharp negative reaction from some quarters; and it was alleged that the decision of the state government was influenced by considerations other than purely administrative in nature. An example of the stinging criticism mentioned, read, "The entire frontier region of Ladakh, as is well known, comprised a single district where Buddhists and Shia Muslims lived in absolute peace and harmony for a considerable period of time. The bifurcation of the district into Buddhist Leh district and Muslim Kargil district for so-called administrative convenience, inevitably lent communal complexion to this uncalled for surgery. This also disturbed the age-old cohesive demographic profile of the region and generated intra-regional strifes from time to time, which were conspicuously absent before bifurcation of the region on July 1, 1979."[6] However, it does remain a fact that the state government did complicate the matters on ground, when it bifurcated the Plan Allocations between the two districts, for the first time, in 1979-80; and in this process, allocated little more money to Kargil district than Leh district. For example, the DDC Leh in his plan document for the year 1980-81; mentioned, "REVIEW OF DISTRICT PLAN 1979-80... The draft annual plan was put up before the District Development Board for approval on the basis of allocations made by the Planning Department. The members of the District Development Board objected to the formula of distribution of the plan funds between Leh and Kargil Districts and tendered their resignations on 1st August 1979. The working period which is very limited in this district had already advanced considerably, but the plan was not yet approved by the District Development Board. The District Administration had no alternative but to get the scheme-wise plan allocations approved by the Administrative Department. Finally, the sanction to the sectoral and schematic plan was issued by the District Development Commissioner on 30.8. 1979."[7] Notwithstanding the justifications forwarded by the concerned quarters; this move further exacerbated the matters and an agitation, on this very point, took place in Leh for a major part of the summer of 1980; in which various demands were added later, including that of Union Territory status for the region. The two prominent facts over the past decades have been, that the existence of Kargil as a separate district is a matter of reality and apart from Zanskar area; the other two places where Buddhist population is concentrated, in this district, are Wakah and Mulbek and at none of these three areas there have been problems of communal nature.

The inhabitants of Kargil sector are predominantly Shia Muslims. They are simple at heart; steeped in religious ethos and God fearing people. For a few decades after Independence, as an example, there were hardly any property disputes between people in the region as all such matters were amicably settled within the community; with some help from the elders. It is also a fact that till the mid 1970s people did not lock their houses; the doors and windows were just closed and bolted. A lock in the house was then taken as a sort of insult to the entire community; as it was perceived that the person concerned did not trust his neighbors. Even

6 Shridhar Kaul and H.N. Kaul, *Ladakh Through the Ages,* Indus Publishing Company, New Delhi, 1992, p. 262.

7 Govt. of Jammu and Kashmir; District Plan Leh, 1980-81, p. 9.

government officials, from outside the place, followed this tradition. It was only after the people became 'educated and smart'; that the worldly practices of outsiders slowly crept in the life style of these simple folks. Traditionally, the local people have been looking up to Baghdad in Iraq for guidance in theological matters and some of the 'Agas' (few respectable persons in the area who wear black turbans) wielded lot of influence and authority in their respective areas. Three of them have been quite famous and held sway over the people in their vicinity, as also enjoyed immense prestige amongst their followers. They were very important persons till few decades after nineteen fifties. One of them was Aga Ibrahim Shah of Choskore village. He became a Member of the Legislative Council (MLC) and for sometime was also a Vice- Chairman of the Ladakh Development Committee. Another person of this category was Aga Baqar of Panikher; who had a lot of say in the Teh-Suru belt of Kargil. The third – and certainly most famous of this lot – was Aga Haider of Sankoo. There were a number of stories and incidences attributed to him – regarding his unusual spiritual powers – in the decades of sixties and seventies. It was also he who helped Sonam Narboo in completing the Kargil – Leh part of the main road from Srinagar; by asking his large number of followers to work on this project. Over a period; and mostly coinciding with the spread of education and modern ideas among the people, this phenomenon of Agas exerting a lot of power and influence over the locals has considerably declined.

As an institution; the Islamia School of Kargil was the single most influential organization in Kargil area. It remained so till the rise of Ayatollah Khomeini in Iran in 1979. Soon thereafter, some younger people in Kargil organized the Khomeini Memorial Trust (KMT); which became a rival institution to the Islamia School. Slowly, with the increased pace of development in the area, the hold of both these organizations declined; more so after LAHDC, Kargil came into being in 2003.

The leading and eminent personages from the Leh area have been four and each one of them shaped the destiny of their people in the formative decades after 1947. These men of rare qualities were Kushok Bakula; Sonam Narboo; Rigzin Namgyal Kalon and Chewang Rinchen. They provided leadership to the entire Ladakh region in religious and spiritual, administrative, social and military fields respectively. Much has already been mentioned about the personality and military exploits of

Chewang Rinchen; therefore, a brief biographical portrayal of the other three is given in the following paragraphs.

The prince turned monk, Kushok Bakula, was indeed a person with many qualities. Within and also outside Ladakh; he was hailed as a learned religious scholar, visionary political leader as also a consummate diplomat who always strived for building a harmonious society and worked for uplifting the common man. Personal humility was a hallmark of his personality; in spite of the fact that he was perceived as an extraordinary combination of a monk, administrator and politician. Kushok Bakula, some of his followers also called him "Bakula Rinpoche", was born in the royal family of Matho, to Raja Nangwa Thayas and Rani Ishey Angmo, on 21st May 1917; with the family name of Thupstan Chognor. At the age of four he was identified to be the reincarnation of the 19th Kushok Bakula of Spituk and Sankar Monasteries. After getting the formal recognition of this from the then Dalai Lama; this young boy of tender age was shifted from Matho palace to Spituk Monastery and the Lamas there took over the responsibility of his grooming and religious teachings. After learning the basics of Buddhist theology and rituals for few years; in 1925 he was sent to Tibet for higher studies in the religious philosophy and metaphysics. There, in the famous Drepung Monastery he diligently pursued and practiced the learning of a higher order for almost a decade and half; before returning to Leh in 1940s as an acclaimed Buddhist scholar.

Being a monk; he could not actively take part in the military operations in and around the Leh area during the critical months of 1948; but actively extended moral and material help to all those fighting for the region. A part of the Spituk Gompa was converted into a kind of canteen and first aid centre to provide free rations and medical help to the army personnel. In the middle of 1949; Jawahar Lal Nehru and Sheikh Abdullah visited Leh and on their persuasion he agreed to join active politics – considering this route to be more effective for the speedier emancipation of his poor and backward people. He was appointed as the President of the newly formed district unit of National Conference in Ladakh. Later, he was elected uncontested, as the MLA from Ladakh constituency and inducted as a Deputy Minister in the State Cabinet. He continued in this capacity for good over ten years; when G.M. Sadiq became head of the government in J&K and elevated him to the rank of a State Minister. When Sadiq converted the National Conference into Congress; Kushok Bakula, along with his supporters joined the Indian National Congress in 1965; and he was made President of the Ladakh unit. Subsequently he was elected as a member of Lok Sabha from the Ladakh constituency and remained a M.P. for two terms. He also had the privilege of being a Member of the Minorities Commission for over a decade. In the course of his long years of public service Kushok Bakula emerged as a political leader and a Buddhist scholar of eminence. In the latter capacity he was known internationally. In 1989, he was appointed as India's Ambassador to Mangolia. In this role he earned lot of laurels both as an able Ambassador as also a great teacher for the resurgent religious people of that country; and managed excellent relations between the two countries. He was awarded Padma Bhushan for distinguished services to the nation; in 1990. Kushok Bakula breathed his last in 2003; a venerated scholar of Buddhism and highly acclaimed political personality. Throughout life, he tirelessly worked for the upliftment and betterment of his people in this far flung area.

Sonam Narboo, was born on 27th July 1909 in a farmers family, in Skara village on the outskirts of Leh. Right from the beginning he was a keen and bright student; completing his eighth class in the Government Middle School, Leh. For further studies he went to Srinagar and finished his graduation on a scholarship given to him for being outstanding in studies. After this, he was selected for the training of Naib Tehsildar. But fate had something else in store for him. During this training, he saw an advertisement for admission for engineering degree in England and applied for it. Narboo got selected for this course and also, on the strength of his academic performance, obtained a scholarship from the state government. In 1942 he got the degree of BE from Sheffield University. On his return from England, he was appointed as an Assistant Engineer by the State Government and posted in Baramulla, in the month of July 1942. His dedicated work in the Domel area of the district attracted positive attention of the authorities and he came to be considered as an outstanding engineer in the service of the State. Sonam Narboo got married to Palzes Angmo in 1946 while still being in Baramulla. Many decades later; the then Superintendent of Police there, Man Mohan Wazir, fondly recalled that the young couple had their first meal, in that area, at his residence.

In the month of February 1948, Sonam Narboo accompanied a small contingent of the Indian army belonging to the 2nd Dogra Battalion, under the command of Major Prithi Chand. It was in the middle of a severe winter and these people had to cross over Zojila pass, on foot, in the sub-zero temperature. This march involved great hardships and acutely tested the endurance of every person in the small team. After long marches in tough conditions, the party finally reached Leh on 12th March 1948. Sonam Narboo took in hand the task of constructing a rough landing ground for aircrafts on the long plateau between Leh town and Spituk Gompa. He was ably assisted in this work by a local Overseer of the State PWD, named Babu Dorje. The local people also came forward to help this effort by providing adequate labour and Narboo had been allocated a grant of rupees thirteen thousand for this project – a part of this money also he saved and deposited in the State Treasury. This combined effort paid handsomely and within a month of his arrival in Leh, the landing ground, of approximately 2300 yards length, was ready to get the first aircraft; so sourly needed then – as the Pakistani raiders had advanced perilously close to Leh town. It was more than a month later that the first Dakota of the Air Force landed in Leh on 24th May; with Maj. General Thimayya and Air Commodore (Baba) Mehar Singh as the two VIP passengers. Leh had been literally brought back from the brink; and a large amount of credit for this does belong to the efforts of Sonam Narboo. As a quiet and dedicated worker; he joined back his official duty at the earliest possible opportunity.

Two years later, in 1950, he was promoted as a Divisional Engineer (now called Executive Engineer) and posted at Ramban; from where he competently supervised the snow clearance work on the mountainous portion of the Jammu – Srinagar road; more specifically in the Pir Panjal range. In this rank he served in different stations, including Kishatwar and Anantnag. In 1958, he was elevated to the rank of Superintending Engineer and posted in his home town of Leh. Here, apart from other construction projects; the most prestigious work he took in hand was completing the road connecting Kargil with Leh. This he successfully achieved and Srinagar to Leh road was opened for vehicular traffic in August 1960 – just in time to meet the Chinese aggression in Ladakh region. He left the state government in 1963 and soon thereafter his services were requisitioned by the Border Roads Organization as Chief Engineer of Project Chetak. In 1965 he was appointed as the Development Commissioner Ladakh and in that capacity he took up a number of developmental projects in hand. Two years later, when he left this assignment, Sonam Narboo was nominated as a Member of Legislative Council (MLC). In 1970, the Government of India appointed him the Charge d' Affairs for Mangolia; later that post was upgraded to that of Ambassador. Finally, in 1975 when Sheikh Abdullah became head of the State Government, Sonam Narboo was inducted in his team as a Cabinet Minister in charge of Public Works Department. He remained a Cabinet Minister till his death in February 1980. His multifarious achievements also included an award of Padam Shree by the Government of India.

Sonam Narboo was a simple hearted man; straight forward in his professional and personal dealings. Standing solidly behind his subordinates for genuine reasons – and against undue criticism – was his strong point. He was a person of dedication and devotion; honesty and ethical values. Coming from an humble background, he rose to the very top of his profession becoming a Chief Engineer in the state PWD, as also held the same rank in the BRO. In 1975 - and till the end of his life – for almost five years, he performed the prestigious role of a Cabinet Minister. This gave additional opportunity to serve people of the state; specifically his own Ladakhis. During his long professional and political life; he successfully undertook a number of projects for benefit of the local people. However, Ladakh will forever be grateful and indebted to him for the construction of airfield in Leh in 1948 and completing the Kargil – Leh section of the main road from Srinagar in 1960. Both these projects have been of immense strategic value to the region. It is a huge compliment to the achievements of Sonam Narboo that just after his death; his only son, Pintoo Narboo was made a MLC and inducted in Sheikh Abdullah's cabinet as Deputy Minister for Tourism and Protocol.

The next name in this select category is that of Rigzin Namgyal Kalon; who certainly was a towering figure in the social life of Ladakh region for more than half a century. He was born on 9th December 1923 in the famous family of Kalons. The word 'Kalon' signifies a title meaning a senior minister. It is said that during the time General Zorawar Singh occupied Ladakh in 1830s; an ancestor of Kalons had considerably helped him in unifying and efficiently administering the region. In recognition of these services, he was given this title; which his descendants continue to enjoy. The Kalons have traditionally been rich and influential in the area. They have owned a lot of property in Leh and Nubra areas; as also carried on a lucrative trade with Tibet. Chewang Rigzin Kalon, the father of Kalon Sahib, was a member of Praja Sabha organized during the reign of Maharaja Hari Singh; led a delegation in 1946 on behalf of the King of Leh to His Holiness the Dalai Lama in Lhasa; he also headed the LBA during the crucial period of Pakistani raiders in Ladakh in 1948.

The real worth of Rigzin Namgyal Kalon came to the forefront during the darkest period of this region in 1948; when the Pakistani raiders, from the Gilgit area, almost reached the gates of Leh. He greatly helped Major Prithi Chand and handful of his soldiers, to successfully raise hundreds of local Scouts in Leh and Nubra. He provided free rations and also footwear to them out of his own resources. The existence of Ladakh Scouts today is a great tribute to his tireless efforts and the heroic deeds of this band of committed men during those fateful months of 1948. He and his father were equally successful in ensuring the safety of Muslim population in and around Leh area during those eventful months. His equally significant contribution to the local milieu has been growing and selling of vegetables as a cash crop to the army units deployed in Leh area. Kalon Sahib breathed his last on 8th April 2002. A tribute to him was written by a son of the soil, Kachu Asfandyar Khan, who was then the Deputy Commissioner of Rajouri, and published under the heading "Hero of Ladakh Passes into History". Paying handsome accolades to him, the author mentioned, "… Being a man of immense sagacity and vision, Kalon Sahib has contributed a lot for the overall development of the people of Ladakh, especially the farmer class. He introduced the cultivation of vegetables as a cash crop on modern line and persuaded other farmers to go in for such crops… Though he never took part in active politics of Ladakh, whenever the people of Ladakh faced any grave problem, he never shirked his responsibility and like a beacon of light guided the people towards safety… Though he is no more with us, the loving memory of his magnanimity, his simplicity, his vision and wisdom will guide us in building a modern Ladakh based on the principal of peaceful co-existence…"[8]

The most significant achievement of Kalon Sahib has been to start and nurture the cooperative movement in Ladakh. This was comprehensively described by him as, "…How much our efforts help the army in saving money can be gauged from the fact that if fodder is airlifted it costs Rs. 58 per kg. Whereas we provide the same at Rs. 8 per kg., and that too Alfa Alfa grass which is one of the most nutritious animal feeds in the world… I have put in considerable efforts and personal involvement in making this

8 The Daily Excelsior, Jammu, dated 14th April 2002. The author, Kachu Asfandyar Khan later became DDC of Kargil district.

experiment a success. Having been in contact with this cooperative venture from day one; other members have left its functioning to me for the last thirty five years and I have been working without charging any money from the Society for my efforts. On the other hand I am spending over rupees ten thousand, per year, from my pocket in undertaking journeys to Srinagar, Delhi, etc. in connection with society's work. I earnestly feel that if the management of any cooperative venture is dedicated and purposeful, the experiment should succeed. I can take legitimate pride in not only making the cooperative movement a success but in also being a pioneer in growing vegetables on commercial basis in Ladakh. In fact I learnt it from my father who was visionary in this matter. When I started growing vegetables on large scale, people use to make fun of me and some would even curse me for not making proper use of my land. But at the end of the day I am a very satisfied and happy man. Every person does a lot in fact for his own family; but having done something for the society gives me pleasure and pride in my own self. Increased money from lands has meant prosperity and education amongst general public. This also discouraged people from selling their lands. I am sure this movement will not only be sustained but would further pick up..."[9]

The increased and sustained pace of progress in the Ladakh region during the nineteen seventies came about because of two developments in the area. Firstly, as has already been explained, the structure of district administration came to be stabilized and secondly, due to the focused attention of the Ladakh Development Board, about genuine requirements of this vast land. It is true that most of the work at the ground level was performed by the government officials; but concentrated attention of the Board, and through it, involvement of the head of the government at the state level was certainly a positive element in the whole scheme of things. The Board was a conduit through which considerable good of the region flowed; and it was also an effective way to involve opinion leaders of the region into the developmental strategy that the state administration followed in their day to day executions. Though, this model did have its flaws and shortcomings; as has been reflected in a contemporary note made by an official, posted in Ladakh, in the middle of 1974. It read, "...The apex body for development in Ladakh is the Ladakh Development Board, headed by the Chief Minister, and assisted by the department of Ladakh Affairs at the secretariat level. The Board has two vice Chairmen, one

9 Interview with Rigzin Namgyal Kalon in September 1998.

from Kargil and the other from Leh area. All development activities are sanctioned by this LDB. Now, what is the competence of the non-official members of this body? These people are generally a conglomeration of men nominated from various regions of Ladakh; not by virtue of their expertise in any field, but they are there because they are known to the powers that be... The LDB meetings are full of instances where the members fight amongst themselves to get a path, a bridge or a school building in their area of influence; and not as a part of a well thought out plan but in a disjointed effort and on a random basis... It is also not uncommon, for a member, to demand the job of a peon or equivalent class IV post for his own person...The most suitable word that comes to mind is *adhocism*..." Notwithstanding such strident criticism; the fact remains that the LDB managed to perform essential functions of development fairly well. The pace of activities – all over Ladakh - did pick up substantially when the Chief Minister took personal interest in these matters; which happened for example in the first few years of Sheikh Abdullah's stewardship.

Within a few months of his taking over the reins of power; the LDB was reconstituted by a Government Order No. 1357- GD of 1975 dated 8th July 1975. This body was headed by Sheikh Sahib himself as a Chairman; with Sonam Narboo, Minister for Ladakh Affairs, as the Vice- Chairman; and comprising fourteen eminent persons as non official members of this body; all belonging to the Ladakh region. This time the LDB proved a more effective instrument of progress for the whole area; and credit for this belonged to the Chief Minister and Sonam Narboo. Men at the top did make all the difference. Concentrated efforts were made during these years to focus attention on the priority sectors of Communication – roads, paths and bridges; Education; Health and Tourism facilities with handsome dividends. These have certainly been major drivers of development and economic prosperity of any region.

It needs to be reiterated that both the state government and district administration became more and more development oriented for the region; from the beginning years of 1970s. However, the hard fact remained that on the ground; a lot depended on the person of the chief executive, in this case the DDC. This was more true, particularly so in the far flung region like Ladakh; where supervision and oversight from outside was always minimal.

Fortunately, the DDCs in Ladakh in the decade and half starting from 1970; were all competent and hand-picked officers who were capable of maintaining and increasing the pace of developmental activities in the region. After bifurcation of the place in two districts, in July 1979, the DDC Kargil was also carefully chosen by the state government in the initial years. Sheikh Sahib as the Chief Minister and Sonam Narboo as Minister for Ladakh Affairs, used to take personal interest in this regard and hence for five years after 1975; Ladakh received focused attention at the highest levels of the state government. But, after the demise of Sonam Narboo in February 1980 and virtual incapacity of Sheikh Abdullah, beyond 1981, due to serious illness; things started changing for the worse in Ladakh. The area to suffer first was Kargil district; where local political personalities started playing favorites and officers at various levels – starting from DDC downwards – were picked up and posted there not on the basis of inherent merits but on extraneous considerations. This proved calamitous for the area. In Leh district as there were no such suspicious considerations; things carried on well for some time. With the advantage of hindsight, it can be said that this happened for a few years on the basis of "developmental momentum". By the middle of 1980; Leh district also began suffering on account of wrong choice of officers, especially that of DDCs. This got duly reflected in the slower pace of development in the region; as also resulted in serious law and order issues that cropped up in that peaceful area. In the second half of 1980; the whole of Ladakh was engulfed in a sort of crisis of development paralysis. Emergence of law and order situations and deployment of police forces; so unknown in the region; became increasingly common.

This sad turn of events did not take place over a short space of time; but was a long drawn process of over few years. The political developments in the Valley after the death of Sheikh Abdullah; followed by jockeying for power in the family and the party; had considerable negative fallout on the Leh as well as Kargil districts. The only silver lining in this gloomy scenario was that the Ladakh region did not get adversely affected by the growing terrorism in the Valley – as also for few years in the Southern parts of the Pir Panjal range – in spite of strenuous efforts of some quarters. For this; people of Ladakh deserve compliments in good measure.

A Comprehensive Analysis of Socio-Politico-Economic Scenario in 1970s, 1980s and 1990s

a) Infrastructure.

In the seventies there were four main crossings over Indus river; and these were at Khaltsi, near Alchi, Choglamsar and Chumathang in the form of steel Bailey Bridges at each of these places. Twenty years later, one could see more than ten such crossings, of all types, over the same mighty river; and of course numerous bridges and culverts in the entire region. Infrastructural development in Ladakh, during last three decades of the previous century, has really been impressive. By the end of the closing years of the 1990s; there existed an impressive net work of roads and tracks covering the entire region of Ladakh.

The main road in the region, of course, has been the Srinagar to Leh connection; passing over Zoji La, Dras, Kargil, Namik La, Fatu La, Khaltsi, Saspol and Nimoo. This road was opened to vehicular traffic in August 1960. By 1990s; two other links came up between Kargil and Leh. These were Kargil, Himboting La, Silmo, Batalik, Gurgurdoo, Khaltsi and Kargil, Khangral (short of Bodh Kharboo on the traditional Kargil-Leh road), Chiktan, Sanjak and then crossing over the Indus to meet the Batalik-Khaltsi road. After the proposed tunnel at Zoji La is completed; this route would be open for traffic between Srinagar and Leh throughout the year.

Other prominent road connections in the Kargil area have been Dras-Mushkoo; Kargil-Sankoo-Panikhar-Rangdum-PenziLa-Padam and Padam-Karsha plus Padam-Zangla. There also exist a number of roads and tracks, of different sizes and qualities linking smaller places in the district.

The alternative main artery from Leh connects it with Manali in Himachal Pradesh. This road starts from Leh and passes over Upshi, Thaglang La (17550 ft.), Sarchu, Baralacha La, Keylong, Rohtang Pass and then to Manali. This link is open for vehicular traffic only during the summer season; as it gets blocked in winter due to heavy snow fall at Rohtang, Baralacha and Thaglang high passes.

Significant road connections from Leh town to the outlying areas include the Leh-Nubra and Leh-Nyoma sections.

The Leh-Nubra road starts from Leh and goes over Khardung La (18380 ft.) to Diskit – the headquarters of Nubra sub-division and from there along the river to Turtuk (a village liberated in 1971). From Diskit internal road connections lead to a number of places up the Shyok valley and upstream of Nubra river right up to the Base Camp of the famous Sia-Chin Glacier.

There are two links from Leh to the sub-divisional headquarters of Nyoma; and in a way, this forms a sort of biggish loop – comprising the road from Leh, Sakti, ChangLa (17350 ft.), Tangtse (Darbuk), Lukung, Chushul, Tsaga La, Nyoma, Chumathang, Kharu and back to Leh. The Lukung – Chushul section of this road passes along the famous Pangong lake.

There are also two important subsidiary links from Nyoma to Hanley and Nyoma to Phukchey- Damchok. Both these are road worthy.

From Chumathang; internal roads – which can easily take vehicular traffic – lead to the well known Tsomo Riri lake; as also to Puga valley and then to Tsokar lake, from where it meets up with Leh – Manali road; on the other side of Thaglang La.

Of course, there is a large network of internal roads in the Leh area connecting the main arteries with important places like Timisgam, Alchi, Sumdo-Chiling, Likir, Taru, Pheyang, Sabo, Skara, Chochoot, Hemis and the like.

b) Education.

From times immemorial in this region, the concept of education consisted of teaching and acquiring life skills and surviving techniques in the existing harsh climate and adverse conditions. The resources in terms of cultivable lands, the animal population and bounties of the nature; were extremely limited and therefore; expertise of the people inhabiting this area lay in how best to manage within the limited means available; and also feel satisfied, if not happy, with their lot. By all accounts, including the written records of travelers in this far flung area, the population of Ladakh has led a happy life – feeling contended with their resources and means available. This has been reflected in the looks of satisfaction and happiness writ large over the faces of the locals; both men and women.

The first primary school for modern education, as the term is generally understood, was started in Leh by the Moravion Christian missionaries in 1889. This was followed, four years later in 1893, by the state government opening its first primary school which was established in Leh town. The first middle school started functioning in 1925 and the first high school, located in Leh, in the year 1945. By that time the education department of the state had opened enough educational institutions in the region, to justify posting an Inspector of Schools in the Ladakh area, with headquarters at Leh. After Independence, not much increase in educational facilities took place in the region for the first two decades. Thereafter, the expansion in the number of schools, at all levels, was marked and basic educational facilities reached almost all farthest corners in the next twenty years or so. The region saw first higher secondary school in 1970 and colleges started functioning in Leh and Kargil in 1994. In this sector of huge land mass and very limited population; there has always been a running competition between the concepts of 'spread' and 'number of beneficiaries'. However, in the field of education; the coverage of the department even in the farthest corners has remained impressive. For this a large amount of credit legitimately belonged to the education department, various DDCs and the enlightened local leadership. The elder segment of the local population, though they themselves did not enjoy the benefits of education, were always very eager and insistant that the young boys and girls of the area were empowered with the tools and skills of reading and writing. For them, education and connectivity – in that order – always received priority over other sectors of development. This positive attitude has paid handsome dividends over the years; more so in the Leh sector, where people realized the importance of education, earlier and more acutely, than their Kargil brethren. About benefits of this fast spread of education facilities; a perceptive local observer expressively mentioned, "Consequent to the opening of a large number of elementary schools and two high schools, a generation of youths fluent in Hindustani (Urdu and later Hindi as well) and reasonably proficient in English language had provided the initial crop of modern-educated and formally trained teachers, doctors, engineers, white-collared workers and other technical hands to man the positions available in the region of Ladakh in the second half of the 20th century. Such positions were earlier almost entirely manned by persons from the Kashmir valley".

By 1979-80, as per official records, the Leh district had 209 educational institutions of all types; in which total enrolment came to 6604. The expansion programme was going ahead even then; more so at the primary level where the attention was focused on covering the unreached segments of population. For example, nine primary schools were opened in 1979-80; and the next year this number was eleven. Among 431 teachers who were then working in the district, 256 were trained and 175 listed as untrained. This was a typical problem in that area where initially local candidates, though not highly educated, were employed to cope up with the fast expansion of educational services in the far flung area; places where non locals were not willing to serve. This difficulty was progressively resolved by starting a Teachers Training School, at Leh, where such untrained teachers were provided requisite tools to upgrade their skills and come up to the expected standards; in addition this institution also functioned as a medium for in service training of teachers.

Like other areas of the state, this part also faced the twin problems of drop-outs and single teacher schools. To induce parents to send their children to schools and also keep them there; some incentives in the form of free supply of books, free supply of uniforms and scholarships to promising students were started in the late seventies and early eighties; with encouraging results. These helped considerably in making a positive impact on increasing the rolls and reducing the dropout rate. It was also observed that single teacher schools, particularly in the interior areas, did face difficulty especially when the teacher had to get his salary from the respective 'pay centre' or proceed on leave. To deal with such eventualities; a concerted effort was started, in the late seventies, by the district administration to progressively reduce the number of single teacher schools – by posting an additional hand there. These long term measures did make a positive difference over a period of time.

A typical problem for Ladakh region had been the ever rising demand for opening higher educational institutions in almost every locality; irrespective of the number of student population. Otherwise, it was argued, that the boys and girls would not study beyond the level at which the facilities were locally available. This issue was duly reflected upon and commented in the Plan Document of Leh District for the year 1980-81, as "...There are few pockets in the district where the facilities of High School or Higher Secondary School are not available. The students of these areas were persuaded to get themselves admitted in the existing High School or Higher Secondary School by providing them the hostel facilities in the shape of monthly scholarship at the rate of Rs. 75/- per month for a period of nine months in an academic year. This facility is available to 9th, 10th and 11th class students...provision of hostel scholarships to students of 9th Class and above staying in various hostels, instead of opening new High or Higher Secondary schools has shown encouraging results..."[10] It also goes to the credit of the non-official members of the District Development Board that they had agreed to and also approved this formulation; and such a scheme could serve as a model worth emulating in other areas also.

The acute desire of the local people to get the best of education for their children, irrespective of the stakes involved, was duly reflected in the discussions of their representatives as non official members of the District Development Board. One episode comprehensively underlines this passion and appetite for literacy and learning. This happened in the month of August 1980, during the discussions about annual plan for Leh district. One point which was debated for about two hours concerned providing science education to students, across the area, in the early classes. The local members insisted that they unanimously want this facility at the middle school level. For this, they said, it was absolutely desirable that every middle school had at least one science graduate teacher. The District Education Officer and the DDC, both pointed out that though this was a very positive attitude, but fulfilling the parameter was simply not possible because so many science graduates were not available in the district. The non official Board members were insistent in their request on this count and would not agree to go to the next item on the Agenda unless this issue was satisfactorily resolved. Notwithstanding reasoned explanations to the contrary; they literally dug in their heels and persisted on the need to meet this requirement. An exasperated DDC then pointed out that the only way to resolve this issue was to recruit almost about a hundred science graduate teachers from outside Ladakh. A lengthy discussion on this sensitive issue followed; as the matter pertained to hiring of new hands for the posts of teachers, which belonged to the 'district cadre'. Any effort to get teachers from outside the district had its own implications. At the end of this session; it was resolved unanimously that the DDC Leh be authorized to formally request the Divisional Recruitment Board Kashmir, which had the jurisdiction over Leh district being technically a part of the Kashmir division, to recruit requisite number of science graduates as teachers, temporarily for a period of five years. This was to be done on contractual

10 District Plan Leh – 1980-81, pp. 12 and 15.

basis. Within this period of five years; the DDB expected that sufficient number of local science graduated would be available in the district, to carry on this good work.

The point to be remembered is that even though local recruitment was a highly emotive issue; the non official members of the DDB gave higher priority to the acquisition of knowledge of science by students at young age; even if meant getting qualified people from outside. During the winter months that year; the hiring of teachers from the Valley was fast tracked and by the next summer, every middle school in Leh district had at least one science graduate teacher; thus effectively meeting demand of the locals to get science education for their wards at an early stage. This incident duly reflected the emphasis placed on acquisition of knowledge, by the local people there way back during 1980.

The story did not end there; but had an interesting sequel. The officer who was DDC Leh then; got posted as Divisional Commissioner Jammu, five years later. In that capacity; once while he was attending the meeting of the District Development Board of Doda district, a similar problem of teaching science at every middle school of the district came up for discussion. After sometime, the Divisional Commissioner Jammu shared his experience of an identical situation in Leh and suggested that the non official DDB members consider following a similar solution. After hearing him out, the local members one after the other objected to this course of action; emphasizing that they would rather not have their wards learn science than to get teachers from outside the district – even for a short period on contractual basis. Comparison between the two regions of Leh and Doda could not be starker; as also the stress laid by locals on acquisition of knowledge by young people.

It is therefore not surprising that the people of Leh district, population wise, have done better than other districts of the state; including that of Kargil. Over the last few decades this region has done exceedingly well in expansion of educational facilities; as that is of a very high priority amongst the locals. An intellectual from Leh has thoughtfully opined, "However, there is a need in the region, as in other parts of the country, to encourage creative learning in schools and colleges by cutting on the widely prevalent rote learning practices. The tests and examinations are required to be so structured as to disincentives degree acquisition through rote learning. This calls for conscious overhauling of the education and training curricula and examination system by education planners within the framework of a national policy. It is gratifying that some efforts in the past by the private sector and the civil society in this area have resulted in many Ladakhi youths managing to compete for decent government and private sector jobs outside the region. Spread of education and healthcare services has doubtlessly helped the people of this remote region to harness their latent potentials."

c) Health.

In Ladakh, people traditionally had deep faith in the Amchi system of medicine (also known as the Tibetan medicine). It was mainly based on locally available herbs and other material. The role of Amchi was considered very significant in this holistic and customary healthcare scheme. For centuries every major village and hamlet had their own Amchi. Until the early fifties, Amchi medicine used to be the only kind of treatment available to the sick people in Ladakh and it is still considered, quite widely, effective and affordable system of healthcare which is organic in nature without any toxic side effects. It has been a long standing custom that villagers, in lieu of treatment would provide livestock, agricultural products and field labour to the Amchi; but today they pay a small fee to the Amchi for their services and medicine. In order to preserve and promote this age-old therapy; the Ladakh Society of Traditional Medicine (LSTM) was established in 1999. Initially, it was sponsored by an institution from France; but later it became an independent Ladakhi non-profit organization, which has been playing an active role in revitalizing the Amchi systems. LSTM also operated an Amchi clinic in Leh for foreign and domestic visitors and residents wishing to receive treatment or learn about the Amchi medicines.

The Allopathic Medicare in this vast region started in 1940 when the first medical centre was established in Leh. Later in 1950, four dispensaries were started in Leh, Dras, Kargil and Khaltsi. Except in Leh; no doctor was available in these dispensaries and only para medical staff would man them. The Leh dispensary where one Medical Officer, one Pharmacist, one Nurse, one ANM, one Vaccinator and one Class IV staff were posed; was popularly known as "Shifa Khana" and provided only outdoor patient facility. In later years the infrastructure, manpower and equipment augmentation started taking place.

In 1963, a fifteen bedded District Hospital Ladakh came into existence in Leh town. It was established in the premises where the CMO office shifted in the early 1980s. Soon, in 1965, three local Medical Officers joined this facility. By 1970, the doctor's strength in this hospital had risen to seven and it became a 20 bedded hospital providing OPD and IPD services; with commensurate supporting staff. It also had the services of specialists in medicine, surgery, gynaecology, ophthalmology, anesthetics and tuberculosis disciplines. This hospital, at the old location, was also equipped with normal component of equipment; including a laboratory with microscope, Dental Chair and an X-ray Machine. Almost twenty years after its inception; the location of the District Hospital was shifted to the 100 bedded SNM (Sonam Narboo Memorial) District Hospital at Leh; which has since then been the highest grade medical facility for the local population there. Work on this project was started in the middle of 1970s and completed and commissioned in 1980. It was initially without the provision of central heating system, but had the facilities of all major medical specializations. Most of the staff like doctors, nurses, para-medical personnel and others had been locals themselves. There were teething troubles and difficulties in the first few years; and a local specialist doctor remembers, "The Operation Theaters (OTs) were cold during winter season; scalpels and other operating instruments would stick with skin due to extreme cold. These had to be kept in the clean, boiling water to keep them warm…sometimes due to lack of trained 'anesthetist'; this work was managed by surgeon or other senior or specialist doctor… once, for a broken leg after it was fixed; the doctor had to get a silk string from the market and put stones at the other end to work as 'weights'…similar improvisations were resorted to for lady patients requiring C-Section deliveries…in the ultimate analysis commitment, dedication and patient welfare were the guiding principles for the doctors; particularly local doctors…". By the end of 1980s, the bed strength of SNM hospital was raised to 130 which was enhanced to 150 ten years later. In the closing years of last century; facilities like central heating, uninterrupted power supply, piped gas supply and running water were added to the this institution. The SNM Hospital at Leh undoubtedly became the best District Hospital in the entire J&K state; in terms of equipment, facilities, cleanliness and dedication of the staff. The march for improvements continues. The Ladakhi traditions of hospitality and warm welcome have seeped into the general working culture of this hospital; thereby resulting in very cordial relationships between the doctors, the medical staff on duty, the patients and their attendants. This is something which such government institutions, in other parts of the country, can learn from this hospital.

From the pitiable figure of one state healthcare institution in 1947, the coverage of entire Ladakh area has been impressive over the decades thereafter. As a representative sample; in Leh district itself the healthcare system expanded a lot and by the year 1999 it had 137 medical institutions. These included one District Hospital, one SDH, one CHC, 14- PHC, 84 – MAC, and 36 FW Centers. Other statistical details, in the year 1989, included 2138 Indoor Patients; 95038 Outdoor Patients; 211 major operations and 3336 minor operations performed and 45 doctors on rolls. Ten years later, in 1999, these figures were 6481; 257489; 518 and 10566; and 55 respectively. The doctors and paramedics in this area have been quite dedicated in their job. Despite harsh climate and inaccessibility during winter months, they have done good work in reducing morbidity of different diseases and also arresting infant and maternal mortality rate. The maintenance of records pertaining to various family welfare goals and targets especially with reference to institutional delivery system, anti natal care, immunization and other indicators is quite impressive. In fact, the Health Secretary of J&K State during his field visit to this district in September 1999 was pleasantly surprised to find that detailed and up to date registers were meticulously maintained at the village levels by the local health professionals. They were indeed contributing a lot in generating awareness about various health issues, programs and schemes in almost a missionary spirit. The relations of doctors, paramedical staff; with patients and their attendants in various health institutions have been very cordial. They often behave in a friendly manner and the patients and their attendants are respectful to the health professionals. Apart from cultural values; it appears the traditional Amchi system in which Amchi was respected professionally as well as spiritually, has definite bearing on the behavior pattern in hospitals.

Similar expansion in Health Institutions and provision of services to locals is also discernible in Kargil district. Thus, across the entire Ladakh region the availability of health cover has been praiseworthy, considering the overall scenario and the services provided by the health professionals to local population, of a high order.

d) Animal and Sheep Husbandry.

Animals have always been an integral part of the Ladakhi life, economy and household; and not just a commodity. Total livestock population of the entire region was little over three lakhs, as per live stock census of 1972. The famous species of this area are the Pashmina bearing goats; mighty Yaks; the Zos and Zomos (crosses between Yak and Cow) and Zanskari horses; famous for their amble trot and sure-footedness. Exotic wild life, though not often seen, is found at higher altitudes. The most common variety under this category is the wild ass, locally called as Kiang, moving in large herds in the pasture lands of the high altitude Chanthang area. Extremely famous, as also elusive and almost extinct, varieties are of 'snow leopard' and 'black necked crane'. The livestock is generally reared all over Ladakh; but Changthang belt has always been famous for its Pashmina goats. It is located in the Nyoma sub division of Leh district and the average height there varies between 12,000 to 16,000 feet. In the lower altitudes, sheep and goats are commonly reared for wool and meat; as also horses and ponies for load carrying in the mountain trails. Though Ladakh is rich in animal wealth; but the productivity of these animals is lower as compared with the stock found in other parts of the country. This is mainly due to the characteristics of local breeds, high altitude and its effects. Over a number of decades after the 1960s; the Animal and Sheep Husbandry departments have been engaged in constantly improving the breeds; animal health cover; investigating diseases; production of improved stud stock by importing exotic varieties from abroad and then getting them acclimatized to local conditions. Some foreign species, like the Russian Marino, did show encouraging results.

Pashmina Goats

The world famous Pashmina wool – it is supposed to be the softest, as also the warmest, wool across the globe - comes from the Pashmina goats that are reared in the high altitude pasture lands at the Changthang plateau, which is a part of Leh district. The average height of this area is above fifteen thousand feet. Only very sturdy animals can survive and flourish at this altitude and the harsh climate of the belt. Pashmina bearing goats are one of such species. In fact, it is a miracle of the nature that these animals grow on their body and below the normal hairy coat, a special layer of fleece that enables them to withstand the very severe winter of the region. After the winters are over and the spring season heralds; these goats naturally shed this special woolly coat. But before that happens; the owners of these goats take out this wool using specially designed combs and store it separately. These shedding by the goats are primarily the famous Pashmina wool and each goat averagely yields about 4 to 6 ounces of fiber each year; but at this stage the main product is mixed with goat hair also which is normal in the combing process. At the first point of sale; the Changthang rearers dispose of this coarse woolly mix itself and leave it to the subsequent buyers, up the Pashmina trade, to further refine this produce which ultimately ends up in the form of much sought-after *Shawls* bearing the same name. Over the centuries, the nomads of Changthang have been selling raw Pashmina to various traders without any value addition; either *in situ* or anywhere else in Ladakh. Converting this raw material into the final product is a very laborious process and even a simple plain shawl, without any embroidery on it, involves 200 to 250 man hours. It was in the 1960s that the state government established two Weaving Centers, one each in Leh and Kargil, with a view to train the local artisans in making better use of their resources and produce improved quality of Shawls, Carpets and other articles for which the basic material was available in Ladakh itself. The main skills imparted in these Weaving Centers related to the weaving of carpets, from the local wool, and shawls, made from the Pashmina wool. But, the Pashmina shawls produced there remained coarse and of low quality. For example in the early seventies, a Pashmina Shawl in Leh or Kargil was available at around rupees one hundred and fifty; whereas in Srinagar and beyond these fetched prices in the range of thousands of rupees. The two main ingredients which considerably enhanced the value of Pashmina wool; related to the removing of hair from the wool as also spinning the wool into as fine a thread as possible. Both these activities were labour intensive and required expertise which the trained artisans, mostly belonging to the Kashmir valley, had acquired over many generations. This was where Ladakh could not compete with the craftsmen from the Valley.

In the late 1970s an effort was made by Ladakh administration to impart upgraded skills to the local weavers. The plan was to make lucrative offers to some Kashmiri experts to come to Leh and teach the local artisans the art of separating hair from the Pashmina wool; spin the resultant wool into as thin a thread as possible and then weave this product into a fine Shawl which would command a high price in the market. For over a year and despite the strenuous effort of the local officers, at various levels, it is interesting to note that not even a single artisan from the Valley agreed to come to Ladakh to teach the art and craft of making high quality Pashmina products to the local craftsmen. After a couple of years; this futile effort was quietly dropped.

e) ***Postal and Telecom Services.***

The Postal and Telecommunication facilities in Ladakh, like anywhere else in the world, have undergone revolutionary changes in the 20th century – more particularly towards the end. In the early years Ladakh had only rudimentary postal services in the region; and that too mainly for the delivery of government communications and matters related to military and strategic issues of the J&K state and the government of India. The arrangement was entirely based on a set of "*Harkaras*" or the Dak-Delivery men. They were all paid employees of the establishment; who moved day and night – without any stop – between Srinagar and Leh. It was a primitive but extremely effective arrangement; which worked well. The distance from Srinagar to Leh was then usually covered by private individuals in twenty one days. For the official 'Dak' this very route took four days flat. Such was the efficiency and efficacy of the system that it is famously said that once the British Joint Commissioner in Leh was unhappy because his official mail was "full three hours late". The local Post Master was reprimanded for this lapse and had to explain the delay. Except on unusually bad weather days over the Zoji La during winter season; this tight time table was strictly adhered to round the year. That explains the existence and proper maintenance of Dak Huts at Gumri and Meenamarg in the Zoji La area; during the pre-1947 period. The important official correspondence between any two points in the region, in those olden days, was carried on through special messengers; who were also efficient and moved with speed.

For the record it may be mentioned that the Kargil sub-post office was opened on 18th July 1884; and few years before that only a departmental branch post office existed in Leh. One Branch Postmaster with another Buddhist language knowing Postman to assist him; would cater for the postal needs of the entire Leh sector. The first Branch Postmaster in Leh was reportedly a person named as Wazir Shamsher who was a resident of Skardu. Even those days, the periodic inspection of this far away postal outpost was carried out from Srinagar. For anecdotal interest, it may be mentioned that the first such visit there was made by Mr. F.B. Oslia;

Superintendent of Post offices, Kashmir Division, in March 1886. Another review of this place was carried out by Sh. Gokalchand, Inspector Post Offices, in May 1895. This person recorded an interesting observation that firewood was supplied at the rate of one and half Maund per rupee. Details of one more check are available pertaining to a visit of Superintendent Post offices Kashmir Division on 22nd July 1901; who found that one stamp of 1/2 Anna was missing from the stock. The Leh facility was upgraded to the status of Sub Post Office in 1901 and remained so till 1947; though postal services were started in Mulbek and Khaltsi in 1936. The Leh Sub Post Office was further upgraded to the status of Head Post Office in 1974; and from June 1979 became a separate Postal Division. The Padam SPO became functional in 1981; and it had the distinction of being the farthest sub-post office from its account office in the entire country. After Independence, the expansion of postal services in Ladakh has been quite impressive; considering the low population figures of the region. For example in 1950 it had 3 Sub Post Offices and 35 Branch Post Offices; which figure was 11 and 74 respectively in 1983 – and by the turn of the century these became 14 and 93.

Till 1947; there existed only one telegraphic line between Srinagar and Leh; but it functioned efficiently throughout the year. In the 1930s this facility was extended from Kargil to Skardu. Also there was a telephone connection available to Wazir Wazarat Ladakh; who could speak with his Tehsildars in Kargil and Skardu. For few decades after Independence the progress in the field of telecommunications was rather tardy. Almost forty years thereafter, the Telephone and Telegraph department was supervised by a Sub-Divisional Officer with headquarters at Leh; for the entire region. This status was upgraded as an independent Division in February 1983. Till then, only manually operated telephone exchanges worked in Leh and Kargil; with a small facility in Dras also. It was later that automatic exchanges were installed in various locations. But by the turn of the last century; the telecom facilities in Ladakh made impressive strides with Satellite Communication systems made operative in the closing years of 1980s. Thereafter, almost spectacular positive changes took place; culminating, over a time, in the large scale use of the mobile phones and related services.

f) Solar and Geo-Thermal Energy.

Looking at the sky – during the day and at night – is an experience of its kind in Ladakh. May be it is due to the effect of high altitude or general absence of dust in the atmosphere or both; but the sky is incredibly blue in that area. If one is to understand what 'sky-blue' colour means; he just has to see the overhead canopy in Ladakh. It is so much clear and true to the name of the colour. Also it is a treat to look at the dark sky full of stars during the night – particularly in the moonless period. The whole scene creates a virtual three dimensional effect. One can actually see that a particular star is nearer to the viewer than another one which is much further away. Another peculiarity in that area is the fact that it is hardly ever cloudy, even during the winter season; and at an average for 300 days in a year the entire region gets lot of sunlight in the day time. The unusual sunny weather and huge uninhabited land tracts make Ladakh an ideal place for the effective harnessing of solar power. Efforts in this direction started rather late; the first one towards the end of seventies. It is also a fact that Solar Technology is still in a developing stage in India; and not much progress has been achieved in this sector.

The pioneering work in this field was done in Leh by Prof. (Dr) Chaman Lal Gupta in 1979. He was earlier teaching in the then Roorkee Engineering College, Roorkee. In the late 1960s he took pre-mature retirement and permanently shifted to the Aurobindo Ashram, Pondicherry. But he kept his interest alive in scientific studies; particularly in the field of solar energy. J.R.D. Tata, recognizing his talents, encouraged him and requested that while continuing his work in the Aurobindo Ashram Pondicherry; he could also collaborate with the Tata Energy Research Institute, Bombay. It was an offer which Prof. Chaman Lal gladly accepted. About his introductory work in Leh; in the field of solar energy, he prepared a comprehensive note in April 2019 describing his performance there. In this document; Chaman Lal ji recalled, "My solar work in Ladakh began rather indirectly. The project of retrofitting two houses with Passive Solar Heating in Leh, was initiated by Ms. Helena Norberg-Hodge from Germany, a linguist scholar well versed in Ladakhi language. It was financed by Intermediate Technology Industrial Services (ITIS) London. Architect Costis Stambolis was the architect appointed and Dr. C.L. Gupta of Tata Energy Research Institute, Field Research Unit, Pondicherry (me) was appointed a consultant to the project. This project was completed and monitoring done from October 1979 to April 1980.... Tata Energy Research Institute agreed to provide part of the finances so that it could be possible to monitor the project performance over a winter period with the active collaboration of the research staff of TERI Field Research Unit at Pondicherry. Mr. Sonam Dawa, Superintending Engineer, PWD of Leh very kindly agreed to oversee the monitoring and maintenance of the instruments installed in the experimental houses as well as conventional ones for comparison... Ladakh, a high altitude land of desert and snow is one of the most remote and rugged regions of the world. Most people are subsistence farmers; who live in villages that comprise up to hundred houses. Resources are used to the utmost and frugality is almost a tradition. People do not generally complain about hardships.... However, one vital need people have is for relief from cold. The traditional Ladakhi house is a massive construction of rectangular plan. The walls built of stone or sundried mud bricks, are from 30 to 50 cm thick. Due to scanty rainfall the roofs are flat as opposed to usual inclined roofs in the mountains. Since early seventies access to glass from Srinagar resulted in windows growing larger culminating in *Shelkhang or glass room* which gets very warm in the day time due to direct sun light coming in.

"Due to fairly high altitude, clear skies, shortage of fuel and remoteness of the area; passive solar systems seem the ideal means of space heating. The obvious choice for solar space heating in Leh was a solid glass wall system... Two such glass wall systems were installed, one on each of the rooms at Shambala and Karakoram Hotels. A green house system adjoining the solar room was also put up. The systems were ready by beginning of October 1979. Principles of solar heating by such systems are well known.... To monitor thermal performance of the passive heating systems, mercury-in-glass thermometers with an accuracy of 0.5 deg C were installed in each of the two rooms... Systematic data were obtained for 5 months from December 1979 to April 1980 for the solar heated room at Shelkhang at Karakoram and the weather station set up for this purpose. The winter of 1979 was not particularly severe by Ladakh standards and selective heating differentials of the order of 8 deg C and above (through out twenty four hours) were observed during coldest months of December and January when Sun is in lowest elevation and solid solar wall was most effective.... Fuel wood is scarce in this area because of dry climate and cold desert type terrain. Kerosene oil is also expensive and scarce. People do need to heat minimum one room. The heating season considered is December to April, when local people will normally heat rooms, if they can afford to obtain the fuel needed.

"Net savings per family in heating fuel if solar passive system is retrofitted are estimated to be the order of one kilo litre of kerosene oil or six metric tons of fire wood per heating season for normal massive housing construction used and for reasonable comfort standards at 18 deg C. For South oriented rooms, solar space heating in Ladakh is effective....While doing the experiments in Hotel Karakoram & Shambala, I was asked one day by the Venerable Head of SOS Childrens' Village (of Tibetan Refugees) at Choglamsar, if I could do similar work for the children at SOS village, Choglamsar. I agreed and got a funding for them of Rs. One Lakh from Tata Energy Research Institute in Bombay.

"In one of the SOS village homes, we fixed a frame work of double glazing on the two bedroom walls and extended the veranda to make a solarium. The solarium had a sloping curtain of blankets under the roof. This was opened in the day time to let the sun in and pulled back in the evenings so as not to let the heat go out. The temperatures of -3degC in the building during the night went up to 12degC after the blanket curtain was pulled back to shield the glass roof from losing heat. In the day time also, the temperatures became so comfortable that the children removed their jackets and kept them aside. We knew we had succeeded and I got as a gift the school badge fixed on my jacket by a six year old child. Since then all the twelve buildings of SOS village at Choglamsar have been retrofitted. Apart from the technical service; I have since those days lifelong friendship with some of the Tibetan monks for which I am indeed grateful.

"We had also made a solar still to produce distilled water for the batteries used in vehicles. We had taken care to use and train local carpenters and masons. Now, we hear that there are many such buildings around Leh right up to the famous Hemis monastery. We also trained a PWD engineer Mr. Matin Tak who continued to supervise solar work in his spare time...On the research side, we made a mathematical model to predict the temperatures of retrofitted buildings like this, which was presented at the International Solar Energy Congress at Brighton, U.K. It was truly a success story which enhanced the building practice in Leh region...Seeds that were sown in seventies have blossomed over these years; the entire region has turned solar.... Also there is an active Ladakh

Autonomous Hill Development Council which is engaged in meaningful renewable energy projects".

In the month of August 1979 Prof. Chaman Lal, who was in Leh in connection with his work on solar energy, met with Deputy Commissioner Leh. He apprised the D.C. with his work and emphasised the great potential for the tapping of solar power in that area. The DC was quite impressed with his presentation and both agreed to work together in future. As a beginning, the district administration sent a junior engineer of PWD for training in Pondicherry with him, for one month in December 1979. This officer on return also brought a specially designed 'solar cooker' with him. He arranged a demonstration for the DC and few officers in Leh in the month of January 1980. It was a clear and sunny weather that day. There, under the bright sun light and when the temperature hovered around minus ten degrees centigrade (-10 degrees C); the JE was able to bake a cake in his solar cooker. He proudly shared a piece each with those present there; and the cake was unanimously declared a tasty fare. In that practical way, he was able to explain – rather convincingly – the efficacy of solar power to the gathering of officers; as also its huge potential if harnessed properly, for the entire Ladakh region. Unfortunately, the district administration failed to keep up the interest and in the years to come; work in this important field perceptibly declined instead of picking up. But, as a happy spin-off; the concept of solar heated rooms picked up in the region. Thereafter in Ladakh, a large number of homes – particularly those owned by more affluent people – have at least one room kept warm during the winter season by making efficient use of solar energy. Inside these spaces; even during the middle of winter when the outside temperature is sub-zero, it is pleasant and cosy. One can feel comfortable even in the normal summer clothing. But once the sun goes down, the temperature plummets – naturally.

Equally promising, as also similarly neglected, is the field of geo-thermal energy in this region. Theoretically it holds considerable potential but the practical applications of this comparatively new field are yet to be fully realized. In Ladakh there are three known places where the efficacy and benefits of this form of energy is openly on display. These locations are Puga and Chumathang (in Nyoma sub-division) and Panamik (in Nubra sub-division). There is a natural Geyser in Puga; where the water gushes out many feet high at periodical intervals. In the early seventies of the

20th century, the J&K Minerals Ltd – a company of the State Government - had installed a pilot plant there for the extraction of Borax. It worked successfully for sometime; but when the top man interested in this kind of work retired from government service; this initiative was also quietly buried. It was never revived again. Similarly, almost during that period, a senior functionary of the Geological Survey of India (GSI) had planned to install an experimental unit of one megawatt generation of electricity based on geo-thermal energy, in Puga. This initiative too did not fructify.

At Chumathang and Panamik, the existence of hot springs has been known for a long time. The availability of hot water there, at very high temperatures, even during the peak winter season of Ladakh, adequately indicates the huge reservoir of locked up power under the top hard crust. If properly channelized, these places have the potential of becoming focal points of booming technology with considerable side benefits.

The Agitation of Summer of 1980

Right from the beginning, that is after 1947, when the new democratic government took over the reins of the state administration from Maharja's dispensation; relations between Ladakhis and the state government have been 'suspicious' at the best. However, the simmering discontent in the region over continued neglect and slow pace of development remained under wraps; primarily because Kushok Bakula – the widely recognized voice of Ladakh then – was not assertive enough in his criticism of the new rulers. This was mainly due to the fact that he was not only the district president of the ruling National Conference, but also a member of the Legislative Assembly and, in addition, part of the state cabinet. To be fair to him, he tried hard to get his people their due share in the growth process by working, as also occasionally raising his voice, from within the system. This way there were no signs of an organized protest in the region on this neglect and through the fifties, things appeared to be quiet and peaceful – at least outwardly. The first time this bottled up discontent spilled over was in the mid-sixties and the protests continued, though intermittently, for next few years. This phenomenon has been explained as, "…The history of our struggle goes back to 1964 when the first organized effort of Ladakhis against Kashmiri domination and exploitation under the leadership of Rev. Kushok Bakula manifested itself in a demand for NEFA type central administration. A similar agitation was launched in 1972, under the leadership of Rev. Lama Lobzang and

Thupstan Chhewang demanding Central Administration for Ladakh…"[11] Thupstan organized black flag demonstrations against Mir Qasim, when he visited Ladakh in 1972 as Chief Minister of the state. For this, he and his associates were arrested and this agitation was suppressed by the government. Ladakh remained peaceful for most of the remaining decade and in this intervening period; the entire region saw unprecedented growth as also developmental activities. The next agitation, as also a hiccup in the growth process, started in the summer of 1980. There was an interesting and provocative reason for this.

The erstwhile single district of Ladakh was divided into two units of Leh district and Kargil district on 1st July 1979. While allocating the resources for 1980, the first plan year after the bifurcation, the state government gave rupees nine lacs more to Kargil on the plea that it had little more population than the Leh district. This logic was not acceptable to the people of Leh district; headed by their opinion leaders, among whom the prominent name was that of P. Namgyal, who had by the beginning of 1980, become a Member of the Parliamentary. They collectively argued, and rightly so, that when the state government goes to the Planning Commission of India for getting funds allocated for the State Plan; it asks for additional resources on the premise of the larger area of the state. By the same consideration; Leh district having a larger area than Kargil, it should get more money for its annual plan than Kargil. On this point an agitation was started in Leh, in the beginning of summer of 1980. The DC Leh also took up this matter with state authorities, particularly the Planning Commissioner; for token enhancement of allocations to Leh and increasing it by an amount to make it larger than the funds given to Kargil district. He assured senior officers of the state government that once this was done; the agitation in Leh would get withdrawn. But, his requests also did not evoke a positive response from the state headquarters; and the demonstrations in Leh continued – getting more vociferous and even violent – with the passage of time. Within few months, the agitators added more demands to the earlier one only; including direct administration by the Centre and Scheduled Tribe status for the entire region. At its peak the agitation had resulted in injuries to a number of civilians as well as policemen. Once the situation took such an ugly turn that a violent mob burnt down the Tehsil office and threatened to ransack the DC office also.

11 Part of the background note issued by the organizers of National Convention on the Ladakh Issue, New Delhi, March 18, 1990.

This resulted in the police firing few shots to disperse the crowd and by evening, the army was called in to assist the civil administration in the maintenance of law and order. The overall situation in Leh was indeed tense.

The state government ultimately took notice of the rising tempers among the local population and sent a cabinet sub-committee to negotiate with the agitating Ladakh Action Committee led by P. Namgyal, MP. This cabinet sub-committee was headed by D.D. Thakur, the finance minister, and his other two colleagues were G.N. Kochak and G.M. Shah. They arrived in Leh in the beginning of January 1981 and stayed there for three days; having a series of meetings with the LAC. The local people headed by Namgyal, put forward a series of demands which were heard and discussed patiently by the visiting dignitaries. At the end of parleys the main stipulations of the local delegation boiled down to greater regional autonomy; promotion of tourism; fairer allocation of central funds to the region and Scheduled Tribe status for all people of Ladakh. The cabinet sub-committee assured the LAC that the state government would carefully and sympathetically consider these demands. In particular, it agreed to support to the central government; the claim of the region for a ST status. Regarding allocation of funds; it accepted the suggestion that this be done by following a concrete formula based on scientific data of the region. As an interesting sidelight; it may be mentioned that the initial 'agreement' was drafted and read over in the open house by D.D. Thakur – himself a legal luminary and a trained mind in such matters. On objections by Namgyal and party; he handed over the drafted statement to them and said that they would meet again after one hour; during which time the LAC could go over the contents of the paper collectively and offer suggestions for improvement. When both sides reassembled after the given interval; Namgyal almost apologetically handed over the document back to D.D. Thakur and said that he and his people have no suggestions to offer and accept the solemn promise of the state government as given therein. Thus the mission of the cabinet sub-committee ended on a positive note; to the satisfaction of all concerned. Based on the assurances given; the LAC agreed to suspend its agitation. Thorny issues appeared to have been sorted out satisfactorily and an atmosphere of peace prevailed in Leh. It turned out to be a false calm.

Soon after the cabinet sub-committee left; and as seen from the LAC point of view, "the state government once again did not honour its commitments and instead played the usual game of delaying tactics". The common meeting ground between the two sides had shrunk to be almost negligible. Consequently, the LAC declared in a press statement on 14th May 1981 that unless the government implemented the assurances given by the cabinet sub-committee, the people would resume their agitation on an even more intensified scale. Nothing tangible came from the government side; and the LAC once again took to agitational path including *Dharanas* and public meetings at various places. The list of demands of LAC also increased. The district administration and the state government treated the developing and increasingly adverse situation as purely a law and order issue and dealt with the whole thing as such. Resultantly, the actions of the police and magistracy, at various levels, appeared repressive and high handed to the other side. Towards end of the year a delegation of the LAC, accompanied by Kushok Bakula and P. Namgyal, M.P., met the Prime Minister Indira Gandhi in New Delhi and briefed her about the situation in Leh. They also requested her to intervene in the matter. However, it was more than a year before she could come to Leh and Kargil. In the meantime, the situation in Leh went on deteriorating. Matters came to a head on 24th January 1982, when to control a violent mob; the police resorted to lathi-charge and also to firing. In this action, two people got killed and some others were injured. The two casualties further angered the agitators; and district authorities responded by imposing curfew in Leh and areas around. The army was also called in to stage a flag march through the town and assist the civil administration in the maintenance of law and order. The cremation of the two persons who had died in the police firing took place four days later on 28th January; and in paying tributes to them the people from other communities also joined. After the cremations; district administration re-imposed the curfew; and later invoked section 144 of Cr.P.C. to prohibit gatherings of more than four people at one place. The ding-dong struggle continued, with neither side willing to give up. It appeared to be the beginning of a long haul.

From 1973 onwards; Ladakh launched itself on a trajectory of unprecedented development and growth. This trend received further impetus by opening up of the region to tourism, in July 1974. It literally transformed into a vigorous progressive mode; be it in the infrastructure sector, expansion in all government departments and related activities or advancements in social areas like education and health; and providing increased avenues of employment to the local youth. But the agitation of 1980 put a brake on this thriving growth. The whole thing started on a seemingly petty issue – marginal difference in the annual plan allocations between Leh and Kargil districts. Over time, the protests evolved into other matters confronting the region; till the agitation gained its own momentum. The protests and demonstrations – at various places and levels – went on for the next fifteen years; till 1995. Apart from having a retarding effect on the development process of the whole region; it put the traditional communal amity of the area under severe strain and spoiled the happy relations between Buddhist and Muslim communities. The resultant bitterness has continued ever since - may be at the subterranean levels - but the traditional closeness is still to be revived. The agitational mode also put the local population, of the Leh district, in a confrontationist trajectory with the state government and district administration. Though things started improving after 1995; and the developmental activities picked up once again; but the scars on the social fabric remained discernible. Ladakh would, at least for a long time, never be the same again.

CHAPTER VII

The LAHDC

Genesis and Roots

Right from the beginning, in fact, from the very end of 1948 when the crisis created by the Pakistani raiders and troops was successfully resolved and with Leh and Kargil regions becoming safe once again; relations between the locals of Ladakh and the state government have remained strained. The contemporary scenario has been well described as, "…, the Ladakhis were suspicious of the sort of treatment they would get at the hands of the popular government in J&K that had taken over from the Maharaja. One reason for this was that the leaders of the Kashmir region who were the new rulers had not involved them in their struggle against the Dogra order. There was no political inter-action between the two regions till 1947. In fact, looked from the Ladakhi perspective, it seemed as if the Kashmiri leaders were guided by parochial sentiments as well. That is why the Ladakhis felt that a method should be evolved to pave their way out of J&K and link them directly with India as a UT. They were apprehensive that with just two seats (their number has since doubled) in the Assembly of 76 at that time their voice would never be heard… Their worst fears were to come true soon. The devastation caused by the Pakistani raiders followed by an unprecedented famine in the Zanskar region had shaken the Ladakhis in 1948. They were shocked when the financial relief personally sanctioned by the then Prime Minister Jawaharlal Nehru was not distributed to them by the officials of the State Government. There was oppression at every level with the State Government shutting its doors on Ladakh…"[1] As a logical sequel to this thought, a deputation of Ladakhis met Prime Minister

1 *Border Affairs*, New Delhi, Jan – Mar, 2006, p.20.

Nehru on 4th May 1949. It was not easy those days to traverse the long distance between Leh and New Delhi and this group covered the route up to Manali on the horseback and from there by road to their destination. There they formally presented a memorandum seeking direct rule of the Centre in the entire Ladakh region. This written statement strongly put forward the point as "...We seek the bosom of that gracious mother (India) to receive more nutriment for growth to our full stature in every way... Will the great mother refuse to take to her arms one of her weakest and most forlorn and depressed children..." This document was drafted by Shridhar Kaul, well known locally as 'Pandit Dulloo', who was officially an Inspector of Schools for the entire area; but in his personal capacity was then a friend, guide and philosopher of these people and he remained in that area for years together. He did most of the talking in front of the Prime Minister. He was provided significant inputs by Kushak Bakula and Chewang Rigzin Kalon, the latter was then President of Ladakh Buddhist Association (LBA). This document is of considerable archival value and is often cited as the beginning of the demand of Ladakhis for direct rule by the government of India, way back in 1949; sort of a precursor to the developments over the coming times.

For the next two decades; interests of the whole region were watched by Kushok Bakula, who also provided effective leadership to Ladakhis. His impassioned speech in 1952, in the J&K Assembly denouncing the State Government - of National Conference of which he was a part then – for ignoring this vast land tract is still remembered in Ladakh. In a way, it can be said that he planted the seeds of the demand for Union Territory status in that area; more firmly in the collective local psyche. His subsequent call for '*Delhi Chalo* – March to Delhi' evoked good response from the people there. A lady from one of the villages was then said to have wondered aloud as to where would she tie up her sheep and goats once they reached Delhi – even then a big city. Kushak Bakula also led the demand for a 'NEFA type' central administration during the early 1960s; and was partly successful in this endeavor though the system remained in place only for a few years. He genuinely felt that Buddhism as also Ladakhi culture could survive and thrive only in India.

By the beginning of the seventies; the number of educated Ladakhis had grown large and so also their demands for rights and privileges started increasing. This gave rise to local unrests at one hand and on the other; the mantle of leadership passed on to younger hands. Two names surfaced prominently in this behalf; that of Lama Lobzang and Thupstan Chhewang. Of these two, the latter was arrested for organizing black flag demonstrations against the state Chief Minister, Syed Mir Qasim, when he visited Ladakh in the summer of early seventies. "On June 25, 1973, in a statement Lama Lobzang, then spearheading the movement, charged the Kashmir Government with totally neglecting Ladakh and pitting one community against the other in the region. Young persons returned to Leh after studying in colleges in Srinagar, New Delhi and elsewhere only to find that there had been no progress on the home turf. They also noticed that the local inhabitants were being ignored in the matter of employment. No popular head of the State had cared to visit Ladakh for more than twenty-five years."[2]

But this phase of Ladakhi agitation did not achieve much, nor did it last long. There were two reasons for this. Lama Lobzang was staying most of the time outside Ladakh, in New Delhi and Thupstan joined the staff of Sonam Narboo, on his becoming a Minister in the Sheikh Abdullah cabinet in 1975. Thupstan Chhewang was to loom large over the political landscape of Ladakh, from the mid-1980s for more than twenty years; as his life description would indicate. He achieved the personal distinction and regards amongst the locals, notwithstanding the influence of two powerful and highly respected personalities in his life; an affable person with an endearing personality as also possessing transparent honesty coupled with unimpeachable integrity. His wife, Sarla, is the local princess; an offspring of the famous Namgyal dynasty. Kushok Bakula has been his maternal uncle.

Thupstan was born in Shey village on 1st September 1947. He received his basic education in the Primary School at Shey and then shifted to Srinagar under the care of his maternal uncle Kushok Bakula; then a minister in the state government. He did his matriculation from the Mahabodhi Intermediate College in Sarnath, Varanasi and passed the Higher Secondary examination from Delhi. Thereafter, for the graduation he enrolled in the Ramjas College of Delhi; completing it in 1967. Later, he got admission in the Law faculty of Delhi University and completed the LLB in 1970. Subsequently, for some time, he practiced in Jammu as a junior to the well known advocate R.P. Sethi – who later rose to

2 *Border Affairs*, New Delhi, April – June, 2008, p. 7.

become a Judge of the Supreme Court of India. He then went to Ladakh and there took part in active politics; mainly stressing for the grant of Central Administration to Ladakh. He energetically led demonstrations against the state Chief Minister, Mir Qasim and was arrested along with his associates. Thereafter, he left active politics for a few years and first worked as Public Relations Officer to Sonam Narboo, then PWD Minister in the state government – for about two years, joining in 1975. In 1978, Thupstan was selected as a Programme Executive in the AIR Station at Leh and worked there for almost ten years. He resigned from this post to join a local NGO and turned a full-time political activist. Thupstan was elected as President of the Ladakh Buddhist Association (LBA) in 1986. For the next over two decades, there was no looking back; as his personal and political graph registered constant ascendency; though initial years were difficult and full of struggle. He became the first Chairman and Chief Executive Councillor of the Ladakh Autonomous Hill Development Council (LAHDC) Leh in September 1995; and after remaining in that position for nine long years, resigned and successfully contested the Lok Sabha election in 2004.

As mentioned earlier; the agitation in Leh started in the summer of 1980 - after a peaceful period of about seven years - on a relatively small and certainly resolvable issue of allocation of few lakh rupees more to the newly created district of Kargil; as compared to the Leh district for that year's annual plan. The planning department of the state government refused to make any changes in the figures of initial allotment. This, in spite of the assurance of the Deputy Commissioner Leh that he would persuade the local leaders to call off their protests once the amount given to Leh was suitably enhanced. Seen in the larger perspective; this stubborn and inflexible attitude of the higher functionaries of the state – particularly of Kashmiri officers – reflected their disdain and, at best haughty indifference, towards the people of Ladakh. This is exactly what the Ladakhis had been feeling and saying right from 1947 onwards. Over a time, this single demand expanded to include the ST status for the region; greater regional autonomy and direct rule of the Centre – in that ascending order – and the stir continued. The Ladakh Action Committee (LAC) was able to mobilize ever increasing support of the population by the month and the public demonstrations grew more vocal; as also violent at times. Particularly after the parleys conducted by the Cabinet Sub-Committee in January 1981 did not produce any tangible results; the local agitation was stepped up. The subsequent clashes with the local administration and the police resulted in the death of two people on 24th January 1982; with the result, that situation in and around Leh became very tense. This further incensed the entire local populace and galvanized the disturbances few notches higher. These developments also created considerable pressure on the state government. In the meantime; on the death of his father the redoubtable Sheikh Abdullah, Dr. Farooq Abdullah was sworn in as the Chief Minister of J&K on 8th September 1982. The new CM made an announcement in October, little over a month after taking over, conceding Schedule Tribe status for Ladakh from the state government side and assured the people there that he would soon write to the government of India in this regard. But, nothing tangible came out of this promise also. Sometime later Kushok Bakula and P. Namgyal, the local MP, met Prime Minister Indira Gandhi; briefed her about the deteriorating situation in Ladakh and requested her to visit the region to see things herself. She came to Leh and Kargil, on 14th April, 1983 and promised that New Delhi would look favorably about any demand for ST status. However, she did not make any specific announcement in the matter. This visit by the Prime Minister herself considerably raised the local expectations; but their optimism faded away when no forward movement was made by the Centre in this regard.

A year later; there was another change of guard in J&K. G.M. Shah came to power as the new Chief Minister on 2nd July 1984. The Shah government was supported in the Legislature by the thirteen MLAs who had defected from National Conference; in addition to those belonging to the Congress. It was a coalition government. Shah became Chief Minister with the reputation of being an acerbic personality, short on patience and niceties but an efficient administrator and a competent political executive. Within the next two months, the new Chief Minister met the LAC in his office in Srinagar; heard their demands and assured that the state government would support their request of ST status to Ladakh. To his credit, G.M. Shah kept his promise and soon the formal recommendation from the state government was sent to the GoI. But, the years moved by and on the surface nothing much appeared to have happened. In New Delhi though; the whole process was not indeed stalled, however, matters were going ahead at a snail's pace and being sieved through various bureaucratic processes. In the meanwhile, there was another change in the state government when the Congress withdrew support from G.M. Shah on the grounds of communal violence; reducing his government to a minority in the Legislature. The Shah ministry was dismissed on 7th March 1986, and Governor's rule imposed under Section 92 of the Jammu and Kashmir Constitution. This development, the people of Ladakh thought, put further spokes in their demand for the ST status; stimulating their agitation some more as also inducing the leaders of the region like Kushok Bakula and P. Namgyal to increase their efforts in the national capital – including meeting Prime Minister Rajiv Gandhi and apprising about the current situation in Ladakh and the need to concede this demand at an early date.

As per the census figures in 1981, the Buddhists constituted a majority in Ladakh region with 51.2 percent of the total population. However, in view of the positive recommendations of the state government and taking forward the course of action by the Central Government; a special census was conducted by the Registrar General of India in 1987. This indicated that the total population of the region had increased to 1,71,351 of whom Buddhists were 78,896, which worked out to be 46 per cent. Thus, it appeared that this community had lost its majority status, in the area, for the first time. This fact also must have weighed at the back of collective psyche of the people and the LBA; though there is no apparent or explicit evidence available in this regard.

Finally, almost after a decade of constant agitation, the Presidential notification with regard to ST status for Ladakh was issued on 7th October 1989. This was positive culmination of a decade long struggle of Ladakhis; almost a gift to the local populace as the measure was to benefit more than ninety percent of inhabitants. Apart from being the fulfillment of a long standing demand; the measure was to help the Ladakhi youth achieve their dreams and also accelerate the pace of development of the region. The very next day, Kushak Bakula – who had assiduously followed this case – wrote a letter of thanks to the Prime Minister Rajiv Gandhi. Invoking the memory of his grandfather Jawaharlal Nehru, he is reported to have mentioned, "…It was Panditji's wish to see Ladakh flourish in its pristine glory and take rapid strides towards development. You seem to be instrumental in transforming that wish into a reality…."

But, on a different plane; it was the case of a positive measure taken up too late and also without extracting any political or social reciprocity. Back in Leh district things had been going on from bad to worse; more so from the middle of the year 1989. There were socio-economic-political reasons for the unsavory developments that had been taking place there; and the first one to take hit was traditional cordial relations between Buddhists and Muslims – a virtual bulwark against any kind of obscurantism. Ladakh had remained a peaceful area for centuries together. For a long time Ladakhis, irrespective of religion and sects, enjoyed congenial and amicable relations. Matrimonial alliances took place; not only among the common people but also in the royal families. Many Muslim princesses married with some of the Rajas of Namgyal dynasty. Similarly, some Ladakhi Buddhist princesses were married to Muslim Rajas of Baltistan. Discords and disputes in the name of religion were quite unknown in the region. However, by the end of 1960s – more so because of the rising expectations of the people, demographical profile of the area and virtual stagnation of the region – certain resentments and grievances started affecting the mind of Buddhists of Ladakh. They were of the opinion that conversions were being made by way of marriages with Buddhist women. In addition, they thought that most of the important business in Leh was dominated by the Muslims and in spite of being a minority there; these people were getting much more favorable treatment from the Kashmiri officers in respect of stuck up cases, allotment of contracts and the like. The chasm between these communities did not develop suddenly; the discontentment and resentment had been building up slowly and over the years. However, the initial signs of smoldering conflicts were either not detected or, worse, ignored by the community elders as well as the administrative set-up at various levels.

The deterioration of communal relations was also due to the interplay of a number of factors; most significant being the process of slow but definite change in the social and economic balance between the Buddhist and Muslim communities. For a long time, before 1947, the trade in this area was dominated by those actively engaged in operating on the Central Asian axis. Most of these people, although belonging to different areas, were Sunni Muslims. For them Leh was a convenient halt, resting place as also a change-over destination. Some of them also married local Buddhist women and their off springs did profess the same religion. They also, as a community, possessed better business and trading skills. Consequently, even though the Muslims in Leh and areas around were not so large in numbers; traditionally they always had an upper hand in economic activities. This balance was maintained roughly up to the 1960s and the Muslims continued to enjoy a more dominant position. They were also perceived having better access to the bureaucracy and political executive in Srinagar – and this particular aspect was seen as a continuous process. With the increase in developmental activities and education facilities; the Buddhists gradually improved their social and economic position. Tourism generated income also enabled these people to enhance their financial status. Still, it took decades for the socio-economic balance to swing in favor of the Buddhists. This tipping of scales tended to increase antagonism between the two communities. The Muslim population wished to preserve its old position while the Buddhists strove to enhance the social and economic gains it had already made; as also endeavor to exercise greater influence in the conduct of affairs of the area. Both sides, therefore, reacted with greater resolve to the social and economic changes that were inevitably taking place. Also by 1989, the militancy activities were in the upswing in Kashmir valley and quite possibly this too had a negative effect on the minds of the local Muslim population; particularly the younger lot which certainly was more hot-headed. In the context of a gradual but definite change in the socio-political milieu; it was necessary that accommodation and wise counsel prevailed in the region. For this to happen, enlightened social leadership was required amongst both communities; which unfortunately was missing at that crucial time. The administration also can not absolve itself of the blame for the incremental increase in unfortunate incidents and breach of communal harmony in the region.

In the first half of June 1989, two incidents of communal overtones took place which further deteriorated the situation. On 6th June, Parvez Ahmed, President of Muslim Youth Association got into a scuffle with a Buddhist young man at Jivastal park about eight kilometers from Leh. It was the same place where His Holiness the Dalai Lama performed the Kala Chakra ceremony in 1976 and since then this location always had a special significance for Buddhists of the area. Luckily, before it could take an ugly turn the situation was diffused by local intervention. Few days later; an altercation broke out in the only civil cinema house in Leh between two groups; when few Buddhist youth started smoking, which was objected to by some Muslims. Before the matters could go out of hand, the police intervened and brought the situation under control. However, while dispersing both groups indulged in stone throwing on the properties owned by the other sect. This further inflamed an already tense situation. Things came to a head on 7th July evening when Rigzin Jora,

General Secretary, Congress (I), was roughed up in Leh bazaar by Parvez Ahmed, President of the Muslim Youth Association. After this, the latter was taken to the Leh Police Station. For some inexplicable reasons; he was released by the police and this further incensed the local Buddhists who had gathered in good numbers around the Police Station. To control the situation, the administration imposed curfew in the town, which continued for the next few days. This was the effective beginning of the breaking up of age old traditional Buddhist- Muslim relationship of harmony and tolerance. The LBA announced and enforced social ostracisation of the Muslim community; something unheard of till then. The chasm became deeper and wider with each passing day. When the situation became normal, from the law and order point of view, the curfew was lifted on 12th July. But the social boycott continued; and the LBA strictly enforced it.

At this juncture, an effort was made by P. Namgyal, who was then MoS Parliamentary Affairs, Government of India. He visited Leh on 8th-9th July and used his good offices to organize a Peace Committee consisting of representatives from the Buddhists and Muslim communities. Namgyal, accompanied by other elders and respectable persons, also visited some villages to persuade community leaders there to maintain peace and harmony; and this helped to diffuse the communal tensions. But, the relief was temporary. On 15th July, the LBA withdrew its members from the Peace Committee on the grounds that the purpose for which it had been set up was served. The situation was back to its old precarious and ticklish uncertain dimensions. However, a week before this on 10th July, the Divisional Commissioner Kashmir and DIG Police came on an official visit to Leh. They reviewed the developing ground situation; also met with respectable citizens of both communities. The LBA asked for the appointment of a commission of enquiry to investigate into the series of events that had taken place during the past about two months and because of which the overall things had come to the existing sorry state. The LBA also cautioned the visiting officers that if their request was not met within a reasonable time, it would launch an all-out agitation to press for its demands. Nothing substantial, of political nature or relating to law and order, came out of this visit. The LBA took this as a sign that the state government had chosen to do nothing to restore confidence amongst the local population and probably meant to treat the whole matter as a purely law and order issue and deal with it as such. Consequently, the Buddhists of Ladakh came out on the streets in full force under the banner of LBA demanding ST and Union Territory status for Ladakh.

One significant offshoot of the two senior officers' visit was that the top level changes were made in the district administration. The new incumbent, Verghese Samuel took over as Deputy Commissioner on 19th July. A week later, Ashok Gupta assumed office as the new SP of Leh. These officers, having had to join in the midst of disturbed conditions; took some time to get acclimatized and settle down. Even otherwise, in the best of times, in Ladakh it inevitably took little longer to become familiar with the contours of the area and provide the district administration with the required level of leadership. With the arrival of the new team; things did show an improvement in the beginning but the situation nose dived again, in the first fortnight of next month.

On 7th August, the LBA had called for a *bandh,* in the entire district, to press for their demands; and it turned violent. The most unfortunate incident of the day – which had the potential of further heightening communal feelings in the entire region – was the burning of three houses belonging to Muslims in Shey village and the injuries sustained by a Muslim lady of the same locality who eventually died. As a result of the happenings of the day; curfew was imposed in Leh town by the District Magistrate late in the evening. The Army was also called in to assist the civil authorities. Leh and areas around continued being patrolled by the Army for many days; as adequate police force was not available with the district authorities. The police presence was subsequently augmented by the state government by sending additional contingent from Srinagar. Also, disturbed by the flared up communal feelings in an otherwise harmonious region, the state government deputed a senior and seasoned administrator; S.S. Rizvi – a highly experienced and competent IAS officer of J&K cadre who had been the Deputy Commissioner of Ladakh during 1977 and 78 – on a fact finding mission. He visited Leh between 8th and 12th August; carefully studied the existing situation and filed a very comprehensive report on his return to the sate headquarters.

Syed Rizvi's incisive and searching comments included, ".... It may be mentioned that a part of the sense of neglect among the Leh people arises from the geography of the area, the problems of communications, and the fact that the Buddhists form a very small minority among the population of the state as a whole... The most serious damage that has occurred from the events of the recent past has been to social and communal relations in the district. There have been agitations and violence in Leh district before, as well as possibly undercurrents of communal feeling. But never in the past has there been the kind of serious violence between Buddhists and Muslims as witnessed this time... The district administration is making efforts to talk to community leaders separately to persuade them on this point. Depending on their success, leaders of both the communities would need to meet together formally and make efforts at restoring communal relations. There is no alternative to this, as this is the only durable means of ensuring communal amity in the district. In a fraught situation, every effort in the right direction helps. It may be mentioned that on the evening of 8th August 1989 Sh. Samphel MLA condemned the communal violence, and his statement was announced over Radio Kashmir. Sh. Thupstan, President of the Ladakh Buddhist Association, in discussion with me also stated that, the hard attitudes of the younger elements notwithstanding, the Association would assist in restoring communal harmony.... Taking an overall view, there does appear to exist an enabling set of conditions in which to attempt the restoration of communal relations. Very determined efforts have to be made at all levels to achieve this end... The important point is that the interplay of changing social and economic conditions, arising from political forces, has to be taken into account when deciding on action to be taken to restore normalcy. In the long run, it is only when the leaders of both communities genuinely commit themselves to restore communal harmony, when they allow wise counsel to prevail, and when they accept the need to accommodate each other in the process of social and economic change, that communal harmony on a sustained basis can be achieved... There is no alternative to making the most determined and committed efforts in this behalf. Failure in this effort can only have the most disastrous consequences for communal relations in Leh district, and this will certainly have wider ramifications elsewhere in the State... It may be useful at this point to record discussions I was able to have with various people in Leh. I met members of the Muslim Association, and a large number of respectable people, including serving and retired government servants, who constitute the intelligentsia and help to mould the public opinion. The President of the Ladakh Buddhist Association, whom I had requested to meet me, did not originally do so, although he did send his regrets. However, after the arrival of Sh. P. Namgyal, Hon. MoS for Parliamentary Affairs, on 11th August 1989, he did, after meeting the Hon. MoS, eventually come and meet me. As mentioned above, the younger elements in both the Buddhist and Muslim communities tend to take a hard line. But almost everyone I spoke to was shocked and upset about the communal violence that had occurred. There is general agreement that the issue of people's demands should be separated from that of restoring communal amity. In any case, the Muslim Association had also endorsed the demands, including the declaration of the region as a Union Territory…"

Shri Rizvi also made disparaging comments about the functioning of administrative machinery in the district, indicting it of inefficiency and corruption; by mentioning "…the senior levels of the district administration were not manned by committed, honest and neutral officers, and as a result the district administration does not deliver." He also pointed to the deficiency in the ranks of the district police and strongly recommended that its presence be strengthened. In addition, an almost prophetic observation was included in the concluding part of his report, which said "Granting of divisional status to the Ladakh area, with the appointment of a Divisional Commissioner and DIG Police. This would restore the integrity of the Ladakh area which was broken by the division of the old Ladakh district into the districts of Leh and Kargil." The state government, however, took no action on the detailed report of S.S. Rizvi.

As mentioned earlier, the LBA imposed a social and economic boycott of Muslim community and strictly enforced it. Such a drastic measure was never even contemplated in the area before. This step caused a lot of anguish, as also discontent, to the wise and prudent people on both sides of the divide. Anybody found disregarding the boycott was in turn ostracized. It brought a lot of distress and grief to the right thinking people in general and families with mixed religious denominations, in particular. Even on solemn occasions like marriages and deaths; this restriction remained in place. This unfortunate state of affairs was to last for a little over three years.

Towards the 20th August the situation showed some signs of improvement as the elders of both communities appealed for maintaining traditional harmony and resolve all differences peacefully through dialogue. But, matters came to a head again on 27th August when a group of protestors came out of the Jokhang temple in Leh and staged a token of protest in defiance of Section 144 of the Cr.P.C.; which had been imposed in the town. In the altercation and scuffle that followed; the police deployed in the area opened fire on the crowd. This resulted in the death of three people – namely Tsewang Dorje, Nawang Rinchen and Tsering Stobden – as also injuries to some others. This incident vitiated the atmosphere further and soon afterwards, Leh town plus area around were put under curfew and the place handed over to army for maintenance of law and order. The local administration and the state government acted tough; arrested prominent Buddhist leaders including the LBA President Thupstan Chhewang, and took them to Srinagar. A number of Muslim youth leaders were also arrested. There was, understandably, a sense of consternation among the people and public anger did show itself in different ways. On 2nd September, state government employees in Leh went on an indefinite strike in support of the LBA agitation. The district administration virtually came to a halt. The Buddhists and Muslims were becoming even more polarized. After sustained efforts and series of discussions among the community leaders of both sides; some semblance of peace and public order gradually returned by end of the month. The veneer of normalcy, however, was quite thin and even a small provocation from either side could change the situation. The uneasy peace did hold on. After some time all those who had been arrested and taken to Srinagar, were released and came back to Leh.

Things in the Valley began sliding badly in the second half of 1989, keeping the state government occupied with managing the day to day happenings there; leaving it with very little time or attention to monitor the serious developments taking place in Leh. For all practical purposes; Ladakh had again become a place of only marginal interest for the people at the helm of affairs in the state; and the management of the situation there was left in the hands of the district administration Leh and the normal official channels. There was no political initiative taken during those critical months. The onslaught of militancy was engulfing the Kashmir valley – and also kept the state government busy with managing it – when, on 21st August 1989, Mohammad Yusuf *alias* Yusuf Halwai, one of Block Presidents of National Conference, was shot dead by militants in broad daylight in downtown Srinagar. It was a serious challenge posed to the National Conference; but the party or the government did not pick up the gauntlet. Barely a fortnight before the assassination of Mohammad Yusuf, the Jammu and Kashmir Liberation Front, the main militant outfit at that time, had issued an ultimatum to the National Conference workers to quit the party. This was followed by targeted killings, abductions, extortions and threats to the NC cadre. A good number of party workers and office bearers started leaving the party and issued public statements – generally through the local newspapers – of this intent. In the second half of 1989, the NC leadership not only lost its control over the party apparatus but became increasingly ineffective in providing meaningful governance in the state. Its political ally and the coalition partner the Congress, undergoing its own existential crisis in the centre, could do nothing more than merely being a fellow traveler.

It was under such an overall gloomy situation – and as mentioned earlier – the President of India formally promulgated the Constitution (J&K) Scheduled Tribes Order 1989, dated 7th October 1989, which declared eight tribes of Ladakh as Scheduled Tribes. This certainly was a very major and favorable measure for Ladakhis as it benefited more than ninety percent of the population there. But since this step was taken by the Centre without securing any political reciprocation or *quid pro quo*; the LBA continued with its agitation demanding Union Territory status for the region. In a bid to end this agitation, New Delhi took the initiative and tripartite talks took place in Leh on 29th October. These culminated in the signing of an agreement by P.P. Shrivastava, Additional Secretary in the Union Ministry of Home Affairs; Ashok Jaitly, Additional Chief Secretary J&K Government and Thupstan Chhewang, the President of LBA. The talks were conducted in the presence of the Union Home Minister Buta Singh and two ministers of J&K government; represented by Mangat Ram Sharma, Transport Minister and Mohd. Shafi, Agriculture Minister. A formal notification issued on this occasion read,

"The initiative taken by the Hon'ble Prime Minister Shri Rajiv Gandhi and the Hon'ble Chief Minister of Jammu & Kashmir Dr. Farooq Abdullah, to restore peace and normalcy in the Ladakh region was greatly welcomed by the Ladakh Buddhist Association. The visit of Union Home Minister Sardar Buta Singh, Shri Mohd. Shafi, Agriculture Minister of J&K and Shri Mangat Ram Sharma, Transport Minister of J&K to Leh on 29th October 1989, was also welcomed and greatly appreciated. It was further agreed that a meeting would be held very soon after the General Elections.

1. To find a satisfactory and mutually acceptable solution to the problems of the people of Ladakh region. In this context the Memorandum of the Ladakh Buddhist Association, which

includes the demand of Autonomous District Hill Council, was received for detailed consideration.

2. To discuss the developmental needs of the people of the region so that an integrated tribal sub-plan could be formulated to be implemented within a specific time-frame.

3. In all these matters the Central Government would lend its good offices to the State Govt. at all stages.

4. The Ladakh Buddhist Association agreed to withdraw their agitation and the demand for Union Territory Status.

5. As a matter of goodwill, the state govt. agreed to withdraw all cases in connection with the agitation, except those involving serious offences. Prohibitory orders would be withdrawn immediately.

6. Efforts would be made to create an atmosphere of harmony and brotherhood and a sense of security among the people and measures will be taken to rehabilitate all those who have been affected during the agitation in which Ladakh Buddhist Association will render all possible assistance."

Thus, this three-way meeting of 29th October did prove useful in the sense that it laid the basis of later granting the Autonomous Hill District Council to Ladakh as also keeping this landmass as a part of the J&K state. Within these parameters all future developments were to take place. These parleys also brought down the existing tension, by a few notches, as the agitation was formally taken back by the LBA. But the boycott of the Muslim community continued as hereto before; and the text of the agreement also did not make any specific reference to this aspect. Sardar Buta Singh did offer elderly advice to the local leaders, particularly to the younger lot, and urged them to iron out the differences with the Muslims and maintain their traditional brotherhood and also work for re-establishing harmonious relations. As a senior political executive of the country, he is also reported to have cautioned, "Unless and until, the Muslims would not co-operate the cause, the government could not consider your demand."

As an agreed follow up to this accord; a meeting was held on 10th January 1990 in which fifteen representatives of the LBA took part; with the Joint Secretary, Ministry of Home Affairs representing the Government of

India and a team of senior State Government officers. The intention of the state officials was to find mutually acceptable solutions to the outstanding development needs of the region, including plan outlays, employment and recruitments in the government service and related administrative matters. However, the representatives of the LBA insisted at the meeting that they wished to discuss only their demand for setting up an autonomous district hill council for Leh district and nothing else. They also mentioned that a commitment in this regard was made to them by no less a person than the Union Home Minister himself. The state officers, on the other hand, asserted that they were not aware of any such promise or assurance by the Hon'ble Minister. The document of agreement of 29th October only stated that the memorandum of LBA "... was received for detailed consideration." The group of officers representing the state government kept on insisting that all development related issues of the LBA could be fully and objectively met under the provisions of the Panchayati Raj Act of 1989. The State Government was of the opinion that the objectives of the LBA would be met in a better way through this Act than what they had suggested in the structure of the Hill Council. The LBA, however, refused to discuss any matter other than the setting up of an Autonomous Hill District Council. Thus there being hardly any meeting or common ground between the two sides of the state administration and the LBA; the meeting ended without achieving anything worthwhile.

Even otherwise, by this time the situation in most parts of the state were fast deteriorating and the government losing its grip over the administrative set up. The conditions had started spiraling dangerously downwards since the month of December when militants kidnapped Rubiya Sayeed – the daughter of the then Union Home Minister Mufti Mohammad Sayeed – followed by subsequent developments. The final scene of this politically charged drama got enacted on 19th January 1990. On that day Jagmohan was appointed the new Governor of the state replacing General K.V. Krishana Rao (Retired) and Dr. Farooq Abdullah and his party ministers resigned in protest. Governor's Rule was imposed under Section 91/92 of the State Constitution on 19th January; which was later followed by promulgation of the President's Rule in the state from 18th July 1990. In this background and the fast changing environment; the problems and people of Ladakh received much diminished attention of the state and the central governments.

Governor Jagmohan had intended to pick up the thread once again and had fixed a meeting with the LBA on 19th February 1990. Four days before that, a background brief was sent to the Governor by Ashok Jaitly, Additional Chief Secretary and Planning Commissioner of the state. After outlining background details and issues involved in the matter, including the failed meeting on 10th January, his memorandum mentions towards the end, "… If there were still some further amplifications in the Panchayati Raj act to meet the special needs of the Ladakh region, these could be discussed at a subsequent meeting. However, the representatives of the LBA declared that they would be prepared for further discussions only if the State government first accepted the demand for the autonomous hill council at least in principle. Any further discussion would only be restricted to the details of such a hill council and the modalities for bringing it into existence…After the meeting – of 10th January - the matter was reported in detail to the State cabinet who decided that the demand for an autonomous hill council could not be accepted because it would result in similar demands from other parts of the State and would definitely endanger the integrity of the State which was not in the national interest. At the same time, the State cabinet appreciated the need to provide some special consideration for the Ladakh region in terms of decentralization which could be done under the Panchayati Raj Act. It was approved that the Act could be amended, if necessary, to provide for greater decentralization in respect of Ladakh region – this would include both Leh and Kargil districts. There has been no further dialogue with the LBA subsequently…"

It so happened that due to the worsening law and order situation in the Valley, this meeting of Governor with LBA had to be postponed and no further date was fixed. The matter, in any case, was firmly in the court of New Delhi, which – as Ladakhis conceived – was much more favorably disposed off towards the aspirations of Ladakh than the J&K government. The LBA was sanguine that their outstanding issues would be sympathetically considered by the Centre. After about a fortnight – on 5th March 1990 – Kushok Bakula, as Indian ambassador to Mongolia, wrote a formal letter to Prime Minister V.P. Singh; giving background details of the LBA agitation, including its demands and requesting for his early attention. This communication had some interesting details, which included, "…I am writing these few lines regarding Ladakh which, for the past some time, has been undergoing a very strained and difficult period of its history. The Buddhists of Ladakh have been for decades subjected to discrimination and neglect at the hands of successive State Governments in Kashmir…I had apprised the previous Government as well as Home Minister, Mufti Mohd. Sayeed about the simmering discontent… In view of their past experience with the State administration, the agitating Buddhists would not agree to participate in any discussion for a settlement without a representative of the Government of India also present in the talks. Accordingly, an agreement was signed in November *(Sic)* last in Leh in the presence of the then Union Home Minister and two Cabinet Ministers of the State… It promised solution to the problem facing the Buddhist minority and an early consideration of the demand of the LBA. It may be mentioned here that by this time, the LBA in the overall national interest, had dropped the demand for UT status for Ladakh and would be satisfied if a Darjeeling type District Council is given to them. I am also a witness to the agreement…Ever since my joining as Ambassador here; I have been watching the developments in Ladakh with great concern. It appears that the feeble voice of Ladakh is unable to make any impact on the Government whose compulsions in the Valley seem to out-weigh the vital interests of Ladakh. I may, however, emphasize that making Ladhaki interest a scapegoat on this account may not be in the overall national interest… I request that the demand of LBA for District Council as agreed upon be kindly conceded early. Such a step, I am sure, can alone bring peace in the region. I shall be grateful if you kindly intervene in the matter and help in finding an early solution to this important matter…"

The Prime Minister, it appears that based on the above letter advised the J&K Governor to interact with Ladakhi representatives. Jagmohan met the LBA in the middle of March 1990 and during the course of discussions clearly told them about his inability to take any positive decision in view of the changed situation and the fast worsening security scenario in the state; particularly in the Valley.

The LBA took the initiative to plead its case in New Delhi and for this purpose organized one day deliberations in that city – designated as National Convention on the Ladakh Issue – on 18th March 1990. Interestingly, the Organizing Committee of this conclave consisted of well-known and distinctive people like Prof. M.L. Sondhi, five MPs, P. Namgyal - Ex Minister and Lama Lobzang – Member National Commission for SC & ST; with Thupstan Chhewang acting as the Convener. The Resolution passed in this meeting included, among other things, "The National

Convention on the Ladakh Issue that met in New Delhi on Sunday, 18 March 1990, fully supports the democratic aspirations of the patriotic people of Ladakh and demands that the Committee on Kashmir recently appointed by the Government of India must also look into the grievances of the people of Ladakh who have been subjected to discrimination and oppression by the successive Governments of J&K. The Convention is of the firm and considered view that the only solution of the problem lies in granting Union Territory status to Ladakh (Leh District) and this alone will also fully ensure national security interests in a sensitive and strategic region of the country… The Convention notes that even after the long standing demand of the people of Ladakh for being declared as Scheduled Tribes was conceded by the Central Government in October 1989, this has not brought about any change in the plight of the Ladakhi people… The Convention draws the attention of the nation to the fact that the Constitutional safeguards provided to the minorities have been denied to the Buddhist population of Ladakh in the matter of protection to their religion, language and culture… The Convention appeals to the Government of India to amend the Constitution, if necessary, to give Union Territory status to Ladakh (Leh District). The tripartite agreement reached in October 1989 having ended in fiasco due to insincerity of the erstwhile State Government, it is imperative for the Government of India to take initiative to find a lasting solution to the issue of statutory recognition of Ladakhi identity and political aspirations. In this task the Ladakh Buddhist Association and the people of Ladakh are ever willing to extend their cooperation."

The LBA was thus able to put its point of view before a much wider audience – people of the whole country – from the national capital.

Meanwhile, during the first half of 1990, conditions in the state were continuously on the decline; in a way worsening by the day. The few months after Jagmohan took over as Governor of J&K, represented a very bloody and chaotic; to some extent bewilderingly wild face of militancy violence in Kashmir. Some of the significant incidents during this period included eight people killed in firing by security forces in Srinagar on 22nd January followed by Director Doordarshan Srinagar, Lassa Koul, being shot dead by the militants on 13th February. Thirty people were killed in firing incidents at Zakura and Barzala by-pass in Srinagar on 1st March. The Kashmiri Pandit mass exodus from the Valley also took place during this period. On 24th March, Independent ex- MLA Mir Mustafa – a highly respected person – was kidnapped by Hizbul Mujahideen and killed four days later. This was followed by the kidnapping of Kashmir University Vice-Chancellor Mushir-ul-Haq along with his private secretary; and HMT General Manager H.L. Khera on 6th April. Khera was killed by his captors on 10th April; whereas the Vice Chancellor and his private secretary were murdered the next day. These four killings spread a wave of anger and consternation through the Valley; but the mayhem continued. On 21st May Mirwaiz Maulvi Farooq was also shot dead by militants. The public outpouring of hurt and rage could have been channelized by the administration against the militants; but – on the contrary – fifty people were killed when panicky security forces detachments opened fire on the mourning procession. Three days later, Jagmohan demitted the office of the Governor. Jagmohan has been an administrator of proven merit with commendable achievements to his name. But, he was not a person well equipped to handle the prevailing security and law and order situation. Still, he bore the full brunt of the rising wave of urban insurgency, as it was then developing, and manfully tried to hold the fort. The next in succession was G.C. Saxena (fondly called 'Garry' by his friends and colleagues); who took over as the new Governor of J&K on 26th May, 1990. The significance of Saxena's nomination and his traits have been described, at one place, as, "The appointment of Saxena as the Governor was a shrewd move since he enjoyed the trust of all parties – and particularly of the Congress (I) and Rajiv Gandhi, who had a very high regard for his professionalism… Saxena, was suave in his behavior and gentle in his words, but hard-hitting in action."[3] He began an agonizingly slow process of rejuvenating the state administrative structure block by block and slowly brought back the system on rails. In the process, Saxena also devoted attention to the happenings in Ladakh.

In his characteristic style, Saxena studied and got briefed in details about various aspects of the Ladakh issue and the outstanding matters. After that, he met a delegation of LBA in Srinagar in the month of June 1990; had a detailed and fruitful interaction with them. He treated these people with courtesy as also conducted discussions with polish and diplomacy. During the course of deliberations, it was impressed upon the LBA representatives that even though the Government of India remained sympathetic to them and continued to support the desire of the people of

3 B. Raman, *THE KAOBOYS OF R&AW*, Lancer, New Delhi, 2007, pp 218 and 189.

Ladakh to retain their distinct cultural identity and to have an effective say in the running of affairs affecting them; their larger political demands could not be immediately resolved. He told them, tactfully, that they may have to wait till the situation in the Valley was brought under control and the political process started in the state. The Governor also assured them that he would effectively deal with their other problems and issues connected with the state administration; including development matters and delivery systems. He also appealed to the LBA delegation to end the social boycott of the other community. However, the situation did not improve much; although the tempers in Leh region and general level of tension prevailing came down perceptibly.

The Ladakh Buddhist Association kept on blaming the Government of India for having backed out of the promise to give them an Autonomous Hill District Council for Leh. Though they kept up the social boycott of Muslims as a pressure tactics; the bitterness and violence witnessed in the second half of 1989 was not in evidence from the later part of 1990 onwards. The Governor again met the LBA, led by their President Thupstan Chhewang, on 19th November 1991. This meeting took place in a cordial atmosphere. In nearly the three hours long and free exchange of views; the LBA reiterated its demands for providing adequate safeguards for preserving the identity and aspirations of the people of the region. It underlined the need for and sought a framework wherein the elected representatives of the people would have an effective say and involvement in all matters of the area. The issues of the setting up of an Autonomous Hill District Council as also the possibility of application of the Sixth Schedule of the Constitution; specifically came up for discussion. The Governor agreed and assured the delegation that the entire matter would be examined in its totality and various options evolved will be included for discussions and consideration at the next meeting; likely to be held in a few months time. He once again called upon them to terminate the boycott. In a friendly advice, Governor Saxena cautioned the LBA that unless they did this; no government at the Centre would take serious steps to meet their demands. By this time; the LBA had also seemed to realize that they had come up against a wall and that the social and economic boycott of the Muslim community was sticking out as a negative point against their interests. But the LBA also did not want to retrace its steps without credible guarantees from the empowered source – which under the existing circumstances was the Government of India. The LBA also comprehended that efforts in this regard would have to be accelerated with greater vigour and positively before the popular government got re-installed in J&K. Thus it was sorely caught between the propositions of expediency and positive measures; but sufficiently understood that traditional brotherhood and harmonious relations – which had always been a hallmark of Ladakh – would have to be restored early. Consequently, the LBA increased its efforts in New Delhi and for this also used the good offices of some prominent Ladakhis and other influential well wishers. Practically, everyone was of the opinion that perceptible progress on the LBA demands could only be made by the Government of India after the communal harmony and traditional brotherhood between Buddhists and Muslims is restored in Ladakh. The LBA, while agreeing in principle with this line of thinking, were looking for credible guaranty and binding assurance that the promised Autonomous Hill District Council would be granted to the region.

Finally, a breakthrough was made in this respect. In a tripartite meeting between officers of Government of India, the State Government and representatives of the Ladakh Buddhist Association; the social and economic boycott of the Muslim community was lifted on 29th November 1992. Following this; the Muslims under the aegis of LMA (Ladakh Muslim Association) agreed to cooperate in the struggle to achieve the Hill Council status for Ladakh. For this purpose a coordination committee came into being, comprising the LBA and LMA, to jointly fight for the cause. Almost simultaneously, several rounds of talks took place between officials of the Government of India and the State Government on this issue; in which various measures and alternatives were considered. The officials were looking for a formulation which would meet the demands for autonomy and a more forceful say of locals in the administration of the region; as also at the same time ensure that the entire J&K State remained an effective single unit. Taking an over-all view of the issues involved it was generally agreed that the ideal arrangement for granting autonomy to Ladakh region should have the following attributes;

- Ladakh should remain a part of the J&K state. While separate arrangements for Kargil and Leh districts need be made; the entity of Ladakh as a region should also be preserved.

- The set up of autonomy should be based on features which are unique to the region so as to enable the state administration, in future, to effectively resist demands for similar arrangements from other parts of the State.

- The contours of the proposed structure should be durable and not amenable to dilution or change by the State Legislature.

It was within these parameters that various alternatives were put on the table and discussed in details, by the concerned authorities, with a view to arrive at the most plausible solution. At the official level, the following five alternatives were taken up for consideration:-

(i) U.T. Status.

(ii) Application of Schedule VI to Ladakh.

(iii) Declaration of the region as 'Scheduled Area' under Schedule V of the Constitution.

(iv) Regional development Board.

(v) Autonomous District Hill Council.

The recourse topping the list, the UT status, was straight away not considered feasible as this was bound to lead to a breakup of J&K into more than one unit; and this possibility was not acceptable to the Centre. In addition, it was rightly thought that the State Government and the State Legislature would also be vehemently opposed to the very idea. The Sixth Schedule, the next item, was then applicable to only the states of Assam, Meghalaya, Tripura and Mizoram; all located in the North East region. It was felt that extension of this provision to J&K would not only create legal difficulties and involve complex administrative measures, but was likely to become controversial; such a move could also trigger similar demands from other regions of the country. Considering the possibilities of such problems, this idea too was dropped. Declaring the Ladakh region as a 'Scheduled Area' under Fifth Schedule of the Constitution of India; was also not recommended because such a course could only be taken under the provisions of Article 244 of the Constitution of India and this was not applicable to the State of J&K. In addition, extending this Article to the State would have the same set of problems as in the case of Sixth Schedule. Next in the zone of consideration was the possibility of constituting a Regional Development Board. Such a step, it was thought, would fall short of the local demand and –in addition- might give rise to similar requests from other parts of the State, particularly in Jammu region. Hence, this alternative was also not found practicable and not taken up for detailed consideration. Therefore, of the five different recourses mentioned hereinbefore; the first four were not found workable and appropriate for one reason or the other. By this process of elimination; the choice of the recommended measure, therefore, zeroed on to the last and fifth one, that is, an Autonomous District Hill Council. This was found to be a workable proposition for many reasons; and officials of the central and the state governments began working on the outlines of this arrangement in right earnest.

While crafting out various details; two negative points did emerge. One was that the experience of a similar experiment in the form of Darjeeling Gorkha Hill Council, in West Bengal, had not been a happy one. Secondly, at a future date similar demands from some parts of Jammu region could not be ruled out. But, considering the overall situation and various parameters; this certainly was the most effective and also least bothersome recourse. There were, of course, certain distinct advantages in this respect too. This scheme could very well be accommodated within the existing constitutional framework of J&K and no amendment to either the State Constitution or the Constitution of India was required. Ladakh also had a predominantly tribal population; and to that extent this region was indeed different from other parts of the state, so therefore it would be very difficult for any other area or segment to refer to this arrangement as a precedent. Also unlike the Darjeeling venture; the four MLAs of Ladakh were certainly on good terms with their counterparts in the State Legislature and the political executive of the State. Therefore, even though the provisions of the proposed statute could be, in principle, diluted by the State Legislature; in practical terms the eventualities of such a thing happening for the disadvantage of Ladakh, were indeed meager and insignificant. In view of the fact that Ladakh comprised two districts of Leh and Kargil; it became necessary to plan for two Councils for the area with an Inter District Advisory Council or such similar mechanism. Since, the State was then under President's Rule, the proposed Act had to be moved in the Parliament for passing. A year after the revocation of the Presidential proclamation under Article 356; the statute needed re-enactment by the State Legislature. This was not thought to be a big issue at all. Based on these stipulations; a proposed Legislation was prepared by the Central and State representatives and put up at the appropriate quarters for consideration. In the entire exercise, the then Union Home Minister S.B. Chavan played a leading and active role.

At the political and official levels; the people in the Government of India were keen not to repeat the mistake of October 1989 and this time extract a *quid pro quo* from the local representatives; before making a formal announcement of such a noteworthy plan. After tying up various loose ends – which also involved a series of parleys with the LBA leaders; a concluding round of discussions was held on 14th April 1995. The record note of this significant meeting was jointly signed by the Joint Secretary, Department of J&K Affairs, GoI and Commissioner- Secretary, Ladakh Affairs Department J&K Government. It contained the following two paragraphs:-

"The Union Home Secretary, Shri K. Padmanabhaiah, the Chief Secretary, Government of J&K, Shri Ashok Kumar, Shri C. Phonsog, Joint Secretary, Department of J&K Affairs, Government of India and Shri Verghese Samuel, Commissioner Ladakh Affairs Department, Government of J&K had a meeting with the members of the Coordination Committee for the Ladakh Autonomous Hill Council on 14. 4.1995. The Union Home Secretary recalled that tripartite agreement between the Central Govt., the State Govt. and the Ladakh Buddhist Association was signed as early as in October, 1989, whereby it was agreed to constitute an Autonomous Hill Council. Since the legislation for this is required to be done by the State Government, the agreement provided that the Hill Council would be formed soon after the Elections to the State Assembly in December 1989 were held. The Home Secretary mentioned that, however, certain other events and developments had overtaken the State as well as the country as a result of which the President's rule had to be imposed in the State in January 1990 itself, which is still continuing. Both the Central Govt. and the State Govt. had to divert their entire attention to the fighting of militancy in the Valley. In these circumstances, the question of formation of the Ladakh Autonomous Hill Council did receive a setback. While agreeing that there was a delay in the formation of the Ladakh Autonomous Hill Council, he assured that the Government of India and the State Government are fully committed to the formation of the Ladakh Autonomous Hill Council. He also mentioned that the Government had to look at the issues from various angles which took time. Now all the issues have been sorted out, and a proposal would be put up to the Cabinet in a couple of days. He assured the Committee that in his judgment the enactment of the legislation for forming the Autonomous Hill Council should not take more than a month. He as well as the Chief Secretary J&K have also assured the Committee that when the legislation is passed, steps would be taken to constitute the Ladakh Autonomous Hill Council within two months thereafter.

"The Govt. officials mentioned that the formation of this Council which is the long standing demand of the region should accelerate the pace of development in the area. The Union Home Secretary referred to the tremendous potential for tourism in the area. Even though the inflow of tourists in the last five years has increased substantially the infrastructure could not keep pace with it. He gave an example of the development of tourism in the Rocky Mountains of the USA and mentioned that there is a need to add much more infrastructure. In view of the foregoing, the Coordination Committee decided to call off the proposed intensification of the Agitation."

Thus the long struggle of the local people for their recognition as a distinct entity came to a happy and significant conclusion with the 'in principle' agreement to formulate the Ladakh Autonomous Hill Council. Some formal measures and steps were left to be taken at various levels; for which provisions were made and procedures worked out in the next few months. Thus the promised time frame was generally adhered to. The State Government consequently prepared a final draft of Ladakh Autonomous Hill Development Council and sent it for approval to the Government of India. This was then vetted in the Union Home Ministry under the guidance of the Home Minister, S.B. Chavan and the relevant Act was placed in the Parliament to be passed; as the State was still under President's Rule. After the Parliamentary concurrence, it was submitted to the President for his consent. On 9th May, 1995, the President of India approved the Ladakh Autonomous Hill Development Council Act. Under the Act, the District Council was to comprise 30 members, including 26 elected and four nominated by the Governor from principal minorities and women in the district. There was also a provision for Members of the Council to elect a chairman, who would be designated as the Chief Executive Councillor. The four other Executive Councillors were to be be nominated by the CEC; from among the elected councilors.

In the body of the Act, 'Reasons for Enactment' significantly mentioned: "Ladakh region is geographically isolated with a sparse population, a vast area and inhospitable terrain which remains landlocked for nearly six months in a year. Consequently, the people of the area have had a distinct regional identity and special problems distinct from those of the other areas of the State of Jammu and Kashmir. The people of Ladakh have, for a long time, been demanding effective local institutional arrangements which can help to promote and accelerate the pace of development and equitable all-round growth and development with regards to its peculiar geo-climatic and locational conditions, and stimulate fullest participation of the local community in the decision making process. It has widely been accepted that decentralization of power by formation of Hill Councils for the Ladakh Region would give a boost to the developmental activities in Ladakh and meet the aspirations of the people of the said Region. The present measure was taken to achieve the above object."

Understandably, after promulgation of the LAHDC Act, there was great jubilation in the entire area. As a natural follow up, the state administration conducted the elections under this new law on 28th August 1995 and the elected Councillors took oath of office in a public swearing in ceremony. This function was organized in the Polo Ground at Leh on 3rd Sept 1995. Thupstan Chhewang was elected as the first CEC of LAHDC of Leh district – he was to function in that capacity for nearly next nine years. The Executive Councillors included Sonam Dawa, retired Chief Engineer, M. Akbar Ladakhi, Nawang Rigzin Jora and Tondup Sonam. Undoubtedly, it was a significant development which heralded far reaching positive consequences for the entire area. The rally at the Polo Ground was a sort of 'victory celebrations' by the large gathering present on this occasion. There it was announced on behalf of the Ladakh Buddhist Association that the LBA would revert its socio-religious activities, as before, and the LAHDC would function on the democratic lines. Interestingly, some speakers did mention that the ultimate solution to Ladakh's grievances was only the grant of a UT status and the current dispensation was just a stepping stone in that direction.

Later, reflecting on this momentous development Thupstan Chhewang wrote, "...However, mercifully, there was no serious misunderstanding among Ladakhi Buddhists and predominantly Shia Muslims... There was a tripartite agreement among Ladakhi leaders and Central and State governments paving the way for the constitution of an elected LAHDC on September 5 (the actual date, as per the records of LAHDC Leh, being 3rd September), 1995. The formation of the Council has indeed encouraged the participation of people in managing their affairs. There are more welfare and development projects being executed now than ever before…"[4]

No similar Council was established in Kargil district; it was to take another eight years for the same to materialize. This process has been vividly described by Fayaz Ahmed, a student from Kargil studying in the Jawaharlal Nehru University (JNU), New Delhi. He read a paper on the subject; in a seminar organized in the capital by the Institute of Peace and Conflict Studies, on 1st February 2013. This presentation included, "… In case of Kargil district, the leaders of Kargil not only refused to support UT status for Ladakh but also rejected the offer for an autonomous Hill Council status, essentially to mark their solidarity with the Kashmiri mainstream politician; especially with the National Conference. It was widely perceived then that acceptance of the AHC by Kargil would not have been appreciated by the Kashmiri politicians, despite the fact that the vast majority of people in Kargil supported the idea of an AHC. However, things changed with the passage of time in July 2003, with the coming of the coalition government of PDP and Congress to power. They approved the formation of AHC also in Kargil. As a result an Autonomous Hill Development Council was established in Kargil district as well. This formation of LAHDC Kargil was one of the most remarkable developments in the history of Kargil…"

When the elected government came to power in the State in October 1996; the constitutional requirements mandated that this Act would lapse after one year unless passed again by the State Legislature. The needful was done as the State Government was in agreement with the principle of this arrangement. Consequently, the Ladakh Autonomous Hill Development Council Act, 1997; as passed by the Jammu and Kashmir State Legislature received the assent of the Governor on 8th October 1997. It was, "An Act to provide for establishment of Autonomous Hill Development Councils and an Inter-District Advisory Council in Ladakh region of Jammu and Kashmir." Main provisions of this statuette, other than the CEC, Executive Concillors and Members which were the same as mentioned hereinbefore, included the following:-

4 Border Affairs, New Delhi, April – June 2008, pp. 7and 8.

1. Section 1. (3). It shall be deemed to have come into force with effect from 1st June 1995.

2. Section 3. There shall be an Autonomous Hill Development Council for each District.

3. Section 4. (3). The sitting members of the Legislative Assembly of the State of Jammu and Kashmir and the sitting members of the House of the People representing the Assembly or the Parliamentary Constituency, as the case may be, in which the district is situated shall be ex-officio members of the Council constituted for the district.

4. Section. 11. Every member shall, before taking his seat, make and subscribe before such person as may be appointed by the Government in this behalf an oath or affirmation according to the prescribed form.

5. Section. 14…the term of a member, elected or nominated shall be five years unless the Council is dissolved under section 52 and shall commence from the date appointed by the Government for the first meeting of the Council after a general election.

6. Section. 15. If a person who is already a member of the Council is chosen as member of Parliament or State Legislature his seat in the Council shall, on the date on which he takes oath as such become vacant.

7. Section. 16. A person shall not be qualified to be a member of the Council unless he is an Elector.

8. Section. 21. Every member shall be entitled to such allowances as the Council may with the approval of the Government determine.

9. Section. 25. The members of the Council shall at its first meeting after a general election elect from amongst the elected members one member to be the Chairman.

10. Section. 29. (1) There shall be Executive Council consisting of –

    (a) the Chairman who shall be the Chief Executive Councillor; and

(b) four members to be nominated by the Chief Executive Councillor from amongst the members of the Council;

Provided that at least one member shall be nominated from amongst principal religious minorities in the district.

11. Section. 36. The quorum necessary for the transaction of business at a meeting of the Executive Council shall be three members.

12. Section. 38. Deputy Commissioner of the district shall be the Chief Executive Officer of the Council.

13. Section. 40. All Government employees in the district except the judicial employees and police personnel shall be deemed to be the transferred employees on such terms and conditions, to be notified by the Government from time to time; provided that the terms and conditions of service of an employee of the Government transferred to the Council shall not be varied to his disadvantage.

14. Section. 42. (1). Save as otherwise provided in this Act, all land within the district, on the constitution of the first Council, shall stand transferred to such Council.

15. Section. 44. The Government shall provide funds under the Plan and Non-Plan Budget to the Council to be credited to the Council Fund as per budgetary requirement as approved by the Government.

16. Section. 50. The Government may in consultation with the Councils of Leh and Kargil by notification in the Government Gazette constitute an Advisory Council to be called the Inter District Advisory Council consisting of such number of persons as it think fit for advising the council –

    (a) on matters of common interest to both districts;

    (b) on the measures to be adopted for resolving differences between the Councils; and

    (c) on the measures to be taken for preservation of communal harmony in the Ladakh region.

The Assembly elections took place in J&K in October 1996, after over six years of Governor's and President's rule. The election results brought to power National Conference government headed by Dr. Farooq Abdullah. The new administration did publically support the idea of LAHDC for Ladakh region; but inwardly saw and placed itself, more or less, in an adversarial position. In the initial stages of its functioning the LAHDC needed all the support and guidance of the more experienced state apparatus. The same was not only denied but the State Government certainly proved unhelpful in its attitude, policies and governance systems. It was decidedly negative to the LAHDC Leh; which was then in existence. However, things did improve after a period of six years when the next Assembly elections took place in October 2002. The National Conference government was replaced by the PDP and Congress coalition ministry headed by Mufti Mohammad Sayeed. The new government not only established LAHDC in Kargil district; but also made both the units – in Leh as well as in Kargil – function much more effectively and without any undue interference from the State Government. In addition, the new set up considerably enhanced the remunerations of Council members including the office bearers. It also granted the status of a Cabinet Minister to the CEC and that of Deputy Ministers to the Executive Councillors.

Overall Assessment

However, the fact remains that the LAHDC – right from CEC downwards – kept grumbling against the State Government for lack of facilities and delegations; right from the inception of the new set-up in 1995 to the end of the century. Its emasculation was considerably effective. A dispassionate evaluation of this system of local governance, particularly in the initial years, does indicate the following points:-

- Many subjects were not clearly defined whether they came under the purview of the Hill Council or the State Government. Quite often senior functionaries of the State, including Ministers, would issue instructions to all the districts including Leh and Kargil without taking into account the authority of the Hill Council. This led to avoidable conflict and confusion.

- The functioning of the LAHDC remained comparatively much smoother when the State Government was of the same political party. But, when the two belonged to different parties; the State

Government often tried to undermine the authority of the Hill Council.

- The Executive Councillors have certainly been considered important components of the LAHDC structure. The resources at their disposal and their personal staff did not adequately reflect this trend, at least in the first few years.

- There has been some confusion and overlap in the functions of Panchayats and Council members. This aspect needs careful and deliberate consideration. The relations between Councillors and Sarpanches have, by and large, remained cordial. This has been due to dominance of one political party among Councillors and the election of Sarpanches on non-political basis. However, in case of any change in this situation; the political affiliations of these two categories could become a source of friction. Also, under certain schemes, the funds are directly transferred from Center to the Panchayats. Consequently, in these sectors, Panches and Sarpanches wield more influence at the grassroots level and would not take kindly to any interference from Councillors. On the other hand, the Councillors feel more important because in each of their constituencies there are three to five Sarpanch halqas. This certainly is an issue with a potential for unpleasant and adversarial situations.

- The LAHDC Act has a provision for the constitution of an Inter-District Advisory Council. Its early establishment cannot be over emphasized.

All the same; the fact remains that notwithstanding some nagging difficulties – particularly in the initial years – the LAHDC has certainly come out as a sort of model structure for effective governance at the grassroots levels.

On the balance, all things considered, LAHDC has been an admirable example of democracy working effectively at the ground level. Some initiatives of the Hill Council – particularly in the education and environmental sectors – have been appreciated even outside J&K. The efficiency and transparency in the functioning of LAHDC has decidedly set an example. It has also helped in preserving the distinct identity and cultural heritage of Ladakh. Certainly the decentralization of power as well as a system of checks and balances – both integral parts of this setup – ensures a genuine democratic participation. This formation can fruitfully become an example to be emulated in other parts of the country.

Commenting on some of the negative aspects of the LAHDC and its actual functioning over the years, a local Ladakhi, Tsering Dorje observed "… Less said the better about our legislative powers. We can't frame rules with respect to matters directly under our control and concerning our people. Likewise the funds are transferred to us late. The Comptroller and Auditor General of India has brought out this grim reality in one of its recent reports…Time and again we have reiterated at every forum that gross discrimination in development and employment opportunities has compelled us to seek a Union Territory status. Right from the day Jammu and Kashmir had acceded to the Union of India we have been agitating for the acceptance of our request. Many times it appeared that we were reaching our target. However, we were persuaded at the last moment by successive governments in New Delhi to put off our stir "in wider national interest". In retrospect we find that we have been made a pawn on national and international chessboard… Our argument for Union Territory is based on our distinct profile beyond the mighty Himalayas. We have a unique ethnic, cultural, religious and linguistic identity. Moreover, we are a large territory with a scattered population. Our strategic importance is only too well known to be elaborated. We thus feel that only a self-governed political superstructure can guard our overall interests…"[5]

As the Ladakhis feel, particularly the people of Leh district, their main demand right from the beginning of Independence has been direct administration from the national capital. In other words, the grant of UT status for the region. The local people still perceive the LAHDC being a stepping stone towards that end.

5 Border Affairs, New Delhi, April – June 2007, pp. 22 and 23.

CHAPTER VIII

Assessment of 20th Century in Ladakh

From 1900 to 1999, the hundred years have been a century of change in this sleepy region. Much has happened in Ladakh during this period and the usually laid back lifestyle of this area has now given rise to almost a bursting level of activity. This enormous transformation has mostly taken place from the 1960s onwards. In fact, from the beginning of the twentieth century Ladakh can be classified as having passed through six distinct phases. The first one, which lasted the longest, can be said to taken place from the beginning of the century till 1947. For more than a millennium before this period; peoples' life patterns in Ladakh had almost stood still. From the beginning of the twentieth century till Independence in 1947 few things did change, though in small doses, in this region. Orderly establishment of postal and telegraph services – and also later some telephone lines, regulated flow of trade and traffic on the 'silk route' as well as beginnings of educational and medical services in the region were some of the more significant accomplishments of the administration during that period. One of the enduring contribution or in a way reminder of the silk route travelers, is the addition of a dish called "Yarkandi Pulao" to the local cuisine of Ladakh. As the name suggests; this recipe must have originated in or around the city of Yarkand in Central Asia. The traders and other people on the silk route trail were fond of making this single dish meal; which was delicious, not much time consuming and also wholesome. This is almost a gift of that era to the local populace.

In spite of these few changes; life in general was spent at leisurely pace till late October 1947 when Maharaja Hari Singh, the ruler of J&K, acceded with the Union of India. With this began the next stage lasting for more than a year; which in its wake brought lot of difficult time for Ladakh.

1948 was a particularly bad and trying year for the entire region. The tribal raiders mixed with elements of Pakistani Army started bloody trail of occupation, loot and rapine with Gilgit in the beginning of November 1947; moved on to Skardu and by the end of May 1948 these people had captured the whole of present Kargil district and moved on to occupy Leh. The raiders were practically knocking on the doors of that town. Leh was barely saved by timely arrival of the Indian Army reinforcements and also credible defence efforts of local population; particularly the doughty defenders of Leh and brave plus hardy fighters of Nubra valley. Contrary to the general believe; the peace-loving Buddhists of this region transformed themselves into courageous and determined combatants. Stories of heroic exploits of these warriors were narrated and also heard with interest in Ladakh for many decades thereafter. By the end of 1948; all Pakistani raiders were pushed back and the whole of present Leh and Kargil district areas cleared of the invaders. Though Ladakh was saved literally from the skin of the teeth; Gilgit and Skardu regions were lost to the Pakistanis.

The next stage, lasting from 1949 to 1962, was really a dark period for the region. Ladakh was almost a forsaken territory by all those concerned with welfare and development of the region. The Government of India practically washed its hands off – with elements of the army also withdrawing from this area. Similarly, the J&K State Government paid scant attention to this belt. The flourishing trade routes to Central Asia and Tibet were first choked and then fully blocked; plunging the entire Ladakh region to terrible monitory loss; considerable reduction in the employment of men and animals and pushing it into a pall of gloom and despair. It was China which took advantage of this state of neglect and spread its tentacles there; mainly in the region of Aksai Chin.

The fourth phase can be termed as The Awakening and it roughly coincided with the duration from 1962 to 1974; in fact starting with the Chinese aggression of 1962. This adverse development in fact proved beneficial to the area. It was no more to remain a neglected part of the country. Besides heightening of the strategic importance of Ladakh for the national defence; the area was incrementally covered with a network of roads and vehicle-worthy tracks coupled with introduction of modern telecommunication systems. All these brought the population of this remote belt face to face with modern ways of life. Ladakh started receiving unprecedented attention of the Central as well as State Governments;

leading to progress on all fronts. This was in fact water shed period between the old and the new in this region.

Ladakh embarked on a path of considerable growth from the early years of 1970s; but since this region was declared open for tourism in July 1974, thereby facilitating unhindered movement of people to and from the area – the era of 'development trajectory' including sudden surge in tourism related progress and growth – can be said to have begun from this year of 1974. Even though the process continues till the present as also would remain so in the foreseeable future; decade of the seventies was really a period of high progress for the region. Comments of Kalon Sahib, in this regard, are very valid. He observed, "...Probably Sheikh Sahib also realized the mistake of neglecting the development of Ladakh during his first tenure; so when he returned to power in 1975, he nominated Sonam Narboo as one of his three ministers along with Devi Dass Thakur from Jammu and Mirza Afzal Beig from Kashmir. Sonam Narboo opened new vistas of development in Ladakh region. We can never forget him for what he has done for the people of this region. The airfield at Leh was constructed by him in 1948 which proved crucial for the defence of this land. After this, he was the man who constructed the road link from Leh to Kargil which opened up this land locked place. Finally, after his appointment as a minister in 1975; a decisive push was given to developmental activities in Ladakh..."[1] Notwithstanding disturbed conditions in the area from 1980 onwards for almost a decade and half; the high growth trajectory – both in Leh as well as Kargil district - continued in the last three decades of the century.

The sixth and final phase for Ladakh in the twentieth century relates to the granting of two Hill Development Councils in 1995; as also establishment of the LAHDC Leh after elections during the same year. Even though this was a watered down version of the local demand for a Union Territory status; the formation of LAHDC Leh gave a decisive push to progress and growth of the area – which was henceforth put in a high gear.

A number of social changes took place in the local societies, during this period. The most discernible of these have been as follows:-

- Polyandry system has been stopped.

1 Interview with Rigzin Namgyal Kalon in September 1998.

- Though inter-marriages do take place occasionally; their number has reduced drastically. In particular, marriages between Buddhist girls and Muslim boys have been decreased to the lowest minimum.

- Considerable increase in the awareness about education in the whole area. Even though there has been substantial addition in the number of educational institutions in the region; there is an ever increasing demand for higher centers of learning and greater spread on the ground.

- Similar is the case with medical institutions and rising awareness about treatment facilities and provisioning of greater health related services.

- Some well educated Lamas have left their traditional role and preferred to lead a house holder's life.

- The people, in general, are changing their traditional vocations and instead preferring government employment or any other white-collar jobs.

- Young generation prefers the Indian or western life style over the traditional Ladakhi way of living.

The views of two prominent Ladakhis, about the overall socio-economic milieu prevailing in the region; are remarkably relevant. According to one, "… There have been three important changes in Ladakh in the past half a century; prosperity, learning as well as acceptance of Science and Technology as a tool of development and Lamas entering into politics… Today if anything happens to any of our monasteries there are enough records, photographs and films which will help us to recreate the same structure and ambiance brick by brick and layer by layer…"[2] On the same topic, views of C. Phonsog – the first I.A.S. officer from Ladakh – are more elaborate and he has opined, "Over the second half of the twentieth century, Ladakhis had experienced an unprecedented general assimilation into the main stream of Indian nation-state like no other ethnic minority. Since independence in 1947 and the State's accession to the Indian Union, Ladakhis have come to participate in the vicissitude of the country shoulder to shoulder with people of other regions of the country. Post-1947 Ladakh

2 Interview with Tashi Rabgias on 12th September 1998.

has, therefore, become meeting ground of two very different cultures, Ladakhi and Indian, and thereby the crucible for a new and, hopefully, a more sublime culture in which the best of both can be said to have been fused. Thus, before the evolution of Ladakhi society had gone far in the 20th century, the revolutionary impact of Indian civilization and culture has been upon it which, with all its pluses and minuses, has come for a harmonious mingling with the former... Human capital development for a place, particularly an isolated region like Ladakh where economic opportunities are limited, can hardly be overemphasized. Ladakh region with a population of over two lakhs constitutes about 60% of J&K State's geographical area. However, 90 percent of this land is not available for any economic activity. The region's population has grown from about 75 thousand in 1951. With these geographical, demographic and ethnic situations; Ladakh has its own unique problems. Livelihood avenues in different sectors of the economy in the region are extremely limited and cannot keep pace with the growing population. Therefore, in order that economic opportunities keep pace with the growth in population, planners are required to assign still higher priority to human capital development by improving medical, educational and training facilities; including their standards. The effort has to be aimed at enabling Ladakhi youth to compete for suitable jobs outside Ladakh – in the state and the country, and even abroad..."

Changes in Socio-economic life

Three major institutions – or ways of life – in Ladakh have remained more or less steady during the course of twentieth century. These are the monasteries; the primacy of agrarian economy and importance of the nomadic people. These have survived many transformations which have taken place in the region during this long period; more so in the later fifty years which heralded a number of improvements and changes. The Ladakhi monastery has played an important role in the physical and spiritual growth of Buddhism; and has been generally described as, "... It has not only been a centre of learning for Buddhist philosophy, history, literature and language; but also a sanctuary for Buddhist paintings, printing and making statues...A Thanka is a Tibetan Buddhist religious painting drawn on fabric. Originating in India, Thanka was introduced into Tibet as early as the eight century. From there it came to the Ladakh region. The painter would invariably follow the rules of scale-perception as laid down in the Buddhist scriptures; as this has been believed to ensure in it the insertion of the Divine Spirit. The act of consecration is carried out by the Lamas when the Thanka is being installed in a monastic shrine or household chapel. The elaborate ceremonies and consecration rites are believed to have transformed these into objects of veneration. Most major colors used to paint a Thanka are available in Ladakh itself. Vermilion is obtained from Nubra; lime-white from Zanskar; yellow from Khaltsi, brown from Markha; red lead is obtained from vermilion itself and green is extracted by copper oxidation".

In times of distress in the region; monasteries in the past have also functioned as big providers and opened their granaries for free distribution of food amongst the needy population.

Agricultural

In spite of the fact that only one crop is grown there in a year; Ladakh has always been self sufficient in food grains. This was particularly so till the early sixties when the road connection between Srinagar and Leh was established; enabling the administration to get food grains from outside the region. Also, though unaware of the principles and benefits of a balanced diet including the mineral and vitamin contents of the food intake; traditional Ladakhi meal has consisted of wholesome and well balanced diet, over the centuries. It is very rare to find an undernourished child or adult there.

In the whole region – both Kargil as well as Leh district – religion and politics often get mixed. The people are intensely religious and their lives as well as activities are inextricably mixed with religious ceremonies and institutions. Also, traditionally the monasteries have owned large chunks of land and thus dominated the economic setup in the region; impacting on the social, cultural as also political life of the people. Stratification of the society in Ladakh is quite perceptible and hence it is not surprising that – at least in a few decades after 1950s – the politics and religion were largely dominated by socially and religiously important personalities. Therefore, in the initial years after independence; the political outfits were deeply impacted by religious establishments.

Other than farming and attendant agricultural activities; animal rearing has traditionally been a very important occupation in the economic life of Ladakh. The agriculturist as well as the nomadic population reared a good number of animals; in each household for meat, milk, fiber and subsidiary activity to agriculture operations. Animal manure also played a significant role in the enhancement of yield in a limited land-holding peasantry scenario; which in turn ensured food security in the region. In the later part of the century, increasingly more means of livelihood became available to the population; thus also diversifying the otherwise traditional twin segments of agriculturist and nomadic existence. Over a period; larger numbers of people are opting for non-traditional occupations and generally live more happily than ever before.

Some good things in Ladakhi society have fortunately remained unchanged. For example the welcome given and courtesies shown to guests; adherence to traditions and customs and the tasty local cuisine; all this has been preserved by the community. One peculiarity of the inhabitants – and which has also not undergone much change – pertains to their attitude to taking a bath. At one end of the spectrum are the inhabitants of Dah-Hanu area – supposedly of pure Aryan stock and widely believed to be descendents of some elements of Alexander's army that stayed back – who are reported to seldom take bath during their entire lifetime. For the rest, very interesting comments have been made by a keen observer as, "The local people are not very particular about the need for a daily bath. This habit, it must be admitted, is partly due to weather and partly due to the low economic standard of life. Though spring water is plenty and is available at hand, it is too cold for bath for nearly six months in a year. On account of the high cost of firewood, heating water for bath is something which few people can afford and consequently baths are few and far between… Luckily for people of the Nubra valley there are some hot water springs near about Panamik village. These sulphur springs are a great boon to the people nearby and 'Iharjeys' or local physicians sometimes accompany their patients over long distances to have a dip in these springs. A bath in these sulphur springs is considered to be a good cure for various types of diseases particularly rheumatism. The 'Iharjeys' always mix the hot water of the sulphur spring with cold water, in such proportion as he deems fit, and then the patient takes his bath."[3] Even though these observations were made during the period of 1950s; things have not changed much during

3 Maj Gen Rajendra Nath, PVSM (Retd), *Strategic Ladakh,* Vij Books India Pvt Ltd, New Delhi, 2016, pp. 66 and 67.

the subsequent decades of the century and local customs remain, more or less, unchanged in this regard.

Pastoral

Living conditions in the higher reaches, where people generally lead a pastoral existence or the life of 'wandering shepherds'; have not changed much in the twentieth century. Changthang – literally meaning the high plateau – is primarily the pasture area of Leh district and lies in the Nyoma sub-division; with an average height of over 15,000 feet. Because of being located so high, temperatures fall very low during the winter months; even from the Ladakh standards, though the snow precipitation in this belt is quite low. The area is primarily inhabited by nomadic groups called Changpa – residents of Changthang – in the local parlance. These people are basically of the Tibetan stock and are believed to have migrated from the Western Tibet areas along with livestock some centuries ago; probably in the search for better pastures. Traditionally they are good in livestock rearing but know little about agriculture. About managing the livestock; they have invaluable experience and wisdom acquired over the centuries in this field. This also includes the expertise in treating the animals through use of locally available plants and materials. As vegetables hardly grow in the area; meat is a big part of their diet. They generally try to fatten the animals as much as possible during the summer months so that the livestock can face the long, bleak and harsh winter better. Also because traditionally these people have been living on the edge; every member of the family contributes to the collective effort and distribution of work in the family is meticulous.

For major part of the year, they lead a wandering existence with their animals and also the family depending upon the availability of pastures. The area ordinarily has no dearth of summer grazing but winter season is a problem. Things have become even more difficult after the illegal incursions of the Chinese; particularly in the fifties and sixties. This has been a great setback to the traditional life of the Changpas. During the long and harsh winters, these people lead a lot more settled life revolving around a small house or a make-shift structure, stocked with necessary provisions. February and March are generally the breeding period for the animals and the young 'kids' are susceptible to an untimely snowfall. To overcome this problem; the administration tried to help by giving these people sheets of polythene free of charge, in the late seventies, to build rudimentary "kids-sheds". They were advised to erect stone walls around a dugout and cover it with the polythene sheet to use this as a kind of safe house for the new born kids to shelter them from the plunging temperatures as also untimely snowfall. This experiment did prove successful.

Broadly speaking, there has been no material change in the lifestyle of these people over the centuries; but things have been slowly transforming in the last couple of decades. Due to increased educational facilities and enhanced opportunities in the employment sector; a growing number of Changpa youth are leaving their traditional vocation and moving to alternative avenues. This tendency is likely to increase in the coming times. Looking into the future; two seemingly opposite trends appear in sight. On the one hand increasing pressure on the available grazing lands is discernible; simultaneously there is also a growing demand of the special woolen fiber – a bounty of nature at this high altitude – the *Pashmina*. The most likely scenario in the coming decades indicates that the rearing of Pashmina bearing goats will be done in a more scientific way and also in an increasingly settled manner. This would most likely mean that Changpas, as a distinct group, lead a more cohesive community life. Hence the next, twenty-first, century would be of immense significance to these people; whose life has remained unchanged for such a long time.

Changpas do speak Ladakhi; but their dialect differs considerably from other parts of the region. The local fabrics like the wool and particularly *Pashmina*, have considerable possibilities of up gradation and improved production as also greater marketing potential with much higher technological intervention. As it is, Ladakh has the justified reputation of being the home of best Pashmina producing goats in the world. This germ plasma, a gift of the nature due to special environment of the belt, can be a great asset to Ladakh as also hold considerable commercial value.

NGO Culture

An interesting development that took place in this region in the late eighties and nineties; pertains to the emergence of public spirited bodies in Ladakh. These indigenous NGOs, headed by SECMOL in Leh, have played a significant role in the spread of quality education in particular; as also protection and preservation of culture and environment in general. The trend has also given rise to a strong ecological movement in Ladakh; with fairly good results. However, as a matter of interest, it may be mentioned that the first non-government organization to work in Ladakh was not a local outfit, but a component of the multinational establishment, based in England, called Save the Children UK. They started working in and around Leh in the year 1978, supplementing the children diet with a programme called Leh Nutrition Project. The scheme worked successfully for many years in the area. More than the actual work, their philosophy had considerably greater importance for this region. Sir Robert Folkes, was the first Programme Director of this project; he was an Englishman who stayed and worked in Leh for years. He once made a very relevant and perceptive observation, as "I think our greatest success was to familiarize Ladakh with the concept of NGO action. Prior to our arrival, it was generally believed that both relief and development were something that should be done by the government. At the same time, we at least began to sow the seeds of the idea that communities could do more for themselves in a modern sense...If you like, we were trying to expand the 'development imagination'." There is now a very active and thriving set of NGO groups working in Ladakh and in all likelihood more will follow. This is true of both Leh as well as Kargil districts. This vibrant sector arrived on the scene – and also flourished – rather late. But it collectively holds great promise in its fold. Ladakh, with a vast landscape and myriad potentialities, abundant solar energy being a premier one, is an ideal place for much greater development of the NGO system.

Afforestation

Ladakh has no natural forests in the sense this word is understood in other parts of the country. There are only scattered plantations which can be termed as 'community forestry' and some ostensible efforts of the forest department. Today there are more green patches in the belt than ever before. An aerial view would depict islands of green in an otherwise barren vastness. Water being a scarce commodity; plantations could only emerge and survive along river banks or *nallahs*. Whatever little come under the nomenclature 'plantation', comprises only two varieties of willow and poplar. These are also popular amongst the locals because these have good timber value and are used in the ceilings as well as roof thatching; in addition to giving good returns in a comparatively short duration. The difficulty in Ladakh is that being a cold desert with very meager precipitation; water is scarce and land along the water-body banks is highly prized for growing crops and vegetables. These are much more remunerative and hence preferred by the locals over forestry or community plantations. Therefore, in Ladakh, trees can only be grown in areas which are not considered good for agriculture or vegetable cultivation but have all the same some availability of water. So far, in Ladakh, only alfa-alfa grass and poplar and willow have been grown with success. However, the green cover has perceptibly increased in the region in the last few decades and it holds good promise for the future.

Seabuckhthorn is almost a wonder plant of the area. According to a locally based Defence establishment, called FRL (Field Research Laboratory); Ladakh has about 11,500 hectares of area under seabuckthorn and another 30,000 hectares where seabuckthorn comes mixed with other plants. Virtually every part of this plant has a utility. The berries are a very rich source of vitamin C and so is the juice; apart from being tasty. The oil from seeds too contains abundant vitamins and minerals which make it ideal for use in medicine and cosmetic industry. The leaves are an excellent fodder for animals and the dried thorny branches are also used locally as fence along the fields to prevent entry of grazing animals. Besides, the roots fix nitrogen and thus add fertility to the soil in addition to being effective soil binder. In fact after Ladakh became well known as a tourist destination, more so in the nineties; seabuckthorn along with Giri-oil[4] almost became Brand Leaders of the place.

Infrastructure Developments

Roads and bridges have always received a high priority, and rightly so, in the overall development plans for Ladakh. Particularly 1970s onwards, the two major rivers of the area; Indus and Suru have been dotted with numerous motor able and foot bridges. The same is true of the smaller streams in the interior areas. It is a fact that, till late seventies the people of Padam, used to cross the fast flowing Zanskar river over a shaky rope bridge made of local shrubs and twigs. Such like things have, over the years, become a matter of the past. Also, in addition to the main link road connecting Srinagar to Leh; a comprehensive network of internal roads has been laid out in the whole region. The more important roads in this category being Kargil-Padam; Kargil-Batalik; Leh-Deskit; Leh-Nyoma; Nyoma-Darbuk and the like.

4 It is the traditional oil extracted out of the kernel of local Apricots in Ladakh; and is reportedly as good as the almond oil for body massage. In the olden days Giri-oil was also used as a cooking medium in the region; especially in Kargil area.

The building constructions in the government sector have generally followed the Kashmir pattern of a stone and cement structure, topped up with a sloping tin roof. This was probably so because most of the senior engineers posted in Ladakh came from the Valley; though keeping in view the very low temperatures of the belt, some parts of the building particularly the lower portions were sometimes given a mud plaster coating and then white washed. The change to a much more eco-friendly and local type of construction started to take place towards the end of the seventies decade. This shifting of emphasis primarily came about when a local engineer, Sonam Dawa, became head of the PWD works there in the rank of Superintending Engineer (he later retired as a Chief Engineer). The first government building based on the local design and architecture, was the district meeting hall at Leh. It was a single storey structure with traditional mud covered walls, local design and painted windows with flat roof protruding on all four sides; just as in the houses around. This edifice came up next to the DC's office; a double storey construction made up of stone and cement walls with a sloping tin-roof. The contrast between the two could not have been more stark and telling. It is a matter of record that the subsequent structures in the whole of Ladakh followed the local design and style in an increasing manner.

Much has already been mentioned about the spread of education and related infrastructure in the region. Till the nineties, though, the local education facilities were limited to the Higher Secondary level. It was only in 1994 that a college each came up in Leh and Kargil where the local youth could study up to the graduation level. The subjects offered by these colleges were limited as the number of students was quite low – with a majority of the concerned lot preferring to go to institutions outside the region. On the other hand; the enrolment was low only because the choice of subjects offered was quite limited. It was a classic situation of like the 'egg and hen' and this stalemate was to continue for few more years.

About the spread of health institutions and the efficacy of health education; these topics have been mentioned earlier in considerable details. All the same, the coming up of SNM District Hospital in Leh, in the late seventies and its expansion as well as consolidation of services – in the subsequent years – was not only beneficial to Leh district but also a thing of considerable advantage to the population of the entire Ladakh region. Another establishment of notable significance for the whole area;

was the opening of an All India Radio station in Leh in the seventies. It further helped that, in the beginning, this was headed by people known by their competence in the field of Broadcasting. In the early years of its existence, the Leh AIR station was under the stewardship of Zubair Rizvi; who was not only a competent professional in his own right, but also an Urdu poet of national repute.

A notable institutional organization to come up in Ladakh during the 20th century has been the Indian Astronomical Observatory at Hanley. With the Hanley monastery as its nearest neighbour; this establishment stands at a height of above fourteen thousand feet. Situated in the middle of a large valley – locally called Nilamkhul - this observatory is located on the top of a hillock named by the parent body as Mt. Saraswati. The search and reconnaissance for a suitable site 'to study the meteorological conditions over the Indian subcontinent in the Himalayan and trans-Himalayan regions' started in September 1993. After a detailed analysis of six different places all over the country, the location at Hanley was finalised in January 1995 and thereafter the work on this project started; which took few more years to complete. Cloudless skies, night brightness, coupled with low atmospheric water vapours make this an ideal site for optical, infrared, sub-millimetre and millimetre wavelengths. In these and other related fields, the Hanley location is an ideal place for further extensive studies. The main installation there is a 2-m optical infrared telescope; which is remotely operated from a distant place called Hoskote, in Karnataka. In addition; several site monitoring instruments have also been positioned, which is a continuing process.

Like education and health; Ladakh also made considerable strides in the agriculture, animal and sheep husbandry sectors particularly after the 1960s. The farms established by the government departments at Chanspa, Matho and Khumathang need special mention. A multi dimensional and comprehensive analysis of activities in these sectors and their impact on the local society has been made by a perceptive observer, in the following words, "Before the advent of tourism in Ladakh, the only way of survival and in fact the main industry in this area was agriculture and agro based activities. This has been so for centuries. During the sixties, people also started making some money by selling surplus vegetables and fodder etc. to the army. But this involved hard work and substantial exertions. Now, it is distressing to see the fertile lands at times lying fallow or being built upon to make quick money through the growing tourism trade. This on one side has made the hardy, industrious Ladakhis to look for easy money and no tiresome activity; on the other the days of hard working, hard drinking and hard enjoyment seem to have been relegated to a distant past. A group of outside doctors have diagnosed a change in the lifestyle of locals to a more sedentary living and hence increase in the related ailments. This includes well-known maladies like high blood pressure, diabetes and heart ailments; even amongst younger people. Something never heard of earlier."[5]

Telecommunications was another field in which considerable progress was made during this period in Ladakh. However, for more than three decades after independence; the services in this sector almost remained at the primitive level. Even though there was extensive internal connectivity in Leh, Kargil and other urban clusters; the telephone exchanges were operated manually and a subscriber had to be connected to the required number by an operator. There was no STD facility available and all trunk calls had to be booked and routed through the telephone exchanges. All this took a quantum leap in the year 1980 and virtually a new beginning was made when Leh was connected to major cities of the country through satellite based communication system. Telecom services never looked back since then and one technical improvement followed another. By end of the century, Ladakh had almost come abreast with rest of the places; in so far as services in this sphere were concerned. Of course, the era of mobile phones and related advancements were still a few years away.

Electricity has been the inevitable fountainhead of comfort, progress and prosperity of any society in the 20th century. Ladakh has been no exception to this percept; even though regular power supply has been missing in that region for most of this period. It was only during the last four decades that electricity made an appearance on the scene. In the 1960s Diesel generated power came to Ladakh for the first time; and it was confined to a small number of urban centers like Leh, Kargil, Nyoma and Diskit. Being based on Diesel – a commodity that had to be transported all the way from Srinagar during summer months and stocked, *in situ*, for the long winters – the availability of electricity even in these few towns was for a few hours in the evening; and that too for lighting purposes only. All the same, it was a luxury for the benefitted population;

5 Interaction with Col (Retd). Wangdus Kalon on 8th November 2018.

even though they longed for a better source of power and free flowing electricity – as in other parts of the state and the country. Therefore, it was almost natural that when planned development of the region was taken in hand for Ladakh; one of the first important undertakings was for power generation in the form of Stakna Hydel Project based on the Indus; about forty kilometers upstream from Leh. This turned out to be an almost ill-fated venture and as the years went by, there were design modifications – including specifications for the generation equipment – resulting in a cycle of time over runs and cost escalations.

More than two decades later the Stakna went on stream, in the year 1986, as the first hydel power project in Ladakh providing 24 hour supply to a small population for nine months of the year. At the peak, it generated 4 MWs of power through two turbines of 2 MW each. However, right from the inception, it was facing difficulties due to severe problems of siltation and thus frequent damaging of underwater parts. This project was later closed, immediately after the commissioning of Nimoo – Bazgo Hydro Electric project in 2012 and recommended for fresh look from various technical angles.

On the similar lines a Hydel project was taken in hand in the immediate vicinity of Kargil town – called Iqbal Hydel scheme. It was named so because of the Power House being located near a bridge over Suru river, which was christened as Iqbal Bridge. The work on this scheme began in the beginning of 1970s; and it was initially envisaged to produce one MW of electricity. Later it was revised and generation capacity enhanced; resulting in time and cost revisions upwards. This project was ultimately commissioned in the year 1995; with three generating units each having an output of 1.25 MW. Thus the Iqbal project turned out to be having an installed capacity of 3.75 Mega Watts. However, because of constraints of the Indus Water Treaty and flow in the Suru river; mostly this scheme is under operation with a load of 1.25 MW, feeding part of the Kargil town. Thus at the end of the twentieth century; two important hydel projects – namely the Stakna and Iqbal - had gone on stream in Ladakh region.

In addition, there have been a good number of mini hydel projects in this vast area; particularly in the Nubra valley and the 'sham' belt of Leh sector between Nimoo and Batalik where almost perpetual mountain streams provide enough water to keep these going. The oldest amongst this category is the Nurla mini hydel project; which was commissioned in the 1960s and is certainly the first of its kind in the entire Ladakh area. Added to this, as already mentioned, is the huge and untapped potential of solar, geo-thermal and wind energy; making the power sector a vibrant and attractive strategy in the future development plans.

Tourism

The number of tourists visiting Ladakh has grown exponentially from a mere 527 in 1974 to around one lakh by the end of the twentieth century. But tourism in this region remains seasonal and unpredictable; quite a lot influenced by the conditions prevailing in the Valley. This became clearly apparent by these numbers going down significantly in the beginning years of 1990s; when militancy reared its ugly head in Kashmir. Even otherwise, it is not easy to sustain this inflow beyond a particular point or figure; due to corresponding demands of water and energy supply as also increased garbage waste. Therefore, on the balance it can be easily surmised that Ladakh undoubtedly needs quality and not quantity tourism. But, this aspect as well as developing a responsible form of tourism is not a small order. This challenge would remain to be in focus for many decades to come.

Another connected issue pertains to much greater diversification of tourist related activities with a view to ensure that this whole gamut is widely dispersed all over the region and does not remain confined to mainly the two focal points of Leh and Kargil. This would ensure much greater benefits to a larger number of locals as also wider spread of tourism activities. It is in this context that the local administrative structure needs to lay much greater emphasis on the concepts of 'home stays'; trekking and mountaineering activities. The consequent change of focus is not only difficult to achieve, but may also be resisted by the current beneficiaries. For much larger benefit, and also seen from a more practical angle, there is no alternative to adopting this strategy. The recent changes in government policies in allowing tourists to visit more areas in the hinterland are also loaded in favour of initiatives of this kind.

LAHDC

In addition to opening of Ladakh to tourism; the other step of the government which profoundly changed the region, was the grant of LAHDC status and this form of local governance in Leh and Kargil. As already mentioned, this was a sort of half-way solution to the demand of Union Territory status by the local population. Apart from other advantages of this form of administration; the LAHDC gave confidence to many a young and aspiring public figures in the matters related to native governance problems; as also prepare them for bigger roles at the state and national levels. Tourism and LAHDC structure - between them – have effectively pitch forked Ladakh from a remote and backward region to a visible and upcoming area with considerable promise.

The Ladakh Scouts

Of the many changes in Ladakh during the 20th Century – more so in its second half – a very significant transformation has been that of 'Nubra Guards' from the strength of one battalion of J&K Militia to its metamorphosis into Ladakh Scouts over a period of few decades. Today, Ladakh Scouts have the distinct honour of being one of the youngest and highly decorated regiments of the Indian Army with proud traditions of valor and sacrifice. It has registered notable rise and expansion; as also illustrious achievements. In a short span of little over half a century; Ladakh Scouts have been awarded Battle Honours of Turtuk and Batalik as also Theatre Honour Kargil; besides a large number of gallantry awards. It has distinctly grown into a strong and potent organization of redoubtable reputation.

Their story began with the birth of Nubra Guards in 1948 when the Pakistani Raiders penetrated the undefended Ladakh region. The people of Leh and Nubra areas volunteered to take up arms to defend their land, homes and hearths. They were enrolled into the Nubra Guards and National Guards; depending upon their age and location. The younger lot and coming from Nubra valley were selected for the Nubra Guards; whereas older persons and those belonging to Leh area were organized into National Guards. The Nubra Guards were given military training under the supervision of Major Prithi Chand and formally raised as 7th Jammu and Kashmir Militia on 15th August 1948 at Leh, under the command of Lt. Col. Prithi Chand – as he had been promoted from the rank of a Major. After the immediate crisis of 1948 were over and this unit became officially battle worthy; they were deployed all over Ladakh. Apart from other gallantry awards, Jemadar (later Colonel) Chhewang Rinchen of this unit was awarded the coveted Maha Vir Chakra in the 1948 war. In the closing years of 1950s, when the Chinese threat was increasing in the region; another battalion of the J&K Militia, consisting of Ladakhis and named as 14th Jammu and Kashmir Militia Battalion, was raised in Srinagar on 2nd May 1959. This unit, under the command of Lt. Col. Prahlad Singh was airlifted to Leh in May 1960. It was during this period that the pattern of deployment of these Militia units was changed by the army headquarters, in the background of enhanced Chinese incursions. The Militia companies were withdrawn from Pakistan border and assigned to establish posts along the borders with China in the forward locations like Phobrang, Chushul, Demchok, Koyul and Fukche.

In the wake of 1962 Operations; some other units of the army took over responsibility of manning some of the forward defences and both these battalions were deployed on the border in Demchok and Daulat Beg Oldie (DBO) sectors. These brave men fought valiantly against the Chinese as also against heavy odds, and for acts of gallantry; they were awarded 4 Maha Vir Chakras and 10 Vir Chakras. The then Lt. Chhewang Rinchen was also decorated with a Sena Medal during this war. After these operations were over; the Government of India decided to reorganize the Ladakhi troops of J&K Militia under a separate set up. Consequently, the Ladakh Scouts were raised by merger of 7th and 14th J&K Militia on 1st June 1963 with Lt. Col. RM Banon as their first commanding officer. They had been created "primarily for executing a specialized role of operating behind the enemy lines and cause maximum attrition. They were expected to operate generally in company groups." However, due to various operational factors; the soldiers of Ladakh Scouts continued to be utilized in the conventional role of occupying the forward defences. Few years later; another reorganization of this force took place and under this scheme the Ladakh Scouts were grouped into a Headquarters; eight Rifle Companies; one Signal Company; one Training Platoon; one Administrative Platoon; a Depot Company and Records Office. The Headquarters of Ladakh Scouts along with training and administrative organs were located at Phyang, near Leh, while the rifle companies were stationed in the three sectors of Nubra valley, Karakoram and Indus valley. This was the effective nucleus around which future expansion was to take place.

During the 1971 Indo-Pak war, the main task of Ladakh Scouts was to defend the Nubra valley against any Pakistani incursion from the Baltistan side. On the beginning of hostilities, in the first week of December, four rifle companies of Ladakh Scouts combined with elements of locally raised

Nubra Guards – together named as Dhal Force – were constituted and placed under the command of legendary Major Chhewang Rinchen. This group was intended to also undertake restricted offensive actions to keep the enemy off balance. In spite of limited strength of troops; the Ladakh Scouts splendidly rose to the occasion and exploited the operational successes achieved under a brilliant and inspirational commander. They captured a number of enemy locations, including a mountain top called Point 18402, its height in feet, which is the highest post ever conquered in history of warfare. The triumphs of Dhal Force also included the liberating of Turtuk area, which had been under the illegal occupation of Pakistan since 1948. During this war, the Ladakh Scouts were decorated with a number of gallantry awards including one MVC (Major Rinchen – in his case it was the second Maha Vir Chakra), four Vir Chakras, two Shaurya Chakras and two Sena Medals. Besides, they were also accorded the Battle Honour of 'Turtuk 1971'. Little over a decade later, in 1983; Ladakh Scouts were reorganized into Headquarters Ladakh Scouts based at Phyang along with Indus Wing at Karu and Karakoram Wing located at Partapur.

Ladakh Scouts were among the pioneers when formidable heights were occupied in the Siachen Glacier region in 1984; they were the first ones to get inducted there. Havildar Chhering Mutup of the force was awarded Ashok Chakra in this area; for his exceptional gallantry. Many posts of Siachen, now manned by Indian forces owe their initial occupation to the brave soldiers of Ladakh Scouts.

In the Operation Vijay also; which lasted for over two months from May to July 1999; Ladakh Scouts participated actively. In fact, the first success was achieved by them on 30th May 1999 in area called Rockfall, under the command of Major Sonam Wangchuk. He was awarded a Maha Vir Chakra for his bravery in this action. These troops operated very effectively in the Chorbat La area; thwarting intrusions and pushing back enemy from tactically important features in the region and across the watershed. The troops from the two wings were mixed and often operated in hazards terrain and difficult battle conditions. In these engagements, they were awarded one Maha Vir Chakra; six Vir Chakras; fifteen Sena Medals and fifteen Yudh Seva Medals. In addition, Battle Honour 'Batalik' and Theatre Honour 'Kargil' was conferred on the Ladakh Scouts. Consequent to and in recognition of the valiant actions and courageous display of bravery during these operations; the Government of India decided to restructure this unit into a regular Infantry regiment. Thus in the year 2000, its Headquarters at Phyang was named Ladakh Scouts Regimental Centre. First and second battalions of Ladakh Scouts originated out of Karakoram Wing; whereas third and fourth battalions of Ladakh Scouts were raised out of Indus Wing. The fifth battalion was added to this number, a year later.

Ladakh Scouts is one of the most decorated regiments of the Indian army; in spite of coming so late on the scene. It has garnered a tally of 605 Gallantry and Distinguished Service Awards; which include one Ashok Chakra, three Param Vishisht Seva Medals, ten Maha Vir Chakras (including one Bar), twenty six Vir Chakras and seventy five Sena Medals. Their achievements in the field of Mountaineering are also impressive and entail the scaling of peaks like Kanchenjunga (1977), Saser Kangri (1979 and 1987) and Mamostong Kangri (1988). During first decade of the next century; the men of Ladakh Scouts reached the top of many well known peaks including Mount Everest.

Their famous Battle Cry of KI KI SO SO LHARGYALO (Victory to God); reflects the collective faith and determination of the regiment. General V.P. Malik, the Army Chief in 1999 mentioned about these troops as, "The Ladakh Scouts acquitted themselves with an inspiring tenacity of purpose and indomitable courage and played a stellar role in the Batalik Sector… In recognition of the outstanding valour of their men and their sterling performance, the Ladakh Scouts were awarded the Unit Citation and, later, in a special ceremony at Leh, I presented them with the Chief of Army Staff Banner. I also approved their request to recognize the Ladakh Scouts as a full-fledged regiment of the Indian Army and put them at par with all infantry regiments of the Indian Army."[6]

In the years and decades to come; it is expected that the Ladakh Scouts would add further laurels to their already formidable list of achievements.

The Kargil War of 1999

The next few paragraphs take a brief and broad overview of the 1999 Indo-Pak war: fought primarily in Kargil and some parts of Leh districts. Much has already been written about various aspects of these operations

6 General V.P. Malik, *KARGIL,* HarperCollins Publishers India, New Delhi, 2006, p. 203.

and almost all details stand extensively covered. Here is not an attempt to critically analyze the happenings before, during and after the conflict of 1999. But, these events taking place virtually at end of the century in Ladakh; are too important for the region to be missed without comments. Hence some mention need be made.

At the outset; it is significant to remember that no part of the predominantly Shia population of Kargil district supported the game plan of Pakistan, nor Pakistan ever succeeded in clandestinely making inroads into Kargil. The people there have steadfastly remained uncooperative with the ISI and its militant organizations. If anything, the colonial type of rule imposed by Pakistan government on the people of Northern Areas alienated the Kargil population even more. The pattern of Pak troops' infiltration across the Line of Control in this sector and occupation of some positions clearly indicate that they entered our area in such a manner so as to deliberately avoid any contact with the local people.

In most of the accounts pertaining to this period; one finds that not much has been written about travails of the local population as well as the problems faced by the civil administration and their exertions during this difficult and trying period. It is generally believed that the problems for people and administration there started with the unprovoked military adventure of Pakistan in May 1999. But, the difficulties in Kargil actually began almost two years earlier. It was on 13th April 1997 that Pakistanis shelled Kargil town for two hours creating large scale fear and scare amongst the local population. Then after a gap of six months this aggravation was repeated on 28th September. But the next day, things really became desperate when within a span of two hours, between two and four p.m., almost sixty shells landed in the town resulting in the death of ten persons and inflicting injuries on thirteen others. This practically turned Kargil into a ghost town; seriously disrupted the functioning of civil administration and put an unbearable burden on the already overloaded medical services. The seriously injured patients were managed and operated upon with the active assistance of the army doctors and by sharing their facilities. This shelling continued intermittently through the whole of 1998 targeting the Kargil town and parts of the Srinagar – Leh national highway in the Drass sector. Some segments of this road around Drass were visible to the enemy and it brought down fairly accurate artillery fire on the vehicles moving there, thus seriously disrupting the winter stocking, troops movement and regular maintenance of the Indian Army in the entire Ladakh sector.

During the winter months, corresponding roughly with the period between November 1998 and February 1999 there was respite from the Pakistani shelling. This period the district administration utilized to tie up loose ends and further increase its preparedness to meet unforeseen situations. Even though at this stage nobody could predict the exact nature of Pakistani mischief as it later unfolded, but one thing was certain that the dreaded shelling would be resumed with nauseating regularity during the summer of 1999. By March that year the Deputy Commissioner's office was shifted from its regular location at Baroo, about two kilometers from the town, to Suru View Hotel in Kargil. This served twin purposes. It was now much closer to the population of the district headquarters and was also at a safer place; being located in the shadow portion of the town, as viewed from the Pakistani side. Assured of safety everyone could work there in peace. However, this arrangement was not to last long.

Towards the end of April the regularity and intensity of Pakistani shelling increased to a menacing level making the Deputy Commissioner to think about moving his headquarters, once again, to a totally safe and yet not very far away location from the town. About ten kilometers south of Kargil, down the Suru valley, a 50 MW Hydel project was under initial stages of construction at Chutuk village and some office as well as residential units had been completed by the project management. He now decided to shift the important components of the district administration, including his office, to Chutuk. That is where the entire set up remained till the situation stabilized in the whole district. He also ordered moving of the civil hospital from the centre of Kargil town to the TB hospital premises at Titichumik, couple of kilometers to the south. Thus as the things began hotting up in Drass and Batalik sectors as well as in Kargil town during the month of May; prominent constituents of the district administration, including medical facilities, had been very sensibly and with appreciable foresight, shifted to much safer locations from where these could function unmolested and without much disturbance.

It is now evident that Pak Army regulars, along with some elements of Lashkar-e-Toiba and Hizb-ul-Mujahideen were responsible for crossing the LoC and occupying important heights as well as areas of tactical importance right from Mushkoh valley in Drass to Chorbat La in Batalik and beyond to Turtuk in the north. The exact timing of this ingress and preparation of defences in each location is still not precisely determined; one can safely premise that this was managed during the autumn of 1998 and the spring of 1999. The infiltration appears to have taken place in two phases. The first and the deliberate one must have commenced sometime during the summer of 1998 and culminated in preparation of regular defences, stocking and arrangements for occupation of these new posts during long and harsh winter. In the next phase; the intruders either took possession of some of the Indian positions un-held during the winter months before these could be re-occupied by our troops as per established routine, or moved forward and laterally from the prepared defences to enlarge the arc of infiltration. Even by the beginning of May 1999, when our forces on the ground became aware of the broad contours of Pak designs and the situation was pretty serious and grim, from the Indian point of view, the extent of Pakistani ingress had not been fully realized. By the middle of May, the army was discovering fresh Pakistani held positions on an alarmingly regular basis spanning the entire Kargil sector.

Over the years many accounts, especially from the Indian side have been published which give a fairly accurate account of the force levels employed and the conduct of military operations. In this context, a special mention can be made of the book "*Kargil: Turning the Tide*" authored by Lt. Gen. Mohinder Puri, PVSM, UYSM (Retd) who was then commanding 8 Mountain Division there and gives a first-hand account of the war. The Pak manpower in this sector appeared to be about eleven battalions comprising elements of regular army, Northern Light Infantry units, SSG troops and militants of different outfits. The Indian Army also reportedly deployed 300 Artillery pieces, including 100 Bofor guns. The Air Force logged 550 strike missions, 150 reconnaissance missions and 500 escort missions. In addition 2185 helicopter sorties were also put into operations. The cost of the conflict in monetary terms for India has been projected as 1100 crores. In terms of manpower, the most precious national resource, Indian losses were 527 all ranks killed and 1363 wounded. Pakistani casualties were estimated to be 1042 killed (Indian estimates); Pakistani official figure being 453 killed.[7]

The American pressure, wide spread condemnation from the world community including China, coupled with Indian forces increasingly

7 www.wikipedia.org/wiki/Kargil War #Casualties. Accessed on 24 May 2016.

gaining an upper hand on ground, forced the Pakistani army to start withdrawing its elements from middle of July and fully vacate the Indian territory before the end of the month. "Operation Vijay" was declared a success by the Indian Prime Minister.

Notwithstanding the advantage of initial surprise gained by the other side, it goes to the credit of Indian army that after the details of infiltration became apparent and seriousness of the incursion evident; it reacted swiftly and decisively, without taking any more chances. According to an estimate almost five additional brigades were moved into the area of conflict, almost post-haste, along with sufficient artillery components. The logistics for such a large scale movement and maintenance thereafter were also managed competently.

The entire operations have been neatly condensed as, "...The middle of June was most anxious period of the war and possibly the closest when we came to enlarging the conflict area...Most of the credit for victory in Kargil, quite deservedly, goes to the bravery and dedication shown on the battlefield by soldiers and young officers. They were upfront, not hesitating to make any sacrifice to uphold the regimental and national pride and dignity. On the basis of great determination, high morale and brilliant junior leadership, our troops performed superbly. There were countless acts of gallantry, displays of steely resilience, single-minded devotion to duty and tremendous sacrifices."[8]

Overall handling of the problem and emerging scenarios, both at military as well as the political levels also came under criticism. The accomplished commentators ranged from senior retired army officers to noted journalists and experts on security related matters. One knowledgeable opinion succinctly described the Pakistani game plan as, "Pakistan relied primarily on troops from the Northern Light Infantry because soldiers from this regiment are mostly young local men from the mountainous regions of Skardu, POK, Baltistan, Gilgit and the North West Frontier Province. They are fully acclimatized to military activities at high altitudes. They were ordered to shed their uniforms, put on *salwar kameez,* grow beards and wear skull caps...Most of the military operations were carried out by regular Pakistani officers and soldiers...The Force Commander Northern Areas (FCNA) and the higher command of the 10

8 Op. cit. 5, pp. 146 and 155.

Corps of the Pakistan Army provided command and control and back up for the military operation."[9]

However, one year after the Kargil episode, in June 2000 a series of write-ups appeared in the Pakistani print media. Some of them made scathing criticism of the handling of Kargil operations and also asked for a comprehensive inquiry into various aspects of the debacle; including role of the army there. Two representative samples are reproduced. "The Kargil story begins in the September of 1998. Brigadier Surinder Singh of 121 Infantry Brigade had ordered, as has been the usual routine, his troops to descend from the heights of Kargil. Every winter, half a dozen battalions of Indian troops came down leaving behind some ten dozen well-stocked posts.....On the other side of the LC, it was going to be a busy winter. The force commander (Northern Areas), headquartered in Gilgit, commanding Pakistan's NLI; along with his superior the commander of 10 Corps in Rawalpindi, had set their eyes on unheld Indian posts around eight kilometers across the LC. In October 1998, by the time the withdrawal of Indian troops was complete, there was a change in command at the Pakistan Army. General Jehangir Karamat had to go and Lieutenant General Pervez Musharraf took over as the new Chief of the Army Staff... General Musharraf visited the Northern Areas twice during the winter of 1998-99....People in the know must have included the COAS, commander 10 Corps, the Force Commander Northern Areas and DG ISI...Pakistan's aim behind Kargil was to 'Internationalize the Kashmir issue'. It backfired both internationally and domestically. The entire civilized world took it as an act of 'aggression'. Even China told Pakistan to back off. Within the Pakistan Army it proved to be highly divisive. Young army officers felt deeply betrayed."[10] On the same day demand for an inquiry was made in Dawn as, "There has almost been a universal demand for an inquiry commission to investigate the Kargil venture and this should be accepted. We have had too many convulsive happenings in our history left unexplained, most notably the fall of East Pakistan and the Ojhri Camp disaster. A beginning should be made."[11]

A very scathing condemnation was made by Lt. Gen. Shahid Aziz (Retd), a former Corps Commander of Pakistan army, as "Kargil, like

9 J.N. Dixit in Indian Express dated 22nd July, 1999.

10 Farrukh Saleem in an article in NEWS dated 18th June 2000.

11 Lahori in DAWN dated 18th June 2000.

every other meaningless war that we have fought, brings home lessons we continue to refuse to learn. Instead, we proudly call it our history written in the blood of our children. Indeed, our children penning down our misdeeds with their blood! Medals for some, few songs, a cross road renamed, and of course annual remembrance day and a memorial for those who sacrificed their tomorrow for our today; thus preparing more war fodder for our continuing misadventures…" He further graphically described the Kargil combat in the following words, "An unsound military plan based on invalid assumptions, launched with little preparations and in total disregard to the regional and international environment, was bound to fail."[12]

Two eminent former officers of the Indian Army have thus commented on these operations, "The war in Kargil will go down in the history of India as a saga of unmatched bravery, grit and determination displayed on the battlefield by the Indian Army; a symbol of great pride and inspiration."[13] The second one mentions, "The Indian soldier asks for very little and is prepared to give his all in the cause of duty, for his officers and comrades and for his battalion, whose colours he so proudly serves. The casualty figures speak for themselves. No country could have asked more of its soldiers and no soldier could have given more for his country than those who fought and died or survived severe wounding, than those who fought in the Kargil Heights in 1999… Kargil, with its intense cold and treacherous terrain, the demands it made on every last ounce of strength and will power, mountaineering skill and courage, was perhaps the greatest challenge the Indian soldier has had to face in recent times. A legacy of great gallantry and devotion to duty has been left behind, which future generation of soldiers will be hard-pressed to surpass."[14]

The 1999 war was the last major event of the twentieth century in Ladakh. This was the fourth time since Independence that Pakistan started a war with India. The other side, though, had the initial advantage due to gaps in intelligence and less than adequate surveillance at the local level; but the Indian army reacted swiftly and wrested the initiative soon

12 The Nation, 6th January 2013. This article is also available in the Blog of Gen. Aziz at: "gen-azizshahid.blogspot.com".

13 Op. cit. 5, p.9.

14 Amarinder Singh, *A Ridge Too Far,* Motibagh Palace, Patiala, 2001, pp. xxiv and 231.

and thereafter called the shots. Both, militarily as also diplomatically Pakistan was chastened and its lies exposed before the world; including its operational and strategic weaknesses.

Op-Sadhbhavna and Army – Civil Relations

After the 1999 operations; various army units posted in Ladakh undertook different activities to help the local population. Credit for introducing this concept of 'Sadhbhavna works' belongs to Lt. Gen. Arjun Ray, who was posted as the first commander of newly raised 14 Corps. Headquarters of this Corps, which came into being just after the war, was based in Leh and it controlled all units located in Ladakh. During the mid-nineties this officer – Arjun Ray, then as a Brigadier – was posted as BGS, a high ranking staff officer in the Srinagar based Chinar Corps; which at that time commanded all the troops in Valley as well as Ladakh. That is where he had come to acquire the first hand knowledge of this formulation and its efficacy. The Sadbhavna works were started in early nineties in the Valley; and it produced encouraging results. According to one of the erstwhile commanders of the Chinar Corps; the philosophy of this concept is, "Sadbhavna is not a tactical or strategic manoeuvre by the Indian Army. Rather, it is a resolve by men in uniform to come closer to the populace and develop a bond of mutual faith and trust which a soldier enjoys across the country. As people realize the futility of an unrest which has given nothing more than misery to them, the Army has successfully ventured into a more humane domain of Winning Hearts and Minds through a simple yet challenging military civic action."

In the post Kargil conflict period; various units of the 14 Corps undertook substantial developmental works in the entire Ladakh region. Gen. Arjun Ray was quite impressed with the whole hearted support of the people of Kargil to the military operations against the intruding enemy; therefore a large number of Sadbhavna works were carried out in that district during his tenure. Under the Operation Sadbhavna many initiatives were started which yielded good results; although the priority areas were primary education, health care, community development, information technology and empowerment of women. According to a published report, "In health care, the Unit medical officers visit villages and move house to house checking patients, who are either too sick to come to a central place or are too shy to be seen by a doctor at a place other than their own house... Patients requiring special medical attention are referred to the field surgical centers or to the General hospital at Leh. For major surgeries and for other complex treatment, the patients are flown to the Army Hospital at Chandimandir or to the PGI Chandigarh at the army's expense."[15]

According to this journal, the Deputy Commissioner, Leh observed "With genuine care and concern, the Army has nursed the development of this region". Thus, the military participation in the issues of importance to the local population certainly resulted in building the rapport between the people and army to serve multiple purposes.

The relationship between army and the civil population in Ladakh has always been cordial and warm; an example to be emulated in other parts of the country. This aspect was comprehensively elucidated by Kalon Sahib as "Our relationship with the army is not limited to providing troops a cup of tea which one finds in other places; but is based on much deeper bond where both the local population as well as the army play complimentary role in the functioning and existence of each other. We co-exist with mutual love and affection. There has never been any bad blood with the local population and the army right from 1947 onwards."[16] A seamless bond amongst these two entities has been built and nurtured over many decades to the mutual benefit of both sides.

In August 1989, when the communal situation had taken an alarming nose-dive in Ladakh; the state government had deputed a seasoned and senior IAS officer there for an on the spot study of the developing grim situation. Shri S.S. Rizvi, spent four days from 8th August 1989 in Leh. He knew the entire area, as also the local dynamics, very well; having been the Development Commissioner of unified Ladakh district during 1978-79. On his return to Srinagar, he filed a detailed report of the situation to the government. In this appraisal he made an almost prophetic recommendation as, "…5. Granting of divisional status to Ladakh area, with the appointment of a Divisional Commissioner and DIG Police. This would restore the integrity of the Ladakh area which was broken by the division of the old Ladakh district into the districts of Leh and Kargil." In the last Para of his overall evaluation; he proffered sage advice to the policy makers which remain strikingly relevant even at present. He mentioned, "The basic problem in Leh appears to be the perception that the legitimate aspirations

15 *Epilogue*, Jammu, November 2007, p.26.

16 Interaction with Rigzin Namgyal Kalon in September 1998.

of the area, in which Buddhist aspirations are the critical element, are not being met. The Buddhists are a small minority in the State – less than one lakh in a population of over 60 lakhs. Their sense of disadvantage is also heightened by the fact that they live in inhospitable climatic conditions and in an area which is difficult to access by road, since the only road-link with the rest of the State crosses the Zoji-La which remains snow bound for about six months of the year. The people of the area have for long had a sense of neglect. It is important that this sense of neglect and their sense of being thwarted in meeting their aspirations be assuaged. This has to be done keeping in view the changing social, economic and political balance between the Buddhist and Muslim communities, analyzed above. Political action has to be taken in such manner that the two communities are enabled to adopt wise counsel and make such accommodation as will give satisfaction to both. Unless this kind of accommodation is made mutually by both communities, communal peace and sanity on a sustained basis may be impossible to achieve."

The division of Ladakh region into two districts of Kargil and Leh in 1979, did adversely impact on the homogeneity of the area. These fissures have acquired greater prominence over the years; more particularly due to lack of meaningful efforts on the part of political and community leaders. The gap created by this separation of districts was further accentuated by political movements of late eighties and early nineties. The declaration of ST status and LAHDC by the government did give considerable advantages to the general people; but the schism which developed in 1979 turned into greater mistrust, suspicion and differences over the years; more so as the two entities moved forward on community lines. A perceptive local observer comprehensively summarized this milieu in the following words, "…It is unfortunate but a fact that differences still persist between the twin districts and yet none of the two seem ready at first to approach the other so as to reconcile the differences and reach at a common understanding. A provision for Inter-District Advisory Council is there in the Chapter IX of the LAHDC act 1995 but no such council was constituted till date. The provision was meant for resolving such political discordances and such an arrangement is much needed at this juncture. The time has come when the rationality over emotion, commonality over differences and community interest over individual interest must prevail in both the districts."[17]

17 Sonam Angmo, *Daily Excelsior*, Jammu, 13th August 2019.

The planned as also visible development of the region; more so in the last three decades of the twentieth century created its own dynamics; including some with unintended consequences. The emergence of Leh and Kargil as twin and main growth centers of the region further accentuated the developing socio-economic scenario. This resulted in the phenomenon of considerable rural to urban migration creating immense pressures on all the expanding urban hubs like Leh, Diskit, Kargil and Padam. Smaller towns of the region, for example, Darbuk, Nyoma, Khaltsi, Sankoo and Dras were just a step behind. This on one side resulted into an unplanned growth of these places and, on the other, exerted tremendous strain on the limited civic facilities available. This trend has continued unabated since the 70s and would prove to be a significant challenge to the urban planners in the decades to come.

Particularly 1970s onwards; an increasing number of educated locals came to occupy important and key positions in the district administration. They also proved an inspiration to the following lineage of youth, leading to an increasing number of people going in for higher and technical education. The generation in Ladakh in the post-independence India – more so two decades thereafter – can be termed as a bridge between the old Ladakh, lost in time, and the new, vibrant region. Ladakh has considerably benefitted from cross cultural current, facilitated by the modern communication links established between this area and the outside world. It would not be off the mark to collectively call these pioneers as the "bridging generation" between locals, the country and the world. Since Ladakh got linked by road and air with rest of India; the people of this region have learnt to integrate modern with the traditional, very imaginatively. Hopefully, this happy trend continues; even though it is really a tall order.

The region is well connected by road and air at present. New developments are taking place almost regularly; thereby enriching the area incrementally. The challenges are certainly huge and somewhat problematic; more so due to Ladakh's remoteness, difficult accessibility as also environmental constraints.

CHAPTER IX

Post-Script

The LAHDC Kargil constituted in 2003

After the promulgation of LAHDC Act in the middle of 1995 and election to the Council, held under it for Leh district in September the same year; nothing much of significance happened in Ladakh in the field of socio-political evolution. The ground situation there remained almost unchanged during the remaining years of the last decade of the century. Of course, the 1999 Indo-Pak war did take place in Ladakh; but that episode belongs to a different category. On the political front though; a lot happened at the state level. The elections to the State Assembly were successfully conducted in Sept-Oct 1996; almost four months after holding efficacious parliamentary polls in the state. This saw the end of over six years of Governor / President's rule in J&K and return of a popular government at the head of administration. In this election the National Conference easily formed the State Government, headed by Dr. Farooq Abdullah as the Chief Minister. The party won a total of 57 seats; narrowly missing the two third majority in a house of 87 MLAs. More importantly; it emerged as the single largest party in the Assembly in all three regions of the state. In Ladakh, it won three out of four seats; that of Kargil, Zanskar and Nubra; conceding only the Leh constituency to the Congress candidate. However, notwithstanding a resounding popular mandate in all segments of the state; the government did nothing to benefit this region or take steps to befriend the Ladakhis. If anything; the people in power tried to put roadblocks in the smooth functioning of LAHDC Leh; which needed not only their support but also hand holding during the initial years of this experiment. The state government also failed to conduct the council elections and put in place the LAHDC Kargil; even though the same was mandated in the Act.

After six years, the normal life of the House, State Assembly elections were held in Sept – Oct 2002. It threw up surprising results; with the ruling National Conference failing to cross the majority line. In fact it fell quite short of the halfway figure of forty-four. The results of main political parties – including the newly formed Peoples Democratic Party (PDP) of Mufti Sayeed – were; National Conference – 28 seats, followed by Congress bagging 20 and PDP registering victory in 16 constituencies. In the rest; other parties and Independents were declared winners. This hung Assembly led to considerable political activity and discussions between various political groups. By the end of October that year; the Congress and PDP hammered together an agreement to form a coalition government – heading the state administration for three years in turn; with the support of Panthers Party; the CPM; some Independent and other members. For the first three years; leadership of the establishment was to be headed by Mufti Sayeed of PDP. The people in power – both at political as also administrative levels – took the initiative to reach out to the Ladakh region. This certainly was a refreshing change to the local population. The administration headed by Mufti Sayeed opened a process of dialogue – at different levels - with the opinion leaders of Kargil and persuaded them to actively participate in the local elections to the Council there. On 10th July 2003, elections to the first LAHDC Kargil were held and swearing in of the Councilors took place on 9th August 2003. So, with these events happening; the LAHDC Kargil was duly constituted. Establishing the Kargil Council was not as showy and elaborate affair as its Leh counterpart eight years ago. All the same, it provided a valuable lesson to the people of Kargil in the sphere of local self-government and accelerated the process of developmental activities in the district. Also, the local population there realized importance of the decentralization of planning and implementation process. The Mufti government also delegated additional and sorely needed powers to the two bodies; to make these more effective on ground, as well as to further facilitate their functioning. In addition; the state government also issued orders granting the status of a cabinet minister to the CEC of the Council and that of a minister of state to each of the Executive Councilors. In comprehensive terms; actions of the Mufti government were to make friends with the Ladakhis; without making any distinction of religion or political affiliations. For the first time in decades;

the local population felt that they had an active voice at the highest levels in the state. Also there was one cabinet minister from Ladakh in the state government.

Since then the elections to both the LAHDCs have been held at the mandated regular intervals. In the year 2013; two students of JNU New Delhi – one each belonging to Leh and Kargil districts – made quite insightful observations on this system of governance. These included, "…Initiatives of the Hill Councils have been hailed across the nation. Leaders of national and regional political parties which have their presence in Ladakh cite the LAHDC as the best example of local governance…also appreciate the effectiveness and efficiency of the LAHDC and the level of transparency in Ladakhi society…Ladakh has a distinct identity, cultural heritage, ancestral knowledge and wisdom to be preserved…"[1] In a similar vein another speaker mentioned, "…The first general election for the LAHDC Kargil took place in the year of 2003…It was again a struggle for power between the traditional religious and political elites and not among the common people…The second election took place in 2008… In comparing these two election results, we find that the prevalent traditional power structure were further strengthening and exerting itself more strongly…The social progress and success of democracy can be measured in terms of its representation of the underprivileged. Sadly, women form a huge section of this group of the society and the under representation of women in these structures speaks volumes about the existing patriarchal, feudal value system prevalent in the society. LAHDC is a case in such a scenario…"[2]

However, the term of this friendly dispensation ended in October 2005; when the headship of the state structures passed on to the Congress nominee. Unfortunately, this successive administration reverted to the old policies of neglecting the Ladakh region. Consequently, disillusionment and disaffection was back in the local circles. The first major sign of the changing times became evident in 2007, with the formation of Ladakh Union Territory Front (LUTF) headed by Thupstan Chhewang. This outfit started organizing and mobilizing people for its demand of a Union Territory status for Ladakh region. It was not difficult, politically, to reach

1 Tsewang Rigzin, a student of JNU, presenting his paper in a seminar organized by IPCS, in New Delhi on 1st Febuary 2013.

2 Fayaz Ahmad from Kargil. Rest of details are same as above.

out to people at the grassroots level; as this issue had been kept alive for the past six decades. Almost by virtue of a 'ripple effect'; support for this demand was mobilized. Fortunately, the assertions, gatherings and symbolisms of the LUTF activities did not have any communal overtones. The leaders of this undertaking, at no stage did or said anything against the national grain on this issue. Perhaps that is what kept it alive and gave strength. After the LUTF came into being; this region was convulsed by different developments and minor agitations for the next over one decade. Ultimately, on 5th August 2019; things got changed irrevocably when Ladakh was declared a Union Territory. In a way, it was the culmination of a seventy year old demand raised for the first time in May 1949; when the Ladakhi deputation called on Prime Minister Nehru in New Delhi.

Ladakh Vision 2025 – a document made in the year 2005

Encouraged by, and in the wake of, Ladakh centric friendly policies of the Mufti Sayeed government towards this region; the LAHDC Leh prepared an exhaustive twenty-year plan for overall development of the region. This paper, put together in the middle of 2005, was titled "Ladakh Vision – 2025". The main reason for undertaking this detailed exercise has been mentioned therein as, "Ladakh is a society in transition. Isolated from the rest of the world for much of its existence before it was thrown open to mass tourism in the mid-1970s, the region is caught in a whirlwind of change today. As the new lifestyles, practices and social mores enter the Ladakhi community against a backdrop of centuries' old indigenous traditions and culture, uncertainty and confusion reign supreme in the minds of the region's local populace. To remedy this situation, there is a need to evolve a framework…." (page – i).

This document was unveiled for thread bare discussions in a "Two Day Consultative Workshop" organized in one of the big and well furnished halls of the Sher-e-Kashmir International Convention Complex (SKICC), Srinagar, on 9th and 10th May 2005. It had four technical sessions, to deliberate in detail the various issues raised therein, by experts on the subjects – in addition to the Inauguration and Valedictory functions. The Inaugural ceremony was certainly the main attraction of this gathering and it was addressed by four important ministers of the state; namely Rigzin Jora – belonging to Leh – Minister Science & Technology; Muzaffar Hussain Beigh, Minister Finance / Planning & Ladakh Affairs; Pt. Mangat Ram Sharma, Deputy Chief Minister and the Chief Minister

Mufti Sayeed. The Valedictory session was attended, among others, by the Chief Secretary of the state who himself had been a former Development Commissioner of Ladakh. The state government promised all help in the implementation of the main contours of this plan and issues raised during the technical discussions.

In the Vision paper; impassioned plea was made on two important counts. The first referred to the need to evolve a frame work which facilitates Ladakhi people to seamlessly integrate the old with the new. The second reason alluded to the rapid decline in the region's natural resources in the recent past and thus the need to halt any further deterioration by developing a suitable set of preventive measure. It further stated, "... Isolated from the rest of the world till as little as forty years ago, Ladakh today faces unprecedented challenges to reinvent itself and its traditional society, so as to better fit into the mosaic of the modern world. At the same time, it has a need to retain its unique identity by keeping alive the essence of the traditions and culture that were passed down to it by the earliest generations of Ladakhis. A fine balancing act is therefore required, and it will not be possible to achieve it without first putting down all that needs to be done. A Vision is thus imperative... Ladakh's fragile ecology has also been under tremendous strain in recent years... the original inhabitants of this region lived in perfect harmony with their surroundings and espoused a lifestyle based on contentment and sustainability. If we do not take urgent steps to remedy the situation then it may soon be too late. For this reason too, a Vision becomes essential for Ladakh today." (page-1 of 67). In addition; an appeal was made to the state government for enhanced resource allocations; after working out the details for implementations of various points mentioned in the Vision Document.

Apart from other things; the paper forcefully pushed for four major subject matters. The first one pertained to land based economy and comprised agriculture, horticulture, livestock and allied sectors; the emphasis being on attaining internal self sufficiency in food and related items. It also highlighted the need to conserve water resources of Ladakh for drinking as well as for irrigation facilities. Simultaneously, stress was laid on the conservation and protection from pollution of this important asset – of water - for the region. Also, keeping in view the peculiarities; lay of the land including vast, barren and sun-drenched tracks of Ladakh; considerable stress was laid on meeting the local power and energy demands by following a strategy which gave due weight to conservation and renewable technology. The fourth point referred to the Conservation of Natural Resources – and has been well mentioned therein as, "Despite being a resource challenged region, Ladakh is home to a rich and diverse ecology. Unfortunately, Ladakh's precious natural heritage has been facing severe pressures in recent times, mostly at the hands of unaware individuals or, worse still, people that knowingly harm the environment for shortsighted monetary gains. The need of the hour is to educate people, introduce appropriate legislation, and lay due emphasis on the use of renewable energy in the region. (page-iv)."

This report comprehensively dealt with twelve major aggregations of issues confronting the entire area. These were grouped under the headings of Land Based Economy; Information Technology; Small Scale & Cottage Industries; Tourism; Urban and Rural Infrastructure; Water Resources; Power & Energy; Health & Environment; Education; Conservation of Natural resources; Social & Cultural Values and Micro Level Planning & Governance. To get a compact and overall flair of these topics; it would be useful to go through some of the more significant views expressed in the Vision paper. These representative samples include, "Ladakh is getting excessively reliant on the outside world for critical needs such as food…If things are not remedied soon, Ladakh may find itself in dire straits."(page-3 of 67); "The IT sector enjoys a place unlike any other in the modern world. Ladakh would do well to stay in step with developments in the IT sector." (p-8); "To connect tourists to the unique cultural heritage of Ladakh without endangering its fragile eco-system, while at the same time scaling up tourism to contribute to the economic and social well being of the people of this region." (p-14); "Rural Ladakh is the real face of Ladakh. There has been a massive rural-urban migration pattern in Ladakh in recent times. It is of the utmost importance to arrest this pattern; since the very survival of Ladakh's traditional lifestyle depends on it." (p-25); "To transform Ladakh from an energy deficient to an energy surplus region and supply the local population with reliable, affordable and quality power, by tapping renewable energy sources available in the region to the maximum possible advantage." (p-35); "Education has a critical role to play in the development of any society. In Ladakh, the importance of education is even more marked because it was a neglected sector in the region for many years before the authorities finally woke up to its importance. There is therefore a need to make up for the lost time." (p-

41); "Despite its remoteness, harsh climatic conditions and aridity, Ladakh is endowed with unique resources: boundless solar energy, clean air and water, a rich diversity of wild and domesticated plants and animals, vibrant cultures and indigenous knowledge. The wise use of these resources and the generally healthy state of the environment are the main legacy of the people of Ladakh over centuries." (p-45); "It is of the greatest importance that we try and arrest this decline in the social and cultural heritage of Ladakh, if the region is to retain its original identity. The preservation of traditional values systems, revival of ancient cultural practices and greater support at the institutional level for social and cultural issues are some of the measures that need to be taken in this regard."(p-50); and "It was in 1995 that the LAHDC Act came into existence in the Leh district. This event marked a watershed in the history of development planning in the J&K State, as for the first time the power to set development priorities and approve plans in accordance with them had been devolved to a district-level elected body. In recent times, the constitution of Halqa Panchayats in Ladakh is another breakthrough in the devolution of the planning process further down to the grass root level. The challenge today is to evolve effective mechanisms for dovetailing the LAHDC and Panchayati institutions in Ladakh. Legislative measures to bring these two lobbies together need to be evolved. Perhaps most importantly, the political will to usher in these changes is required." (page- 54 of 67).

Even though the proceedings were conducted by the CEC of LAHDC, Leh, Rigzin Spalbar, and his associates; it was well known in the administrative circles of the state that the entire two-day event carried the unmistakable stamp of Thupstan Chhewang; and the almost 75 pages long "Ladakh 2025 Vision Document" was inspired and its preparations guided by him. This, in fact, lays down the general direction and guidelines which may need to be followed in the development of Ladakh region; as also the possible pitfalls that should be avoided.

Quite a long time ago, in the summer of 1979, K.K.Nayyar – the Station Director of the then Radio Kashmir, Srinagar and a well known name in the broadcasting circles of the nation – visited Leh and recorded a long interview of the Development Commissioner Leh. During this interaction, he voiced his concerns aloud about the negative influences of the ever expanding tourism sector and that this phenomenon may ultimately have negative and unintended effects on the traditional Ladakhi life. The officer, at the other end, expressed his firm conviction that though the increasing activities in the tourism trade did have some negative fallout; he strongly believed that as a people the Ladakhi society was traditional at heart and would always retain their age-old customs, ethos and cultural values. Over two and half decades later, in the year 2005, this Vision Document – reflecting the combined wisdom and aspirations of the Ladakhi people – also emphasized the need for adopting a developmental strategy to seamlessly combine the twin requirements of material progress on the modern lines and retention of all that is good in the old and traditional system. It also indicated the direction in which the future advancement and growth should take place in that region.

Now that Ladakh has been made a separate Union Territory; the local administration – Lt. Governor downwards – would be well advised to give a good reading to this Vision Document, which provides a road map of comprehensive development of the region in quite a challenging environment. It covers almost all the sectors in which progress need be made in the area. The overall cost of this venture is going to be quite heavy and, with a limited population, it is not possible for this area to internally generate the required resources. Ladakh comprises a number of societies and groups; all having traditional set of survival mechanisms and skills which need to be preserved. The big challenge is to harmonize the seemingly opposites of traditional ethos and modern living. This arid and sparsely populated zone is no more the responsibility of the J&K administration; but needs to be now seen in the greater national perspective. After all, the very future of Ladakh is at stake.

In this context, it would be pertinent to quote Arun Joshi writing in The Tribune of 9th March 2020; who opined “The Indian nation is the only nation for them. The nation must now state this in the clearest of terms. And, now with the UT having become their destiny, they deserve special treatment – their terrain is tough, beyond the imagination of those who see Ladakh on the map. These are not just colours and graphics on the paper. They are real people with unique identity, and preserve unique identity with passion and its glaciers are the source of life for millions. That is what Ladakh is and promises to it should be honoured to instill extra confidence in the new system”.

Hydel Projects – Nimoo-Bazgo and Chutuk

The power scenario in Ladakh during the entire twentieth century has remained bleak; notwithstanding the much touted and publicized Hydel projects of Stakna in Leh district and Iqbal in Kargil district. The Stakna project with an installed capacity of two units of 2 Mega Watts each was commissioned in 1986; and Iqbal scheme went on stream, having three units with generating capacity of 1.25 MW each, in the year 1995. But, both these were frequently plagued with recurring technical problems and practically made very little difference in providing assured electric supply to the local consumers; who continued to depend on the diesel generation to light up their houses. From 1960s onwards; the residents of important towns in Ladakh were used to getting few hours of power supply in the evenings, purely for lighting purposes, through the locally installed diesel generators. It was a very costly affair for the government as the running cost of diesel based electricity was heavily subsidized and only low, fixed charges levied on the consumers. In addition, winter stocking of this commodity also had to be arranged by the administration; making the whole operation messy, not very dependable and costly. At its peak; the biggest generating station was for Leh with an installed capacity of one MW and smaller sets – with varying generation potential – were established at locations like Kargil, Dras, Sankoo, Khaltsi, Nyoma and Diskit etc.

However, the power sector in Ladakh received a real stabilizing boost in the second decade of 21st century; with two major Hydel projects in the region going on stream; and providing great relief to the common man. The first one was named Chutuk project. With an installed capacity of four units of 11 MW each; it was fully commissioned in 2013. The barrage of this scheme is located upstream at Sarze village and the powerhouse made on the right bank of Suru River, near Chutuk village – and hence the name. The powerhouse is located underground at the end of a 10.02 kilometer long head race tunnel. The generation during winter season, comes down to as low as 8 MW. This drop is due to the decreased discharge of Suru in cold weather and the provisions of the Indus Water Treaty (IWT); which allows only 'run of the river' schemes on Indus and its tributaries and prohibits building of storage dams there.

Another major power project in the area is named Nimoo-Bazgo hydel scheme; in Leh district with installed capacity of three units of 15

MW each. It is also a 'run of the river' power project on Indus River, situated near the Alchi village; involving construction of a 187 ft concrete wall across the river, without any storage facility, to comply with the stipulations of IWT. This project has a firm capacity of around 20 MWs due to decreased discharge in the river during winter months and also the IWT obligations. The Nimoo-Bazgo was inaugurated in 2014 and, along with Chutuk, has rightly been named as a major development plan in Ladakh.

Even though the firm generation capacities of these two hydel projects are sufficient, for the time being, to meet the electricity requirements of the locals already connected to the grid. But keeping in view enhanced demands of the future and increasing network of new lines and consumers; the long term solution lay only in connecting this region with the national grid and thus bring Ladakh on par with other parts of the country. This task was taken in hand by the Power Grid Corporation of India Limited (PGCIL). After years of sustained work the PGCIL was able to complete the 339.61 Kilometer long 220 KV line connecting Alusteng sub-station at Srinagar with GIS station at Leh. This important link passes through four sub-stations located at Dras, Kargil, Khaltsi and Leh. This connection with the national grid now enables easy evacuation of surplus power during the peak generation period of these projects; as also makes it possible for the PGCIL to dispatch requisite amount of electricity to Ladakh in the low generation winter months. As of now, all the High Transmission (HT) power lines follow the over ground route to Kargil and Leh; passing over some of the high and snow covered mountains. This can be tricky as also undependable during the cold season. Some experts believe that to make this part of the grid more secure and reliable; an alternative and additional underground transmission line could be laid which passes through the proposed Zojila tunnel; may be inside a special duct made for this purpose. In any case, this region getting connected with the national power grid is certainly a major development which is bound to play a significant role in the future prosperity of the entire belt.

The hydel power potential of Ladakh is indeed considerable and a detailed survey in this regard needs to be undertaken. No doubt due to the national obligations under the IWT; the Indus and its tributaries have a cap on their dormant power generation capabilities, particularly during the winter season when the water discharge in all water bodies gets reduced considerably. Even then, a series of 'run of the river' schemes can be planned and executed; wherever water currents facilitate such projects. During the summer months; when the generation is high and possibly more than the local consumption; the excess electricity can be siphoned to the national grid. Similarly, in the cold climate when production of power is low; any shortfall in demand of the region can be met by that much additional import.

In this background; the analogy of 1,000 MW Pakal Dul hydel project comes to mind. This scheme is located in the Kishatwar district of Jammu division; and it has a storage dam on a river that is tributary to the Chenab – the waters of which are allotted to Pakistan under the IWT. Notwithstanding objections of that country; India insists that this project is fully covered under the provisions of the Treaty and no clause of it is being violated. On the same premises; it needs to be seen if there is a similar possibility in any of the Ladakh rivers.

The future of micro-hydel systems is also bright in this region. The entire belt has a large number of streams – based on discharges of snow on the mountain tops – which come gurgling down the slopes to meet bigger rivers. Many of these are almost perennial in nature; and even if smaller projects are planned on them during the summer months, that much electricity would meet requirements of the areas around. The potential of few of such streams have been harnessed in the past; but in view of much larger generation capacities of Chutuk and Nimoo-Bazgo undertakings, this aspect is practically forgotten. There is certainly a need to revive interest in these programmes; and to remember that the earliest power generation project in Ladakh was a micro-hydel scheme located at Nurla village, few kilometers from Khaltsi towards Leh. It used to generate enough electricity, in the early 1960s, to meet lighting requirements of the people around - particularly those belonging to the nearby Timisgam village. The *Shaam* area of Leh and Nubra valley are eminently suited for this purpose.

Power Potential of Ladakh

In the years and decades to come; power scenario in this area has the potential of being very positive and optimistic. This would be particularly so when other sources of energy are increasingly exploited in the region; including immense potential of solar generation, fuller utilization of hydel capacity and possible capabilities of the geo-thermal and wind energies. The entire Ladakh is literally sitting over a huge potential and virtual treasure of solar energy – waiting to be harnessed. Solar power is about the conversion of energy from sunlight into electricity. This conversion takes place generally through the use of Photovoltaic cells. The technology for this purpose has been known to the scientists for over a century but the same has been prohibitively costly as compared to other sources of power generation. The unpredictable variations of the fossil fuels in the international market and the fast depletion of these resources; under the crust of the earth – including coal – spurred further research in the field of solar energy during the last few decades. This has lead to a further decrease in the cost of generation per unit; and solar power is increasingly becoming competitive with the same based on fossil fuels and coal etc. In addition, this is a low-carbon technology and also harnesses renewable energy from the sun – which is virtually inexhaustible. With more focused research across an increasing number of nations; the power scenario based on the solar energy is likely to become still cheaper as also have greater acceptability across the globe. Ladakh has two big advantages in this regard. It has huge tracts of uninhabited land and an average of 95 percent sunlit days in a year; even at the height of cold season when the lowest temperature varies between minus 20 to 40 degrees Celsius. Surprisingly, in the winter months all over the place, including highland areas, when the highest daytime thermometer reading is in the negative and the weather is shivering cold; it is bright and sunny from dawn to dusk. Ladakh and sunshine are almost synonymous. With these natural advantages, and more research in this field; it is not difficult to visualize a number of huge and inter-connected solar power generating stations in Ladakh, producing electricity for the local consumption as also siphoning off the excess production to rest of the country through the national power grid.

Apart from the hydel and solar based power potential; the region is also endowed with geo-thermal energy. Of course, this technology needs further fine-tuning in our country but it should be remembered that the area has at least three identified places where hot water is naturally available; even during the peak of winter. These locations are, Puga and Chumathang in Nyoma sub-division and Panamik in Nubra sub-division. The number of such locations is likely to increase - as also the extent of locked up energy under the upper crust of the earth – after a proper survey is taken in hand.

Many locals do believe, particularly the older lot, that Ladakh is literally sitting over a big deposit of geo-thermal energy waiting to be uncovered.

This region also boasts of considerable wind energy; particularly in some specified areas as also during certain periods. This resource too can be exploited for power generation and to give other benefits to the region. However, further investigations are required to work out the exact extent of this asset; the technology required and economics of such ventures.

For working out the correct policy mix and developmental strategy; it is important to realize that power is the most precious resource as also crucial for betterment of the entire region. Also, it is a great challenge to make available regular and affordable electric supply keeping in view remoteness of the region, scattered population and long distances involved. For this; more emphasis on renewable energy and decentralized systems of generation and distribution would be of considerable help. All this would need to be attempted keeping in mind the local environmental factors and the fragile eco-system of the area. In this regard, it would help to quote from the Ladakh 2025 Vision document; which at page–33, mentions "The way forward for Ladakh with respect to its power and energy requirements clearly lies in the field of renewable energy sources. The potential for solar and micro-hydel generated energy exists in abundance in Ladakh, and even geothermal and wind energy possibilities are present in certain pockets. These should be tapped to the maximum possible advantage. Other measures that could be adopted alongside to improve the power situation in Ladakh include the setting up of a decentralized power generation and distribution network, fostering a culture of energy conservation in Ladakh, and streamlining the administrative machinery looking after power in the region".

Connectivity to Ladakh

The connectivity to Ladakh, and importance for keeping the region accessible to vehicular traffic throughout the year, came into prominence during the 1999 war with Pakistan. Efforts are afoot to make this dream a reality. As of now, this region is connected with rest of the country along three axes. These being the traditional Manali-Leh and Srinagar-Leh routes and the, few years old, Tilel (also sometimes spelled as Tulail) to Dras link. The last one is about 120 kilometers long vehicular road constructed by the Border Roads Organization (BRO); and movement thereon is restricted to the army traffic only. In fact it is an extension to the already existing Srinagar-Bandipur-Gurez and Tilel route; which is used by army as well as civilian traffic. This axis, also like the other two, gets closed during the winter season due to heavy snowfall in the intervening two high passes. One is called the Razdhani Pass, located between Bandipur and Gurez and the other – Kaobal Gali – situated on way from Tilel enroute to Dras. Work is going apace on the other two connections to Leh; with a view to make further improvements in the riding surface and other road engineering aspects on these roads. Let the eastern link be examined first.

The Manali – Leh highway is about 490 kilometers long; of which 230 kms lie in Himachal Pradesh and the rest of 260 kms fall in Ladakh territory. It remains open, at an average, for four and half months from May or June to the middle of October. This road remains snow covered during winter months, because of four high passes enroute. Starting from the Manali side these are Rohtang Pass having a height of 13,051 feet and situated between Manali and the district headquarters of Keylong. The second obstacle on this road is Baralacha La, with a height of 16,500 feet; for this a steady climb starts from Darcha itself. The next high place to be negotiated is between Sarchu and Pang, called Lachung La at an altitude of 16,616 feet. While approaching the top, a traveler gets breathtaking view of 22 hairpin bends called Gatta loops at an average height of 13,750 feet. The fourth high pass on this road is Taglang La; which is 17,480 feet high and situated between Tsokar Lake and Upshi village. Of these four high altitude passes; currently the work on Rohtang tunnel has been taken in hand.

The tunnel at Rohtang pass in now called Atal Tunnel; named after the former Prime Minister Atal Bihari Vajpayee on his birthday on 25th December 2019. It is a fact that works on this project was inspired by him during the time he was at the helm of affairs. With a length of 8.8 kms, it is certainly one of the longest road tunnels in the world at that height – 10,171 feet. When completed; it is expected to reduce the road distance by forty six kilometers and travel period by about two hours onwards. Work on this project formally began on 28th June 2010 under the supervision of Border Roads Organization. Excavation of this tunnel was completed in October 2017, when both ends of the tunnel were physically joined. After that it was occasionally also used for emergency services, like the evacuation of patients in serious conditions during winter months when the main pass is closed due to heavy snowfall and helicopter evacuation was not possible due to bad weather. Other physical features of this project include a two way passage; with a riding surface of 33 feet wide and fitted with modern facilities, including CCTV surveillance and an emergency tunnel for inspection and contingency evacuation. The present completion target of this ambitious scheme is around 2021.

The Rohtang tunnel would significantly reduce the distance and time of travel – including serpentine traffic jams seen at present – between Manali and Keylong, Lahul and Spiti areas. This would also provide yearlong connectivity amongst these locations; giving a major relief to the local inhabitants who would otherwise feel locked up and face many difficulties during the winter months. However, completion of this project would not result in the year long link between Manali and Leh. For that to happen; one would need to understand the salient features of Manali-Leh route as it exists at present. There are three different ways to ensure through the year connectivity to Leh; and two of these pertain to this axis. One course of action would be to plan for and execute three tunnels, enroute to Leh on this road, at the intervening high passes of Baralacha La, Lachung La and Taglang La. Alternatively, a new link needs to be established from Darcha to Padam and from Padam to Nimoo. From Nimoo to Leh is a short distance along the existing all weather road. This certainly is a longer route; but the advantage would be that the link can remain open throughout the year.

The shortest and the least time consuming as at present, all weather road link to Leh, of course, would be along the existing over 440 kms Srinagar – Leh highway. For this to happen; two long tunnels would be required on this alignment. One is called 'Z-Morh tunnel' near Gagangir village, which is few kilometers short of Sonamarg from Srinagar side. Work on this project is already in hand and more than fifty percent completed. The other major undertaking would be to construct an all weather tunnel more than 14 kms long; between Baltal and Minamarg, below the Zoji La. The project planning of this venture is also in an advanced stage. Once completed; this existing axis will ensure the year-long road link between Srinagar and Leh. This would be vital; not only for the civilian population of Ladakh region but would also considerably enhance the capability of the Indian army deployed along the Pakistan and China borders in that area.

There is an interesting background to the undertaking of these two ambitious works in hand. In June 2005, the then Prime Minister Dr. Manmohan Singh came on a visit to Ladakh and spent few days there, based in Leh. He was accompanied by a team of senior officers including his Principal Secretary 'Kutty' Nair. The Chief Engineer of Project Himank of the BRO, with its headquarters in Leh, was Brig. Amin Naik. His efforts to get the Zoji La tunnel approved through departmental channels – and thus ensuring round the year connectivity to the region - had got entangled in procedural matters and did not make much headway. In virtual desperation; he requested the J&K Chief Secretary to get him an audience with Principal Secretary to the PM, hoping that a positive response from that end would expedite matters. This meeting was duly arranged and Brig. Amin briefed Shri Nair for over an hour. Fortunately, he was able to convince the latter about the feasibility and desirability of all weather connectivity to Leh and substantial benefits to the civilians and security forces alike. A positive interest from the PMO; did expedite matters and in the years to come this dream took a practical shape. The driving force behind this project, Brig. Amin Naik, retired from service few years later, in the rank of Major General and after getting nominated to undergo the prestigious course at the National Defence College, New Delhi. He has been decorated with Sena Medal pertaining to military matters and also an Arjuna award in the field of sports.

The BRO had initially taken a stand against the technical feasibility of Zoji La tunnel. Way back in 1985 when the Chief Engineer of Project Beacon, working on this section of the road, prepared a case for tunnel here; his proposal was not accepted by the headquarters of BRO giving the reason that Himalayan Mountains are young, seismic and avalanche prone; thus the area is not feasible for tunneling. After the Kargil operations in 1999; the need to have a year round connectivity to Ladakh received added impetus. In the month of March 2004; Brig. Naik now posted in Leh as the Chief Engineer of Himank Project resubmitted the case to headquarters of BRO, proposing a new 12 kms long tunnel – on an alignment which was generally avalanche free – along with other technical details. He also argued that at different locations in the same 'young' Himalayan ranges; tunnels of even longer distances were in different stages of construction. This proposal was also shot down by one line response from the office of Director General BRO, which mentioned, "this being seismic area tunnel not feasible". However, convinced of the technical details as also actual practicability of this project and in sheer despair; he turned for support to the Principal Secretary to the Prime Minister in June 2005 when the latter visited Ladakh.

In view of the assertiveness and insistence of the PMO; the Border Roads Organization agreed to give a fresh look to this project and began serious work on making this strategic link an all weather road. While working out details of this scheme; it was realized that in order to achieve the intended purpose; it was first necessary to make Sonamarg accessible during the winter. The road from Srinagar would only be trafficable up to the village of Gagangir; few kilometers short of Sonamarg; due to heavy snowfall in winters on the intervening ridge. In administrative circles this place was known as Z – Morh; although the locals called it *Hung*. This aspect of approachability to Sonamarg, during the peak of winter had earlier escaped notice as the road over Zoji La would remain generally closed from December to April; a period when reaching Sonamarg was not considered crucially important either by the state government or by the security forces. Therefore, any venture to keep the Zoji La open throughout the year; would become useful only when Sonamarg could be reached any time of the season. Therefore, it stood to logic that two tunnels; one each at Z-Morh and Zoji La; had to be planned for and constructed in tandem as also giving preference to the former first. Based on this assessment; the BRO floated a combined tender for feasibility and Detailed Project Reports for Z-Morh Road Tunnel (ZMRT) and Zoji La Road Tunnel (ZRT).

During the year 2012, DPRs of both projects were ready and sent to the Planning Commission for clearance and finances. The ZMRT project got the requisite clearance on Design, Build, Finance, Operate and Transfer basis. It was tendered by the BRO in 2013 and soon the actual work was taken in hand. However, the firm to whom this work was allotted ran into financial problems and thus failed to complete the task. In the meantime, J&K government also raised some environment issues. These problems were sorted out - over a period – and work restarted by another firm in 2015. This company too faced administrative and financial difficulties, resulting in the stoppage of work again in 2018; when forty percent of the project stood completed. The next year, a third company was allotted this work; which is likely to resume in the summer of 2020 with new completion target as the year 2022.

When completed, the technical details of ZMRT would be a 6.50 kms long single tube bidirectional tunnel; with a riding surface of Two Lane traffic. There would also be an Escape Tunnel of similar length for emergency purposes; as well as adequate provisions for ventilation, communications and CCTV. In short it is planned to be a structure with all modern facilities and gadgets.

In the year 2012, when Planning Commission was approached with both ZMRT and ZRT Project Reports; it refused to clear the tunnel at Zoji La (ZRT) on the grounds that the estimated cost of 9090 Crores and completion time of nine years; were both on the higher side and needed a fresh look to rework out the details. Accordingly, this scheme was back on the 'drawing board' and DPR was duly revised. By making some design changes the completion time was reduced to seven years; but the cost estimates remained the same at 9090 Crs. The modified proposal was then cleared by the Planning Commission. Also, during the beginning of 2016, some institutional changes took place. Both the tunnels – ZMRT and ZRT – were taken away from the control of BRO and handed over to the National Highway Infrastructure Development Corporation Ltd (NHIDCL), under the ministry of Road Transport and Highways; for tendering and execution. The work was allotted to IL&FS firm and construction on site began in May 2018. Soon the execution company ran into financial problems and NHIDCL cancelled the tender in May 2019. The bids for ZRT are likely to be invited again sometime in 2020. The overall revised cost is now estimated to be around rupees 8500 crores and the design also revised to two independent tunnel tubes of ten meters diameter each. Of course, the ZRT is proposed to have an escape passage for emergency purposes and other latest technical features like ventilation, telephone, medical and CCTV facilities. On completion, the Zoji La Tunnel will be the longest road tunnel at this altitude in the world; in addition to ensuring the year round and all weather connectivity to Ladakh. This would be crucial and important to the civilian population of the region as well as to the troops deployed in the area.

When the work on the ZMRT and ZRT – the two tunnels – is over; it will affirm the technological prowess of India in the field of tunnel expertise. In this context, it would also be in order to remember and pay a tribute to the dogged determination and technical confidence of Maj. Gen. (Retd) Amin Naik.

Another access to Ladakh surely exists; in the route followed by Gen. Zorawar Singh in the decade of 1830s. This is from Kishtwar – in Jammu division – to Paddar and there from over high Zanskar Mountains to different points in Ladakh. Of course, the famous warrior commander had to completely avoid the Kashmir Valley as the same was then not under the control of his master Maharaja Gulab Singh. The difficulties on this axis are that the entire stretch from Paddar onwards has to be surveyed and constructed afresh and the route would be closed due to heavy snow fall during the long winters. Therefore, for decades to come; the civilian requirements and the defence needs in Ladakh would be well served if the Srinagar – Leh road is made all weather and the existing Manali – Leh and Tilel – Dras links are operationalised during the road opening months.

UT status on 5th August 2019

On 5th August, 2019, the central government made a series of announcements making fundamental changes in the structure of J&K state. It abrogated Articles 35A and 370 of the Constitution of India; thereby abolishing the special status enjoyed by the state till then. It also bifurcated the state into two Union Territories (UT); the UT of Jammu and Kashmir with a legislature and the UT of Ladakh without a legislature. The suddenness of these decisions came as a surprise to very large number of people and political observers; more so those belonging to J&K and specifically the Ladakhis. This demand of Ladakhis – particularly of Leh region - was no doubt seven decades old, but the locals or their representatives did not expect it to be fulfilled so suddenly or in this manner. Historically speaking, one finds that the demand for a direct rule by the Centre was first made in the year 1949, when the first Ladakhi delegation travelled to New Delhi from Leh, via Manali, to meet Prime Minister Jawaharlal Nehru. From then onwards, this requirement underwent cosmetic changes under various leaders and passed through diverse stages. Kushok Bakula was the first leader to raise this issue in various forums across the country. In the nineteen sixties the Ladakhis were prepared to accept NEFA type of administration in the region; which was again converted to their earlier request for direct rule from the Centre. After Kushok Bakula; the mantle of leadership was donned by P. Namgyal, former Union Minister of State, who took the issue forward. During the mid-eighties onwards Thupstan Chhewang became face of this UT demand. The local struggle on this count did partly succeed when the region got two LAHDCs – one each for

Leh and Kargil – in 1995. These two were also respectively constituted in 1995 and 2003. It is on record that the LAHDC Leh representatives, while taking oath of office in September 1995, made public statements that the LAHDC structure was a stepping stone to their main demand of a UT status. To further add impetus to this request, Ladakh Union Territory Front (LUTF) was also launched by the locals in the first decade of the twentieth century. It was therefore surprising for any outside observer, that when this long pending demand was finally conceded on 5th August 2019; the initial reaction of locals was not of jubilant ecstasy and joyous celebrations but that of astonishment coupled with bewilderment. There were few reasons for this unusual response.

The Ladakhis felt, and justifiably so, that they were not taken into confidence or consulted before such a far reaching decision was taken by the Centre. In a way, it was a classic case of doing the right thing in a wrong manner. Connected with this was also a lurking suspicion that the region was made a pawn in the larger canvas of political considerations of the union government in addressing the issues related to the state of Jammu and Kashmir. Seen in this context; the benefits to the region became quite incidental. Also, the new UT status was without any legislature; which meant there would be no MLAs and to that extent the bargaining power of the locals with the governing instruments would get restricted as compared to the earlier dispensation. Then, there were unresolved questions of spheres of functioning and inter-dependence between the UT administration, LAHDC and Panchayati Raj structures. These were some of the perceptions due to which the kind of celebratory eruptions expected; did not take place even in Leh area.

Ladakhis also did not much appreciate the speech given by the local MP, Jamyang Tsering Namgyal, in Lok Sabha just after the declaration of UT; where he unequivocally supported this move by the central government and enthusiastically welcomed the step. A typical reaction came from Rigzin Spalbar, a former two-time CEC of LAHDC Leh; who made this statement to a national magazine, “Ladakh is a majority tribal habitat population and a resolution would need to be passed either by the Hill Council or the Governor that non-tribal people cannot buy land here. In other words, replacing 35A through other means. Either by way of inclusion in Schedule 6 or some other safeguard. I think that the Hill Council will remain empowered and the land should be under its jurisdiction. There are many States in India where non-tribal people cannot buy land from tribal people born there, and it can be applied to Ladakh to protect our interests."[3]

The situation in Kargil district was different. Here the people did not want to go with the Buddhist majority Leh; but also preferred to continue as a part of J&K state, having developed contacts with the Kashmiri leadership particularly after the 1980s. They were confronted with a set of difficult situations. Being a Muslim majority area the people of Kargil felt closer to Kashmir region; but on the other hand, linguistically, culturally and even socially they had greater commonality with the Leh population. In addition, their support to the army and nationalistic feelings; right from 1947 onwards and more recently during the 1999 crisis, have been appreciated at all levels. This dilemma of conflicting pulls was resolved by the UT decision of the Government of India. However, the people of Kargil had some genuine skepticism and apprehensions about their place in the new dispensation of a separate UT; and were keen on clarifications in this respect. Even in Leh the common man, especially the younger generation, raised some doubts about the UT set up and questions regarding employment and ownership of land etc. The combined result of this situation was that whereas there were no immediate and marked celebrations in Leh; Kargil people started an all party agitation against the UT, spear headed by a Joint Action Committee (JAC), in which non political and influential local personalities were also included. The J&K administration, which was also responsible for Ladakh during the interim period, reacted swiftly by imposing movement restrictions and internet ban in Kargil. In the days to follow; parleys with the local opinion leaders and the JAC were held at different official levels. These discussions were finally rounded up by the J&K Chief Secretary who drove to Kargil for this purpose. On his assurance that the soon to positioned UT administration would effectively address all genuine concerns of the Kargil people; the agitation was suspended. But the simmering continued.

The newly appointed Lt. Governor of UT of Ladakh, Radha Krishna Mathur paid his first visit to Kargil, lasting for two days from 10th November 2019. During this period; he was briefed by the district officers and also met people across the broad local spectrum, that is, various political, social leaders as well as professional groups and association representatives. He

3 *Frontline*, Chennai, 27th September, 2019, p. 35.

interacted with the local LAHDC and gave a patient hearing to the JAC Kargil, headed by Sheikh Nassir Munshi. At the end of this familiarization trip and holding extensive discussions with a cross-section of people; the LG announced that his administration would deal evenly with both Leh and Kargil districts as two equivalent and identical units of the Ladakh UT. He assured that there would be no marginalization of any region and while there was no plan to introduce a 'durbar move' type system between the two major towns of the belt; the LG, UT Secretariat and IGP office will be established in both Leh and Kargil. The opinion leaders of Kargil reacted positively to the assertions made by the LG and seemed satisfied with his overall analysis of the situation and proposed line of action. Since then there has been no trouble in the region and hopefully this situation would continue in the future also. Another positive development was a statement issued by the JAC that Kargil people would like to coordinate with LAHDC Leh; the ways to settle vexatious issues like protection of land, jobs and culture of Leh and Kargil areas.

Two representative samples of the local apprehensions about the move to make Ladakh a separate UT reflect the general mood in the region. Sonam Wangchuk, a celebrated social worker of the region, is on record to have said, "…people are worried that their land and environment would not be safe, if large number of people from other parts of the world would start arriving in Ladakh… Ladakh's fragile ecology and environment would not be able to tolerate it."[4] In a somewhat similar vein C Phonsog, the former Chief Secretary of J&K State and currently the Vice Chancellor of Ladakh University, opined "Ladakh can progress provided it utilizes opportunities and also when its fears are allayed once and for all… As the matter stands now, the people of Leh and Kargil districts are both vehemently demanding safeguards for land, jobs and unique cultural identity of Ladakhis by declaring the whole region as a tribal area to help the people of the region get protection available under the Sixth Schedule of Article 44 (2) of the Constitution. The fears in this respect are well-founded and include loss of opportunities, land alienation and loss of the cultural identity of Ladakh valued as unique by both locals and outsiders…Ladakh is already a small but bright patch of the Indian mosaic that instinctively cherishes all that the Indian nation-state, comprising a sixth of the humans inhabiting planet earth, stands for…Ladakhis should

4 *The Tribune*, Chandigarh, 19th November 2019.

certainly try and have a legislature of their own, to reflect their democratic aspirations, when things settle down…"[5]

Thus, taking a comprehensive view of this situation, it may be said that while the Ladakhis generally welcomed the creation of a UT in their region; the concern of locals revolve around issues pertaining to land, employment, environment, cultural identity and legislature. The task of the new UT administration is therefore almost cut out; and a lot would depend on how the new dispensation is able to manage these and related points, as also ensure a better cooperation and coordination between Leh and Kargil districts.

Way Ahead

The UT status for Ladakh is a reality and need be accepted as such by the entire population; which should now work seriously towards making this new and paradigm shift a successful venture. A very crucial element in this endeavor – in fact a matter of decisive importance – is the maintenance of communal harmony in the region. Fortunately, populations of both the districts of Kargil and Leh have had a long tradition of amity and brotherhood between Muslims and Buddhists. This they can proudly boast of not only in terms of years, but in historical antiquity. At the same time, it also must be accepted that both communities – particularly their opinion leaders across the political and social spectrum – should consciously and purposefully work towards this end. They must also accept the bitter fact that communalism did raise its ugly head in this peaceful region during the past four decades or so. There are significant Muslim pockets in Leh district; concentrated in the areas of Leh town and villages of Shey, Thiksey and Chuchoot. Similarly, in the pre-dominantly Muslim population of Kargil district; the Buddhists are concentrated in Wakha and Mulbek villages. In addition, the whole sub-division of Zanskar – with the exception of its headquarter Padam –almost entirely comprises Buddhist population. In this scenario; the element of communal harmony does assume considerable significance.

Whereas, efforts towards this end have to be made in both the districts; the leaders of Leh area have greater responsibility – like that of an elder brother in a family for example – in this respect. This is primarily for three distinctive reasons. The people of Kargil, in fact, never demanded a Union

5 *The Tribune*, Chandigarh, 10th December, 2019.

Territory status for Ladakh. There is nothing on record – ever since the independence in 1947 – to go against this presumption. If anything, to the contrary, the population – the Muslim majority in any case – slowly made efforts for greater integration with Kashmir. Sonam Narboo, many locals believe, was the last leader from Leh area who enjoyed considerable support in Kargil. After his death in early 1980; Kargil started drifting from Leh. This process was further accentuated by the creation of separate Kargil district in the middle of 1979 and subsequent developments. Particularly, during the decade of 1980s; this chasm widened and simultaneously the local leadership in Kargil tried to establish closer links with Kashmir. This trend was also encouraged by the Kashmiri leadership; at times quite unabashedly.

Secondly, an average Kargili – especially Muslim – does not appear to be as jovial and happy-go-lucky as a person from Leh region. The Kargili countenance rather gives an impression of a serious individual weighed in by the worries of day to day existence. This distinction is quite stark, notwithstanding the similar socio-economic conditions of deprivation in the entire region, just after crossing the Fatu La – from Kargil to Leh. From Lamayuru onwards, especially at Khaltsi and beyond, the people look jovial and exude happiness so markedly displayed by the smile and beaming faces. This conspicuous difference exists as a reality and is noticed by any new visitor to the region. The third debilitating feature is the wide gap between people of the two areas in educational attainments; particularly in the fields of higher and technical education. It may be a fact that the state government exertions at the primary and secondary levels; as also the spread of institutions has been almost uniform in both districts. There certainly are socio-economic reasons for this disparity and the people of Kargil – as a group – realized the significance of education rather late as compared to their counterparts. The difference is of about three to four decades; but Kargil is fast catching up in this field, even though it started late.

However, the first two reasons remain valid and strong enough for the Leh leadership to collectively reach out to the people of Kargil and make them equal partners in ensuring that the status of a Union Territory granted to Ladakh region on 5th August 2019, works satisfactorily for both districts. The collective feeling of Kargil people that they have been left behind needs to be accepted and positively addressed. For this to happen;

the maintenance of communal harmony is of greatest importance. Kargil belt has also had a long history and tradition of people professing different religions; living peacefully, in amity and displaying mutual tolerance. To better understand this phenomenon, one needs to ask the Buddhists of Wakha, Mulbek and Muslims of Padam.

In this connection, it will be notable to record the reminiscences of an officer posted as SDM Kargil in the mid 1970s. About a particular village in the area he recollected as, "The Kuksho village in Chigtan valley of Kargil was very unique and popular for exemplary inter religious harmony and composite culture. The beautiful thing was that almost half of the population of the village was professing Buddhism and the other half was followers of Islam. According to the legend and also as recorded in the book 'History of Jammu and the Conquered Territories of Maharaja Gulab Singh' by Hashmatullah Khan and supported by the 'Qadeem Ladakh – History and Civilization' written by Kachu Sikander Khan; village Kuksho was the first settled habitation in 'Purig' region – present Kargil area – which was founded by the Dard prince Tha Tha Khan. He was also founding father of the Gasho Dynasty; and had migrated from the Gilgit area. He, along with followers, came via Baltistan, crossed over Chorbat La; there from entered into Hanu and then arrived at the right bank of Indus River – on the opposite side of Dargo village; which is located just below Kuksho. The time was early spring and chunks of ice sheets were floating on the river. So, Tha Tha Khan and two of his companions crossed the river by mounting upon a big ice sheet and rowing to the other side.

"They then arrived at Kuksho. Seeing lot of spring water and plenty of fertile land around the place; they decided to stay there and cultivate the lands as also establish a habitation at Kuksho. According to a popular fable; there was a stick of 'Birch' tree in the hand of Tha Tha Khan. He planted it on the ground and prayed that if he had the good luck to be settled in that location, then the stick should sprout. Truly; that stick sprouted and overtime became a tree. Subsequently, that place became a grove of Birch trees and is in existence till today. There is a local legend that these trees are the trees of life for the entire Tha Tha Khani clan. If a new baby arrives in that clan then a new shoot sprouts from one of the trees; and if someone dies in that clan then an old shoot withers away.

"Originally, the entire population of the village might have been professing Buddhist faith. But subsequently with the passage of time;

intermarriages as also other social and cultural influences might have prompted some people to accept the Muslim faith. Thus around 1970s, nearly half of the population was Muslim in the village. But, the fascinating thing was that even Muslims had half Buddhist or local names; such as Ali Sonam; Ali Stanba; Chang Khan Mohd; to quote a few examples. It was also worth noting that sometimes one or two members of a family were professing Muslim faith and the rest of the household were Buddhists. It is famously said about the place that major festivals of either community were celebrated by the entire village population together. They used to cook meat etc, in the same pot, though the Muslim members would tie a white thread around their piece of meat that would invariably be *halal*.

"Intercommunity marriage had been common. If a girl there would marry in a family other than her own faith; even then she would not change her name and would continue to be called by her original name. Apart from these matters; the social and cultural gatherings were the true manifestations of a real and exemplary composite culture. In large gatherings, like festivals or a feast; seating arrangements were made in such a way that the Buddhist members would sit on the right side row and the Muslims would sit on the left side row. Local tea and *Chang* (a kind of home-made barley beer) were served on the same table; placed in between and in appropriate numbers. The food would also be served and shared in similar manner. Muslims would take sips of hot tea; whereas Buddhists consumed large amounts of *Chang*. Such gatherings would last for several hours, with time spent on chatting and merry making. There are many such anecdotes about this village."

In the present times of shallow and superficial advocacy of one's own faith; the example of Kuksho type of society is not only a rarity; but also seem like a tale about a fairyland and a by-gone era.

Apart from being a considerable challenge; it is also a big opportunity for the UT administration of Ladakh to create an effective and seamless structure in the entire region, by persuasively taking along the people of Kargil; and in fact obtaining their willing cooperation in this common endeavor. One positive step which will go a long way in ensuring this, is locating the headquarters of some departments in Kargil; after assessing the local needs and discussing various options with responsible people there. This should not pose much problem to the UT administration in terms of logistics and administrative controls. The land routes and internal communications within entire Ladakh area do remain operational throughout the year. Otherwise also, till recently, various heads of departments were, in fact, managing respective activities of their subordinate offices in Ladakh from Srinagar. Doing the same from Kargil would be so much easier and rewarding. The headquarters of Lt. Governor, Divisional Commissioner and I.G. of Police can remain in Leh for most of the year. But they – as also the heads of departments based in Leh – should visit Kargil and areas around quite frequently to take stock of the local needs and solve outstanding issues, on the spot only. This step is expected to go a long way in securing willing help and cooperation of Kargil people in the successful functioning of the Ladakh UT; which indeed has the potential of a bright future.

In this area, well endowed with nature's bounty; the development strategy of Ladakh should mainly be based on the twin sectors of tourism and power generation. These two, if properly and adequately harnessed, have the implicit capabilities to bring substantial growth and prosperity to the entire region. Tourist arrival in this land has grown from little over five hundred in 1974 to a figure of 3.27 lakhs in 2018. But it has a number of difficult kinks that need to be ironed out. So far, the tourism in Ladakh has remained seasonal and unpredictable and the need to make it more dependable can hardly be over emphasized. Also it is a fact that the tourist arrival does become unsustainable beyond a point; as so much extra demands have to be catered for water, power, accommodation and garbage disposal. Therefore what indeed this area needs is more of quality tourism than focus on the numbers. This shift should receive urgent and adequate attention from the local entrepreneurs as well as policy planners. Tourists with higher spending capacity should be preferred in the region. May be Ladakh can beneficially learn from the Bhutan model of tourism; or even improve upon it.

On the issue of power generation; it would be enlightening to read the views of a Ladakhi intellectual. P. Stobdan, our former Ambassador to Kyrgyzstan, wrote in The Tribune, Chandigarh, on 3rd December 2019 as "...Greater attention is needed from the government's side on exploiting Ladakh's huge hydropower potential within the provisions of the Indus Water Treaty. Of the 1,000 MW power potential identified, very little has been exploited so far...Since the formation of the UT, the government, in its single biggest investment proposal, has announced a Rs. 50,000- crore grid-connected solar photo-voltaic project for Ladakh to harness 7,500 MW of solar power. The transmission corridor will be built for evacuating electricity via the Manali route to Kaithal in Haryana. It could be scaled up to 23,000 MW. If it materializes, the UT of Ladakh would become one of India's biggest energy hubs." He further advices, "...Ladakh needn't opt for the industrial path. It needs integration and linkages with national growth centers."

The UT administration will also have to deal with the contentious issue of reconciling the structures of Panchayati Raj and LAHDC; as presently both are operational in the two districts of the area. The Panchayat system is a national formation; with uniformity across the country based on the Constitutional provisions. On the other hand, LAHDC set-up is emotionally important to the Ladakhis; having almost become an organic part of their psyche. Even though there are no serious differences between the Sarpanches and Councilors right now; their respective functions and jurisdictions do tend to overlap. These certainly have the potential of flaring up to a crisis level; and before that happens, is the need to arrive at a mechanism which will ensure harmonious equilibrium between the two. Since the Panchayati Raj parameters have a national character and the LAHDC Act of 1995 / 1997 is only applicable to this region; it would be more workable to amend the latter so that the jurisdiction of both becomes co-terminus. In this arrangement, the elected Councilor could also be taken as the elected *Sarpanch* of the area. This proposed system would ensure better and also more coordinated functioning of the two structures; a national paradigm as also the local set up. It may be risky, for the region, to keep this issue hanging till the situation takes a negative turn.

The Sixth Schedule has been a long pending demand of the entire region; and it became more focused due to the local apprehensions that in the changed circumstances the land and employment related issues need to be shielded to keep away the outsiders. In fact the National Commission for Scheduled Tribes made a recommendation to this effect as per the Press Information Bureau release of 11th September 2019. It included, "The 119th meeting of the National Commission for Scheduled Tribes was held on 11th September 2019 under the Chairmanship of Dr. Nand Kumar Sai to deliberate the issue of inclusion of UT of Ladakh under the Fifth / Sixth Schedule of the Constitution of India. At the outset, the full Commission welcomed the Jammu and Kashmir Reorganization Act

2019 thereby creating the Union Territory of Ladakh comprising of Kargil and Leh districts. The Commission feels that this will immensely help in meeting the cherished aspirations of the tribal people in Ladakh region… The Commission after, careful consideration, recommends that the Union Territory of Ladakh be brought under the Sixth Schedule of the Constitution. The Commission feels that this will help in: (i) Democratic devolution of powers; (ii) Preserve and promote distinct culture of the region; (iii) Protect agrarian rights including rights on land; and (iv) Enhance transfer of funds for speedy development of Ladakh region. Accordingly, Hon'ble Chairperson, National Commission for Scheduled Tribes has written to Union Home Minister as well as Union Tribal Affairs Minister conveying the recommendation of the Commission to include Union Territory of Ladakh under Sixth Schedule of the Constitution of India…" The Sixth Schedule or some other legal or administrative formulation; the fact remains that the government will have to find a method to address apprehensions of the local people regarding land, employment and related issues.

The status of women is another aspect that this region, particularly the Kargil area, will have to pay more focused attention. The abysmally low number of women candidates who were given party tickets in the LAHDC elections, and also ultimately won, is just one indicator. Among the Buddhists; the women have traditionally been treated with respect by the society and also given considerable freedom in decision-making process. But, their role has remained largely circumscribed to house hold matters. This needs to change and they must come out of domestic shackles; and assume their rightful place of prominence in all spheres of life, commensurate with their numbers. In the Muslim society of Kargil; the status of women has traditionally been quite humble and low. For centuries it has remained a strong patriarchic community. Things have started changing slowly there also; but a strong collective and corrective push is required from various social groups, political outfits, religious heads and administrative circles. There is indeed a requirement, in the entire Ladakh region, to give a positive push to further enhance opportunities to women and bring their achievements in the public domain. Their dreams, grit and determination are in no way less than that of the men. For example, not many people would know that, the entire women's ice hockey team of India comes from this region; and that shows their collective resolve to surmount difficulties on the way. Physically, at least in certain domains, they have advantages over the counterparts from the plains. There are no reasons why Ladakh cannot have the likes of Bachendri Pal and Mary Kom. The requisite necessities are opportunities, institutional support and societal encouragement.

A significant level of attention is also required to be paid to the cultural preservation of Ladakh. Under this overarching umbrella, exist a spectrum of sub-cultures pertaining to different tribes and areas; each having a different and distinct identity as also flavor. The people here basically belong to a traditional society; with considerable emphasis on contentment, sustainability and community based cooperation. Preservation of these qualities is not only important in itself – and there is a great need for it – but these are under considerable pressure in view of the modern lifestyle and substantial technological advances. Ladakh's traditional heritage with its accent on community benefits as against personal spaces; is a valuable resource for a much larger domain and needs to be preserved for this reason itself.

In the above background; there certainly are areas which require considerable attention and many interventions at different levels. A specific reason for concern as also requiring urgent remedial measures, as an example, pertains to the migration to Leh town by an increasing number of nomadic people of Changthang. This takes place primarily for two reasons; lack of facilities and amenities in the nomadic areas and anxiety of these people for the education of their children. A good number of young nomads are taking to alternative means of livelihood and as such, increasingly less people are left in Changthang to look after the live stock and keep alive the nomadic culture and traditions. Therefore, for the live stock related sectors to thrive in Ladakh it is imperative to put in place requisite short term measures and long term strategies. The former includes the provision of drinking water for men and animals at summer pastures; breed improvement and training of handlers; feed and fodder banks of appropriate scale for these people; assured relief during calamities; personal hygiene measures and the like. The long term strategy should be based on research initiatives and market interventions for enhanced production of Pashmina wool as also better quality of finished products made locally; to satisfy the national and international standards. All the same; fact remains that the continuing rural to urban migration does present a palpable challenge to the entire Ladakh region requiring appropriate responses. This is significant to prevent a 'ghost village' like situation existing in some parts of Uttarakhand.

Ladakh is also confronted with the twin menace of external threat and internal warning signs; based on hostile neighbors like Pakistan and China on the borders and depleting sources of water for drinking and irrigation purposes. As for the former; it is in the best interests of India that perturbed conditions are not kept for long and the outstanding boundary issues are addressed early through diplomatic and other means. This is as important as the developments on the socio-cultural and economic fronts.

This region depends on glacier fed streams for its sustenance, and not rain fed watercourses as in other parts of India. It has been so, for over the centuries. With the current phenomenon of 'global warming' and very real threat of melting glaciers; it is a moot point as to how long will the people of this area survive comfortably and adequately meet their demands of water. The life giving sources of glacial waters are reducing quite alarmingly. Going 'green' is not only a mindset for locals; but their very survival is on the line. In this battle of ideas some priority sectors consist of; the concept of conservation, agro forestry, herbal cultivation – particularly of the extinct and fast vanishing varieties – green energy from solar, geo-thermal and wind sources; traditional and modern water management techniques giving primacy to building of artificial water bodies in order to trap and keep the glacial melt. These measures will help in building a sustainable environment as also improve ecosystem giving rise to economic and social development in the entire region. All this work will need to be taken up in a mission mode involving environmentalists, economists, agriculturists; as also almost every family of the area. Fortunately, there exists a strong ecological movement, as well as awareness in most of Ladakh presently. This needs to be enhanced and built upon; deliberately and purposefully.

In the second half of the 20th century, Ladakh became a meeting ground of two different cultural streams – Ladakhi and Indian – and hence a crucible for a new and more sublime cultural traditions in which the best of both can be said to have been fused. This is evidenced by the ease with which Ladakhis have taken to Hindustani language; Indian fine arts and music; Indian dress; Indian food habits and the general way of living. In a manner of speaking there has been a short-circuiting from the Ladakh of then and now. The resultant mutation can best be described as Indo-Ladakhi culture wherein Ladakhi vocabulary has been replete with Hindi/

Urdu words and Hindustani has become the second language for young Ladakhis. Ladakhi folk theatre and folk songs are continuously being replaced by Bollywood films and songs. Traditional Ladakhi dishes and staples are steadily giving way to North Indian varieties; and Ladakhi dresses are increasingly replaced by the popular shalwar - kameez as also shirt – pants and jackets. Hence, before the evolution of Ladakhi society had gone far in the 20th century, the full impact of the Indian way of life was upon it; with all its positive and negative aspects. The resultant product has been a harmonious mingling of the two streams; happily impacting the local customs, traditions and culture.

One finds that today the Ladakhi society, unaffected by geographical constraints and extreme cold climate; is literally pulsating with enthusiasm and full of creativity, dynamism and entrepreneurship. It is looking forward to a bright and productive future as in the rest of the country; and democratic traditions of India have certainly taken roots in the remote corners of Ladakh, with attendant benefits to the region as also to the country at large. For the Buddhists, of course, there is an added comfort in India being the land of Buddha.

With justifiable pride; Ladakh can look back on its eventful and splendid past. With equal, if not more, purposeful exertion and expectation, it should collectively fix sights on a glorious and happening future; and find its rightful place in the colourful tapestry of India. Also, in the wake of scramble for progress and lure for modern facilities; there is the real danger of Ladakhi society getting unhinged from its traditional moorings. In this connection, some thoughtful observers believe that the local population will steadily move ahead in the times to come; harmoniously balancing their cultural conventions and modern way of life. These people feel; as long as Ladakhis keep 'Gonchas' and 'Gompas' as part of their collective existence; the native inhabitants would retain their individuality as also societal distinction.

Annexures

Annexure – I

Wajah-Tasmia of some villages of Leh District, in alphabetical order, is given below:

1. Alchi. :- Alchi is a mispronounced word of 'Abchi'. The inhabitants of Alchi were once the followers of Degong Kargyut. On the name of the deity of this sect called Abchi, the village came to be pronounced as Alchi in due course of time.

2. Bazgo. :- There is a stone like the shape of a cow head at Bazgo and the village's name has been kept after this stone. Bam means 'of cow' and go means head; the village name was, in the olden times, written as Bamgo meaning cow's head. This has been turned into Bazgo over a long period.

3. Chuma-Thang. :- Name of this village is after the situation of the place being on a plain near the river. Chu means water or river and Thang denotes a plain area in Ladakhi – hence the name Chuma-Thang.

4. Chushul. :- The area of Chushul was under a lake in ancient time. On drying of the lake a village came into being there, which was called Chushul. Chu means water and Shul means residue.

5. Deskit. :- Des kit means happiness and comfort. This village is located at an appropriate place in Nubra valley; so it has been given this name.

6. Domkhar. :- Domkhar means "A fort at the end of a gorge". The old fort of the village was at the end of a gorge; from that it has derived the name.

7. Hemi. :- The village is called Hemi after a Tibetan word 'Ha'; which is formed on a rock in the ravine of Hemis.

8. Hunder. :- It is also a mis-spelt word for 'Snontar' which means settled earlier. It is said that this village was settled first of all in Nubra valley.

9. Khaltse. :- This is a slightly corrupted version of word 'Khartse'. Khar means fort and Tsa stands for 'just below' in Ladakhi. Location of this settlement is just below the fort there and hence this name.

10. Khardong. :- Khar stands for a fort and 'dong' signifies face in the local language; as such it is called 'faced to the fort' or Khardong.

11. Kharnak. :- This village has been named after the fort Kharnak; which was located in the land in ancient times.

12. Karzok. :- Its original name is Korzot; which denotes a place for keeping rented cattle. As the place has been famous for good grass land and rented cattle are kept there for grazing; it has been named for that very reason. In due course of time Korzot has become Karzok.

13. Leh. :- A watery land is called Leh in Ladakhi. The place where initially houses were built was Chubi; located on Leh – Sankar road just below the Tseme Khar which used to be watery land and it was called Leh due to its watery property.

14. Nimo. :- Nimo means nearby. In ancient times Ladakh excluding Nubra and Changthang was divided in two parts; Stot and Sham meaning upper and lower. Nimo is the first settlement of Sham area, nearest to Leh the capital, and therefore it was called nearest village or Nimo.

15. Partap Pura. :- This is a newly settled village during the reign of Maharaja Partap Singh; and the name of habitation has been kept after that of the ruler.

16. Phuktse. :- This word signifies an upper part of a ravine. As the village is located on the upper part of a *nullah,* it has been called Phuktse.

17. Saspol. :- Sas means vegetable or fruit garden. This village has plenty of fruit trees in the locality. Pol has been added for the word 'Pa' which implies owners. By adding these two words one gets name of the village.

18. Shey. :- Shey has been a distorted version of word 'shel' which means glass. The hills near this habitation give the look of glass; and there from this name is derived.

19. Spituk. :- Spituk has been a distorted version of Spay Thup; which stands for a 'model'. The Gompa on the hillock at Spituk, being a model one, was called Spay Thup. This name has changed to Spituk in due course of time.

20. Stakna. :- The Stakna monastery is located on a hillock which is like the shape of a nose of tiger. So the village has been called Stakna, meaning a tiger nose.

21. Sumoor. :- This is a slightly distorted version of the word 'Soomyur' which signifies three *kuhls.* There are three main *kuhls* in Sumoor village and hence this name.

22. Tagma Chik. :- It is mis-spelt for Stakma Chik. Stakma means a mother tiger and Chik denotes one. It is said that a mother tiger was caught by a man of this village. This news reached the then ruler of Ladakh Raja Tundup Namgyal who kept the name of this village as Stakma Chik for that very reason.

23. Tegar. :- Mis-spelt for Tyagar which means a central fort. It has been called as such due to the location of a fort there that appeared to be in the middle of Nubra valley.

24. Thiksey. :- Not far removed from the word 'Thitse' meaning ten thousand. It is said that in olden times there were ten thousand monks in the Thiksey monastery and as such it was called Thitsey. Over time the village got its present name.

25. Timisgam. :- A slightly corrupted depiction of the word Ting sGang. Ting means deep and sGang denotes high. The palace at Timisgam was located on a high place and rest of the village in deep ravine; hence this name in due course of time.

(Every village has a name and every name has some basis or background. During the process of Settlement; after enquiries from village elders, the basis for naming a village are recorded in the prescribed place in *Shajra Nasab* – a mandatory statement - attached with Record-of- Rights of the village. The same is known as *Wajah-Tasmia.*)

Annexures – II

The following is a compilation of some significant proverbs and sayings of the entire region. These wise percepts and practical dictums handed down the generations, from times immemorial, also represent the unique ethos of the Ladakhi culture. In a way, these are invaluable pieces of Ladakhi folk literature as also repository of ancient and continued wisdom of the area.[1]

1. A mighty person rolls a stone uphill.
2. One who moves forward, and strikes is definitely a warrior,

   One who retreats gracefully is also a warrior.
3. Every child shall experience maturity,

   Every foal shall become a riding horse.
4. If the crow avoids the arrow,

   He may live for hundred years.
5. A quiet person is like a covered vessel.
6. Even a golden stirrup remains under the foot.
7. In a country of blinds, a one-eyed fellow becomes the king.
8. To go to see a festival when it is over,

   And to close the window after the cat has escaped.
9. One who drinks wine has no secrets,

   One who eats meat has no compassion.
10. A goat of the city is far cleverer,

    Than a man from a remote village.
11. Unless one tastes bitterness first,

1 These popular maxims are selected from a book titled, *Ancient Wisdom,* by Kacho Asfandyar Khan, Kacho Publications Kargil (Ladakh), 1998.

The taste of sweetness cannot be judged.

12. One not seated on a proper place,

    Shall have to stand up hundred times.

13. Hundred persons have hundred mouths.

14. Worry is a disease and happiness is a tonic.

15. Brothers share the property of their father,

    Valleys share the water of its mountains.

16. A king is also abused on his back.

17. An unskilled black smith gets no food.

18. One must sow the Rabi crop first,

    Then attend one's father's funeral.

19. When there is no perspiration, there is no gold.

20. Excess of water is harmful for the crops,

    Excess of dogs are harmful for the village.

21. A Yarqandi horse turns its head towards

    Yarqand at the time of dying.

22. To speak is silver and to keep silence is gold.

23. One does not feel thirsty by doing one's own work.

24. The law of the land cannot be overruled even by the King.

25. When the stomach is full, then people sing.

26. Men do not afraid of the hardships of a high pass,

    Women do not afraid of the pangs of delivering a child.

27. When a Kashmiri becomes old his limbs begin to shake,

    When a Ladakhi becomes old his limbs suffer from rheumatic pain.

Index

F

G

H

I

R

S

T

V

W

X

Y

Z

About The Author

Dr. Sudhir S. Bloeria, IAS (J&K- 1968) is an ex- Army Officer having served in the Infantry, The Jammu And Kashmir Rifles, from 1966 to 1972. He took part in the 1971 war with Pakistan, in the Fazilka sector.

An alumnus of the Scindia School Gwalior, he is a science graduate, also holds a Masters Degree in History, and acquired the Ph.D Degree for his thesis on "The Battles of Zojila-1948". A graduate of the National Defence College, New Delhi, he takes keen interest in military history and national security matters.

Important assignments held by him include, Deputy Commissioner, Jammu, Development Commissioner, Ladakh, Divisional Commissioner, Jammu, Principal Secretary to Governor, Secretary to the Government of Jammu and Kashmir in the departments of Food, Civil Supplies, Transport, Forest, Public Works, Health and Medical Education.

Dr. Bloeria was posted as Special Commissioner, Rajouri and Poonch districts during 1990-1992, with the specific responsibility to keep that region free from militancy during that critical period. He remained Home Secretary to the State Government in 1995 and 1996 when Parliament and Assembly elections were conducted in the State after a gap of almost ten years. His last assignment was Chief Secretary J&K Government from November 2002 till his superannuation in September 2005.

In July 2008, when Governor's rule was imposed in J&K, Dr. Bloeria was appointed as Advisor to the Governor. He was instrumental in successfully handling the Shri Amarnath Shrine Board land agitation and, later, conducting the Assembly Elections.

In August 2011, he became the founder Vice Chancellor of the Central University of Jammu, for a period of three years, and relinquished that post in August 2014.

He has authored five books, "*The Battles of Zojila-1948*", "*Pakistan's Insurgency and India's Security*", "*The Dying Terrorism*", "*The Men Who Served J&K*" and "*Peace Process in Jammu and Kashmir*."

CPSIA information can be obtained
at www.ICGtesting.com
Printed in the USA
LVHW020305220221
679596LV00004B/154

who maintained that Muslims and Buddhists had lived together and should die together; hence he exhorted the local Muslims to actively participate in the defence efforts. That paved the way for Muslims' involvement in all future endeavors. Training of the youth and the defence of Leh town was given the highest priority and both these were organized in much more professional and on long term basis. Every hillock around the town was turned into a defensive position, trenches were dug and manned. My father being in charge of the Defence had to go from one height to another height and it was a sight to see him sweating out. He was a short and bulky man."[34] The official history of 1947-48 operations in J&K records these events as, "The Military Governor held a public meeting soon after assuming charge and exhorted the people not to panic or indulge in anti-social activities. He also set up a full-fledged Cabinet including a Prime Minister, a Health Minister, a Defence Minister (who looked after Home Affairs also), a Finance Minister and a Food Minister. The local public men and petty officials nominated to these posts worked efficiently as a team and relieved the Military Governor of much of the work of civil administration."[35]

A comprehensive analysis of Parab's actions in Ladakh would indicate that he forcefully worked on and kept in focus primarily five issues. Out of these the first priority was, obviously, the safety and security of Leh town and its people. This was followed by vigorous action to ensure revival of the moribund civil administrative structure; which he achieved admirably with the help of prominent locals and officials already working there. He also proved to be a careful commander, trained and steeped in the orthodox mode of the military craft; wherein he kept his battalion closely located around Leh in a very effective defensive posture with its command and control systems intact. At the same time he also exhibited the flair for some unconventional tactics considering the long and unguarded line of communications of the enemy forces; mostly passing through areas inhabited by people who were friendly to the Indian army. The guerrilla type of operations, which were conducted under his watchful eye in Leh and Nubra sectors, fall in this category. Lastly, he was also preparing for stocking of supplies at Leh so as to last during the harsh winter ahead; till the next summer. This must have been advised and insisted upon him by the Headquarters Sri Div; notwithstanding the efforts of Indian troops

34 Rigzin Namgyal Kalon, *Op. Cit.*

35 Prasad, *Op. Cit.*, pp. 338 and 339.